D1271852

Poets as Players

Theme and Variation in Late
Medieval French Poetry

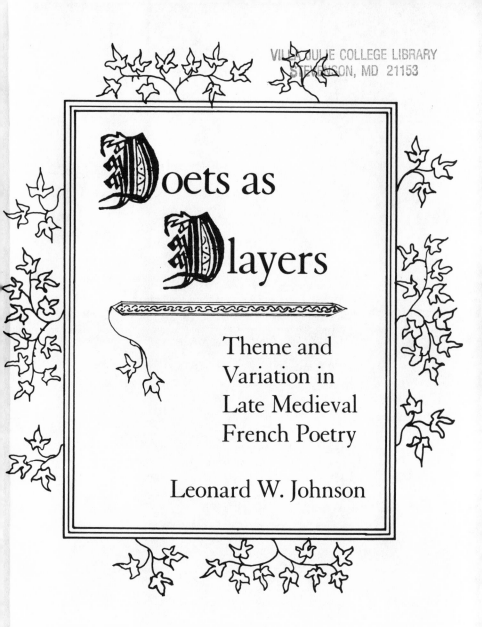

Poets as Players

Theme and Variation in Late Medieval French Poetry

Leonard W. Johnson

STANFORD UNIVERSITY PRESS, STANFORD, CALIFORNIA

Stanford University Press, Stanford, California
© 1990 by the Board of Trustees of the
Leland Stanford Junior University
Printed in the United States of America

CIP data appear at the end of the book

The initial letters used for the title page and chapter
openings come from *Le Jardin de plaisance et fleur de
rethorique*, published ca. 1501 by Antoine Vérard (re-
produced in facsimile by Firmin-Didot, Paris, 1910).

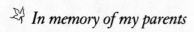 *In memory of my parents*

Acknowledgments

During the lengthy gestation of this book it has been my good fortune to have had the counsel both of present and of future colleagues. To the latter, those graduate students over the last dozen years who have been bold enough to brave in seminars the rigors of late medieval French, I am grateful for the opportunity of testing ideas proposed herein and of profiting by their frank response. My debt to the colleagues at Berkeley and at other institutions who have read the manuscript in its various states is large indeed, and it is a pleasure here to be able to thank especially Leo Bersani, Howard Bloch, Gerard Caspary, Samuel Danon, Marie-Hélène Huet, and Walter Rex not only for their insightful comments but also for their encouragement. Stephen Orgel's advice was invaluable at a critical moment. Helen Tartar, editor for the humanities at Stanford University Press, has been extraordinarily understanding and helpful, not least in enlisting a reader for the manuscript whose name is unknown to me but whom I wish to thank for a report combining perceptive commentary with unusually stimulating critical suggestions for improvement. Finally, my friend Caroline Senour deserves much credit for having so elegantly and patiently seen the text through its many versions, electronic and otherwise.

L. W. J.

Contents

A Note on the Texts

At the price of some slight inconsistency, it has seemed preferable, in quoting late medieval texts from modern editions, to print them as their editors give them, even though practice differs in detail, e.g., the preposition *à* printed with or without the grave accent; the past participle of verbs in *-er* spelled differently (*-é*, *-ez*, *-és*). For readers familiar with Middle French, these differences will present no problems; for others, the translations will be of help. Such variance represents in a way, moreover, the inconsistencies in spelling of the period itself.

I provide translations for all quotations in Middle French. Translating poetry is an endeavor at best frustrating, at worst impossible. Translating these poems has been a decidedly sobering experience. I have tried to give for each text a simple denotative equivalent in prose (which occasionally includes punctuation changes). This inevitably eliminates most if not all of the properly poetical elements I write of in the essays.

oets as Players

Theme and Variation in Late
Medieval French Poetry

Et s'on fait de triste matiere
Se est joieuse la maniere
Dou fait.

And even if one makes poems on sad subjects,
yet the manner of the making is joyous
—Guillaume de Machaut

Prologue: To the Reader

he nature of the essays that make up this book and of the method that informs them can best be characterized, I think, by defining at the outset what I see as their relationship to a certain historical perspective. Although I recognize that my own ways of thinking about literature, like everyone else's, have inevitably been influenced by concepts and emphases current today, it seems to me that a requisite for scholars studying a bygone age is an informed sense of the differences that separate it from their own—and that can thus serve as tools for understanding its specific character. This is as true in the history of literature as it is in the history of art or music or diplomacy. It has presided over many aspects of the present volume. It has dictated, first, the choice of poets: those studied as exemplary here were seen as important writers by their own contemporaries, more than by ours, and that has seemed one good reason for choosing them. Readers may thus be surprised to discover that the two authors usually regarded as the major poetic figures of the time—François Villon and Charles d'Orléans—find little place in these pages, although they lurk, inevitably, in the background, and the readings I propose can apply just as well to their writings as to those of the poets, somewhat less celebrated today, who are my main concern. Indeed, the latter may be better seen, their lineaments more clearly fixed, I think, outside of the giant shadows cast by those whom the nineteenth and twentieth centuries chose as the most worthy poets of the age.

By the same historical token, when analyzing late medieval poetry I have generally aimed at avoiding the imposition, *a priori*, of twentieth-century modes of thought on fifteenth-century intellectual and formal structures: I explore this poetry in order to discover its own aims—explicit or, very often, implicit—and its own character. I try, that is, insofar as is possible (and I am well aware that some critics deny that it is possible at all[1])—to take these texts on their own terms, and not on ours. I try not to make them fit into any one critical scheme, or at least not one imposed from without. Although I have been a spectator of attempts at applying every sort of twentieth-century critical canon to pre-Romantic literature, and although such attempts often yield valuable or interesting results, it nonetheless seems to me that one must first of all learn how to read such texts in a way radically different from the way in which one can read Hugo or Mallarmé or Eluard. I hope that this approach will be compatible with the interests of medievalists and nonspecialists alike.

One conspicuous aspect of medieval literature that must strike even the occasional modern reader as characteristic of its time is the constant use and reuse of certain accepted ideas and certain conventional forms. My central strategy in the chapters that follow will lie in showing the ways in which these ideas and forms are deployed, varied—played with, if you will—by certain poets, in order to assure for themselves the creative place or space that is necessary to any artist. In doing this, I lay no claim to making any systematic survey of the entire poetic production of the fourteenth and fifteenth centuries, or even of any particular genre within that production.

In each of the five essays, however, I treat a different kind of poetry, with "kind" understood now in a thematic, now in a formal sense, using a single poet to exemplify the problems raised by each of these "kinds." As preparation for this study, I propose in the introductory part of the first chapter a brief analysis of the problems that seem to me inherent, for the twentieth-century reader, in the poetry of the time. Once more, be it lyric or narrative, moralistic or dramatic, fifteenth-century verse cannot be read like Romantic and post-Romantic poetry: the rules are different. After this prolegomenon—a warning and a summary that medievalists may wish to skip—I go on to illustrate some of the rules of the poetic game in the work (and particularly in the ballades) of Guillaume de Machaut, the foremost poet of the fourteenth century, whose influence in the next century furnishes a useful illustration of the force of authority and tradition. The first chapter has, then, like the others, the double goal of investigating a poetic mode or genre or form in general, and the work of a single poet in particular.

This poet, in the second essay, is Christine de Pizan, whose play with her persona and with the courtly conventions of formal verse like the rondeau constitute inventive attempts at interpreting the rules. Analysis of repetition and variation in her work, and of their relation to meaning, leads me to consider forms less "fixed" than the ballade, the rondeau, and the virelai.

In the following chapter, the longer, apparently even less formally static poems of Alain Chartier—some including a first person and others excluding it—provide the field for investigating a poetics in which neither intellectual nor psychological nor yet metaphorical originality, as we understand it today, appears to be central to the poet's craft. How, then, does the poet still constitute his own voice and create his own poetic personality?

Often much longer than the longest poem of Chartier, the numerous moral and didactic treatises in verse seem particularly characteristic of the Middle Ages—and particularly un-poetic to modern readers, despite the frequent appearance in them of an apparently individualized "I." The fourth essay, through a reading of *Les Lunettes des Princes* of Jean Meschinot, confronts the problems posed by such poems. Can they, on the one hand, be read as "poetry" in any modern sense? Can one, on the other, find in them any adumbration of the modern lyric first-person persona?

Finally, I consider in the last chapter a group of poems defined not principally by author (although Jean Molinet will in fact appear as a prototypical poet) or by formal criteria, but rather by tone and vocabulary. We shall look at the considerable body of obscene verse, largely ignored by critics and historians but nonetheless characteristic of the time, that reproduces formally the so-called "courtly" genres but does not reproduce their abstract language. It is tempting, in the current critical climate, to see the authors of such poems as subversive of the prevailing moral and social order—whether this view is reasonable or not is one of the questions I shall raise. Another and perhaps more fundamental question concerns the validity of the term "courtly" itself as a literary category.

Although each chapter is thus discrete, they are all related through more than a common chronological base and the effort to explore and elucidate late medieval poetic practice. Both the title of the book and that of each essay have been devised to indicate that the study as a whole turns about a central concept, the concept of poetry as "play"—as an amusing, and more or less gratuitous, enterprise or game, in which both the poet and the public may be players. As Guillaume de Machaut himself points out in the statement quoted in the book epigraph (a statement that is all the more important because of the relative rarity of its theoretical nature in the Middle Ages), even "serious" poetry, of a clear moral or religious inspiration and didactic intent, must be based on this sense of verse-making as a joyous activity, a game. Although I recognize that this notion is hardly novel in contemporary criticism, I shall propose it as a basic metaphor for poetry in the essays that follow in a fashion as little doctrinaire as possible, for I wish to allow to the rich terms "play" and "player," and their corollary "game," every legitimate resonance. (Not every nuance in the fertile semantic field of "play" will be appropriate, to be sure: despite the condemnation of intense rhyme-play as puerile by such twentieth-century prosodists as W. T. Elwert and Maurice Grammont, we shall find that the poems in which it occurs are hardly child's play.)

All games have rules, for instance, and we shall see how the poet-players—with Guillaume de Machaut as a kind of *magister ludi*—codify them, follow them, bend them, expand them. Further, the number of games is legion; thus we shall find late medieval poets playing different kinds of word games, involving, for example, to a degree rarely attained since, puns and the richest of rhymes: they juggle with words in dazzling ways. Sometimes such games, by presenting us with riddles, invite us to participate, to become decoders of meaning. Playing on the (consecrated) words of proverbs, a favorite pastime of those poets known as the Grands Rhétoriqueurs, is another way of winking at the reader.

At other times, what one finds is the poet indulging in the play of wit, either crudely, through sexual jokes and allusion, or more delicately, like Alain Chartier, through irony and ambiguity. Sometimes the game is one of blindman's bluff. The reader is blindfolded by the poet, turned this way and that, subjected to a *jeu de cache-cache* in which the poet's identity is hidden, changed, multiplied: Eustache Deschamps speaks in a woman's voice; Christine de Pizan becomes a man; Meschinot hides behind the allegorical figures of the four cardinal virtues. Such play-acting signifies that the dramatic meaning of the metaphor cannot be forgotten, fortified by the French associations of *jouer une pièce, joueur,* and *jeu dramatique.* Some poems of Chartier are clearly farces—*Le Debat des deux fortunés d'amours,* for example, or *Le Debat du herault, du vassault et du villain. La Belle Dame sans mercy,* on the other hand, is high comedy. Other poems, like Meschinot's *Les Lunettes des Princes,* are morality plays, in which the poet casts himself as a player. Identifying the role played by the poet, the place of his or her "I" in its various embodiments, will, indeed, be a major concern in our reading of the texts. And the reader's role as spectator of the play cannot be forgotten.

Nor do the connotations of the metaphor stop there, for we shall find from the outset that one of the chief characteristics of late medieval poetry is the play with meaning, often expressed in more or less subtle variations on a topos or a piece of conventional wisdom. Indeed, play with words often leads to play with meaning, and excessive play with words either to the near-elimination of meaning or, conversely, to its intensification.

In short, since the very notion of poetry as play (and of poets as players) appears to me to be generated by late medieval poetic practice itself, I do not wish to eliminate, either by adopting a particular restrictive critical stance or by arbitrarily limiting its definition, any possibilities which it may offer for the informed reading of the various texts proposed by each chapter. I hope readers will see this approach as productive rather than naïve or indecisive.

They should further be warned that although such texts cannot be fully appreciated without an awareness of their singularly different cultural context, these essays largely—and deliberately— eschew any attempt to find the *reasons* for the poetic practices in that context.[2] My effort, rather, is to see the texts both as the fifteenth-century author wrote them and as the twentieth-century reader must first approach them. It is well known, for instance, that Alain Chartier is not the first French poet to write debate poems, and were I writing a study of that genre, I should certainly pay more attention to their antecedents than I do in the third chapter. My aim is quite different, however: I try not so much to place Chartier's poems in any historical sequence as to define them as related in various ways, prosodic as well as thematic, to other poetry of the same period, and at the same time as characteristic of the work of an individual poet. Once that is accomplished, readers are free to apply to them whatever insights their own particular critical bent may afford, either from literary history or from contemporary theory, or from both.

Here, then, is the final justification of the stance I adopt in regard to these texts: it does not imply that they are not susceptible to analysis other than my own, or that they have nothing with which contemporary criticism may not usefully come to grips. Quite the contrary, for many of the problems they pose have been at the center of current critical discussion: the place of the "I" in fiction and in autobiography, for example; poetic voice; the nature of allegory; the definition of poetry itself.[3] This may come as a surprise to non-specialist readers—but it can only be a healthy surprise. It is these same readers, including not a few students and teachers of literature, who, despite the present-day climate of critical sophistication, still believe—or want to believe—a poet who claims to weep or to whimper, to love passionately, to hate, to pray. One has only to look

at recent studies on the work of the poet known as François Villon to
see that this is true.

Put briefly, the way of reading various poets and various kinds
of poems that I propose is meant to facilitate the moment of encoun-
ter between the text and its reader. It is intended, in other words, not
to close but to open the texts, in all their playful variety.

1 ♁ *Les Règles du jeu*:
Guillaume de Machaut
and Poetic Practice

he idea of finding pleasure in the reading of four-
teenth- or fifteenth-century French poetry could only
have been thought of, until recently, as a professorial
notion engendered by the myopic view of those few
specialists who, unaccountably neglecting the glories
of the epic and the romance or the splendors of the sonnet, were
content to work in the autumnal twilight of what the French trans-
lation of Huizinga's famous study calls the decline of the Middle
Ages.[1] Exception was always made, of course, for two poets, Charles
d'Orléans and François Villon, the Prince and the Pauper, the first
praised, a bit faintly, for the precious refinement of a limited vision
and the second, extravagantly, for the realism and sincerity—the
"modernism"—of his poignant confession in verse. But whoever
wished to venture beyond this conveniently contemporary pair, be
they *amateurs* of poetry, students, or even specialists curious about a
period other than "their own," found unexpected obstacles of vari-
ous sorts in their path. It will be instructive, I think, to remind
ourselves of these obstacles at the outset of this study; we shall find
that, while many impediments have been or can easily be removed,
others remain, which it will be the purpose of this book not only to
define but, in some measure at least, to overcome. I shall begin with
an analysis of problems that seem to me inherent for the twentieth-
century reader in the poetry of the time; lyric or narrative, moralistic

or dramatic, fifteenth-century verse cannot be read like Romantic poetry. After this preliminary *mise-en-garde*, I shall go on, as I said in the Prologue, to elucidate some of the rules of the poetic game in the work of Guillaume de Machaut, the greatest poet of the fourteenth century, whose influence in the fifteenth will already furnish an illustration of the force of authority and tradition. The first chapter, like the others, aims thus at the double goal of investigating a poetic mode or genre or form in general and the work of a single poet in particular.

The first obstacles to reading late medieval poetry can be divided into two categories: those that are historical in nature and those that are textual or linguistic. By "historical" I mean those impediments stemming from the very concept that a "Renaissance" occurred after a long, dark middle age of the arts, and further (at least since Michelet), that such a rebirth was necessary because this middle age had finally reached old age—and death.[2] This Romantic historiographic construct, still very much alive at the turn of this century, was demonstrated brilliantly, with particular reference to northern France, in the study by Huizinga to which I have just referred. After the work's initial appearance in Dutch in 1919, translations into the major European languages (English and German in 1924, Spanish in 1930, French in 1932, Italian in 1940) brought its masterly, dramatic—but ultimately biased—synthesis of life and art in the late Middle Ages to the attention of an enormous public; and they continue to do so.

It would be foolish to deny the extraordinary vigor and conviction of this work, but I can only agree, with Millard Meiss, that the Dutch historian's judgments "remain more influential than they deserve to be,"[3] for while Huizinga generally admired the artists, the Van Eycks and Roger van der Weyden, his contempt for most of fifteenth-century literature is evident: even though he admits that "a new beauty of form was already revealing itself in the literature of the fifteenth century," he contends that this is difficult to perceive and that, in most of it, the form is extenuated and "the qualities of rhythm and tone are poor."[4] If, with unmatched skill, Huizinga points out in his work the crises affecting fifteenth-century society, in which, increasingly, the chivalric ideal was obliged to confront new political and social realities, if he shows the importance, for those realities, of the princely or royal court as an institution and gives a vivid picture of everyday life, yet it may be fairly said that the picture is *too* vivid, made up as it is of contrasts between light and dark, blood and roses, leading to generalizations that can no longer be accepted.[5] Like many other scholars—for I use Huizinga here as an example of an attitude widely shared by historians—he takes little account of differences in generations or regions, or of the immense vitality of France and its people, which after the Hundred Years War was to lead, among other things, to economic revival and large literary production. It is difficult to view these phenomena as the last gasps of a dying civilization.[6] Nor does he accord much attention to the special role of literary language or attempt to apply fifteenth-century canons of taste or literary assumptions to the literature.

Despite his very wide reading and the elegant use to which he put it in *The Waning of the Middle Ages*, Huizinga was not a literary historian, nor did he pretend to be. But critics and historians of literature from Sainte-Beuve to the present have, in their own field, adumbrated or shared his point of view or variations of it, as Franco Simone has demonstrated in his brilliant work arguing for the originality of the fifteenth century.[7] The opinions of Gaston Paris, of Henri Guy, of Gustave Lanson, all of whom saw in fourteenth-century and fifteenth-century poetry a kind of abyss separating the great twelfth and thirteenth centuries from the Pléiade, are still alive in countless minds and manuals. The attitude is easy to find in those school texts that reprint some of the works of the period, where praise is condescending indeed: "If, too often enslaved by form, he [Guillaume de Machaut] sometimes lacks grace and originality and is too fond of the play of allegory, he can also occasionally express his own feelings with sincerity." "[The poetry of Charles d'Orléans] evokes with a somewhat mannered grace, the charm of the seasons, the lure of life, . . . the regret of growing old.'"[8] A perfect resumé of this traditional way of looking at the poetry of the period can be found in the course on medieval literature given by the eminent scholar Gustave Michaut; although they date from 1931, the views expressed are still all too current. He writes of the long "period of transition" between the "real" Middle Ages and the Renaissance, and he characterizes the Italian wars at the end of the fifteenth century as "the end of the Middle Age, which took two centuries to die."[9]

Now taking two hundred years as a "period of transition" appears not only unhistorical but a peculiarly fruitless way of considering the literature of those years, in all its lively variety and abundance. To understand the insidious force of this view of literary history and analysis, one has only to remember that attitude with which, blinded by the light of Classicism, historians and critics until well into the nineteenth century approached most French sixteenth-century literature: it was valid insofar as it "prepared" or "announced" the great literature of the following century. This view is still prevalent among those who find interest in Renaissance tragedy only to the extent that it leads to Corneille or Racine—or, in other words, conforms to literary canons that were not its own. If the poets of the fourteenth and fifteenth centuries—even including the Rhét-oriqueurs—with their rhythmic and linguistic experiments and their growing insistence on the métier of the poet, prepare the way for the Pléiade, and the Pléiade, with its aesthetic humanism and its attentive revalorization of myth, prepares the way for Classicism, we come to a "period of transition" some three (or three and a half!) centuries long, culminating in those forty years or so of the seventeenth century that constitute the "true" Classic age—clearly an absurd framework for French literature.

Happily, it is becoming less and less possible to fit late medieval literature into such a framework. Under the impetus of such scholars as the late Franco Simone and Albert-Marie Schmidt, the literary history of the period is at last being given the kind of careful study that it warrants. Daniel Poirion's monumental study of the evolution of the courtly lyric from Machaut to Charles d'Orléans has been an immensely important contribution to a new understanding of the poets, of the forms they used, and of their artistic conceptions, but his more general volume on French literature from 1300 to 1480 will doubtless have more influence, with its bold panorama reassessing, in an attractive format, the whole range of French literature of the period.[10] And it is a healthy sign that, although P.-Y. Badel admits to a relative neglect of the fourteenth and fifteenth centuries in his popular and admirably brief introduction to medieval French literature, he does so with regret, assuring the reader that "these were not centuries of decline, these genres [i.e., history, theater, Rhétoriqueur poetry] have given literature some of its most beautiful texts."[11] The literary "desert" of Sainte-Beuve and Michelet has, at last, blossomed in men's minds—and in literary history.

With the removal of this historical block, a corollary obstacle can be eliminated as well: the alleged necessity, debated in a long, occasionally lively but more often dreary critical battle, of deciding whether the period in question is "medieval" or "renascent." Once its historical autonomy is recognized, however—and this is now the case—it can be seen as being neither and as partaking of both, as being composed, like all ages, of remnants of the past and adumbrations of the future.[12] The problem is of course complicated by the fact that this period has no name: "pre-Renaissance," like "pre-Classic," is a loaded label; "late medieval" will have to do, I suppose, for the moment. What is important, in any event, is recognizing the original character—political, social, literary—of those two centuries. Dealing with a nameless period can, in fact, be considered an advantage: instead of trying to apply to this age a medieval or Renaissance label from the outside—and neither category is very satisfactory—it appears much more useful, now, to try to see it from within, for what it is by itself.

Politically, it is an era that saw the development of a kind of monarchy that was neither feudal nor yet absolute;[13] socially, the increasing importance of money and the growth of urban centers as well as of a central administration contributed, on the one hand, to a change—indeed, a crisis—in the status of the aristocracy and, on the other, to the consolidation of an ever-expanding upper middle class, often aping the nobility, often becoming integrated into it.[14] From the literary point of view, this period would stretch from the time of such early poets as Guillaume de Machaut (d. 1377), Eustache Des- champs (d. ca. 1407), Froissart (d. ca. 1404), and Christine de Pizan (d. ca. 1430) to the era of Guillaume Crétin (d. 1525), Molinet (d. 1491), Octovien de Saint-Gelais (d. 1502), Jean Marot (d. 1526), and Jean Bouchet (d. ca. 1557). Once one conceives of this histori- cal span as independent, it becomes possible to see it not as a time of decadence but as one of development,[15] not only in the many poetic genres, including the theater, but in prose fiction, in histori- cal writing, and in what one might call the notion of literary self-consciousness, as well. It is clearly time to conclude, with Franco Simone, that "recent research envisages the . . . problems of the French fifteenth century in an entirely new way"[16]—and to suggest new ways of reading the literature of the time.

If, in the light of recent studies, it is relatively easy to remove the historical impediments to reading, it is not always so with those that I have termed textual and linguistic. One must remember at the outset that most of the poetry of the fifteenth century now known to the reading public was not published in printed form until modern times—and even today much of it remains in manuscript. Indeed, the last fact surely accounts for a good deal of the misunderstanding that surrounds the works of the period. The existence of a consider- able body of prose and poetry not yet accessible in print makes it impossible for all but the specialist to have a wholly adequate first- hand notion of the entire literary production of the time. Were this to be true for the nineteenth century, say, it is easy to see that any such precise definition of the evolution of the poetic consciousness and its manifestations as we now have would be impossible: what would one make of the poetry of a century represented only, for example, by *Les Orientales*, *Ruy Blas*, the complete works of Théodore de

Banville, *Les Trophées*, and some poems of Mallarmé, Jules La-
forgue, René Ghil, and Raymond de la Tailhède?
But even if the entire corpus of the poetry were available in
modern editions, these very editions could themselves pose delicate
problems for their readers, as the ones we now have do. Ever since
the massive acclimatization of the printed book, we are used to
thinking, rightly or wrongly, of the text, fixed on the page, as the
exact result of the author's will, in both senses of this word—a legacy
unchanging, unchanged, except by unscrupulous editors or the dis-
covery of a new will. One has only to think of how Montaigne is able
to play with this assumption, claiming—falsely, of course—never to
suppress a clause in his literary legacy, only adding to it, to realize
how early on in the civilization of the book it became accepted and,
indeed, essential: the printed text was, in fact, the guarantor of the
author's good faith (his good will), of his dependability, of his capac-
ity to manipulate his reader. It is only in relatively recent times that,
through various means, some measure of freedom with the printed
text is taken by the author—and is given by him to the reader. One
of the most obvious of these means is the deliberate rearrangement,
or disarrangement, of words on the printed page.

Now poems set down by hand during the Middle Ages present
some of these characteristics of freedom, but in a different way. It is
rare to find a manuscript like the one we have bearing the statement
"Vesci l'ordenance que Guillaume de Machau vuet qu'il ait en son
livre" (This is the order that Guillaume de Machaut wants in his
book).[17] Generally, we cannot be sure either of the order of the texts
or of their preparation under the supervision of their author, and
even when the author is known to have had a hand in them, varia-
tions exist from manuscript to manuscript. The situation is usually
much closer to that found in the poetical works, for example, of
Alain Chartier, which survive in 113 manuscripts, almost all of
which appear to have been copied after his death.[18] So where—or
what—is the "true" text? Is there, in fact, such a thing as an Ur-Text
in medieval literature? The answer to this question, conditioned by
ideas emanating both from the Romantic conception of the absolute

individuality of an author and from the Germanic beginnings of modern Romance philology in the nineteenth century, has always, at least until recently, been a resounding "Yes," with the resulting cataloguing of every known manuscript for any given literary artifact, of the construction of stemmata of manuscript "families," of the reconstruction, even, in some cases of a hypothetical "original" form.[19] But the (re)construction of a fixed Text, it seems to me, can profoundly alter the nature of what was a much less consecrated form, a text subject to variation and to reshaping at the hand of a scribe or by the voice of a performer. I do not mean in any way to disparage the extreme usefulness of the immense philological labor that, since the middle of the nineteenth century, has provided so many editions of medieval texts, printed often with infinite care for indicated variants; I suggest, however, that the Text, hypothetically perfect and thus perfected, may often hide the text(s), and so may constitute, albeit unwittingly, a real series of obstacles to reading. Certainly "a sure text" is a sine qua non for any serious literary analysis, in any period. But might it be that in much of medieval literature, and particularly in poetry, for reasons that we shall see, there are, for any one artifact (if I may use this word again to mean the single original manifestation of a literary impulse), several possible texts, among which it is sometimes, though by no means always, feasible to choose one as being "better," that is, presumably closer to the original manifestation? The operative word in this question is *choose*—and our knowledge that innovation was regularly practiced (and, indeed, encouraged by the oral transmission of the text) should turn the formidable apparatus often found at the bottom of the page in modern "critical" editions from an unattractive obstacle, forbidding in its seriousness, to the affirmation of a playful kind of textual freedom that traditional modern texts cannot have.

One may counter that only the frivolous reader, not the serious student, would be put off by critical apparatus. This may perhaps be so—and yet, in a much more subtle way, an "edited" Text may mask the text, even if there is only one version of the latter, for any editor of a medieval text must make decisions that, originally, were left to the choice of the reader or executant. One of the best known and most

anthologized poems in fifteenth-century literature is found in the
following form in the principal modern edition of the poetry of
Charles d'Orléans (my translation is based on the manuscript version
of the poem, with punctuation added):[20]

XXXI

L E temps a laissié son manteau   [*p. 365*]
  De vent, de froidure et de pluye,
Et s'est vestu de brouderie,
De soleil luyant, cler et beau.   4
  Il n'y a beste, ne oyseau,
Qu'en son jargon ne chante ou crie:
Le temps [a laissié son manteau!]   7
  Riviere, fontaine et ruisseau
Portent, en livree jolie,
Gouttes d'argent d'orfaverie,
Chascun s'abille de nouveau:
Le temps [a laissié son manteau.]   12

The season has put aside its cloak of wind and cold and rain
and has dressed in embroidered clothes of sun, shining bright
and beautiful. There's no beast or bird which in its own lan-
guage isn't singing or crying: The season (etc.). River, spring
and stream are wearing, in pretty livery, drops of silver and of
goldwork. Everyone is clothed afresh: The season (etc.).

In his study of the autograph manuscript of the poems, the
same editor, Pierre Champion, included a photograph of the page on
which this rondeau appears;[21] this is the way one finds it written on
the lower half of page 365, labeled "Rondel 220":

Le temps a laissie son manteau
  de vent de froidure et de pluye
  et sest vestu de brouderie
  de soleil luyant cler et beau
Il ny a beste ne oyseau
  quen son jargon ne chante ou crie

    Le temps etc.

Riviere fotaine et ruisseau
  Portent en livree iolie

Gouttes dargēt dorfaverie
Chascun sabille de nouveau
   Le temps etc.

Even this diplomatic version of the manuscript, with no punctuation and no line numbers, does not, however, represent exactly what one *sees* on the page, for evident thereon are several features that cannot be rendered in ordinary print: (1) it is clear that "220" has been added by a later hand and does not necessarily, therefore, indicate an order decided on by the poet, even though he owned and annotated this manuscript; (2) the letter "L" of the first line is larger than all the others and is enclosed in a square; (3) the letter "R" (l. 8), on a smaller scale, is similarly rubricated but in a more florid style; (4) the words "brouderie" (l. 3) and "luyant" (l. 4) are corrections.

Such a confrontation of the manuscript text and the Text of a modern editor can teach us a number of things. For the single reader of the poem, the order in which it is found may or may not be important, depending on whether or not that reader wishes to see the poem in relation to other poems; in any case, the modern editor's arrangement may be arbitrary—as that of the original manuscript may be. Our conclusion can only be that the relationship of one poem to another, in any given group of poems, must be conceived of quite differently in fifteenth-century poetry than in, say, *Les Fleurs du mal*. Further, the rubricated letters in the manuscript not only add a measure of visual delight to the poem imperceptible in any modern printing of it (the large "L" in Champion's edition does not give the same effect), but underline, in the main, the strophic structure—one finds the same phenomenon, for example, at the beginning of each stanza of the ballades in the Charles d'Orléans manuscript. Beyond this, since there is virtually no punctuation before the end of the poem in medieval manuscripts, all those who read the poem, either silently or aloud, were free to punctuate as they pleased, according to their own interpretation of the text. In other words, readers were their own editors—and they still may be; they need not feel bound by what are, in fact, the arbitrary choices of another editor in matters of punctuation. One recent critic of the Champion edition goes so far as to say that *any* punctuation imposed on the rondeaux of Charles d'Orléans is a betrayal of the poet.[22] This is surely true if the Text in any way obstructs the perception of the text, free on its page—if, that is, the commas, question marks, and semicolons inserted disallow *any* of the possible readings of the text to which the poet may be inviting his reader.

Of course it would be absurd to insist in every case on a mere printed replica of the manuscript: substituting "laissié" for "laissie" and "fontaine" for "fōtaine" can hardly be called betraying the author, since these are merely orthographical changes indicating the same sounds. In the same way, the transformation of "sabille" into "s'habille" and even "sest vestu" to "s'est vêtu," as in many current editions, does not in any way affect the poem, except to make it more immediately accessible to a modern reader.[23] But the sound of "luisant" is clearly not that of "luyant," and "brouderie" may represent a different sound than the modern "broderie," as "orfaverie" was surely different phonetically from "orfèvrerie."[24] These nuances of sound are, if anything, more important in the poetic structure than the insertion of a period instead of a colon. In any case, and despite the fact that what we see as tinkering with texts would in all probability have been seen as a kind of literary creation in the Middle Ages, modern readers should be aware of the existence of a text that, though it may not be the "original," is at least a version that allows them as much leeway for interpretation as it did its fifteenth-century reader—or its twentieth-century editor.

A very important example of this is the choice made in regard to repeating the refrain of a rondeau. One must remember that the basic structure of the rondeau, like that of the ballade and the virelai, the other two major *formes fixes* of the fourteenth and fifteenth centuries, derives from a musical form—at first a dance form—with a simple, fixed structure of two musical phrases that recur in a certain order. Each section of music, conventionally represented in analyses of this poetry by I and II, may of course cover more than one line of verse, but new verses set to a recurring section must have the same length and the same rhyme scheme as the original verses. Even when there is no real musical setting—and this is the case for the majority of rondeaux in the fifteenth century—there is an implied one, and the basic order of recurrence remains fixed. It is clear from the musical settings that, in the rondeau, the refrain takes up both sections I and II and is stated at the outset; that that part of it corresponding to section I is repeated after new verses occur, also corresponding to section I; and that the poem ends with a repetition of the full refrain. If one adds to the underlying, unvarying, *musical* structure the verses of the *poetic* refrain, indicated here by superscript R, the form of the rondeau can be understood according to the following schema: I^R II^R I I^R I II I^R II^R. Thus the shortest possible rondeau must have eight lines, and its rhyme scheme would be represented in the conventional way by the following pattern, in which capital letters stand for the refrain lines: AB aA ab AB.

The problem arises with rondeaux of more than eight lines— in which, in other words, either I or II, or both, stand for sections of more than one line of verse, for in many of the manuscripts, the copyists did not recopy more than two or three words of the beginning of the refrain, followed by "etc." An example of this can be seen in the manuscript version of "Le temps a laissie son manteau." What does this "etc." represent? Does it mean, at the half-repetition point, that all of section I (AB), that is, lines 1 and 2, should be repeated? Or does it mean to repeat only line 1, as Champion has done in his edition? And, at the end of the poem, does it indicate a repetition of I (AB) and II (BA), or, once more, merely I? It is clear that in the fifteenth century, following the complexity brought to music by the *ars nova* of the fourteenth century and the subsequent widening of the divergence between poetry and music, poets no longer felt strictly bound by the musical substructure; they could—and did— shorten the refrain if they so desired, although they always continued to observe the basic pattern of repetition. The problem, obviously, is to know what the "etc." stands for: whether it means to repeat the refrain in whole or in part. The question is a vexed one, and it has been answered in an alarming number of ways by the various editors of fifteenth-century rondeaux. The Text of Champion gives only one answer. To take another example, the refrain of the rondeau "Sot euil raporteur de nouvelle" (Foolish eye, the reporter of news) by

Charles d'Orléans, given simply as "Sot euil etc." in the manuscripts, is printed in four different ways by four different editors.[25] If imposed punctuation can be a betrayal, it is clear that an imposed, arbitrary number of lines for an essential part of the poem is an even graver transgression. I shall not now, in my turn, propose a solution to the problem.[26] The existence of the ambiguity is what the present-day reader of fifteenth-century verse must remember, an ambiguity kept as late as ca. 1501, in *Le Jardin de plaisance et fleur de rethorique*, an anthology printed in gothic type and reproducing poems of Guillaume de Machaut and Eustache Deschamps, alongside the works of such fifteenth-century authors as Alain Chartier, Michaut Taillevent, Charles d'Orléans, and Jean Meschinot; it, too, does not give the entire line of the refrain in the rondeau, using instead, as the manuscripts do, only the first two or three words, followed by that vexing "etc." The printed page inevitably replaces the manuscript, with its call for oral reading and the reader's *formal* participation in the poem; but it does so slowly, and throughout the last part of the fifteenth century, after the introduction of printing, at least in certain types of poems, a measure of textual liberty is left to readers—or, perhaps, a certain knowledge is expected of them—both of which are lost in most modern editions.

The so-called *formes fixes*, the mention of which is enough in many minds to define the poetry of the late Middle Ages, can thus be seen in fact to be much less *fixes* than one may think, for to textual freedom must be added the choices open to oral readers, the *récitants* of the poem, free to embellish it as they wished through intonation, rhythm, emphasis. This is of course true today, as well—but one reads poetry aloud much less frequently than in the fifteenth century. We cannot forget that silent reading, as an activity, was much rarer then than it is now. H. J. Chaytor, in his book on medieval vernacular literature, devotes a chapter to showing the degree to which reading used to imply *saying*, or reciting.[27] The Middle French words *dictier*, to indite, *dictié* (our "ditty"), and *dit*, meaning a poem, keep something of this, as does the modern French expression *dire un poème*. The very casualness, as it were, of the poem on the manuscript page, with its variants from copy to copy, its unrealized abbreviations, its abridged refrains, shows how much the written word was but a substitute for the living poem, embodied only by the voice of an executant, in the moment of its reading. By "casualness" I do not, of course, mean sloppiness, for some of the manuscripts—especially those containing the works of the poets who enjoyed or were seeking royal favor, like Guillaume de Machaut and Christine de Pizan—are splendid indeed, adorned with brilliant miniatures, illuminated letters, fantastically ornate borders. But here, too, the visual delight seeks to endow the poem with an aura it cannot have in the sober black and white of the printed page.

Nor does such a text imply that other eminently temporal and oral aspect of the poem lost to modern readers without specialized knowledge: music. Not only the rondeau, but also the ballade, the virelai, the lai—all of these forms have a musical origin, and even though music and poetry tended throughout our period to diverge more and more, to go each its separate way, since the days when Machaut united in one person both a superb poet and a composer of genius, music was still never far from the poem; it remains indeed, as we have seen with the rondeau, essential for an understanding of its structure. Many poems were still being set, on the one hand, and the musical qualities of language were, on the other, acquiring new importance, as we shall see.[28] The union of poetry and music, which, with humanist nostalgia, Ronsard and J.-A. de Baïf would make some effort to recapture in the sixteenth century, was in our period already broken. Indeed, this very rupture was one of the characteristics of the time, and both its recognition and its denial were to bring consequences of importance for the evolution of music as well as of lyric poetry.

Another kind of music, now neglected or forgotten, is present even in the nonlyric genres, in the narrative *dits*, even in moral and political poems: this is, of course, the pronunciation of the words themselves, and the rhythm of the lines. If part of the latter—what might be called the microrhythm of the individual line—can be assured by the poet through the meter and the placing of stresses, the reader, then as now, was still free to create the poem's macrorhythm, to read it more or less slowly, accelerando or ritardando. From evidence in Froissart and Deschamps, Daniel Poirion believes that contemporary poetic declamation was rather slow and solemn, emphasizing significant pauses within the line and at its end.[29] What has changed most radically, however, in the creation of the music of the verse is the pronunciation itself; the entire acoustic tonality of a fifteenth-century poem, when its pronunciation is modernized, is obviously different from what the poet intended it to be. Although the phonetic history of a language before the advent of the phonograph can only be imperfect, enough is known to make it possible to reproduce with fair accuracy the sounds of Middle French. Even though the language of Machaut, say, is doubtless further from modern French than that of his contemporary Petrarch is from modern Italian, or that of Chaucer from modern English, it is still relatively simple to identify those features in which Middle French differs most radically from present-day speech.[30] If we return for a moment to the example of Charles d'Orléans's celebrated rondeau, the first two lines alone can illustrate this.

Le temps a laissie son manteau
De vent de froidure et de pluye

1. The three nasal vowels in "temps," "manteau," and "vent," which sound the dominant phonetic note, were not pronounced simply [ã], as in modern French, but [ã] followed by pronunciation of the nasal consonant, as it still can be heard in some regions in southwestern and southern France; the [n] in "son" was likewise sounded after the nasal: [õn].

2. The spelling *-eau* in "manteau," of obvious importance because of its place at the rhyme, represents a triphthong [ɛao], which is reduced during the Middle French period to a diphthong [ɛo] or [eo].[31]

3. In the next line, the [t] of "vent" may be sounded if one pauses after the word, although normally it would not be pronounced before a following word beginning with a consonant.

4. The [r] in Middle French (e.g., "froidure") is still trilled or rolled as in modern Italian or Spanish; the uvular [ʀ], so characteristic of modern French, was not used.

5. The spelling -oi- in "froidure" indicates the sound [wɛ] instead of [wa] as at present; one has only to think of the occurrence of the words "moi" and "joie," for instance, in lyric poetry, of the imperfect tense, spelled with -oi- (there seems to have been a popular Parisian tendency to use [ɛ] in the imperfect, however), and of infinitives in -oir, to realize the enormous phonic importance of this difference.

6. Finally, the so-called "mute" e [ə] of modern French is never mute in Middle French (e.g., "pluye"); it is always sounded at the end of a word, except before a following word beginning with a vowel (although even here one occasionally finds a hiatus), and, within a word, it is even sounded in hiatus before a vowel, as in "aperceu," for example, or "veoir."

It is not at all my intent here to describe with any semblance of completeness the pronunciation of Middle French. What I mean to suggest by the foregoing demonstration is, much more simply, the importance of recognizing the aesthetic consequences of a phonetic system that differs in striking ways from the modern French system. This realization is, of course, just as important for sixteenth-century poetry, though we often forget it.

The historical and textual problems we have been considering can, in sum, be seen as primarily problems of *awareness*; once they are defined, or exposed, it is not hard to solve them. Let us assume, then, a few ideal readers, historically and linguistically sophisticated, convinced of the autonomy of the period as much as of that of the texts, who wish to increase their knowledge of fifteenth-century poetry, based on a reading of the best available editions. Those readers will discover, first of all, a growing number of recent editions not only of the major poets but of several poets who have never heretofore received modern editorial attention; ample proof of this is furnished by the bibliography at the end of this book. One further example of renewed interest in the period is significant here. Beginning in 1906, Pierre Champion directed a series of publications entitled "Bibliothèque Littéraire du XVe Siècle," which in its nearly forty volumes produced important contributions to the literary history of the period as well as many editions of texts. It ceased publication around 1930 but was revived in 1975, under the direction of Jean Dufournet; like the other series, it will include both texts and literary studies.

But after reading, say, among others, Kenneth Varty's anthology of Christine de Pizan's poems and Robert Deschaux's new edition of the poems of Michault Taillevent—the first of the complete works of this important Burgundian figure[32]—even our ideal readers may be disheartened, for what do they find? On the one hand, a discouragingly massive number of poems written in the same form—rondeaux, ballades, virelais—or in strophes of varying rhyme schemes but apparently pedestrian meter and, on the other, the endless repetition of the same conventional themes, embodied in the same conventional images: unrequited, and therefore unhappy, love, contrasted with a smiling spring landscape; plaints for unfaithful lovers; the endless enumeration of the beloved's physical and moral beauties; dreams filled with allegorical journeys, figures, architecture; banal disquisitions on Fortune . . . and the apparently total lack of anything resembling sincere, individual emotion on the part of the poet. In other words, more obstacles, albeit more obvious ones, to reading with pleasure. It is time to attack such problems as these in a more direct, less abstract way than we have done so far. This can be done most usefully by considering the work of Guillaume de Machaut who, although he died in 1377, remains clearly a master for the following century. In an age when tradition in literature was the obverse of what it is now, when, indeed, it was a positive value, he stands in a much more direct relationship to Octovien de Saint-Gelais (d. 1502) or even to Jean Bouchet (d. ca. 1557), for example, than Baudelaire does to the Surrealists, although the filiation between the latter is, since Marcel Raymond's persuasive study, hardly questioned.[33] A further advantage is the existence of good editions of Machaut's considerable poetic and musical production, together with a number of recent studies of both.[34] We can thus command an overview of the entire corpus of the work of the poet-musician whose practice shaped that of his successors for at least 150 years after his death. It should be possible to find in his works valuable clues for the reading of fifteenth-century texts.

It is easy to divide Machaut's poetical works into two parts; Machaut did this himself, in fact, in the sumptuous manuscripts prepared under his supervision for his royal or ducal patrons.[35] Most of the lyric poems are grouped in a section called, appropriately, *La Louange des Dames*, which in its fullest form presents nearly 300 examples of the chant royal, the ballade, the rondeau, and the virelai, composed throughout his creative life, from the mid-1320's to the mid-1370's.[36] The rest of his poetry consists of twelve *dits* or narrative poems, written beginning probably in the early 1340's and continuing into the 1360's, some addressed to various patrons, command performances or consolatory meditations; *Le Voir-Dit* (1363–65), a verse narrative containing some prose letters, which purports to be the autobiographical "true story" of the poet's May-December love affair with a young poetess; and *La Prise d'Alexandrie* (ca. 1370), a chronicle in nearly 9,000 verses of the life of Pierre de Lusignan, king of Cyprus. These works run to some 45,000 verses in all, a considerable literary output indeed, especially when one sets them beside his musical compositions: nineteen monodic lais; the celebrated Messe de Notre-Dame (ca. 1364), the first complete polyphonic setting of the Mass to survive; twenty-three motets and a hocket; and settings, both monophonic and polyphonic, for numerous poems (thirty-three virelais, forty-two ballades, twenty-one rondeaux).

Aside from this musical production, then, it is easy to see that there are two main divisions in Machaut's work—the lyric poems and the others. This same division may be found, in varying proportion, in the work of many of his successors: Froissart, Eustache Deschamps, Christine de Pizan, Alain Chartier, even François Villon. The poems of Charles d'Orléans, by contrast, are almost entirely lyric, while other poets, like Martin Le Franc and Octovien de Saint-

Gelais, neglect the lyric genres. It is tempting—and traditional—to call these two divisions "lyric" and "didactic" or "narrative"—but these labels are only satisfactory if a certain caution is observed. The term lyric can serve to designate one division if it is used in its strict sense of a type of poetry in which the formal arrangement of verse permits a musical setting, real or implied, and not in the looser sense of poetry purporting to communicate personal feeling, and in particular, the emotions caused by love. In the broader meaning, the term is inappropriate not only because the poets of the time do not as a rule express, in any Romantic way, their own feelings in the "lyric" genres, but also because these genres are used for many subjects besides love. Even in *La Louange des Dames*, where the great majority of pieces are love poems, a half-dozen have other themes; in such authors as Deschamps and Christine de Pizan, while certain ballades, for example, may perhaps indeed express the poet's personal sadness at growing old (Deschamps), or at being left a widow at an early age (Christine de Pizan), many others are satiric, didactic, or religious; and Charles d'Orléans's enormous collection of rondeaux contains many poems whose subject is not courtly love.[37] This is true throughout the century, as even a cursory glance at *Le Jardin de plaisance* will prove.

The division in Machaut's work, then, as in that of many poets who followed him, is really between poems in fixed forms—whatever their subject—and generally much longer poems, written in "unfixed" forms, that is, without any real or possible musical setting. One would be tempted to see this division as characteristic of late medieval poets, were it not for the fact that it is also characteristic of a number of sixteenth-century poets, including Ronsard, the bulk of whose work, though we tend to forget this, is not made up of love poetry. But it is useful, if surprising, to place him in the line of descent of French poets of the century preceding his own, for the clear distinction in much of their work between lyric forms and nonlyric forms makes more understandable and less disconcerting, perhaps, the division in his own between his sonnets (with their strictly set number of verses a much more "fixed" medieval form than many of the variations on the basic rondeau or ballade that we shall consider), his odes, and, to some degree, his chansons, and his lengthy philosophic, descriptive, and historical poems.

The importance of a formal rather than a subject basis for distinguishing two kinds of poetic discourse is fundamental to an understanding of the poetry of the time, as we shall see further in the chapter on Alain Chartier, who used both kinds, and again in the discussion of the work of the entirely narrative verse of Jean Meschinot's *Les Lunettes des Princes*. A closer look at the Machaut corpus can reveal other points of departure for reading, as well. After about 1370–71, Machaut added to his collected works a kind of "Prologue," made up of four ballades totaling 114 lines, followed by 181 lines of octosyllabic rhymed couplets.[38] It thus represents, in its formal aspect, the work of the poet as a whole, with that characteristic division with which we have just been concerned. It can serve to remind us, too, incidentally, that this division was not absolute, for there are some other texts like the "Prologue," in which the poet inserts examples of the lyric genres in longer narratives. This practice is an old one in medieval literature, going back at least to the early thirteenth century and *Guillaume de Dole* of Jean Renart.[39] Machaut follows it first in *Le Remede de Fortune* (ca. 1342–57), in which single examples of each of the principal lyric genres form a kind of *ars poetica* embedded in a verse narrative illustrating the vagaries of Love and Fortune. He uses the mixture again most notably in *Le Voir-Dit*. François Villon does it as well, of course, in *Le Testament*. As Ernest Hoepffner noted in his edition of the narrative works, the "Prologue" also epitomizes all of Machaut's poetry from the point of view of subject and treatment, for we find in it allegory and didacticism, references to love and to the poet's art, and the person of the poet himself as Narrator.[40] Since the "Prologue" constitutes one of the earliest statements on poetic theory in French,[41] and since it predates by at most a third of a century the period of our concern, it is of evident significance for this study. It will therefore be instructive to look at the text in some detail. (I use the text in *Poésies lyriques*, 1: 1–13.)

It opens with four ballades, each with the usual three stanzas, disposed two by two according to their formal structure. The strophes of the first two are each made up of nine lines, all of which are decasyllabic save the fifth and seventh, which are octosyllabic. The second two consist of ten-line strophes of decasyllables, except for the fifth line in each, which is octosyllabic. The rhyme scheme remains the same for all four—a b a b c c d c D—with the addition of a tenth line in the *d* rhyme in the third and fourth ballades (this is, of course, the refrain). The architecture of these forms is played off against the arrangement of the subjects of the four poems. In the first, Nature comes to encourage Guillaume to form "nouviaus dis amoureus plaisans," and to this end introduces to him three of her children, Scens, Retorique, and Musique. The second ballade consti- tutes the poet's reply to Nature: he is willing to do as she asks and grateful for the help she brings. Having overheard Nature's request, the god of Love, in the third poem, brings three of his children to give Guillaume the subject of his *dits*; they are Dous Penser, Plai- sance, and Esperance. It is to Love that the poet addresses his second reply in the fourth ballade, stating his gratitude and his intention to spend the rest of his life serving love and poetry. In the first and third, then, the refrain states three gifts: in the first, those of Nature, necessary to whoever wishes to master the technical art of poetry; in the third, those that provide the lyric artist with his understanding of his subject, love. In both of these, there is an insistence on Nature's having formed Machaut "à part"—that is to say, he was born a poet, "gifted" with the natural gifts of the poet. The refrains of the second and fourth ballades express the devotion, lifelong in both cases, of Guillaume to his craft—"Tant qu'en ce mont vous plaira que je vive" (As long as it pleases you that I live in this world) he says to Nature—as well as to "la louange des dames," which he claims that he shall pursue "A mon pooir, tant comme je vivray" (With all my strength, as long as I live). The whole allegory of these four ballades, then, far from being the sterile rhetorical exercise it is often indis- criminately labeled, presents in dramatic fashion the poet's con- frontation with the imperatives of his own nature and the source of his inspiration.

The rest of the "Prologue," in octosyllabic couplets, is an expla- nation of this allegory and of how the poetic nature must operate to make poetry of the *matere* (ballade 4, l. 7) given by Love. Machaut takes up each of the gifts of Nature and Love in turn and expands it—but in an order significantly different from that in which they are presented in the ballades. In the first sentence of his explanation, which takes up twenty-three verses, he agrees to use his talents for the honor and praise of ladies by writing "dis et chansonnettes / Plainnes d'onneur et d'amourettes, / Doubles hoqués et plaisans lais, / Motes, rondiaus et virelais / Qu'on claimme chansons baladées, / Complaintes, balades entées" (poems and little songs full of honor and love-sport, double hockets and pleasant lais, motets, rondeaux, and virelais, which are called *chansons baladées*, complaints, *balades entées*). These are the lyric genres, then, in which he will write, using all his feeling and understanding: "y doy mon sentement / Mettre et tout mon entendement, / Cuer, corps, pooir et quenque j'ay" (I must put my feeling into it, and all my understanding: heart, body, strength, and everything I have). The results of this—the results of the right kind of love, really—will give him a happy heart and an elegant, distinguished, gracious turn of mind. He knows through his poems ("mes dis") that once one has chosen to praise ladies, the right thoughts must automatically follow; otherwise his work would be undone: "Et s'a autre chose pensoie, / Toute mon oeuvre defferoie" (And if I thought of anything else, I would undo all my work).

There immediately follows a most important passage that points the way, I believe, to an explanation of much in the poetry of the following century that seems strange to a modern reader. Let me quote it at some length.

> Et s'on fait de triste matiere,
> Si est joieuse la maniere
> Dou fait, car ja bien ne fera   45
> Ne gaiement ne chantera
> Li cuers qui est pleins de tristesse,
> Pour ce qu'il het et fuit leesse.
> Mais quant li cuers est pleins de joie,
> Il se delite et se resjoie.   50
> En faisant son chant et son dit
> En douce Plaisance; et s'on dit

Que li tristes cuers doit mieus faire
Que li joieus, c'est fort a faire,
Ne je ne m'y puis acorder.   55
Car quant Souvenirs recorder
Fait l'amant par douce pensée
La tres belle et la bien amée
A qui il est mis et donnez
Et ligement abandonnez,   60
Plaisant ymagination
Met en son cuer l'impression
De sa douce plaisant figure
Et dous Pensers qui la figure,
Dont son fait cent fois embelist: 65
Sages est qui tel vie, eslist.

Mais quant li tristes ymagine
La grant biauté, la douceur fine
De celle qui n'a de li cure,
Dont li venroit envoisëure,   70
Que elle aimme un autre que li?
Je ne me tien pas a celi,
Qu'il a tant de dueil et de rage
Que c'est merveille qu'il n'enrage,
Ou qu'il ne se tue ou se pent,   75
Ou que d'amer ne se repent;
Si qu'il ne porroit nullement
Riens faire se joliement
De sa matiere dolereuse
Com li joieus de sa joieuse,   80
Pour ce qu'il n'a riens qui l'esgaie
Ne matiere lie ne gaie,
Et s'a desir et poure espoir
Que sa doleur empire, espoir.

And if one writes with sad subject matter, even so the
manner of the poem is joyous, for never will the heart that is
filled with sadness write well or sing gaily, because it hates and
flees gladness. But when the heart is filled with joy, it is de-
lighted and rejoices in making its song and its poem in sweet
Pleasure; and if it's said that the sad heart should write better

than the joyous one, that's difficult indeed, and I can't agree with it. For when Memory makes the lover remember, through sweet thought, the very beautiful and well-beloved woman to whom he is committed and given over and given up by allegiance, pleasant imagination puts in his heart the impression of her sweet pleasant face and sweet Thought, which portrays her, as a result of which he embellishes a hundred times his poem: he is wise who chooses such a life.

But when he who is sad imagines the great beauty, the elegant sweetness of the lady who cares nothing for him—how could he be happy that she love someone other than him? I don't hold with that one, for he is so mournful and so furious that it's a wonder he doesn't go mad or kill himself or hang himself, or doesn't repent of loving; so that he could hardly write anything so prettily with his painful subject matter as could he who is joyful with his joyous material, because he has nothing that makes him merry nor subject matter either happy or gay, but has desire and the poor hope that his pain will grow worse, perhaps.

Unlike most authors of poetic treatises following him, until Du Bellay's *Deffense et illustration* in the middle of the sixteenth century, Machaut throughout this passage not only emphasizes the making of the poem, which is a *fait* as well as a *dit* (see ll. 43, 45, 51, 65, 78); he also defines the frame of mind necessary to the poet, the manner of "making" the poem. Even if the content, the matter, is sad, yet the manner must be joyous if the poem is to be entirely successful, for the sad heart cannot create as easily or as well as the joyful one (ll. 43–52, 65, 77–80). Love, which provides the subject of the poem, also, if it is of the right and joyous kind, illumines artistic creation through Esperance, Plaisance, and Dous Penser. Poirion translates these terms on a literary level as imagination, reverie, and contemplation,[42] and this is certainly helpful, but one must further realize that these are technical terms, taken from Machaut's vocabulary of courtly love. They are to be found again, for instance, in *Le Remede de Fortune*, where Douce Esperance is contrasted with Desir: it is the former that brings joy to the true lover.[43] Desir, on the other hand, as Machaut explains a few lines later in the "Prologue," is coupled with "poure espoir," the opposite of Douce Esperance, and brings pain (ll. 83–84). The three, essential for combating common desire, work together within the heart of the poet to bring him the pleasure of the memory of his beloved's face and actions and of the future bliss that she can dispense and for which he hopes.[44] The result of all of this is creative joy (ll. 56–65), an ebullient, quasi-religious fervor, not unlike the "joy" of troubadours, which finds its natural expression in love poetry.[45] In the following chapter, we shall see that this joy may express itself in a poem with a sad theme—Machaut recognizes this in the first line of the passage above. We shall also find that this joy is closely allied to poetic play, that in the fifteenth century *joie* and *jeu* are inevitable components of poetry. What the chapters of this book will, in fact, try to do is to formulate, as Guillaume de Machaut is doing here, some of the rules of the game of poetry, *les règles du jeu*.

The second half of the "Prologue" deals with the three gifts of Nature; the musician in Machaut accords to Musique the lion's share of the verses—almost three times as many as he gives to Retorique and Scens. He first shows how Musique is closely related to joy, for music creates joy whenever it is heard; it brings harmony out of discord; used in the services of the Church for praise and thanksgiving, it is divine, capable of miracles, present, through the heavenly choirs, in Paradise. There is behind this passage the long tradition of music as a cosmic force, created by the turning of the spheres.

Retorique is not accorded such exalted status: "Retorique versefier / Fait l'amant et metrefier, / Et si fait faire jolis vers / Nouviaus et de metres divers"; ll. 147–50 (Rhetoric makes the lover versify and metrify and thus causes fine verses to be written, original and of divers meters). There follows a list of the various kinds of rhyme— "serpentine," "equivoque," "leonine," "croisie," "retrograde"—and of the lyric genres. Retorique also allows the lover-poet to "adorn" his language "Par maniere plaisant et sage" (ll. 151–58). Finally, Scens governs the whole process and appears to mean artistic intelligence.[46] The poet returns, briefly, to an evocation of the joy necessary for artistic creation and ends his "Prologue" with a prayer that God may grant him the grace of pleasing the ladies.

If, in the ballades, Nature, with her gifts, precedes the God of

Love, with his, it is the other way round in the rest of the poem, for both the beginning and the end of the second part are devoted, as we have seen, to defining the mechanism of the creative act and the nature of the poetic personality: both are caused by the right kind of love. In three of the five principal manuscripts in which the "Prologue" appears, it is followed by the earliest narrative poem, *Le Dit dou vergier*, written in all probability some thirty years earlier; in the other two, it is followed by *La Louange des Dames*.[47] Both of these constitute illustrations of the matter, already defined in the "Prologue": *Le Dit dou vergier* presents a lengthy discourse on love by the God of Love himself; the *Louange* is a collection of lyric poems, almost all of them love poems. These and the other poems of Machaut constitute an ample practical demonstration of the operation of Esperance, Dous Penser, and Plaisance, often in their struggle with Desir. But the "Prologue," too, does more than present a theory, for it is at the same time a demonstration of the practice of Nature's three gifts. Musique is only represented by the lyric form of the ballade, four times repeated; there are no real songs, as in *Le Remede de Fortune* or *Le Voir-Dit*, for example. The whole "Prologue," however, embodies Retorique and Scens. Scens presides over the disposition of the parts, the parallelism of the ballades, the lengthier number of verses accorded to Musique in the second part (to compensate, perhaps, for its lack of real representation). And Retorique is of course perceived, as in any poem, in the rhythm and rhyme of the verses but also, and more particularly, in the entire second part of the poem. That part in fact constitutes a superb example of *amplificatio*, one of the ways in which rhetoric can, in Machaut's term—which is that of the medieval rhetorician—"adorn" language. The entire subject of the six gifts of the artist is placed in the context of ethical conduct: the true lover-poet is incapable of slandering ladies because his whole character is enobled by love; this kind of moral elevation is one way of amplifying the subject. It is also illustrated by such "amplification" as the lists of genres and rhymes, the examples of the joyous and the sad lover, the examples of David and Orpheus and Eurydice, in the section on the power of music (ll. 126–43). Guillaume de Machaut is here engaging in the game while writing the rules of play. After him, with the rules codified and exemplified in the body of his work, we shall find that the game can be played in a dazzling number of ways, and sometimes without the framework of love, but always with joy.

That the rules of the so-called *formes fixes* are at once fixed and supple, capable of accommodating a very large number of variations within the basic structure, is a lesson that cannot of course be learned from looking solely at the two examples of the ballade form found in the "Prologue." But when one considers the mass of poems collected in *La Louange des Dames*, this variability within sameness is easy to see. In Wilkins's excellent edition, published in 1972, the poems are grouped by genre, following an analysis of their various structures.[48] This analysis shows to what an extraordinary degree changes in number of lines, length of line, and rhyme scheme permitted diversity within the unity of each form. Although each of the seven chants royaux, the first genre represented, for example, has the characteristic five stanzas followed by an envoy, although all of them use only the ten-syllable line, and although each of the stanzas begins with four lines of *rimes croisées*, none of the seven is exactly alike. One is unique, with an eleven-line stanza on five rhymes, followed by a four-line envoy. The stanzas of two others are each ten lines in length, but the rhyme schemes are different, one of them using five different rhymes and an envoy of five lines, and the other presenting the notable peculiarity of a two-line refrain at the end of each of its strophes, the second line of which returns to cap the three-line envoy. Two others seem very close indeed, for each uses stanzas of nine lines, with an identical rhyme scheme, but one has a four-line envoy and the other differs significantly from it, with an envoy as long as the stanza itself. Finally, the last pair, each built on eight-line stanzas with an envoy half as long, differ only in their rhyme schemes, one of three and the other of four rhymes. There are thus seven different kinds of chant royal in the collection of seven poems so designated.

The envoy is, quite evidently, one of the means used to vary the structure of this form, but Machaut proves that it is not a necessary element in his prestigious playing with a related form, the ballade, for not one of the 206 ballades in the *Louange* has an envoy, although later poets often added one. The variety of structure to be found in these poems, each made up of three stanzas with, in most cases, a one-line refrain at the end of the stanza, is amazing: there are in all forty-four variations! One can only agree with Nigel Wilkins that this is indeed "a clear demonstration that the principle of an underlying fixed form by no means implies sterile uniformity." [49]

Although there is less variety in the sixty rondeaux, since they are by definition restricted to only two rhymes and are, like all Machaut's rondeaux, isometric, there are still seven types, differing from each other in length of line and in overall length. So that, even though only five different lengths of rondeaux are possible, given the musical substructure—those of eight, eleven, thirteen, sixteen, or twenty-one lines [50]—there is room for diversity, and we shall see that Christine de Pizan playfully enlarges this scope by various means. Of the seven virelais in the Wilkins edition, only three share exactly the same structure.

Despite this appearance of variety, Guillaume de Machaut is no great experimenter in the use of these forms, already developed at the beginning of the fourteenth century. But what is important here is not innovation so much as variation. The versatility that creates subtle new patterns within the fixed confines of the given form is not characteristic of Machaut only; it is the rule rather than the exception in fifteenth-century poetry. If one thinks of the theory expounded in the "Prologue," this is, I suggest, the province of Scens, which governs the part of the poet's craft that is responsible for combining into an artistic whole all the poem's elements, be they linguistic or intellectual, elements that are themselves the province of Retorique, just as their setting out in sonorous lines according to a basic pattern is the province of Musique.

The kind of aesthetic pleasure caused by such slight shifts in patterns seems, to our sensibilities, delicate indeed, if not imperceptible. But to deny the very existence of this pleasure is to misunderstand completely the art of these poets who, as Maurice Delbouille reminds us, were less interested in the kind of emotion caused by putatively personal revelation than in the play of form against form and, as we shall see, of content—as conventional as its vehicle—

against form.[51] Thus, as modern readers, we must overcome another obstacle to understanding: we must realize not only that technique is of primary importance to the poets themselves and must therefore concern us, but also that it can be used in an expressive way. Nancy Regalado, writing of the period of Rutebeuf, points out that "the joy inherent in poetry expressed so often in the first lines of many medieval poems is not separated from the desire to sing *well*, and good writing verified that the poet's subject was worthy of attention."[52] The same can be said for Machaut and his successors. This primacy of formal concerns demands, in any analysis of their work, an attentive consideration of all the formal aspects of the text, in an attempt to sensitize our ears enough to recapture the pleasure in structural detail that the very existence of this kind of poetry implies. If it is impossible to catch every resonance fully—and this is doubtless so—we must at least be aware of the place of such formal counterpoint in the poet's task.[53] That this place was of great importance there can be no doubt: what else could Machaut mean by the adjective "nouviaus," when Nature asks him to write "nouviaus dis amoreus" ("Prologue," l. 5)? The "novelty" can be neither in overall form, fixed or otherwise, nor in subject, for both of these are provided by tradition. It can be found, it seems to me, in the very subtle changes he rings on both. Seen in this light, the repetition that is so much a part of fourteenth- and fifteenth-century poetry takes on new significance: in its insistence on novelty—each refrain in a ballade is different from that in another ballade—it becomes an element brought back for the pleasure of the listener or reader or reciter, a pleasure aesthetic, acoustic, or muscular; at the same time it provides another kind of pleasure in its insistence on sameness— each refrain in a particular form, ballade, rondeau, or lai, returning at the same place in all examples of that form, ensures the poem's adherence to tradition and the pleasurable recognition of that tradition by listener, reader, or reciter. Rather than lulling us by their sameness, then, the fixed forms should awaken us to the extraordinarily numerous possibilities they present for subtle variety. Further—and herein lies another impediment—in order to be alive to such phenomena, we must read a considerable number of each kind of poem: in a way, a single rondeau by Christine de Pizan is nearly meaningless unless we know other rondeaux both by her and by other poets, since, alone, it shows neither how it plays with the basic form nor what originality it might have compared with others of the same structure by the same poet. In other words, these poems are not, strictly speaking, anthology pieces—unless they take their place in an anthology of other rondeaux, virelais, and ballades. Such an anthology of late medieval poetry would also have to demonstrate an evolution in form, discernible to varying degrees in the major poets following Machaut.[54]

Just as the variations and evolution of the *formes fixes*, out of context, may be difficult for modern readers to perceive, so the variation—and, to some extent, the evolution—found in the subject matter of these forms may seem imperceptible or unimportant, hackneyed and impersonal, accustomed as we are to the altogether more obvious effects of the emotional shock prescribed by the Romantics. The main subject for the lyric poetry and, indeed, for nearly all the poetry of Machaut, with the exception of *Le Confort d'ami* and *La Prise d'Alexandrie*, is, of course, love. In the narrative verse, it is set around with numerous other themes; in *La Louange des Dames*, it constitutes the center of all but a handful of poems. The title implies this, for ladies are naturally the cause of the kind of love portrayed. This can loosely be described as Petrarchan, if by Petrarchan one means a concept of love in which the beauty of a lady, both spiritual and physical, is seen as the cause of an emotion that may result in a spiritual force (love enobles the lover, inspires the poet), as well as in other feelings (joy, jealousy), with definite physical and psychological effects (the lover hopes but fears, suffers but is ecstatic, trembles, blushes, pales). The lover, in whom joy and sadness alternate, is dominated to a degree by the beloved, who may be married to another and to whom he nevertheless owes unquestioning service and allegiance. In return, he may expect as a recompense true pleasure from the sweet memories and happy expectations that the frequentation or contemplation of the beloved can provide. The trouble with calling this "Petrarchan" is not only that Petrarch emphasizes, to a degree not found in the poets we shall discuss, the spiritual aspect of this force, but that the term, used to refer to French poets of the fourteenth and fifteenth centuries, is anachronistic, for even though Petrarch was an exact contemporary of Machaut, it is doubtful whether Machaut knew his works, and even in the fifteenth century his vernacular poetry appears to have been little known in France.[55] This same concept of love can also be called "courtly," despite recent controversy surrounding that label,[56] for not only does it derive ultimately from troubadour poetry and its evolution in the works of those poets of the *langue d'oïl* connected with various northern courts, but also its main practitioners in our period are themselves either noble—Jean de Garancières, Oton de Grandson, Charles d'Orléans—or court favorites. I prefer to suspend any further discussion of the propriety of the term "courtly love" until a later chapter, for what is important at this point is not so much the label as the concept itself.

Gilbert Reaney, in an article on Machaut's lyric, distinguishes twelve variations on the theme of love in the *Louange*; they are the commonplaces so familiar throughout medieval (and Renaissance) love poetry: the timid complaint of the woman's coldness, the lavish praise of her beauty, the medicine she alone can provide for the lovesick poet, her fickleness and that of Fortune, the danger posed by the *médisants*, the sadness caused by separation, and so on.[57] Although such subjects can be seen as variations on love, it seems to me that since "love" is in this poetry so broad a concept—since, in fact, it most frequently constitutes the entire emotional world of the poem—they may be better seen as topoi within this all-embracing erotic complex, which includes both emotions and images, each susceptible itself of numerous variations.

Now it is unlikely that fourteenth- and fifteenth-century poets were totally incapable of imagining new and "original" ways of expressing the emotions of love; one must therefore conclude that their use of clichés is not accidental at all, but a matter of deliberate choice. This, again, poses a problem for our imagined present-day readers, for our notions of what poetry is have changed radically, and the idea that a poet may consciously exclude what we may think of as the essence of poetic originality and still be a good poet is foreign to us. We must confront, then, this poetry of cliché with some attempt at understanding it: simply repeating that we are faced with commonplaces is not very illuminating. Roger Dragonetti has shown that traditional images and their variations played a dynamic role in *le grand chant courtois* of the twelfth century: far from seeking "originality" in imagery, the courtly poet sought to use the stock provided him by his literary tradition, to show off his mastery of that tradition and its techniques. The cliché was, further, a poetic means of revealing meaning and a channel for poetic inspiration; it also represented a predetermined understanding between the poet and his public.[58] Although Dragonetti finds that in the late medieval lyric this intermediary role of the cliché became less of a poetic necessity and more of a convention, this notion is not entirely without validity in the period that concerns us, for although it may perhaps be more artificial than in an earlier period, the use of commonplaces is still very much a part of the art of writing poetry—and, we must remember, it was to remain so for some centuries. An analogy in contemporary literature can be made between this kind of poetry and a highly conventionalized genre like the "classical" detective novel, where what interests us is not the fact that a murder has been committed and that it will be solved, but rather how it has been committed and how it will be solved, in what manner, that is, the author will use, will in fact vary, the rules of the genre. In other words, the subject of such books is not what is important (there are said to be only seven different basic plots for that other conventionalized modern genre, the Western); this is equally true of the poems of the *Louange*. How the subject—the particular topos or group of topoi—is worked out is what constitutes the poet's craft and what creates the admiration of his public. The "making" of a poem, then, obliges the poet first to choose among all the clichés at his command those he wishes to invest with poetic value, and then to do so by varying them in a number of ways. It is clear that form may here be expressive, that that formal variation of which I have already spoken becomes in the best poets a way to diversify content, just as a prism, turned in the sunlight, reveals different facets, different effects of light. As Dragonetti puts it: "If . . . the argument [of a poem] is such that it offers nothing to grip the audience's curiosity, it then has meaning only insofar as it is capable of becoming a pure formal counterpoint, in which every element, known in advance, gets its value and its brilliance from the whole."[59] Since we have already seen that reading an isolated example can only falsify considerably our understanding of this poetry, the best way to realize this aspect of it is to consider a group of poems by Machaut, each of which uses the same topos, and to try to discover whether they are in fact the same and, if not, how they differ one from another.

What appears to us now as one of the most threadbare commonplaces of medieval literature is the meditation, reflection, lament, or complaint concerning Fortune and its nature. The history of the theme, with the *De consolatione philosophiae* of Boethius as the most important source in the Middle Ages, is well documented;[60] it need not concern us here. Fortune—often personified as a goddess—is fickle for all men; her wheel symbolizes her false and shifting character, for at its turn one may be precipitated from the heights of worldly fame to obscurity, or from utter ecstasy in love to the depths of despair. The figure is remarkably persistent throughout the Middle Ages, in both prose and poetry. Machaut is no exception, and Fortune appears frequently in his narrative works, among which *Le Remede de Fortune* is one of the most important, for not only is it his major version of the traditional consolation piece, but, significantly, it uses this framework to present examples of each of the principal lyric genres and thus becomes a conscious demonstration of the master's skill.[61] It is also present in *La Louange des Dames*, as well as in lyric poems that do not appear in that collection.

Let us try to define this conventional role of Fortune and its poetic presentation in each of several different texts. For our purposes I have chosen five poems that are not only representative of the topos, but very similar in structure as well, for each is a ballade. I am not here concerned with the chronology of their composition, although two of the five come from a manuscript representing Machaut's early lyric production, between about 1324 and 1356, and two others from a manuscript copied later, representing work composed between about 1356 and 1364.[62] The fifth is from the *Ballades notées*; two of the others were also set to music by Machaut and included in the *Louange*; one, with no musical setting, is included in *Le Voir-Dit*. Thus the selection represents in every way a sampling of the ballade as practiced by the poet. Each one has three eight-line strophes, the last line of which is a refrain. All except one include a heptasyllabic fifth line in each strophe; the others are decasyllabic. The exception contains only decasyllabic lines. None add an envoy. Great similarity in form, then—but within this general formal resemblance, there is the same variety of distribution of rhyme scheme and of masculine and feminine rhymes that we already noted in the ballades as a whole. In fact, only two of the five are exactly the same in respect to these two features.

Does this kind of variety-in-sameness exist in the themes of the ballades as well? "Il m'est avis, qu'il n'est dons de Nature" (It seems to me that there is no gift of Nature), probably set to music at an early date, is a good starting point for an answer to this question.* Fortune is in this poem directly the subject of each stanza: after stating the general observation that no one, however gifted by Nature, succeeds "Se la clarté tenebreuse et obscure / De Fortune ne li donne couleur" (If the dark and shadowy light of Fortune doesn't give him color; ll. 3–4), the same truth is reiterated in the last two lines of the first stanza: "Mais je ne voy homme amé ne chieri, / Se Fortune ne le tient à ami" (But I see no man loved or cherished if he's not Fortune's friend; ll. 7–8). There is some amplification of this in the following strophe, in which the falseness of Fortune and her gifts is emphasized, and she is described as a monster full of misfortune ("monstre . . . plein de maleurté"; ll. 13–14). In the last stanza, the poet won-

---

*Each poem will be cited first by its number in Wilkins's edition of *La Louange des Dames* and then by the volume and page on which it appears in Chichmaref, *Poésies lyriques* (here *Louange*, no. 96, Chichmaref, 1: 170).

ders how Reason can let Fortune vanquish virtue and install for so long a time the reign of vice; anyone who wishes advancement is wasting his time "Se Fortune ne le tient à ami" (l. 24).

The musical structure underlines the structure of the strophe, for each is divided into two parts at the end of the fourth line, both by the sense and by the introduction, following the musical repetition of lines 1 and 2 for lines 3 and 4 (i.e., 1 1, where 1 equals the same musical phrase), of the second part of the musical pattern (11), beginning with the shorter, seven-syllable line. There is no real development throughout the poem; Fortune is not seen as creating or adding to the lover's plight, except in the general and quite vague statement of lines 7 and 8 quoted above. What we find, then, is a moral reflection on Fortune and the state of the world, entirely traditional, with only the slight allegorization found in the refrain and in a few other verses, such as line 20, where "les vices . . . regnent com signour" (the vices reign as lords). There is one striking oxymoron—"la clarté tenebreuse et obscure / De Fortune" (ll. 3–4)—and a minimum of rhyming play with words, but the rhymes are, in the main, merely sufficient. Very little attempt is made to relate the falsity of Fortune to the poetic voice that is speaking: the "Il m'est avis" of the opening, the "je ne voy" of line 7, and the "Si me merveil" at the beginning of the third stanza serve rather to generalize than to particularize the reflections. The effect is rather flat; it is the music that makes this a "lyric" piece, not—at least for us—its tone or subject.

"De Fortune me doy plaindre et loer" (*Louange*, no. 45; Chichmaref, 1: 176), written in the same period and also set to music, is quite another case. Only the third stanza resembles those of "Il m'est avis," with the second part of the stanza (and the second part of the musical pattern) introduced by the shorter line, beginning here with a "Mais," after a full stop at the end of line 4. Both stanzas I and II obviously consist, on the other hand, of one long sentence, the sense of which is carried over from line 4 to line 5 in each by enjambments; stanza I can illustrate both:

> De Fortune me doy plaindre et loer
> Ce m'est avis, plus qu'autre creature;
> Car quant premiers encommensay l'amer,

Mon cuer, m'amour, ma pensée, ma cure
 Mist si bien à mon plaisir   5
Qu'a souhaidier peüsse je faillir,
N'en ce monde ne fust mie trouvée
Dame qui fust se tres bien assenée.

It seems to me that I, more than any other creature, must both complain of Fortune and praise it, for when first I began to love him, it disposed my heart, my love, my thought, my care, so much as I pleased, that I should have been at fault had I wished that in this world were to be found any lady so well provided for.

Further, Fortune here is much more particularized than in the preceding poem, for it is immediately connected with the person speaking—or in this case singing—the first line. Someone—the "je" of the poem—has reason both to blame and to praise Fortune. The reasons for praise are set out following the "Car" of line 3; a second "Car" introduces further reasons in the next strophe: the person loved is the fairest Nature could create. Stanza III begins with a sigh, "Lasse," and goes on—with a third "Car" (l. 18)—to show the nature of Fortune through her familiar attribute, the wheel: "Car Fortune qui onques n'est seure / Sa roe vuet [encontre] moy tourner / Pour mon las cuer mettre à desconfiture" (Because Fortune—who is never sure—wishes to turn its wheel against me, to the downfall of my weary heart; ll. 18–20). Another difference in presentation is that whereas in "Il m'est avis" the refrain (with the preceding line) is the simple statement and restatement of the same moral observation, in this poem, the refrain in each stanza is given a different nuance and serves to develop the sense of the complaint. The first time the refrain occurs, it makes the straightforward statement that there never was in all the world a lady better endowed or provided for (that is, more fortunate), with the implication that this is because Fortune has given her her heart's desire. The penultimate verse of the second stanza introduces a different note: "Et pour ce croy c'onques mais ne fu née / Dame qui fust si tres bien assenée." That is to say, "I *think* there never was a more fortunate lady"; the "ce" in line 7 refers to the reason for this, which she has just given in the preceding lines: she has the world's most handsome lover. But

Fortune's wheel turns: in stanza III we are not told exactly what her "desconfiture" is, but one can only assume that it is some amorous *mis*fortune, perhaps the lover's absence. In any case, she brings back the refrain this time as if to remind herself of her luck, in order to have the courage to go on in the face of adverse Fortune; here, three lines lead up to the refrain, given this time a poignant twist (ll. 21–24):

> Mais en foy, jusqu'au morir,
> Mon dous ami vueil amer et chierir,
> C'onques ne dut avoir fausse pensée
> Dame qui fust si tres bien assenée.

> But in faith, until death, I want to love and cherish my sweet friend, for never should a lady so well provided for have any faithless thoughts.

In the musical setting the shifting meaning of the refrain is emphasized in each stanza by the melismatic treatment of the penultimate syllable (-*é*-) in "assenée."

From being the anonymous force to which Everyman is subject in "Il m'est avis," Fortune in this ballade becomes the particular destiny of a particular person, and the reader will already have noticed that this person is not the poet Guillaume de Machaut, but an unnamed woman. The poet here assumes the lady's voice; he plays, in other words, with his persona, delaying recognition of who is speaking in the first stanza until the refrain, although line 7, with its feminine adjective, gives a hint. This poetic surprise explains the pronoun in line 3 ("Car quant premiers encommensay l'amer"), about which—the "him" of the story—the second stanza gives more detail. This is not by any means the only poem in the *Louange* in which the lover who speaks is supposed to be a woman.[63] Indeed, in one of Machaut's most successful chants royaux, "Ami, je t'ay tant amé et cheri" (*Louange*, no. 1; Chichmaref, 1: 223), he plays ironically with this game itself and imagines that the lady who complains about her lover's coldness is ashamed thus to speak because ladies are not supposed to act that way (stanza IV):

> Honteuse sui, quant je parole einsi,
> Et laidure est seulement dou penser,

> Qu'il n'apartient que dame à son ami
> Doie mercy ne grace demander;
> Car dame doit en riant refuser
> Et amis doit prier en souspirant,
> Et je te pri souvent et en plourant.
> Mais en toy truis, quant plus sui esplourée,
> Cuer de marbre couronné d'aymant,
> Ourlé de fer, à la pointe asserée.

> I am ashamed when I speak thus (the very thought is shame-
> ful), for it is not fitting that a lady should ask favor or grace
> from her friend; for a lady should laughingly say no and the
> friend should beg, with sighs—but I am begging you, fre-
> quently and with tears. But in you I find, when I'm most
> tearful, a heart of marble crowned with a magnet, ringed with
> iron, sharply pointed.

The poet, obviously, is not a woman; he adopts, convincingly, the feminine viewpoint in this and other poems and then plays with this conceit. His disciple Eustache Deschamps, in one of his best-known virelais ("Sui je, sui je, sui je belle?") does the same. There can be no doubt that this is a form of poetic play for both authors. We shall see in the next chapter, on the other hand, that for Christine de Pizan, as a writer asserting both her status as a woman and her status as an author, the use of a person of the opposite sex can take on a se-riousness and a complication that it does not have for them. But even for Guillaume, I think one can go further: this clearly false but apparently real and "sincere" voice cannot represent the man Ma-chaut. Should we not, then, be wary of the "I" who allegedly speaks in the other poems? Even though the voice may be a man's, nothing obliges us to identify that man, that "I," with Guillaume de Ma-chaut. Conditioned by the ways we have thought about poetry for two hundred years, one is tempted to object that surely the emotions expressed can be real, even if the first person of the poem and the circumstances surrounding it are a fiction. This, however, is pre-cisely what, surely, is not the case in the fourteenth and fifteenth centuries. The emotions expressed in love poems, as well as the sentiments, moral or otherwise, set forth in ethical or even satiric poetry (in Villon, for example) may themselves be as conventional as

the forms and the topoi that translate them. They are meant to be—
and labeling them "conventional" simply misses the point. To Ma-
chaut such a criticism would doubtless have seemed a kind of surface
compliment; of course he is conventional, deliberately so—but that
says nothing of the skill with which he uses the conventions.

An example of that skill can be found in another ballade in
which Fortune appears and counters the lover's desire. In "Amours,
ma dame et Fortune et mi oueil" (*Louange*, no. 13; Chichmaref,
1: 204), the complaint is voiced by a man: is it Guillaume? One may
think so, especially if one reads the poem as it is inserted in *Le Voir-
Dit*, which purports to be truly autobiographical and in which much
is made, as in this ballade, of the lady's dwelling at some distance
from the lover—in the case of the narrative, allegedly Machaut
himself.[64] But its inclusion in *La Louange des Dames*, where virtually
all of the poems use the conventional or anonymous "I," of either
sex,[65] must cast serious doubt on such a supposition, especially when
one realizes that the poem is a variation on the theme of Fortune,
that it is but one of a number of lover's plaints against the goddess.
This is apparent from the beginning:

> Amours, ma dame et Fortune et mi oueil
> Et la tres grant biauté dont elle est pleinne
> Ont mis mon cuer, ma pensée et mon vueil
> Et mon desir en son tres dous demeinne.
>   Mais Fortune seulement   5
> Me fait languir trop dolereusement
> Et trop me fait avoir peinne et anoy,
> Quant seur tout l'aim et souvent ne la voy.

> Love, my lady, and Fortune, and my eyes, and the great beauty
> with which she overflows, have put my heart, my thought, and
> my will and my desire within her sweet jurisdiction. But For-
> tune alone makes me languish most painfully and gives me
> much pain and torment when I love her most of all and do not
> see her often.

Here the strong attack of line 1, arranged in a chiasmus of two
abstractions (Amours, Fortune), dramatized by a slight allegoriza-
tion, and of two concrete, human things (the lady and the lover's
eyes) present all the active elements of the poem, and the result of

their combined action concludes the first half of the strophe: the lover, with all his faculties, is conquered by the lady ("demeinne," l. 4, shows her dominance, with its feudal resonance). The second four lines, introduced by "Mais," announce the important restriction that, of all these things, it is Fortune alone that makes him suffer, and the refrain tells us why.

The first half of the second stanza takes up again the traditional elements of the erotic situation, all of which, even the lover's "peinne," concur to give him joy; once again, the second four lines mark a restriction, the force of which is underlined not only by the substantives in -*ment* that define the lover's faculties of intelligence and emotion, but also by the enjambment in lines 14–15, where Fortune and her power of annulling all feeling are placed, significantly, at the beginning of the verse:

> De ma dame ne de son bel acueil,
> De mes .ij. yex, d'amours ne de ma peinne   10
> Ne me plein pas, car par euls en l'escueil
> Suis mis d'avoir toute joie mondeinne.
>   Mais tout mon entendement
> Et mes bons jours et mon gay sentement
> Fortune esteint; s'en morray, par ma foy,   15
> Quant seur tout l'aim et souvent ne la voy.

Not of my lady nor of her kind welcome, nor of my two eyes or of love or of my sorrow do I complain, for through them I have been put in the way of every earthly joy. But Fortune extinguishes all my sense and my good times and my happy feelings; and I'll die of it, by my faith, when I love her most of all and do not see her often.

Recalling in the last stanza, with insistence, the role of Fortune, the poet makes of it a real threnody of unhappiness, piling up expressions like "je me pleing et dueil," "desespoir" (contrasted poignantly with "espoir" in the preceding line), "S'en plaing et plour et souspir."

> Car Fortune dont je me pleing et dueil
> Fait que ma dame est de moy trop lonteinne,
> Et si me tolt bon espoir qu'avoir sueil

Et desespoir dedens mon cuer remainne.   20
    Einsi sans aligement
Vif pour ma dame à qui sui ligement;
S'en plaing et plour et souspir en recoy.
Quant seur tout l'aim et souvent ne la voy.

For Fortune, of which I moan and groan, causes my lady to be
too far away from me, and thus it takes from me the sweet
hope that I am wont to have, and despair stays in my heart.
Thus it is that with no relief I live for my lady whose subject I
am; I moan and cry and sigh in secret, when I love her most of
all and do not see her often.

The *rimes léonines* "aligement" and "ligement" restate and
underscore what the refrain repeats for the third time: his pain is
constant and incurable as long as he cannot see her, for he is entirely
hers: "ligement" recalls the feudal service implied by "demeinne" in
stanza I. What one must admire most in this poem is not its subject
matter, but the way that subject matter is structured, given rhythm.
The eyes, all important in perceiving the lady's beauty, dominate the
poem from the first verse to the end; "Mes .ij. yex" in line 10 recalls
them expressly, and their action—seeing, or, in this case, not
seeing—is restated three times by the refrain. The "Mais" of lines 5
and 13 divides each stanza logically in two and is echoed and given a
conclusion by the "einsi" of line 21. The variations in rhythm are
subtle and masterly: the two iambics of "Amours, ma dame," are
followed by the two anapests of "et Fortune et mi oueil"; in line 2, by
way of contrast, there is no major stress in the line until one reaches
the word "biauté," emphasized this time by a cesura after the sixth
syllable rather than after the fourth. This pause after the sixth syl-
lable is unique in the poem, for in all the other lines, the first major
stress must come on the fourth syllable (e.g., l. 3: "cuer"; l. 10: "yex";
l. 14: "jours"; l. 18: "dame"; l. 22: "dame"). This rhythm is some-
what varied, however, at the opening of stanzas II and III, where the
first syllable of "dame" and the second of "Fortune" are empha-
sized—as well, perhaps by the kind of trailing effect created by the
"mute" *e* (which was not mute at all, of course) at the epic cesura as
by the stress that must perforce be given to those syllables when one

recites the text. This kind of rhythmic organization, often seconded by the strong grammatical structure of each strophe (stanza I: "Amours" / "Mais"; stanza II: "De ma dame" / "Mais"; stanza III: "Car Fortune" / "Einsi"), is typical of Machaut, and it brings to his verse that sense of ordered movement one hears in his music. Once more, in this poem, the poet orchestrates, around the conventional theme, a variation whose shifts of emphasis and diction combine with sound and rhythm to produce a pleasure for the reader—and listener—all the more subtle because its elements are known in advance.

This particular poetic game is, in addition, the more interesting in that its conclusion, implicit in the third strophe, concerns the text itself. The secret sighs and cries of the next-to-last line, introduced by a "S[i]" ("Thus it is," "This is why"), are realized in the poem, a *plainte* made from those same sad emotions; they thus generate the text itself. The song is sad. But it is a song, a poem, and therefore a game—and thus joyous. This paradox is itself, of course, part of the game, creates its own ludic sense.

A game of another sort but with many of the same characteristics is found in another ballade, "Je maudi l'eure et le temps et le jour" (I curse the hour and the time and the day; *Louange*, no. 109; Chichmaref, I: 192). In this poem the speaker, in the tradition of the Provençal *enveg*, curses all those things a lover usually praises, including those two eyes he refused to complain of in the preceding poem. There are three sets of curses. In the first stanza, the poet curses himself, along with the time and place he met his lady, the eyes with which he first perceived her sweetness, and his thoughts and emotions. He goes on in the second to curse the lady and her character traits, her early amiability and her later fickleness and pride. The last stanza sums up what he has been saying about himself and her:

> Et si maudi Fortune et son faus tour,
> La planette, l'eür, la destinée
> Qui mon fol cuer mirent en tel errour
> Qu'onques de moy fu servie n'amée.   20
> Mais je pri Dieu qu'il gart sa renommée,
> Son bien, sa pais, et li acroisse honnour

Et li pardoint ce qu'ocist à dolour
Mon dolent cuer en estrange contrée.

And then I curse Fortune and its false round, the planet, the
chance, the fate that led my foolish heart into such error that
ever she was served or loved by me. Yet I pray God that he keep
safe her reputation, her substance, her repose, and that he
increase her honor and forgive her painful killing of my sor-
rowing heart on foreign soil.

The prayer to God to save the lady's honor is surely, like the rest of
the poem, ironic. Fortune, in all its guises—the planet under which
he was born, fate, destiny—is, finally, the cause of it all: "It is just my
fate to be unlucky in love." Once more, in the poem as a whole, a
strong rhythmic attack in line 1 is followed by *reprises* at the begin-
ning of each of the following strophes: "Je maudi l'eure et le temps et
le jour"; "Et si maudi l'accueil, l'attrait, l'atour"; "Et si maudi For-
tune. . . ." The effect of this cascade of curses is augmented by the
use, unusual in the ballades, of only two rhymes. Another rhythmic
variant here is the systematic use in each stanza of a run-on line to
introduce the refrain, creating the effect of a two-line refrain.[66]

In the last poem of the series to be discussed, all these rhythmic
qualities are combined with a particularly delicate choice of expres-
sive rhymes and the juxtaposition of two traditional commonplaces
to produce one of the most beautiful examples of Machaut's art, and
a model of late medieval lyric. This is one of the *Ballades notées*, and
the music for it is also one of the composer's most successful pieces
(Chichmaref, 2: 556):[67]

De toutes flours n'avoit et de tous fruis
En mon vergier fors une seule rose:
Gastés estoit li surplus et destruis
Par Fortune qui durement s'opose
   Contre ceste doulce flour   5
Pour amatir sa colour et s'odour.
Mais se cueillir la voy ou tresbuchier,
Autre apres li ja mais avoir ne quier.

Mais vraiement ymaginer ne puis
Que la vertus, ou ma rose est enclose,   10
Viengne par toy et par tes faus conduis,

> Ains est drois dons naturex, si suppose
> >   Que tu n'avras ja vigour
> D'amanrir son pris et sa valour.
> Lay la moy donc, qu'ailleurs n'en mon vergier   15
> Autre apres li ja mais avoir ne quier.
>
> He! Fortune, qui es gouffres et puis
> Pour engloutir tout homme qui croire ose
> Ta fausse loy, ou riens de biens ne truis
> Ne de seur, trop est decevans chose;   20
> >   Ton ris, ta joie, t'onnour
> Ne sont que plour, tristece et deshonnour.
> Se ti faus tour font ma rose sechier,
> Autre apres li ja mais avoir ne quier.

Of all flowers and of all fruits, only a single rose was left in my orchard: the rest were spoiled and destroyed by Fortune, who harshly sets its face against that sweet flower, to overcome its color and its odor. But if I see it plucked or fallen, never after shall I seek to have another.

Yet I cannot really imagine that the virtue which surrounds my rose comes through you and through your false acts; it is, rather, a real natural gift—and so I think that you will never have the strength to diminish its worth and value. Leave it to me then, for elsewhere than in my orchard never after shall I seek to have another.

Ah! Fortune, who are the pit and well engulfing everyone who dares to believe your false law (wherein I find nothing good or sure, such a deceitful thing it is): *your* laughter, *your* joy, *your* honor are nothing but tears, sadness, and dishonor. If your false turns cause my rose to wither, never after shall I seek to have another.

This is the kind of poetry that invites reading aloud, for the music is there, in the text, waiting to be liberated by the haunting rhymes in -*our*, carefully prepared by "toutes," "flours," and "tous" in the first line and taken up again by the -*ou*- of "doulce" (l. 5) and by the -*our* of "colour" (l. 6) before appearing at the rhyme; the -*ou*- sound is brought back poignantly, in the last stanza, before the rhyme, within lines 17–19 and 22–23. Music is to be found, too, in the contrast between -*our* and -*ier* (the [r] is pronounced in both cases), and between -*uis* and -*ose*. Contributing to the color of these vocalic effects is the subtle play throughout the poem on [f] and [v], voiceless and voiced versions of the same sound, and, in contrast, the discreet alliterations based on the repetition of an identical sound. Nor can one separate the harmonics thus created from the meter and the rhythmic play: the first lines of the first two strophes, with their less marked pause contrasting with the next line with its strong cesura; the significant "Gastés" of line 3 breaking this pattern with its emphasis, as does "Viengne" in line 11; the enjambments of lines 4–5 and 12–13, together with those in lines 17–18 and 18–19, not excessive and yet playing a distinct part in varying for the ear the rhythm of each stanza, as we have seen in other ballades.

Participating in all of these phenomena is the word "Fortune," for not only does its initial letter ally it to that unique "flour" that is the center of the poem, but by its position, followed in each case (l. 4, l. 17) by a lyric cesura (still frequent in the fourteenth century), it becomes the epicenter of the poem, the implacable force against which the poet places the fragility of the rose in an opposition in which the fact that Fortune and the rose are both allegories, belong each to a long literary tradition, becomes of no importance at all to any understanding—or, better, appreciation—of the aesthetic qualities of the ballade. I must here use the adjective "aesthetic" instead of "poetic," since the latter may well imply an awareness of the traditional connotations of the words used. Indeed, the poetic qualities of this ballade are enhanced by the realization that the poet is associating in these lines the immense register (if I can adopt Paul Zumthor's term here[68]) of the Fortune topos with the immense register of the rose symbol. He thus evokes in the most forceful and moving way, backed by the authority of a long literary tradition, the fate of mankind—here expressed in one of its most poignant forms as the fragile beauty of a lady—faced with its destiny, whose mindless course it is powerless to change. When we are in the poet's garden, devastated except for one last rose, it seems that we are far from the general didacticism of "Il m'est avis, qu'il n'est dons de Nature" or the playful irony of "De Fortune me doy plaindre et loer," for allegory and tradition here combine with the persona of the poem to create a dramatic effect that is heightened by the direct address to Fortune—at first a bit mysterious and then made explicit—of stanzas II and III. Yet the lesson remains, indeed is strengthened by the intervention of the poet as a personage; the "dons naturex" of line 12 receives its commentary from the "dons de Nature" of "De Fortune"—and however much the poet wishes to reassure himself, the ineluctable threat of destruction of even the loveliest of nature's gifts lurks behind the interpellation of the goddess, as we know it must. The evocation through the image of the rose of the fragility of human beauty, the reminder of our fate, of the inevitable cycle of life and death to which we are all subject, the poet's sadness before the disappearance of love and beauty— and the expression of these things through superb sound effects, a varied and expressive rhythmic pattern, and a formal structure that is traditional yet perfectly wedded to the sense—create an extraordinarily effective poetic message and link Machaut to the other great lyric artists in French verse.

One of Ronsard's best-known sonnets, which we are accustomed to think of, and rightly so, as one of the chefs d'oeuvre of the Renaissance, can be described in exactly the terms I have just used: [69]

Comme on voit sur la branche au mois de May la rose
En sa belle jeunesse, en sa premiere fleur
Rendre le ciel jaloux de sa vive couleur,
Quant l'Aube de ses fleurs au poinct du jour l'arrose:

La grace dans sa feuille, & l'Amour se repose,
Embasmant les jardins & les arbres d'odeur:
Mais batue ou de pluye, ou d'excessive ardeur,
Languissante elle meurt feuille à feuille declose.

Ainsi en ta premiere & jeune nouveauté,
Quant la terre & le Ciel honoraient ta beauté,
La Parque t'a tuée, & cendre tu reposes.

Pour obseques reçoy mes larmes & mes pleurs
Ce vase plain de lait, ce panier plein de fleurs
Afin que vif & mort ton corps ne soit que roses.

As the rose appears on the branch, in May, in its lovely youth, in its newest bloom, making the sky jealous of its brilliant hue, when the dawn waters it with its tears at daybreak:

Grace in its leaves and love lies hidden, filling the gardens and the trees with scent: but, beaten down by the rain or by excessive heat, it languishes and dies, laid open leaf by leaf.

So in your early and youthful freshness, when earth and heaven acclaimed your beauty, Fate slew you and you lie as dust.

For your funeral receive my sobs and my tears, this vase full of milk, this basket full of flowers, so that in life and in death your body may be only roses.[70]

That the roses of this sonnet are "Classical" and its form Italianate does not make of it, I think, a better poem than Machaut's: its Parque is another disguise of Fortune, its funerary rite another attempt at appeasing fate, the nonstatic circularity of its "rose" / "roses" but another way to express what Machaut does through the repetition of his refrain. I do not mean to suggest that Ronsard is a less-accomplished genius than he has been thought to be or that he is copying Machaut; this would be absurd, for lyric themes and means have never been copyrighted. My intention is quite the opposite: I mean to show that the poetic quality of Machaut's work is of a very high order indeed. Poems of this sort, giving the same kind of aesthetic and intellectual satisfaction, are not rare in Machaut's work; it is their presence that makes it possible to agree with Jean Frappier when he writes that "in Guillaume de Machaut, the expression of love sometimes takes on an almost cosmic magnitude and suggests the harmonies of the microcosm and the macrocosm."[71]

We have seen that in all five poems Fortune is characterized as a great force, finally irresistible; that it is false; that it is responsible for the woes of mankind (mainly those of the lover, but also those of Everyman); that this is, in fact, the conventional Fortuna. But this conventional figure is used differently in each case, it is varied, its importance and place are shifted, utilized in different ways. These variations on a theme, some of them minute, some of much more importance, work together with those variations in rhyme and rhythm, in structure and organization, and in the use of the refrain we have examined, to produce poems that are, as a result, quite different one from the other, even within the single form of the ballade.

That the same kind of skill at combining and recombining given linguistic, rhetorical, and ideological elements within a given yet supple formal framework can be found in the other lyric genres practiced by Guillaume de Machaut should not be surprising, and there is ample proof of this in Poirion's study. For the narrative works, the same is true, within their freer verse structure, as Calin has recently shown.[72] If I have been mainly concerned in these pages with the ballade, it is not only because I do not wish to retrace what these scholars have done and because later chapters will be devoted more particularly to the rondeau in Christine de Pizan and to narrative verse in other authors. It is also because the ballade can provide us with the double conclusion at which this preliminary essay has aimed: as the lyric genre most practiced by Machaut, it can serve as a representative of his accomplishment and importance; as a form that was to lead a vigorous life throughout the fifteenth century, it can remind us of the problems of reading that the foregoing pages have tried to define and can suggest others yet to be articulated.

In all of Machaut's lyric work, then, as well as, in another sense, in his narrative poetry, one can find the triumph of art over accepted limitations of form, language, and emotional content. This triumph is accomplished with a precise economy of means that can be seen, both in large and in detail, in the nearly 3,000 lines of the *Dit de la fonteinne amoreuse*, for example, as well as in "De toutes flours n'avoit et de tous fruis," or in the quasi-mathematical rigor of an eight-line rondeau (*Louange*, no. 264; Chichmaref, 1: 139):

> Sans cuer, dolens de vous departiray
> Et sans avoir joie jusqu'au retour.
>
> Puis que mon corps dou vostre a partir ay,
> Sans cuer, dolens de vous departiray.
>
> Mais je ne say de quele part iray   5
> Pour ce que pleins de doleur et de plour,

Sans cuer, dolens de vous departiray,
Et sans avoir joie jusqu'au retour.

Without a heart, suffering, shall I leave you, with no joy until my return.

Since I must separate my body from yours, without a heart, suffering shall I leave you, with no joy until my return.

But I do not know whither I shall go, because full of suffering and tears,

Without a heart, suffering, shall I leave you, with no joy until my return.

Formal perfection; a subtle use of the return of the refrain, with its delicate contrasts of presence and absence, joy and sorrow; the careful placing of alliterative effects, of *rime équivoque* ("departiray" / "partir ay" / "part iray"); the almost incantatory rhythm of the first verse, with its triple repetition—all of these details show why, even in such "trifles" as the rondeau, Machaut was a master, and at the same time pointed the way toward further formal experimentation, as we shall see in the next chapter.[73]

It is thus precisely the qualities of this poem and the way they work together that point to what appears to me to be a major paradox in the verse of Guillaume de Machaut: it is, curiously, this great musician who, through the intrinsic musicality of his verse, renders lyric poetry capable of existing without music. Or, rather, without what Eustache Deschamps, in *L'Art de dictier*, calls *musique artificielle*, that is, music produced by instruments or the singing voice, as distinguished from *musique naturelle*, the music of the voice "speaking" in meter, that is, in poetry.[74] In this respect he represents to a much greater degree than the poets of the Pléiade do a real turning point in the French lyric, a point at which poetry begins to become autonomous, begins, as Roger Dragonetti has pointed out, to lose its Boethian, mathematical—and musical—connections and to become "modern."[75] This paradox constitutes one of the important ways that Machaut looks forward to the centuries beyond his own.

What was perhaps even more important to the period immediately following, however, was that notion of creative joy which, as we have seen, he expands in the "Prologue" to his lyric poems and of which this last rondeau can serve, finally, to remind us. The voice of the poem tells us twice that the lover will be joyless until he can once more be near his love. Clearly, no resolution of desire, no positive response to a request, here brings the joy that must, Machaut tells us, inform the manner, if not the matter, of the poem. It can only come, as this chapter has sought to demonstrate, and as this rondeau reveals, from the way in which the topos, be it request, complaint, or adieu, is varied, is played with, both with respect to the rhetorical figures with which it is presented and to the formal texture of the poem. In each poem, that is, the action or operation with form and commonplace is not only expressive of the conventional emotion; it also provides space for the poetic "I" to play, with and within the poem, and thus to create. In the following essays we shall investigate ways in which various writers in the fifteenth century play with words and forms in order to create poems, and we shall try to define the space thus left for the subjective poetic personality within a fabric of convention.

2 🦋 Playing with the "I": Christine de Pizan and the Virgin

fter the death of Guillaume de Machaut in 1377, his disciple Eustache Deschamps composed a lament for him in which he defined the triple legacy of Machaut's elegant genius: perfection of form, courtliness of content, musical mastery. All three qualities are implied in the moving first stanzas of his *double ballade*, both meant to be sung at the same time; the message is made the more poignant by the consonance of words and music in the refrain in each stanza:[1]

> Armes, Amours, Dames, Chevalerie,
> Clers, musicans et fayseurs en françoys,
> Tous soffistes et toute poetrie,
> Tous cheus qui ont melodieuses vois,
> Ceus qui chantent en orgue aucunes foys   5
> Et qui ont cher le doulz art de musique,
> Demenés duel, plourés, car c'est bien drois,
> La mort Machaut le noble rethouryque.
>
> O flour des flours de toute melodie,
> Tres doulz maistres qui tant fuestes adrois,   10
> Guillaume, mondains diex d'armonie,
> Après vos fais, qui obtendra le choys
> Sur tous fayseurs? Certes, ne le congnoys.
> Vo nom sera precïeuse relique,
> Car l'on ploura en France et en Artois   15
> La mort Machaut le noble rethouryque.

Arms, Love, Ladies, Chivalry, scholars, musicians, and poets in French, all philosophers and all the poetic world, all those who have melodious voices, those who sometimes sing with the organ and who hold dear the sweet art of music; go into mourning, lament (and with good reason) the death of Machaut the noble writer.

O flower of flowers of all melody, gentlest master who were so able, Guillaume, earthly god of harmony: after your poems, who will be the first among all poets? I can in no way tell. Your name will be a precious relic, for in France and in Artois they will lament the death of Machaut the noble writer.

There is no doubt that the figure of Machaut dominates both poetry and music in fourteenth-century France, and his heritage was to prove an unusually rich one. In the years following his death, there flourished a number of poet-musicians, little known today, practitioners of an *ars subtilior*—in contrast with the simpler *ars nova* of an earlier generation—in which complex musical textures and rhythms seem almost completely to subordinate text to music.[2] None of them attained Machaut's eminence. Others, inheritors of his poetic rather than of his musical legacy, were famous in their own time and are well known today: Froissart, for example, whose considerable literary production in addition to his celebrated chronicle includes, like Machaut's, both lyric and narrative poems. And Deschamps himself, of course, one of the most prolific of late medieval writers in both poetry and prose. In 1403, in another ballade, he praises in turn another, younger poet: "Muse eloquent entre les .ix.," he calls her; "Nompareille que je saiche au jour d'ui" (Muse eloquent among the nine, unmatched, to my knowledge, today).[3] This time, it is Christine de Pizan he praises. Although his encomium is not, perhaps, as dithyrambic as his threnody for Machaut, it is very generous, and the refrain insists on Christine's uniqueness: "Seule en [ses] faiz ou royaume de France" (Standing alone in her poems in the kingdom of France). It is entirely true that, like Machaut, Christine was a prolific writer, and much of her output consists of lyric pieces (using mainly, at first, the forms of which he had given such expressive examples, ballade, rondeau, virelai) and narrative poems of varying lengths, into which, again like Machaut, she often inserted short lyric forms. Unlike the earlier poet, however, she does not limit herself to "Armes, Amours, Dames, Chevalerie." Although these form a large part of the subject matter of her works, she went on to other things. Indeed, once she started writing, around 1394, she seems hardly to have stopped, and in addition to the aforementioned genres, verse and prose *épîtres*, religious, moral, and philosophical poetry and prose, history, translations, and semiautobiographical writing flowed with amazing facility from her pen until about 1418, when she apparently withdrew from active literary life. Her last work, a sixty-stanza *dit*, was written after a long silence, in 1429, in honor of Jeanne d'Arc and the French victory at Orléans.[4]

Now the name of Christine de Pizan is fairly well known, as such things go, in French literary history. But it is not the variety and vastness of her work that bring her whatever recognition she may have. It comes rather from the one celebrated poem by which she is usually represented in anthologies of French verse—"Seulete suis et seulete vueil estre"*—and from her reputation as the first professional woman writer in France and a feminist *avant la lettre*.[5] To suggest that this view of her as a poor but poetic widow lamenting at length the death of her husband before becoming the champion of women's rights is, to say the least, inadequate can come as no surprise to anyone who takes seriously Deschamps's praise of her. Even though there is bound to be some exaggeration in it, for he was, after all, replying to a highly complimentary *épître* she had addressed to him (Roy, 2: 295–301), in which she calls herself his disciple, his estimation of her as a writer is obviously high. And the writer's role is one that, as we shall see, she herself took very seriously. Paradoxically, this seriousness implies, as with Machaut, what I have called the element of play. The demonstration of this in Christine's case is much clearer than in Machaut's, however, for she goes a good deal farther than he in this respect. It is to the investigation of this

---

*Unless otherwise noted, Christine de Pizan's poems are quoted from Maurice Roy, ed., *Les Œuvres poétiques*, and cited by volume and page numbers. "Seulete" is found in Roy, 1: 12.

evolution in the notion of poetic play, play at times very subtle, at times fairly obvious, that this chapter will be devoted, and for which Christine can stand as an exemplar for the rest of the century.

Before beginning to look at some of the ways in which Christine de Pizan modifies the received tradition, we need to consider one problem central to her work, for it has important implications for the play of the poetic persona. The problem is a corollary of the fact that Christine de Pizan represents the first instance in French letters in which we know enough about the author's life, public, private, and even affective, to be sure that some of the poems are "true." We know, for example, that she lived at court, where her father was astrologer and physician to Charles v and Charles vi; we know that she received an education unusual for young women of her time; we know that she was married in 1380, when she was fifteen, to Etienne Castel, who became notary and secretary to the king, and that after only ten years of a happy marriage, her husband died suddenly at the age of thirty-four in 1390. All of this is reflected in her work: a number of poems, for instance, are quite clearly expressions of her grief as a young widow (e.g., Roy 1: 1, 5–15, 147–51). But even here we cannot, of course, be entirely certain of the "real" intensity of her grief, although the nonpoetic confirmation she makes of it in the semiautobiographical work *Lavision-Christine*, as well as in the lengthy poetic narrative *La Mutacion de Fortune*, tends to make us believe the emotion of the lyric poems.[6] But this timid beginning of "biographical" poetry creates the problem, for the "I" of the widow becomes easily confused with the "I" of the lady in the love poems whose lover has left her sad, lonely, and weeping.[7] In the following virelai, for example, it is impossible to tell whether the lady mourns a lover or a dead husband, especially since the very next poem is addressed to a lover who loves "d'amour legiere" and thus causes great pain to his lady (Roy, 1: 101–2):

> Je chante par couverture,
> Mais mieulx plourassent mi oeil,

Ne nul ne scet le traveil
Que mon pouvre cuer endure.

Pour ce muce ma doulour   5
Qu'en nul je ne voy pitié,
Plus a l'en cause de plour
Mains treuve l'en d'amistié.

Pour ce plainte ne murmure
Ne fais de mon piteux dueil;   10
Aincois ris quant plourer vueil,
Et sanz rime et sanz mesure
Je chante par couverture.

Petit porte de valour
De soy monstrer dehaitié,   15
Ne le tiennent qu'a folour
Ceulz qui ont le cuer haitié.

Si n'ay de demonstrer cure
L'entencion de mon vueil,
Ains, tout ainsi com je sueil,   20
Pour celler ma peine obscure
Je chante par couverture.

I sing as a concealment—but it were better that my eyes would weep—and no one knows the travail that my poor heart endures.

I hide my sorrow, for I see pity in no one; the more you have cause to weep, the less you find friendship.

That is why I neither complain nor repine my pitiable sorrow; rather do I laugh when I want to cry, and without rhyme and without measure I sing as a concealment.

It is of little worth to show oneself afflicted, and those whose hearts are joyful think it only foolishness.

So I have no care to show my real desire; rather, as is my wont, in order to hide my secret pain, I sing as a concealment.

The "peine obscure" is perfectly consonant both with the fear of gossip traditional in the courtly love tradition and with the poet's obligation to write verses that will please, even though her heart is sad. Doubtless because she was a woman and had therefore to be more careful of her reputation than a man, she is aware of the public's tendency—then as now—to identify the persona of one poem with that of another, and both with the author of the poems, and Christine expressly denies to her love poems any autobiographical truth.

At the midpoint of the *Cent Ballades* (Roy, 1: 151), probably one of her earliest compilations, she thus defends herself against the possible accusation by "aucunes gens" that her love poetry must be the fruit of personal experience. This, she implies, is naïve, for whoever wants to write beautiful poems must perforce choose love as the subject, since it is the lightest and most pleasing to the public, although she also admits the possibility of poems about noble lives and actions ("belles meurs"), thus referring to another part of her own work:

> Car qui se veult de faire ditz chargier
> Biaulz et plaisans, soient ou longs ou cours,
> Le sentement qui est le plus legier,
> Et qui mieulx plaist a tous de commun cours,
>   C'est d'amours, ne autrement
> Ne seront fait ne bien ne doulcement,
> Ou, se ce n'est, d'aucunes belles meurs,
> Je m'en raport a tous sages ditteurs.

> Because whoever wants to take on the writing of pretty and pleasing poems, either long or short, the sentiment that is the lightest, and that pleases best all those in the common run, is love (or, if it's not that, it's of some admirable actions)—not otherwise will they be written well or delightfully. I refer to the evidence of all wise poets.

The refrain of the ballade makes clear that her own attitude is a professional one, common to all good poets. She reiterates this point, or variations of it, significantly, in the first and last ballades of the series as well. In ballade 1 (Roy, 1: 1), despite conventionally modest disclaimers, her role as a writer is clear:

> Aucunes gens me prient que je face
> Aucuns beaulz diz, et que je leur envoye,
> Et de dittier dient que j'ay la grace;

Mais, sauve soit leur paix, je ne scaroye
Faire beaulz diz ne bons; mès toutevoye,   5
Puis que prié m'en ont de leur bonté,
Peine y mettray, combien qu'ignorant soie,
Pour acomplir leur bonne voulenté.

Some folks beg me to write some pretty poems and to send them to them, and they say that I have the grace of writing verses; but, begging their pardon, I could not write pretty or worthy poems. Yet, because out of their goodness they have begged me to do it, I'll work at it—even though I'm ignorant—in order to fulfill their wishes.

And in the last of the ballades, it is evident that she considers many of these poems, if not all, to be a kind of amusement, an "esbatement" in her word (Roy, 1: 100); for her, as for Machaut, this sort of poetry is, then, a kind of game; indeed, like him, she here often speaks playfully in the voice of the opposite sex. Nor should the fact that many of the poems are doleful lovers' requests, or regrets, or complaints—in the first person—of infidelity, absence, or abandonment blind us, any more than it did with Machaut, to the playful aspect of those poems. That Christine de Pizan's masculine persona takes on another and less ludic meaning will become apparent in the pages that follow. What I wish to underline particularly at this point is that she sees herself entirely as the professional maker of verses—and that this implies, as it does for all such "faiseurs," the nonautobiographical nature of at least her love poetry.

But does not the poet herself encourage our tendency to think of both "I's" in the poems as expressions of their author, particularly when poems of the "personal" kind are found close by those that are "conventional," like the virelai quoted earlier, and when, mainly in the prose works, she goes into a good deal of detail concerning her own life? There certainly appears to be, in any case, some tendency for the personal, autobiographical first person to invade the domain of the traditionally impersonal, conventional, formal first person of the love lyric. To what degree this may be true is a question that must be posed before going on to look at her play with words and rhythms and images, and with that "I" which, Christine assures us, is an other.

In order to answer it, it will be useful to look once more at the example of Guillaume de Machaut. In the magnificently illuminated manuscript of his works copied in all likelihood under his own supervision during the 1370's, there is a lavish use of gold leaf, of capitals ornamented with vines and flowers and sprightly little faces, and of small illustrations, mostly in black and white, within the body of the text. The general effect, as desired no doubt by the poet, is one of extreme richness. Once this has been duly admired, it is interesting to note another aspect of the illustrative vignettes: aside from the superb colored illuminations of the "Prologue," showing Love and Nature presenting their children to the poet, most of the other illustrations are reserved for the narrative *dits*, each of which has its own individual set. There is only one vignette at the beginning of *La Louange des Dames*; it shows a lover on his knees, his hands raised in a gesture of prayer or supplication, entreating (in song?) his lady, who is seated above him on a little hillock.[8]

This iconographical arrangement can be seen as symbolic of the nature of the poet's persona in his lyric and narrative verse. *La Louange des Dames*, despite the variation we have seen, is in one sense a single poem, since its subject is the single, albeit many-faceted, traditional "courtly" love convention of the time; one illustration can thus suffice for the whole situation. Each of the narrative works, on the other hand, tells an individual story—hence their individual sets of vignettes, each illustrating an event in the story. In many of these, the poet appears as a personage. It is in these poems, which Sylvia Huot in *From Song to Book* felicitously terms lyrical narrative (as opposed to the purely lyric), that Machaut's "personality" comes through. This person, this poetic "Guillaume," is, of course, as artificial as the joyous or long-suffering, hopeful or despairing lover of the ballades and rondeaux, but it is artificial in another way. It is not the result of tradition, as the "I" of the love poems is—or at least not of the same tradition. For in his *dits* Machaut gives a new impulse to what constitutes another tradition:[9] he imagines a persona apart from that of the young lover, though not necessarily apart from that of the poet. He is "friend to royalty," "personal counselor," "comforter." Finally, and most notably, in *Le Voir-Dit*, which purports to be autobiographical, he creates, ironically, in William Calin's words, the "garrulous, elderly, inept, cowardly narrator" who fails to operate under the code of courtly love.[10] To these aspects of character, one must add his role as "elderly *poet*," for it is this reputation that attracts the young lady whom he calls Toute-Belle to him in the first place. Until very recently, most critics have taken *Le Voir-Dit* at face value, as the true story, the poetic journal, of the old master's involvement with a bluestocking fifty years or more his junior. It is one of the merits of Calin's study to have demonstrated that, in this work as in the other *dits*, one must on the contrary always be aware of Machaut as a conscious artist, creating fictions, and ironical ones at that. No source outside the poem corroborates the "facts" it puts into play.

Now Christine de Pizan is as successful as Machaut in creating a literary persona. It is, of course, a different one: the poor widow of intellectual bent, forced by cruel circumstance to write for a living. But whereas the older poet confines this kind of individualized persona almost exclusively to narrative, Christine's created character (in both the dramatic and the psychological sense of the word) appears in her lyric poetry as well, and is also confirmed, to some degree, by the nonpoetical, autobiographical accounts she has left— accounts that (despite what is supposed, in *Le Voir-Dit*, to be an exchange of real letters in prose between the Narrator and Toute-Belle) do not exist for Machaut. A very large part of the "I" in Christine's work in the lyric forms is the traditional male "I" of love poetry, transposed—frequently but by no means invariably—to the feminine. Perhaps this very transposition, in fact, which can be seen as normal in the case of a woman writer in the male poets' world of the time (it is easy to discern, for instance, in the much better-known case of Louise Labé), aids in some measure in the contamination of the first person of the lyric mode by the first person of the narrative mode, closer to the historic widow, but still artificial. It is as if the "real" Christine hesitates to intrude on the lyric but, aided, paradoxi-

cally, by her femininity, ends up by doing so, in an ambiguous way. I
say "perhaps" this is true, because this kind of an "I"—the narrative
"I," it could be called—is also abundantly present in the lyric forms
in the ballades of such poets as Deschamps, Villon, and, to a lesser
degree, Charles d'Orléans. Before one concludes too hastily, how-
ever, that these poets are "sincere" (and therefore "modern") because
they write about their true lives and feelings, one must remember
that, with two exceptions—Christine, because of her other autobio-
graphical writings, and Charles d'Orléans, because of his historical
eminence—we know very little indeed about the "true lives" of the
poets of the time. And can autobiography be trusted? And there is no
historical account of the "feelings" of Duke Charles. Is it not far
safer, then, and far more useful for any literary analysis, to posit for
this period, rather than "sincere" or "personal" poetry contrasted
with "artificial," "conventional" poetry, different kinds of poetic
first-person modes, corresponding to different kinds of poetic per-
sonae? These modes coexist in the literary tradition, although one
may predominate at any period over another. The best known of
these modes is, of course, that of the so-called courtly lover; another
may be that of the poet trying to ape the courtly lover, as in *Le Voir-
Dit*; another may belong to the satiric tradition, as in Rutebeuf or
Deschamps or Villon, or to the didactic, as, again, in Deschamps, in
many of Christine's poems, and, frequently, in the Rhétoriqueurs.
Some, particularly the "courtly" mode and the "satiric"—or "bour-
geois"—mode, have been attached by literary historians to one or
another social class; I will discuss the appropriateness of such a
classification in a later chapter. What the example of Christine de
Pizan helps us to understand is that these modes can coexist, and can
be used by a writer professionally—that is, to please her public—
and at the same time to express her own literary personality.

Christine was the daughter of an intellectual and the wife of a
court official, and she herself had an intellectual bent. Though she
began by writing poems in the lyric forms, with love as their center
(and never gave them up entirely; certain ballades date from 1410–
15 [11]), she wrote moralizing ballades as well, and concentrated, in the
latter part of her literary life, on moral treatises in prose. Since she

was dependent on her writings for her livelihood, she presumably sought the favor of her courtly public in so doing, and the considerable number of manuscripts of such treatises as *Le Livre de la cité des dames* (completed in 1405) and *Le Livre des fais d'armes et de cheva-lerie* (1410) are proof of their popularity.[12] Like any author of the age, she needed patronage to be successful. Guillaume de Machaut once again provides a model here, in his relations with the highest level of courtly society: with Jean of Luxembourg; with the wife of King John the Good as well as with Charles the Bad of Navarre; with John, duke of Berry; with Pierre de Lusignan. Christine, like Guillaume, but also like her father and her husband, sought patronage by dedicating various works to such luminaries as Queen Isabeau, the wife of Charles VI; Louis, duke of Orléans; and Philip the Bold, duke of Burgundy, who commissioned her to undertake the biography of his brother, King Charles V. After the duke's death, his son John the Fearless continued to favor her.[13] In *Lavision-Christine* she tells us that the "benign and humble princes" to whom she has sent several of her works read them willingly—more, she modestly supposes, for the novelty of their having been written by a woman than for their worth—with the result that within a short time her books were known "in several regions and different countries."[14]

But in addition to trying to please a public, it is evident that she was also following her own instincts and inclinations as well, and this complicates the picture somewhat, for in such texts as those that refer to the celebrated debate on Jean de Meung's part of *Le Roman de la rose*, or in the *Cité des dames* or *Le Livre des trois vertus*, she puts playfulness aside and speaks firmly and unequivocally for (and often directly to) women, and in the voice of a woman. A way toward understanding both the occasional ambiguity of the "I" in Christine's love poems and her perception of herself and her role as a woman writer in an author's world inhabited entirely by men is provided by a brief passage in *Lavision*. It records the literary and intellectual evolution that followed her wholehearted devotion, after her husband's death, to the arduous study of history, philosophy, and letters and is of a kind that is rare indeed in late medieval (or even in sixteenth- or seventeenth-century) vernacular literature:

Then I began to hammer out some pretty things, at the start rather lighter; and just like the workman who becomes more cunning in his work the more he practices it, thus, continually studying different subjects, my wit, more and more steeped in curious things, improved my style with greater artfulness and more exalted matters, from the year 1399 in which I began, until this year of 1405, in which I still have not stopped. I have compiled in this time 15 principal volumes, without counting the other little poems, which together make up about 70 quires of large format.[15]

This passage seems to me important for several reasons. First of all, it characterizes succinctly the evolution of her literary production, which goes from lighter things ("choses plus legieres") to more exalted matters ("plus haulte matiere")—that is, from the games of love poetry to more serious subjects, treated in a higher style. Second, the precise mention of the quantity of work she has produced gives clear evidence of her pride of authorship. And finally, partly because of this precision but also because of its general tone, the passage has the ring of autobiographical truth (even though she probably began writing earlier than the date of 1399 she mentions[16]). We *believe* Christine de Pizan, here and in the *Mutacion*, because we know that, as far as her widowhood goes, she is relating historical facts, in either prose or nonlyrical poetry. We tend, then, to suspect that a persona very close to the "real" widow is evoked in certain of the lyrical pieces, even though, as we have seen, she denies any autobiographical element to the love poems, referring to the practice of all "sages ditteurs." There is thus some blurring, perhaps deliberate, of the "real" and the conventional poetic "I" in the amatory verse.

Let me put this in another way. On the one hand, in her lyric poetry, Christine appears to foster the closeness between her created persona ("I, grieving widow") and the courtly subject ("I, grieving abandoned lover"), a rapprochement made easier not only because there is loss, solitude, and grief in both cases, but also because the poet is herself a woman (and the identification of the first-person subject with the author is traditional in lyric poetry). Moreover, the verisimilitude of the first ("grieving widow") is further increased by autobiographical details given outside of the lyric poetry.

On the other hand, Christine is so skillful a player of the poetic game of courtly love that she is entirely convincing when, as she frequently does, she speaks with a masculine voice. Here, indeed, she demonstrates, despite her modest disclaimers, that she can beat the male poets at their own game. Yet even when we are convinced by the Amant who speaks in, say, *Cent Ballades d'amant et de dame*, we know that he can only be a fiction, a figment of the imagination of a woman. This fictionality argues, it seems to me, against a tendency in certain current feminist criticism to see all of Christine de Pizan's work in exactly the same light, a very serious light indeed.[17] That she herself did not do so is evident from the passage above. But the same text also assures us that her interests were larger, that the stakes for her were higher, and this is given abundant illustration in the body of works—moral, philosophical, historical, biographical—that she produced alongside the amatory poetry.

Another autobiographical text will illustrate the somewhat paradoxical way in which she set out her role as an author of serious account. It comes from *Le Livre de la mutacion de Fortune*, a poem of nearly 24,000 verses, in the first book of which she tells her own story, using the metaphor of a ship sailing on Fortune's seas, by which she has been buffeted to the point of despair. But then Fortune took pity on her, she writes, and came to her, and "le secours fu merveilleux!":[18]

> Si la Fortune me toucha par tout le corps;
> Chacun membre, bien m'en recors,
> Manya et tint a ses mains,
> Puis s'en ala et je remains.
>   . . .
> Transmuee me senti toute.
> Mes membres senti trop plus fors
> Qu'aincois et cil grant desconfors
> Et le plour, ou ades estoie,
> Auque remis . . .
>   . . .
> Si me senti trop plus legiere
> Que ne souloye et que ma chiere
> Estoit muee et enforcie

Et ma voix forment engrossie
Et corps plus dur et plus isnel.
. . .

Si me levay legierement,
Plus ne me tins en la parece
De plour, qui croissoit ma destrece.
Fort et hardi cuer me trouvay,
Dont m'esbahi, mais j'esprouvay
Que vray homme fus devenu.
. . .

Com vous ouez, encor suis homme
Et ay este ja bien la somme
De plus de .XIII. ans tous entiers.

Her help was wonderful! . . . She [Fortune] touched me all
over my body; well I recall that she felt every member and held
it in her hands, then she departed and I remained. . . . I felt
completely changed. I felt my members to be much stronger
than before, and even that great sorrow and weeping in which
I had been formerly was put aside. . . . And I felt much lighter
than I had been and that my appearance was changed and
strengthened and my voice had become deeper and my body
harder and more active. . . . So I got up lightheartedly, no
longer the captive of idle tears that used to increase my distress.
I found I had a strong and brave heart—which astonished
me—but I felt that I had become a real man. . . . Just as you
are hearing, I am still a man and have been for more than 13
whole years.

In this remarkable description of an allegorical sex change
brought about by the vicissitudes of fortune, Willard sees Christine
as "simply explaining her need to change her role in life and, as she
herself said, to guide her ship across stormy seas, meaning that she
had to provide for her family." [19] Although this is certainly true as far
as it goes, it seems to me that if Christine de Pizan says she became a
man, it also means that she took on a man's role in her writing as well
as in her family responsibilities, for it was by her writings that she
planned to support her family. Her new strength, her "strong and
brave heart," her deeper voice, would be the result of her reading

and study and would find utterance in her serious writing on "masculine" subjects. The paradox is that although in the nonlyrical works she "becomes a man"—that is, treats serious subjects in learned fashion and in a high style—she nonetheless speaks consistently as a woman, from the woman's point of view. Allegorically a man, she yet reaffirms herself as a woman, writing frequently on subjects important to women: in her condemnation of Jean de Meung in the *Roman de la rose* controversy, for example, or in her defense of women in the *Cité des dames*, or in the advice she gives to various classes of women in *Le Livre des trois vertus*.[20] It is thus through establishing her credibility as a writer in the same league as men ("virilis illa femina" is what Jean Gerson, the chancellor of the University of Paris, calls her admiringly in a letter to Pierre Col, one of her adversaries in the *Rose* quarrel[21]) that she affirms her right to her femininity.

In sum, one must distinguish two levels in Christine de Pizan's representation of herself as a writer. On one level, she strongly adopts the stance and tone of the male writer, which she makes her own by speaking in her woman's voice. She accordingly insists on her own authority in her text: she has what it takes, she assures us, to be a writer, and she is rightfully proud of her accomplishments in the kinds of writing that must be taken seriously. Her historical importance as a woman in the masculine world of writing can thus hardly be exaggerated.

But, important as this is in the current necessary reassessment of the feminine voice in literature, it is not my chief concern in this book, and I should like to turn now to the second level, where she is more playful, adopting now the voice of a woman, now that of a man, the better to express in her lyrical verse the endless tension, the give-and-take, of the courtly love tradition. That some of the authority with which she speaks on the first level is occasionally apparent on the second is hardly surprising, particularly since, as we have seen, the distinction between the "real" and the conventional "I" in the lyric mode is not always clear. This has been discussed before, in a somewhat different perspective, by Daniel Poirion.[22] He notes, for instance, the large element of formal play in its relation to her poetic self: "Formal art, virtuosity, serve . . . as an alibi for the poetic 'I'; it operates therein with total freedom."[23] It is exactly this exercise in poetic freedom that I propose to analyze in the following pages. I shall do so mainly through an investigation of the various kinds of poetic play in which Christine de Pizan engages in the verse in which the conventional "I," the nonnarrative first person, is involved, although in passing we shall see that the ludic sense is not absent from the more "personal" poetry, just as the subject—which is of course also the object—of this kind of poetry tends to spill over, as we have found, into the conventional realm. I shall reserve consideration of the opportunities for such play with the "I" in narrative verse for the next chapter, on the *dits* of Alain Chartier.

In order to understand the ways in which Christine creates through form, image, and idea the joy and the *jeu* that Machaut claims are necessary in all poetry, it is useful to imagine a continuum of playful modes, beginning with variations in meaning and proceeding through different stages to variations that are strictly formal, rather than ideological, in nature. We have seen that a topos, often but not always taken from the stock of love conventions—witness the "Fortune" series analyzed in Chapter 1—can be varied through shifts in emphasis, in the use of the refrain, and so on. The same ballades demonstrated that further play could be introduced by the use of different voices, by the disposition of the rhyme, by the arrangement of the lines, and by various other means. To a far greater degree than Guillaume de Machaut, Christine de Pizan explores and exploits the formal possibilities of this continuum, even for "serious" (that is, nonamatory) subjects, and she goes much farther than he, also, in clearly labeling certain poems, by one means or another, as *jeux*. The accompanying diagram outlines what I suggest; it displays the continuum of possibilities, the board on which the poetic game is played out. The two extremes—the limits of the board—are meaning. If, on the one hand, the text is all meaning, all idea, it ceases to be a game—that is, poetry—at all; it is outside the limits. If, on the other, it is all meter, then it is totally devoid of meaning and, lacking

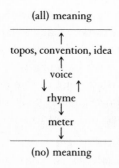

rhyme, in the fifteenth century it is not a poem, either. As the poet, or, to use the contemporary convention, as the poem moves from the top of the continuum toward the bottom, from idea toward meter, it becomes progressively less filled with meaning, less meaning-full, more meaning-less. Another way of saying this is that the poem becomes more and more *detached* from pure meaning. Most of the time, of course, poets play on all of these registers; they use, as it were, the whole playing board, to keep the metaphor. But some seem to prefer one side or the other of it; they tend to one extreme or the other. We shall see, for example, that Christine de Pizan at least approaches the bottom edge, and Paul Zumthor's study of the Rhéto-riqueur poets shows them coming very close indeed to meaning-lessness, though he does not discuss this in a context of play.

In order to illustrate this schema, let me take up some of Christine's nonnarrative poems, beginning with those in which the place of meaning is preponderant and going on to those in which formal elements account for the more important ludic aspect. It would be very easy to demonstrate that, like her master Guillaume de Machaut, Christine composed countless variations on the commonplaces with which the poetic tradition provided her. The ballade expressing the joy of love, or celebrating (or, in the case of a forlorn lover, deploring) the advent of the month of May, or regretting the departure of a lover, the rondeau imploring a return—all of these ring, in subtle ways, stylish changes on their subjects.[24] And in each of these poems, the play with the commonplace, as with Machaut, Froissart, or Deschamps, is not only expressive of the conventional emotion; it also provides space for the poet's literary personality to create itself. But, often, efforts by Christine to assert this poetic self, when it is different from the "I" of the poem—as it always is, we remember that she assures us, in the love poems—are of great subtlety. We can catch some sense of this by reading a seven-line rondeau whose very ordinariness, brevity, and apparent limpid simplicity make any analysis of it seem useless, pedantic, or simply vulgar:[25]

> Amys, venez ancore nuit;
> Je vous ay autre foiz dit l'eure.
>
> Pour en joye estre et en deduit,
> Amys, venez ancore nuit.
>
> Car ce qui nous empesche et nuit   5
> N'y est pas; pour ce, sans demeure,
> Amys, venez ancore nuit!

> My friend, come again at night; I've already told you the hour.
> For our joy and pleasure, my friend, come again at night.
> For what hinders and harms us is not there; for this reason, without delay, my friend, come again at night.

What strikes one first about this poem is its fragility—all is nuance and delicacy and tone—and its conventionality. The poem occurs in a series of rondeaux in which Christine sometimes uses the voice of a woman and sometimes the voice of a man—again, this is play, role-playing, perhaps—to recount the different moments of a courtly love affair, with its joys, its hopes, and its pains. Here it is the woman, courtly but coquettish, secretive but discreetly indiscreet, who repeats for her lover her invitation to love, accompanying it with a reason and a justification. In order for this voice to speak, or whisper, Christine uses, with exquisite skill, all the resources of the various traditions that nourished the lyric at the turn of the fifteenth century. The rites of courtly love are associated with those of formal poetry and its rhetoric to create a poem whose laconic density itself contributes to an effect of spontaneity and freshness.

There is little formal variation. Rather, the three traditional parts of the rondeau form known as the *triolet* are used to underscore the three elements of the invitation: (1) the proposed meeting; (2) the reason for the lovers to meet; (3) the circumstances that will permit their meeting. The traditional refrain of the rondeau, always stated in the first lines and repeated in the middle and at the end, thus takes on three different tonalities: it serves, at the beginning, as a kind of address on the envelope, as it were, of the invitation; then, at the center of the poem, it evokes the nocturnal joys that will be theirs if the lover joins his mistress; and its final repetition expresses the urgent passion of the woman, eager to profit from the absence of her husband.

In the Invitation of lines 1–2, the poetic attack is typical of many refrains of Christine's in its directness and vivacity; it breathes life into the courtly love conventions that inspire the poem and according to which the woman does not name her lover. Her discretion is still to be found in the second verse, coupled, however, with the clever recalling of a previous meeting, "autre foiz." The need for such discretion would of course have been well known to Christine's audience: it is occasioned by adulterous love and the consequent fear of *lausengiers*, or evil gossipmongers.

The Reason for her invitation is immediately furnished in the second couplet, lines 3–4. They should meet in order to have joy and pleasure, "joye" and "deduit." The use of two almost synonymous terms is a rhetorical figure frequently found in the work of the courtly poets, and here it serves to underline the nature of the invitation; "deduit," however, adds a nuance of activity to the joys of love. The refrain recurs, and puts the lover in the center of this little nocturnal play, where it is his place to be.

After having given the reason for her invitation, the woman justifies its urgency in lines 5–7, still with the discretion that is a part of the tradition: her husband—unnamed as such—is absent, and thus the lovers can see each other without danger. Once again, we find two elements that are nearly synonymous but express a nuance, a gradation: it is because the husband is an obstacle ("empesche") that he can hurt them ("nuit"), that he can be, literally, a *nuisance*. Much more than a nuisance, that is: a *nuisans* in the sense of an enemy. The running-on of line 5 to line 6 translates the excitement caused by his absence, and as a result, the voice becomes more urgent: "Don't be late," she lets herself say to her friend, to whom she recalls, one last time, the nocturnal pleasures that await him.

Using a cliché of the courtly love tradition, Christine de Pizan has been able in this poem to maximize the affective aspect of the rondeau form. Its refrain becomes the murmured but urgent entreaty to love. The simple diction of the poem is perfect for this, and no image interrupts the directness of this invitation whispered to her lover by a woman successively flirtatious, sentimental, and sensual. In this brief rondeau, the poet evokes, with an extraordinary economy of means, a whole love story, and she thus allies poetic creativity to *la ronde* of amorous intrigues so characteristic of the court.[26]

To see how exactly the same topos could be amplified by means of another form, another emphasis—this time on the *lausengiers* or *mesdisans*—and the use of other commonplaces to accompany the woman's invitation, compare the following ballade (Roy, 3: 247–48). In one poem all is discretion, evocation, murmur; in the other, the woman is much less discreet and much more long-winded.

> Venez vers moy, tres doulz amy, a l'eure
> Que vous savez et si n'y faillez mie,
> Car mesdisans ja vuellent courir seure
> A nostre amour, dont de paour fremie.
>   Et vous gaictiez   5
> Sagement d'eulx, car ilz sont apointiez
> A nous grever, j'en suis toute avisée;
> Si est mestier que nous en donnons garde,
> Leur maniere m'a esté devisée;
> Ilz nous nuyront, le feu d'enfer les arde!   10
>
> Et ne faillez par trop longue demeure
> Ne par trop tost venir, car endormie
> Ne seray pas, et, se Dieu me seccueure,
> Je vous desir de loyal cuer d'amie,
>   Quoy que sentiez   15
> Pareil desir que j'ay, et que mettiez
> Un abit brun et robe desguisée

Vous pry, amis, pour decevoir la garde
Que ceulx m'ont mis, ce ne m'est pas risée,
Ilz nous nuyront, le feu d'enfer les arde!   20

Tant me tarde, doulz ami, que j'en pleure
Que soye o vous ou une heure ou demie,
Car a autre bien ne sçay ou je queure
Et sans vous suis comme chose entommie.
    Bien agaictiez   25
Ce qu'ilz feront ains que vous vous partiez
Pour y venir, moins seroye prisée
S'on vous veoit, par quoy, quoy qu'il me tarde,
J'ay grant paour d'estre de eulx avisée;
Ilz nous nuyront, le feu d'enfer les arde!   30

Ha! doulz ami, je fusse asegrisée
S'estoie entre voz bras, trop suis couarde
Pour mesdisans et leur faulse visée;
Ilz nous nuyront, le feu d'enfer les arde!

Come to me, sweetest friend, at the hour you know, and
don't fail to be there, because already scandalmongers want to
assail our love, which makes me quake with fear. And care-
fully watch out for them, for they're determined to vex us, I'm
sure of it; so we need to watch out—I've been told about their
ways. They'll do us harm; may they burn in hell!

And don't make the mistake of coming either too late or too
early, because I won't be asleep, and—may God help me—I
desire you with the faithful heart of a friend. Even though you
may feel the same desire that I do and put on the disguise of a
monk in order to deceive the guard they've put upon me, I beg
you, my friend, it's no laughing matter for me. They'll do us
harm; may they burn in hell!

I long so much to be with you, sweet friend, an hour or even
half an hour, that it makes me weep, for I seek no other good,
and without you I'm like a senseless thing. Carefully take
account of what they're doing before leaving to come to me; I
would be less esteemed if you were seen—consequently, de-
spite my longing, I'm much afraid of being noticed by them.
They'll do us harm; may they burn in hell!

Ah, sweet friend, were I in your arms I would be at ease;

I'm very cowardly because of the scandalmongers and their
false aims; they'll do us harm; may they burn in hell!

There is no doubt that much of the difference between the two
poems comes from the choice of form: between the shortest possible
rondeau and a longish ballade stanza. But when the ballade is read
on its own, without comparison, the slight metric variation found in
the fifth line of each stanza is not enough to prevent this poem from
placing itself high on the continuum of meaning, for it is essentially
the *mise en valeur* of the emotional—and conventional—association
that the poet brings to bear on the central convention.

Even were we not to believe her explicit disclaimer of personal
experience, it is highly unlikely that these two poems express some
private affair of Christine's, given what we know of her exemplary
life. Rather than a personal or private "I," the first person in each
seems to be an eye, observant of the foibles of the court, coupled with
an ear and a pen. This is even more apparent in those poems in
which the "I" is a man, that is, when the (female) observer plays at
being the (male) lover, as in the following rondeau (Roy, 1: 170),
which carries the single love story with numerous pairs of players
beyond the tryst evoked in the last two poems to the unfortunate
return of the husband: [27]

> Or est mon cuer rentré en double peine
> Quant le mary ma dame est revenu,
> Qui du pais s'est hors long temps tenu.
>
> Helas! j'ay eu du tout en mon demaine
> Joye et plaisir et soulaz maintenu,   5
> Or est mon cuer rentré en double peine.
>
> Il me touldra—Dieux lui doint male estraine—
> Tout mon deduit, car souvent et menu
> J'estoye d'elle au giste retenu,
> Or est mon cuer rentré en double peine.   10

> Now my heart is in double distress, for my lady's husband,
> who has been away for a long time, has returned.
>
> Alas! I've had in my possession joy and pleasure and con-
> tinual comfort: now my heart is in double distress.

He will take from me—may God ill reward him—all my
delight, for often and often did she keep me in her couch; now
my heart is in double distress.

To the manipulation of the convention of adulterous love,
Christine de Pizan here adds the playful complication of a voice that,
being of another sex, cannot in any measure be "hers." Voice and
convention combine in this rondeau to constitute the message of the
poem: what is said, by whom. Indeed, the fullest message is created,
no doubt, by the addition of the one to the other. Were idea largely
eliminated and only voice to remain (with, of course, the formal
elements necessitated by the prosodic rules of the time), we should be
confronted by a poem tending not toward the upper part of the
continuum, toward more meaning, but very considerably toward
the other end. Such poems exist; they are the *fatrasies* and *fatras* of
the thirteenth, fourteenth, and fifteenth centuries, analyzed so perti-
nently by Paul Zumthor, or later, the *coqs-à-l'âne* of a Clément
Marot.[28] In all of these, although one can identify a poetic voice, it
enunciates lines that make some sense individually but become a
tissue of absurdities when they are strung together by the voice.

The extreme point of this kind of play with the love conven-
tions is reached, however, when there is what can be called a quad-
ruple game in which topos, voice, meter, and rhyme all become
parodies of themselves, are all in play (Roy, 1: 184):

Amoureux oeil,
Plaisant archier.

De toy me dueil,
Amoureux oeil.

Car ton accueil
Me vens trop chier,
Amoureux oeil.

Amorous eye, blithe archer, of you I complain, amorous
eye, for you sell me your greeting too dearly, amorous eye.

Even though the rondeau form is toyed with in these verses, to
a degree beyond that of "Amys, venez ancore nuit," for example, it is

still subservient to the message of the poem—to its topos and its voice. Indeed, the form adds to this message. The very roundness of the rondeau makes a joke of the eye and its arrowlike glances, abetted by the repetition at the refrain points that mocks the lover's obsession with his lady's eye(s), of which there seem to be both one and three. The use of the short four-syllable line is in itself a joke, as is the fact that a woman is the author of this man's complaint, a complaint that is itself ironic, since his "dueil" is not really sorrow but pleasure.

It is not hard to imagine how, through familiarity and constant reuse, the commonplaces of courtly love could lend themselves easily to such varying degrees of playfulness. But what about more "serious" topics, those outside the love convention? We have already seen how at least one cliché of humanist literature—the workings of Fortune and their consequences—could be transmuted into a number of variations. Though Machaut can occasionally play in a frivolous way with a love topos—one thinks, for example, of the rondeau "Quant Colette Colet colie / Elle le prent par le colet" (When Colette kisses Colin, she takes him by the collar)[29]—he does not indulge in such obvious verbal high jinks in subjects from another realm. Christine de Pizan too can adopt common moral and philosophical lessons rather straightforwardly to the ballade form: "C'est souverain bien que prendre en pacience" (The highest good is to be patient), one refrain tells us; "On est souvent batu pour dire voir" (Those who tell the truth are often beaten), avers a second; "Car qui est bon doit estre appellé riche" (The good man should be called rich), teaches another; or "Avisons nous qu'il nous convient morir" (Let us remember that we must die), proclaims the entirely Christian though hardly original thought embodied in the refrain of yet another (Roy, 1: 17, 250, 207, 212). She does not stop, however, with making such *dictons* new and rich and strange by putting them into ballades. A group of 113 quatrains, written, she tells us, for her son, is called *Enseignements moraux* (Roy, 3: 27–54); each one forms a little precept for conduct moral or social, as in the following examples (pp. 29, 35, 41):

Se d'armes avoir renommée
Tu veulz, si poursui mainte armée;
Gard qu'en Bataille n'en barriere
Tu ne soies veü derriere.

If you want a military reputation, see that you join many armies; in battle or barricade, don't be found behind.

A jeux d'eschas n'a jeux de tables
N'a aultres, legiers ou notables,
Ne soies fel ne oultrageux
Et te joue a gracïeux jeux.

In chess or checkers or in other games, frivolous or serious, don't be cruel or unsparing—play the game gracefully.

Fay toy craindre a ta femme a point
Mais gard bien ne la batre point,
Car la bonne en aroit despis
Et la mauvaise en vauldroit pis.

Be sure that you are feared by your wife, but take care not to beat her, for that would vex a good wife and make a bad one worse.

Judging by the number of manuscripts, the examples of conventional wisdom contained in the *Enseignements* had a wide popularity;[30] doubtless their lapidary form had a good deal to do with this. The 101 couplets of her *Proverbes moraux* (Roy, 3: 45–57) reduce such advice, however, to even briefer form; they range from a warning against drunkenness—"Yvresce occit le scens, l'ame et le corps / Et fait cheoir l'omme en villains acors" (Drunkenness kills sense, soul, and body, and causes one to fall into bad company; no. 53)—to the always popular memento mori we have already seen embodied in the refrain of a ballade: "Quoy que la mort nous soit espouventable / A y penser souvent est prouffitable" (Although death is frightful for us, thinking on it often is beneficial; no. 100). Whereas in the ballade the thought is treated differently in each stanza, looked at, as it were, from a different point of view in each, here it is the reduction to a two-line rhymed formula that serves to "renew" the commonplace.

These couplets, too, appear to have been well known, for they were translated into English by Anthony Wyderville, Count Rivers, and published by Caxton in 1477 as *The Morale Proverbes of Cristyne*.

Most of these precepts are taken from such popular compendia as *Les Distiques de Caton*, much translated and imitated in the Middle Ages, in which classical wisdom is easily integrated into Christian teaching. Other poems of Christine's are more singularly Christian: *L'Oraison Nostre Dame* (Roy, 3: 1–9), for example, or *Les Quinze Joyes Nostre Dame* (Roy, 3: 11–14). But the best example in her work of a Christian theological argument made into a game through its language and form is a rondeau made up entirely of one-syllable words, the last of a series of sixty-nine rondeaux in the manuscripts (Roy, 1: 185). This represents the form reduced as far as it will go, the shortest, smallest, most compact rondeau possible.

> Dieux
> Est.
>
> Quieux?
> Dieux.
>
> Cieux
> Plaist
> Dieux.
>
> God is. What? God. Heaven pleases God.

The form is perfect, and for once it is entirely clear from the meaning that the refrain, which in an eight-line rondeau set to music would consist of the first two lines, is here, since no musical setting is assumed, truncated at the end of the poem, producing, as often in Christine's use of the form, a seven-line rondeau. It is equally clear that the poet is playing with the form and its exigencies of rhyme and repetition. Yet the subject is entirely serious: the writer is attempting to define God—not, on the face of it, a very amusing enterprise. But this is play, nonetheless—serious play. There is no role-playing, as when Christine adopts a man's voice, no intrusive female voice, either her "own" or that of another, conventional "I," just the play of word and form with idea, with a perfectly sound theological proposition. The best answer (or one of the best) to the question "What is God?" is, simply, God, happy in his heaven—fideism at its most succinct. One thinks of Herrick's seventeenth-century attempt at the same thing, using the same sort of laconism to make his point:

> God is above the sphere of our esteem,
> And is the best known, not defining him.

Neither poem is frivolous; in neither does the game trivialize the thought. On the contrary. Christine uses the refrain, recurring with inevitability at its proper place in the traditional scheme, to put God at the beginning, in the midst, and at the end of the rondeau. This is where he is in life (or in medieval life, at least): the circle with the omnipresent center and the infinite circumference; the Alpha and Omega of the existence of the poem and of man. It is possible also to find, in the triple repetition of "Dieux," the reflection, expressed with Christine's customary discretion, of the triune nature of God, the Three in One and One in Three.

It is difficult, in this curious rondeau, to distinguish *forme* from *fond*, as one used to be taught to do. Even though one of the interesting things about fifteenth-century poetry is that very often the two are in fact quite distinguishable, this is not the case here, for in this tiny poem we find a superb instance of the total interpenetration of the one by the other that is now what we think a poem is; all the ludic elements are held in a delicate balance. More familiar examples will make this point clearer. In the sixteenth century, for example, in the form known as the *sonnet rapporté*, several subjects are juggled by the poet throughout the poem, each receiving its own series of verbs and qualifiers. Du Bellay plays with this form in *L'Olive*:[31]

> Ces cheveux d'or sont les liens, Madame,
> Dont fut premier ma liberté surprise,
> Amour la flamme autour du coeur eprise,
> Ces yeux le traict qui me transperse l'ame,
>
> Fors sont les neudz, apre & vive la flamme,
> Le coup, de main à tyrer bien apprise,
> Et toutesfois j'ayme, j'adore & prise
> Ce qui m'etraint, qui me brusle & entame.

> Pour briser donq, pour eteindre & guerir
> Ce dur lien, ceste ardeur, ceste playe,
> Je ne quier fer, liqueur ny medecine:
>
> L'heur & plaisir que ce m'est de perir
> De telle main, ne permect que j'essaye
> Glayve trenchant, ny froydeur, ny racine.

> Those golden tresses are the bonds, my Lady, by which my
> freedom was at first o'ertaken; Love, the flame enkindled all
> about the heart; those eyes, the arrow that shoots through my
> soul.
> Strong are the knots; harsh and hot the flame; the shot
> comes from a hand well trained to aim—and yet I love, I adore
> and prize what binds me, burns me, wounds me.
> Thus, to break, to extinguish, and to heal this strong bond,
> this burning, this wound, I'll seek nor knife, nor liquid nor
> medicine:
> The fortune and pleasure that dying from such a hand gives
> me let me try nor sharp-edged sword, nor cooling draught, nor
> feverroot.

Through its interior repetition of topical elements, the poem tends somewhat toward meaning less than it might, for nothing in the nature of love motivates its division into threes. Indeed, to the "liens" and "traits" of the original sonnet by Ariosto that he imitates, Du Bellay adds "flamme" as a third element.[32] Near the end of the same century, Jean de Sponde's well-known *sonnet rapporté* is in this respect entirely different, for its structural principle is motivated by one of the triads of Christian theology.[33]

> Tout s'enfle contre moy, tout m'assaut, tout me tente,
> Et le Monde et la Chair, et L'Ange revolté,
> Dont l'onde, dont l'effort, dont le charme invente
> Et m'abisme, Seigneur, et m'esbranle, et m'enchante.
>
> Quelle nef, quel appuy, quelle oreille dormante,—
> Sans peril, sans tomber, et sans estre enchanté,
> Me donras tu? Ton Temple où vit ta Sainteté,
> Ton invincible main, et ta voix si constante?

Et quoy? mon Dieu, je sens combattre maintesfois
Encor avec ton Temple, et ta main, et ta voix,
Cest Ange revolté, ceste Chair, et ce monde.

Mais ton Temple pourtant, ta main, ta voix sera
La nef, l'appuy, l'oreille, où ce charme perdra,
Où mourra cest effort, où se perdra ceste onde.

Everything swells up against me, everything assails me,
everything tempts me: the world, the flesh, and the rebel angel,
whose wave, whose onslaught, whose deceitful spell engulfs
me, Lord, and weakens and enchants me.

What ship, what stay, what sleeping ear, will you give me
against danger, against falling, and against enchantment?
Your temple in which your holiness dwells, your invincible
arm, and your steadfast voice?

But what is this? My God, I feel many a time still warring
against your temple and your arm and your voice, this rebel
angel, this flesh and this world.

And yet your temple, your arm, and your voice will be the
ship, the stay, the ear, on which that spell will lose its power,
that onslaught will die, that wave will break.[34]

In its organicity, its balancing of the elements of what-is-said and of
how-it-is-said, this sonnet resembles Christine's little rondeau, al-
though its form does not, of course, allow the possibility—exploited
by the fifteenth-century poet—of the exact repetition of whole lines.

Despite its own equilibrium between message and form, this
kind of poem points the way to a second kind in which such a
distinction is much more apparent, because the lusory label is much
more clearly affixed to it. Poems like this extend the notion of po-
etic *jeu*, for they slide away from more meaning, at the top of the
continuum, to less. They do this because they adhere more closely
than the poems we have so far seen do to the notion, evoked in the
previous chapter, of inner repetition. Commonplaces are only com-
monplace if repeated in many poems; a single rondeau is only seen as

a rondeau if compared with many other rondeaux. In the poems that we shall now consider, the emphasis is more on the internal repetition of rhyme or meter than on either their connection with any poetic idea or their relation to other poems of the same or, indeed, of a different sort. This is not to say that such relationships do not exist, for this, we have seen, would be counter to the very nature of the "lyric" genres. But they become of less importance.

There are several ways of labeling such a poem a game. The simplest and most apparent is to indicate its nature by its title, to call it, quite clearly, "game." This Christine does in a group of seventy *Jeux à vendre* (Roy, 1: 187–205). Their title indicates what they are, but it also indicates a certain attitude toward poetry, a particular understanding of its nature. To take a modern example, Valéry's title *Charmes* serves the same double function: each poem is a spell and an enchantment; poetry in general is meant to enchant. Christine's games involve players, like all games; these are the ladies and gentlemen of her courtly public, who propose to sell something one to the other, in a first line of verse. The poem is constituted by this line plus the reply to the proposal. The first *jeu* gives the model for all that follow it (Roy, 1: 189):

> Je vous vens la passe rose.
> —Belle, dire ne vous ose
> Comment Amours vers vous me tire,
> Si l'apercevez tout sanz dire.

> I'll sell you the hollyhock. —My beauty, I don't dare tell you how Love attracts me to you; you can see it without my saying so.

These *jeux à vendre* are, then, obviously *jeux de société*;[35] but they are also poems, inscribed within certain prosodic rules. Although line lengths vary between seven and eight syllables from poem to poem, and sometimes within a poem (as in the lines just quoted), all are made up of rhymed couplets, with sizains predominating in over half.[36] They thus reproduce in their form that variety-in-sameness we have seen as characteristic of the poetry of the time. A certain diversity appears in what is proposed for sale. Flowers, leaves, and herbs constitute the most frequent category (over one-third of the total), followed by birds, animals, and gems; other items include food, musical instruments, structures (a bridge and a fountain), and, in one instance, hair. However varied these objects may seem, the answer to their sale is always drawn from the love convention, be it compliment, complaint, proverbial saying, or advice.[37] Five of the *jeux* can serve to represent the rest (Roy, 1: 191, 193, 194, 197, 205):

> Je vous vens les gans de laine.
> —Je seroie trop villaine
> Se vostre amour reffusoie;
> Car volentiers si j'osoie
> Seroit en vous m'amour fermée
> Par si que de vous fusse amée,
> Car vous estes digne d'avoir
> D'Heleine le corps et l'avoir.

I'll sell you woolen gloves. —I would be too churlish were I to refuse your love, for willingly, if I dared, my love would be sealed up in you, provided that I were loved by you; for you are worthy of having the body and the fortune of Helen.

> Je vous vens la clere fontaine.
> —Je voy bien que je pers ma peine,
> Dame, de tant vous requerir;
> Puis que riens n'y puis acquerir;
> Qu'oncques vous vy l'eure maudi,
> Je m'en vois et a Dieu vous di.

I'll sell you the clear-flowing fountain. —I see that I'm wasting my labor, lady, by entreating you so much, since I'll get nothing from it. I curse the hour I ever saw you; I'm leaving, and I say to you, Adieu.

> Je vous vens le cuer du lion.
> —Vostre cuer et le mien lion
> A tousjours, mais sanz deslier,
> Et pour nostre amour alier
> Par vray serment le promettons
> Et corps et avoir y mettons.

I'll sell you the lion's heart. —Let's link your heart and mine forever, never to be untied; and, so to join our love, let's promise with a true oath and pledge both body and fortune on it.

Je vous vens le chapel de bievre.
—Jalousie vault pis que fievre;
Se ne croiez riens qu'on vous die
Qui vous traye a tel maladie,
Se voulez amours maintenir,
Gaiement et lié vous tenir.

I'll sell you the beaver hat. —Jealousy is worse than the fever, so don't believe anything you're told that may bring you to such a sickness, if you want to maintain love and keep happy and gay.

Je vous vens le levrier courant.
—Pour vostre amour me vois morant;
Ce pouez vous veoir a l'ueil,
Et pitié n'en avez ne dueil.

I'll sell you the greyhound swift. —I'm dying for your love: you can easily see that, yet it causes you no pity or sorrow.

The replies are voiced about equally by men and women; in only nine cases is the sex of the person responding unclear: we have already seen that this kind of role-playing is also characteristic.

One of the most curious features of these little games is that though their form is elegant and the replies often epigrammatic, they are also, in almost all cases, entirely gratuitous. No logical connection ties the lion's heart, say, or the woolen gloves, or the greyhound proposed in a first line to the rest of the poem, which develops on its own, as it were, an erotic commonplace. In only six cases does the first line also represent the stock of courtly commonplaces and determine the content of the poem. No. 8 (Roy, 1: 189) is an example:

Du dieu d'amours vous vens le dart
Qui m'a navré par le regart
De vos beaulx yeulx, dame jolie,

Qui a vous amer si me lie
Que j'en seray a mort livré
Se par vous ne suis delivré.

I'll sell you the god of love's arrow, which has wounded me
through the glance of your lovely eyes, pretty lady, which so
binds me to love you that I shall die if you don't deliver me.

And so is no. 30 (Roy, 1: 195):

Je vous vens le songe amoureux,
Qui fait joyeux ou doulereux
Estre cellui qui l'a songié.
—Ma dame, le songe que j'é
Fait a nuit, ferez estre voir,
Se je puis vostre amour avoir.

I'll sell you the dream of love, which renders happy or sor-
rowful him who dreams it. —My lady, you'll make the dream
I had last night come true, if I can have your love.

Poirion quite rightly points out the gratuitousness of most of
the other poems, and he claims that examples like the foregoing are
more successful than the gratuitous ones, since the first line provides
a symbol, which is then exploited poetically.[38] This would certainly
be true were these poems written in the sixteenth century or later. In
the context of their own time, however, this very high degree of
gratuitousness seems to me to underline instead the lusory nature of
the poetry, in which love exists only as its own expression—there can
be no question here of its sincerity—exists only as the means of
literary creativity, or, perhaps better, of literary activity. Since, except
in the six cases noted, the first line determines only a prosodic
element—the rhyme of the next line—the subject of the reply can
vary to any degree, governed only by the limits of amorous casuistry.
The play, however, is entirely in the *écriture*, and these poems thus
tend toward one of the extremes of poetic writing, an extreme
carried much farther by later fifteenth-century poets, when all
meaning is either banished from the poem or made so ambiguous as
to become meaningless. Thus the *jeux à vendre*, by their formal play
with the love convention, can represent the erotic lyric tradition of

the medieval past handed down through Machaut; but by their detaching of the subjects of this convention, which make up the body of the poems, from any necessary logical connection with their first lines, they look forward to the elaborate play with rhyme and form of the fifteenth-century future, a future that both closes this period in French verse and opens the way to another. And they mirror as closely the important social function of this "courtly" poetry. With little change, one can apply to these poems the description given by Johan Huizinga of the *Inga fuka*, the ceremonial antiphonal songs of central Buru in the East Indian archipelago:

The songs are always in the form of strophe and antistrophe, thrust and anti-thrust, question and answer, a challenge and a rejoinder. Sometimes they resemble riddles. . . . The purely poetic element consists in allusion, the sudden bright idea, the pun or simply in the sound of the words themselves, where sense may be completely lost. Such a form of poetry can only be described and understood in terms of play, though it obeys a nice system of prosodic rules.[39]

In only one instance is there a rent in the social—and anonymous, or impersonal—fabric woven by these curiously sexless sexual games, just as in the larger corpus of Christine's work she denies to all but a relatively few poems the personal element. In the seventieth and last of the *jeux* (Roy, 1: 205), she cannot resist signing her work and making a reference, discreet as always, to her dead husband:

Je vous vens l'escrinet tout plein.
Mon nom y trouverez a plain
Et de cil qu'oncques plus amay,
Par qui j'ay souffert maint esmay,
Se vous y querez proprement;
Or regardez mon se je ment.

I'll sell you the jewel box, all full; you'll find my name clearly in it (and that of the one whom once I loved the most, through whom I've suffered many a care), if you look properly; just see if I'm lying!

Thus she does indeed, at the end, sell us the whole bag of tricks, the entire coffer of poetic gems—and in the "escrinet," as in a coffer, can be found the letters of "Crestine" and "Estien." Once more the narrative and autobiographical "I" breaks through the surface, ever so timidly—but through the evident pressure of pride in artistic activity. Its appearance, even anagrammatic and disguised, is of significance, as we shall see, in the history of French literature.[40]

But that is in the future, and for the moment we are concerned with different kinds of dodges. If the effect of question and answer, give-and-take, is obvious in the *jeux à vendre*, it is even more so in the "Ballade à responses" and the "Ballade à vers à responses." In the former, the first hemistich of each line of the seven-line strophes is made up of a verbal stimulus, and the second brings its response. The whole constitutes a dialogue between a lady and her lover, which begins "Mons doulz ami. —Ma chiere dame. / —S'aconte a moy. —Tres volentiers" (My sweet friend. —My dear lady. —Come close to me. —Very willingly) and continues in this fashion through three stanzas and an envoy. In the "Ballade à vers à responses," the stimulus—command, exhortation, or question—takes up an entire line, and the reply takes up the following one. In both, the playful element is again indicated to a certain degree not only by the titles of the individual dialogue-poems, but by the title of the group of poems in which they figure—*Ballades d'estrange façon* (Roy, 1: 119–24)—which also includes a "Ballade retrograde" and a "Ballade à rimes reprises."

The poems entitled *Ballades de pluseurs façons* (Roy, 3: 189–98) group nine other examples of such variations. They provide, in fact, a small compendium of the ways in which Christine—or any other poet of her time—can play with the material, both linguistic and formal, as distinct from ideological, with which her tradition provided her. Two of the ballades (nos. 1 and 2) are of the "response" sort that we have just seen. They thus represent one possibility on the continuum toward (no) meaning, the possibility of playing with the voice that is supposed to be reciting the verses. Christine indulges in this kind of play throughout whole poems whenever she uses a masculine first person. Another form of this voice-play is to be found in certain series of poems in which one poem "said" by a woman is followed by an answering poem from a man. This is most noticeable in the appropriately titled *Cent Ballades d'amant et de dame* (Roy, 3: 209–317); in a brief introduction the persona of the poet presents the following text as "Cent ballades d'amoureux sentement." Alternating regularly between the Amant and the Dame, as each ballade is labeled, the poems reply one to the other and present, in fact, an entire love story that ends with the death of the Dame and her "lay mortel."[41] We shall see that Alain Chartier uses the same technique, with another ending, in *La Belle Dame sans mercy*.

In what I have called dialogue- or response-poems, this technique is employed within individual poems, with both sexes appearing as voices. It is possible to alternate entire strophes between the lover and the woman (e.g., the first ballade in *Ballades de pluseurs façons*), or regular groupings of verses within a strophe (no. 2 in the same series uses sets of two verses for statement and response). Sometimes only one alternating line is given to him and one to her, and in the "Ballade à responses," as we have seen, even the single line is divided between the two puppet-players of the game.

Following the continuum toward less meaning, another way in which Christine can manipulate the linguistic material is through rhyme, which we twentieth-century readers must remember was of utmost importance in French poetry until very recently. One finds abundant illustration of this in the *Ballades de pluseurs façons*; the first stanza of its "Ballade à doubles rimes" (no. 3) will give the reader a taste (Roy, 3: 191):

> Dame, je pars de vous pale et des*taint*,
> A*taint* de dueil m'en vois, dont je sous*pire*
> En *pire* point qu'onques ne fus ra*taint*,
> *Taint* de couleur mortele qui m'em*pire*,
> Des*pire* doy ma vie qui trop *dure*,
> Car *sure* mort ne me seroit si dure.

> Lady, pale and wan I take my leave, overcome with grief I'll go away; therefore I sigh, caught in a worse state than ever I was, my face colored with a mortal hue that makes me worse. I can but scorn my life, now lingering overlong, for certain death would not be so hard on me.

One cannot say of this ballade that the acrobatics of the rhyme scheme (which I emphasize with italics) make the meaning obscure to any significant degree. What happens instead is that when we read it the peculiarities of the scheme deflect our attention from the meaning, for however brief a moment, more than simple end rhyme would. The play calls attention to itself, calls us to admire its own cleverness, as it were, and in so doing tends to push itself to the fore. This process, as we shall see, can be taken much further. In the next ballade (no. 4), most of the rhymes are rich, or *léonines*, as they were called in the fifteenth century; although once again we have no trouble understanding what is being said—the poem is a woman's complaint on losing her lover—again, our attention is distracted from it by the rhyming game. In a much longer effort of this sort, an astounding lai of 267 "vers léonimes" (Roy, 1: 125–36), the poet addresses Love. Certain stanzas that include very short lines come very close to centering attention almost entirely on form; in so doing, the text *displaces* meaning in a significant way (Roy, 1: 133–34).

> Dont blasmée
> Ne clamée
> Diffamée,
> Ne nommée
> Mau renommée
> Ne fusmée
> Ne dois estre, mais amée
> Et prisée plus qu'autre rien.
>
> Car armée
> Enarmée,
> Affermée,
> Confermée
> T'es et formée
> Bien fermée
> Pour nous, c'est chose informée,
> Ne le nyer n'y vauldroit rien.

On that account not blamed or challenged, defamed or decried, ill-reputed or besmirched should you be, but loved and esteemed above all else.

For an army ready for combat, assured, established are you,

formed firmly for us—that's well known, and it would be no
use denying it.

And the meaning is displaced in a way that points to the third
kind of play on the continuum: play with meter. In the stanzas just
quoted, meaningful utterance is rendered more difficult not only by
the necessity of the rhyme but also by the constraints of the meter. It
is the combination of the two, then, that pushes these verses close to
one of the extremes of the continuum. The *Ballades de pluseurs façons*
provide examples of metric play as well, though they are less extreme
than in the lai. In both no. 4 and no. 5, seven- and three-syllable lines
alternate throughout the three stanzas; in ballade no. 9, the last of the
group, each six-line stanza is made up of the repetition of a group
consisting of two ten-syllable verses followed by a four-syllable
verse; the look is odd. Although isometric stanzas predominate in
the ballades of the time, all the major writers use, to some degree,
this kind of alternation, and metric variation obviously constitutes
one important way of asserting a poetic personality. Thus one can
conclude that if, on the one hand, Christine de Pizan is prevented,
through the desire of her public for poetry playing on the com-
monplaces of love and morality, from expressing her own tragedy in
any very satisfactory way, she can only choose, in the majority of her
poems in lyric form, the ambiguity of a woman—any woman—
bewailing a lost love—any love—with her resultant solitude—the
solitude of all the lovelorn. This can express, albeit indirectly, her
poetic persona. On the other hand, another important part of that
persona—"the *diteur* who delights in her poetic craft"—is ex-
pressed, more largely and less ambiguously, in the very considerable
space she creates for it by formal means throughout her "lyric" verse.

It will not have escaped the reader's notice that the means of
play enumerated in the last few paragraphs follow the continuum in
the figure presented earlier. The charge can be made that it is not
only artificial but misleading to break Christine's poems into compo-
nent parts this way. That would be true were not our model for a
single poem a continuum or playing board on which she, like others,
uses the whole surface; none of the "lyric" poems is played out in
only one way. I have tried, on the contrary, to point out that it is a

question of emphasis, not exclusion. While certain poems tend to emphasize play with topos or idea, others do so with voice, largely through variation coupled with repetition; in others the play that is underlined, even advertised, is with rhyme and meter, again through variation and repetition. It is obvious that these two factors, present in each ludic mode, are more noticeable, for us, when they affect not what is signified, but *how* it is signified, not the message but by what means this message is transmitted. One tendency in fifteenth-century poetry is what appears to us an inordinate development of this principle of repetition and variation applied to the prosodic elements of the poem; we have seen that Christine de Pizan's poems represent an important step in this direction.

By the middle of the century such games, with many variations, were quite common. Zumthor calls some of them, by a happy term, "juggling," and analyzes a number of them in his study of Rhétoriqueur verse.[42] It is not my intention in this essay to offer any such extensive analysis as he proposes. I should like rather, choosing a few examples in the large corpus that has come down to us, to illustrate how tendencies we have found in the poetry of Machaut and to a greater degree in Christine's became major characteristics of fifteenth-century poetry and to suggest how this development can be understood.

Jean Meschinot (ca. 1420–1491), whose lengthy poem *Les Lunettes des Princes* we shall consider in a later chapter, wrote, probably in the 1450's and 1460's, a number of short religious poems as well; this curious huitain is found among them:[43]

> D'honneur sentier, confort seul et parfaict,
> Rubis chieris, saffir très précieulx,
> Cueur doulx et chier, support bon en tout faict,
> Infini pris, plaisir mélodieux,
> Esjouis ris, souvenir gracieulx,   5
> Dame de sens, mère de Dieux trèsnette,
> Apuy rassis, désir humble joyeux,
> M'âme deffens, trèschière pucelette.

The path of honor, comfort unique and perfect, cherished ruby, sapphire most precious, heart dear and sweet, sufficient

succour in all occasions, infinite excellence, melodious plea-
sure, happy laughter, gracious memory, lady of understanding,
purest mother of God, sure stay, humble joyous desire: defend
my soul, most beloved Virgin.

Poetic play with a religious motif is not new to us; we have seen an
example in Christine de Pizan's monosyllabic rondeau "Dieux," in
which the obligatory triple repetition of the refrain was used to
underscore the theological point. Another aspect of that tiny poem's
playfulness is, of course, its very compactness. In Meschinot's poem,
the play comes rather from the opposite, that is, the lines' extraordi-
nary powers of expansion. Its author contends that the poem can be
read "en trente-deux manières différentes et plus, et à chascune il y
aura sens et rime" (in thirty-two or more different ways, and in each
there will be found meaning and rhyme).⁴⁴ Rhyme there is, certainly,
and abundantly. When it comes to meaning, the matter is more
complicated, as I shall endeavor to show.

Once one begins to play with this poem, its expansive nature
begins to boggle the mind. It comes from the fact that, in each line,
there is not one but four possibilities of rhyme; they occur at the first
and last syllable and on each side of the cesura—that is, since the line
is decasyllabic, at the fourth and fifth syllables. The poem, a prayer to
the Virgin Mary, is essentially a list, as litanies are, and the almost
entire lack of syntax (the verb in the last line is the only one in the
poem), coupled with the rhymes at each end and in the middle,
allows each line to be read both backwards and forwards; the rhyme
scheme in all cases is always the same, although the rhymes are
different. Thus the absence of grammatical obstacle—in the form of
conjunctions, for example—and the presence of rhyme at unusual
places make it possible for each line to be read in eight different
ways, the original and seven permutations. I give as a model these
readings of the first line:

    1. D'honneur sentier, confort seul et parfaict
    2. Parfaict et seul confort, sentier d'honneur
    3. D'honneur sentier, parfaict et seul confort
    4. Sentier d'honneur, confort seul et parfaict

5. Sentier d'honneur, parfaict et seul confort
6. Confort seul et parfaict, d'honneur sentier
7. Confort seul et parfaict, sentier d'honneur
8. Parfaict et seul confort, d'honneur sentier

If each line is thus rearranged, the result is, of course, eight different readings of the poem. This entire operation can be repeated beginning with the last line and working back to line 1, which thus becomes line 8 (this is called, in the terminology of the time, a "retrograde" poem), giving eight more readings. Further versions are possible by making a mixed-meter poem of sixteen lines, eight four-syllable lines (made up of the first part of each original line), followed by eight six-syllable lines (made up of the second part of each original line), and then by the reversal of this. Or one can make four poems of quadrisyllabic lines and four poems of hexasyllabic lines. And so on. As the author tells us, this *oraison* "se peult dire par huit ou seize vers, tant en rétrogradant que aultrement" (can be said in eight or sixteen verses, either going backwards or otherwise).[45]

If one is tempted to dismiss as puerile a poem like Christine's rondeau "Dieux," how much more childish must this numerico-verbal juggling act seem! But we must take a second look I think. In the first place, its title—or its subtitle, given at the end of the last paragraph, which mentions that it can be read as a huitain or as a sixteen-line poem—advertises it as a game, but its subject assures that it should be taken as a *lusus seriosus*, like Christine's definition of God. And as in that poem, besides the obvious play with rhyme, there is an interplay between the formal aspects of the prayer and the meaning, although in a quite different way than with the patterned repetitions of God's name in the rondeau. This time the form corresponds, not to any fixed poetic genre, but rather to the liturgical form of the litany, and it has the two elements present in this form, praise and entreaty ("litany" comes from Greek *litaneia*, "entreaty"). In this case, the encomiastic aspect far exceeds the other; it expands, in fact, to monstrous proportions, so that what seems at first a mere virtuoso *tour de rime* becomes a kind of poetic act of perpetual adoration, in which the praise of the Virgin never ends. Meschinot has carefully matched what his poem-prayer sets out to do with what it is prosodically capable of doing. Aside from the one plea in the last line, no inflection of meaning beyond the simple juxtaposition of laudatory synonyms for the Virgin would be possible; having chosen to emphasize the play of rhyme to such an extreme, in other words, the poet must necessarily give up much complexity in what the verses signify. But serious in his role as poet, he compensates for this to some degree by attaching the prayer to the tradition of Marian praise, which brings its own meaning with it. Thus he saves the poem from becoming meaningless, a mere laundry list of attributes.

The danger of the poem's becoming simply a list is not entirely avoided by Jean Molinet (1435–1507), a poet who was also fond of juggling, in another prayer addressed to the Virgin, a poem in which all the words of the first stanza begin with "M," all those of the second with "A," all those of the third with "R," and so on through the five stanzas, spelling out "Marie." Here are the first two strophes of this acrostic:[46]

Marie, mere merveilleuse,
Marguerite mundifie,
Mere misericordieuse,
Mansion moult magnifie,
Ma maistresse mirifie,   5
Mon mesfait masculeux me matte,
M'ame mordant mortifie;
Mercy m'envoye m'advocate!

Ardant amour, arche aornee,
Ancelle annuncee, acceptable,   10
Arbre apportant aulbe adjournee,
Accroissant avoir aggreable,
Astriferent aigle, attraictable
Accoeul, amorti ayemant,
Azime aspirant, adorable,   15
Ancre agüe, ames attirant.

Mary, marvelous mother, pure pearl, merciful mother, much exalted dwelling, my wonderful mistress, subdue my shameful misdeeds, mortify my remorseful soul, send me mercy, my advocate!

Ardent love, precious coffer, handmaiden proclaimed, ac-
ceptable, tree bearing the awaited dawn, increasing our agree-
able treasure, star-bearing eagle, alluring welcome, tender
lodestone, unleavened bread inspiring, adorable fast anchor,
inviting souls.

Since Molinet is constrained very little by either rhyme or meter,
beyond the usual requirements of verse—each strophe is made up of
eight octosyllabic lines with the same scheme, although with differ-
ent rhymes in each—since, in other words, he chooses to play on the
other end of the board, the immediate meaning of the poem is hardly
affected at all, is hardly pushed toward meaning less than it might,
that is. Paradoxically, of course, this relative adherence to meaning
denies to the poem the richness of ambiguous meaning; the poet
forgoes the effect produced in Meschinot's expandable huitain and
gives us instead a more finite litany, where the repetition of the
letters is used to create, but to a lesser degree, the impression of the
repetitive praise that he seeks and that tradition demands. "Praise-
of-the-Virgin" as a topos is here, then, subjected to variation through
repetition; the originality comes through the poet's choice of *what* to
repeat—in this case, the successive letters of her name.

Another kind of originality, closer to what we have seen in the
Fortuna poems of Machaut and to what Christine does with the
commonplace of the lovelorn lady, can be seen in the other sort of
variation this poem so copiously provides, that is, on names or at-
tributes of the Virgin. What strikes us as the quaintness, curiousness,
or simply ludicrousness of the poem comes from Molinet's having
combined the very ancient Christian practice of this kind of litany
with a deliberately intense and obsessive sort of alliteration—in
itself an even older technique in poetry—to produce his acrostic,
thus showing at once his skill as a poet and his intense devotion to the
cult of the Virgin Mary. But I must correct the second part of that
last statement, or at least refine it, for what the poem seeks to
demonstrate is obviously not only the poet's craft—what poet, of
whatever time, does not want to do this? and we have seen that
Machaut and Christine de Pizan are both proud *faiseurs*—but *an*
intense devotion to the Virgin. Just as the poet-in-love can be a

fiction, so of course can the poet-in-love-with-the-Virgin. Devotion to the lady can be—nearly always is—a poetic mode, and the same goes for devotion to the Lady; the important thing is to create from it a mood. It is to create the same mood of devotion—Marian or otherwise—that Meschinot and Molinet use different ploys, employ different game strategies, as we have seen.

A curious *dictier* by Molinet provides proof of the essentially fictive nature of this sort of poetry and of the poet's relation to the subject (which is also the object) of the poem. "Dictier qui se poeult adreschier soit a la vierge Marie ou pour un amant a sa dame" is the way it is described in one manuscript (A poem that can be addressed either to the Virgin Mary or by a lover to his lady),[47] and that is exactly what it is. Throughout the fifteen stanzas, the apostrophes to the lady, the often metaphoric description of her beauty, the praise and prayers of the persona speaking could, in fact, be applied either to the Virgin or to the chaste and beautiful woman of the love convention. A two-stanza sample is enough to demonstrate this:[48]

De tous biens plaine et de beaulté l'exemple
Estes sus terre et nul ne vous en passe;
Vous exedés toute imaige de temple
De chief, de corps, d'yeux, de bouche et de temple;   60
La plus des plus estes et l'oultrepasse;
Toute beaulté que nature compasse
N'est emprés vous sinon obscure et palle,
Et vous estes clere et tousjours lealle.

Et pour ce point vous voeus tribut donner   65
D'ung coeur navré que je vous sacrifie;
Ne me voeulliés du tout abandonner,
Mais moy du tout guerir et guerdonner
Des biens d'amours, que les siens perlifie;
Ma deesse, que j'aime et glorifie,   70
Secourés moy: conclusion finale,
Ma volunté sera tousjours lealle.

Full of all favor and the very example of beauty are you on earth, and no one surpasses you; you transcend every holy image in face, body, eyes, mouth, and forehead; you are the best of the best, the paragon; next to you, every beauty that nature encompasses is but dim and pale, and you are bright and always faithful.

And on this account I want to give you the tribute of a broken heart, sacrificed to you; don't utterly abandon me, but utterly heal and reward me with the riches of love, who enriches his own. My goddess, whom I love and glorify, help me. The final conclusion: my love will always be faithful.

It is clear that the poet is here offering an example of what he could imagine as the feelings of a devout Christian praying to Mary or of a passionate lover addressing his beloved—and he is offering as well an example of what he can do to express the mood of adoration, devotion, and supplication that is identical in both cases. The use of the indefinite article in the descriptive title's "pour un amant a sa dame" is significant, I think, for it underlines the general nature of the emotions expressed—it is, in other words, another way of announcing the poet's relation to his poem, the kind of distancing that we have found manifested in different ways throughout this chapter and that we are seeing as playful.

If this is true, where does this *dictier* fit on the continuum of meaning? It is obvious the poet is here making a deliberate play on meaning, and the result is a poem that means exactly twice as much as, say, a straight versified form of the *Ave Maria*. It does not do this through any intrinsically prosodic process, however, as in Meschinot's huitain or Molinet's acrostic, for the possibility of bringing a double meaning to the poem is allowed by literary and religious conventions or traditions "outside" of the poetic text.[49] Unlike Meschinot's endless litany, "inside" of which rhyme is all-important, the poem does not have to rely on the intervention of those exterior circumstances to guard against the threat of meaninglessness. On the contrary, the poet takes advantage of such conditions to push his poem toward an increase in meaning, albeit limited and well defined—there are always exactly two meanings for each part of the message, because of the two codes that are behind the text. The problem is here rather the opposite: how does the poem support its double load of meaning and still remain a poem? The answer is not hard to find: it keeps its poetic quality through rhyme. It does so, however, in a relatively unobtrusive way, compared with the poems of Machaut and Christine we have read. Even though the rhyme scheme of the fifteen strophes is identical, the rhymes fitted to this scheme are not; each stanza presents a different series of rhymes. But we also find that nearly all of these rhymes are *rimes riches* and, further, that the rhyme in *-alle* occurs in the last two lines of every stanza, with the final line varying but always ending with the adjective "lealle." In the latter case, it is not the richness of rhyme that counts, but rather its repetition in each stanza. Not only that, but the poet has found fifteen words rhyming with "lealle" and has been able to combine them with it in some meaningful fashion. To put it another way, here certain formal elements—beyond the minimal ones of ordinary rhyme and meter—operate both within the constituent lines of an individual stanza (*rimes riches*) and between the last two lines of each stanza (repetition of *-alle/lealle*) to ensure a poetic fabric worthy of the reputation of its maker.

But even with the quality of the rhymes and the repetition of the same ending word across the stanzas of a fairly lengthy poem, we are far from the formal play of Christine de Pizan with which we began this chapter. Yet the path that leads from one to the other has not been difficult to follow. All the verses we have considered have exemplified their authors' effort to wrench language as far away as possible from prose—that is, from "ordinary language." The most obvious way of doing this is through rhyme and meter, especially if the poet is willing to forgo, to varying degrees, the message that the very arrangement of words into syntactic groups implies. This means allowing a certain gratuity to enter language. In the examples from Christine I have analyzed, she has done this largely through literary artifacts in which conventions of rhyme and meter and their repetition work to create units that resemble other units and thus constitute formal genres, the so-called *formes fixes*. We have seen them as playing boards of meaning on which the numerous plays possible to the poet can be usefully charted.

But what happens when such formal conventions (always excepting meter and rhyme) do not tell us that we are reading or hearing a rondeau or a virelai or a ballade, do not, through variation, allow the poets who choose not to follow them to make their language "poetical" in the same way? Meschinot and Molinet, in the poems we have considered, point to the answer to this question. The following chapter will seek to provide a fuller response through the "narrative" works of Alain Chartier.

This answer will necessarily involve another factor that has been made apparent in the poetry of Christine, as well as in the *dictier* of Jean Molinet: the poetic game, the play, often complex, with idea and voice as well as with prosody, leads one inevitably to the persona—and not the person—of the poet. We must not look for the text to produce the same sort of emotion as the one we expect from a modern poem, for that is not what the poet sets out to do. What such texts do aim to produce, through conventional means, are certain reactions: even Christine's "bereaved widow" or Molinet's "poor sinning soul," like Machaut's "distraught lover," are designed to that end. "Of course we all love the Virgin—but look at all the ways I can say it!" says Meschinot. "Look how well he plays the game!" says the reader. Such a poem tells us about the poet's skill in manipulating language in a "poetic" way; it does not, as we have seen, tell us anything about his real devotion, any more than Christine's love poems tell us true stories. We would do well to remember this when we read Villon's poem to the Virgin (which, moreover, is his mother's prayer); it cannot tell us, a priori, much of anything about his "real" religious attitude. But that does not prevent the Villon *oraison* from being a beautiful poem. The effect desired by this poetry can best be summarized, it seems to me, in the term "wonder": wonder at the miracle of poetic language. And the literary personality of each poet can perhaps best be defined through the careful observation of how this miracle is produced.

3 ❧ "Je est un autre":
Alain Chartier and the Game
of Love and Death

lain Chartier (ca. 1380–1430) is one of the few writers of the fifteenth century whose reputation survived the disdain of the intellectual and artistic avant-garde of the sixteenth; an edition of his works appeared in 1617.[1] But this reputation rested less on his work as a poet than on his fame as an orator in the "classic" style, "lointaing immitateur des orateurs," as he modestly puts it in *Le Quadrilogue invectif*.[2] Today, the situation is reversed; that treatise is nearly all that even the avid reader of French literature generally knows of his prose, and he is remembered, instead, as the author of the poem *La Belle Dame sans mercy* and of little else. Although his literary production is far less extensive than that of a Froissart, a Deschamps, or a Christine de Pizan, like theirs it divides itself into prose and poetry. The verse, which will be our concern in this chapter, consists of a group of twenty-eight rondeaux and ballades and ten poems, of varying lengths, in forms that are in the main nonlyric, though they include two lais and a series of thirteen ballades that together constitute a single work.

Chartier's relatively limited literary production may be due, at least in part, to the fact that he held the high office of *notaire et secrétaire du roi* at the court of the Dauphin, later Charles VII, and as such was much occupied with chancellery business. He served several times, moreover, as a royal ambassador, to Sigismund of Hungary and to James I of Scotland.[3] He thus appears, from what little we know of his life, to have been a dedicated public servant, faithful to the sovereign and used to involvement in contemporary events and to life at court. The passionately patriotic prose of *Le Quadrilogue* seems to reflect his political career, as do *Le Curial*, his prose treatise on court life, and on a more abstract level, the unfinished *Livre de l'esperance*, written largely in prose but with an admixture of verse.

This apparently rather direct relationship between life and literature is more problematic, however, when one looks at his poetry. The collection of twenty-eight short lyric pieces is built entirely on amorous themes, with only one exception—and that is a ballade, unpolitical in nature, each line of which has the character of a proverb, or *dicton*. It is the only one in which the poet's persona does not complain, or praise his lady, or recount some misfortune in love; Chartier in these poems shows mastery of the "courtly" mode, with its anonymous "I" at the center and its variations on a theme. Some of the allegories dramatize with great effectiveness various moments of the amorous adventure and anticipate the poetic language of Charles d'Orléans: "Acouché gist en lit de Desplaisir / Mon dolent cuer" (Couched in a bed of displeasure lies my sorrowing heart; rondeau 6); "Au feu! Au feu! Au feu, qui mon coeur art / Par un brandon tiré d'un doulx regart" (Fire! Fire! Fire!—which burns my heart with a torch lighted by a soft glance; rondeau 19); "J'ay un arbre de la plante d'amours / Enraciné en mon cuer proprement" (There is a tree of Love's planting rooted in my very heart; ballade 25).* As Daniel Poirion has pointed out, Chartier's debt to Machaut is undoubted; rondeau 19, for example, with its opening "Au feu! Au feu!," recalls Machaut's "Hareu! hareu! le feu, le feu, le feu."[4] But Chartier differed from his predecessors in one important respect. In his work, the poems in lyric form are few indeed, and although they are of a high order poetically—and by that I mean that their formal technique is faultless, and that the organization and

---

* All references to Chartier's poems are to the texts in J. C. Laidlaw's excellent edition, *The Poetical Works of Alain Chartier*.

imagery and sonority of each poem show the same care in their relationship one to another that we have already noticed in Machaut and Christine de Pizan—they demonstrate neither quite the elegant economy of the fourteenth-century master nor the intense ludic variety of his feminine follower. Most of the rondeaux, for instance, are at least sixteen lines long, and there is, in the way of diversity, no poem in which he "speaks" in a voice other than that of his own sex, as Machaut, Deschamps, and Christine had all done. Instead of demonstrating formal versatility or any desire to manipulate his audience through modifications of the poetic voice, what Chartier seems to be doing in the lyric pieces is to provide proof of a solid competence in the making of poems in conventional mode that allows him to play mostly at the level of imagery, rather than at that of tone or voice or form.

He is much more interesting in the ten longer poems, for they display considerable variety in nature and can be categorized in a number of different ways. They range in length from *Le Livre des quatre dames*, with its 3,531 lines, to *Le Lay de plaisance*, an apparently early effort comprising only 196 verses.[5] From the point of view of their subjects, three of the ten define a concept or defend a principle and have a clear moral or didactic intent: *Le Lay de plaisance*, *Le Lay de paix*, and *Le Breviaire des nobles*. *La Complainte* is related to them in that it too is organized around one intellectual notion, that of death. Only one poetic voice speaks in these poems: in two of them it is the voice of the poet; in *Breviaire* there is no first-person voice at all, and in *Paix*, Paix herself addresses directly the "Princes nez du lis precieux" (Princes born of the precious lily; l. 7). In the others—*Le Debat des deux fortunés d'amours*, *Le Livre des quatre dames*, *Le Debat de reveille matin*, *La Belle Dame sans mercy*, *Le Debat du herault, du vassault et du villain*—a multiplicity of voices is introduced alongside the poet's own, and the questions raised in each poem are debated by these voices, with no voice coming out very clearly as the winner. It is possible to assimilate to this group *L'Excusacion aux dames*, written by Chartier as a defense of his position in *La Belle Dame sans mercy*, which had been criticized in a letter sent to him by certain court ladies.[6] It thus assumes also the nature of a debate or at least of one side of a debate.

I shall limit myself in this chapter largely to the eight poems—that is, all but *Breviaire* and *Paix*—in which Chartier uses a first-person voice in various ways. This limitation is not as arbitrary as it may seem, for the "I" of these poems will provide a bridge with the "I" of the shorter, lyric forms that have until now mainly concerned us. Further, this first-person subject both links these poems together and gives us, at the same time, one way to distinguish between them. It allows us, in other words, to apply one of the principles that became clear in an earlier chapter, that is, the radically non-anthologizeable nature of medieval poetry. This comes, the reader will recall, from the fact that each piece—be it rondeau, ballade, lay, or what have you—belongs, in a way that modern and contemporary poetry cannot, to a body of similar pieces, works that it resembles and from which at the same time it must distinguish itself. In the first two chapters, we saw how such distinctions were made.

Whether this principle also works for poems that have generally been characterized as *dits* (that is, as "narrative" poems, in opposition to the lyric, sung or not) is one of the questions I shall address in the following pages.[7] Let us first, however, ask ourselves how this authorial "I" might afford us a means by which these eight poems may be seen to exhibit some common character.

We can begin by noting that in a considerable number of them, Chartier's awareness of his role as a writer is evident—and it is that same professional awareness we have found in the work of Machaut and Christine. By this I do not mean the mere presence in our eight poems of an authorial "I." Nor, it should now be clear, do I mean that, in five of the eight, the "I" is characterized as sad and mournful, for one reason or another (in three of them, it is obvious that it is because of unhappiness in love); we know from our readings of earlier poetry that this implies no necessarily autobiographical intent.

His own authorial consciousness comes through, instead, in the place he assigns himself or, rather, his persona, in these eight poems. In five of them, he writes ostensibly of what he has "heard" or "overheard." The presentation of this convention is somewhat different in each of the five. As "seul clerc present," in the castle where *Deux Fortunés* takes place, he is asked to write up the debate so that it can be submitted for arbitration to Jean de Foix: "Et je qui yere / Seul clerc present, escoutant par derriere / Tout le debat, les poins et la maniere, / Fu lors requis par courtoise priere / Que je l'escripte" (And I, who was the only learned person present, having overheard the entire debate, the arguments and the way of it, was courteously asked to write it down; ll. 1231–35). After having eavesdropped on the two knights in *Reveille Matin*, he also writes down what he has heard, though on his own initiative: "Si mis en escript ce qu'ilz dirent / Pour mieulx estre de leur butin, / Et l'ont nommé ceulx qui le virent / Le debat Reveille Matin" (So I put into writing what they said, the better to make it part of their spoils. And those who saw it named it "The Wake-up Debate"; ll. 365–68). It is interesting to note, in the last two lines, the presentation of the work, which he is at the moment ending (line 368 is the last line), as an already finished text. This evidence of the highly literary nature of his enterprise can be found again at the end of *Quatre Dames*, where after hearing the arguments of the four women, the narrator suggests that their case be submitted to his lady for judgment, a suggestion they accept. He then returns to Paris, where he delivers to her the very book he is writing:

> Pourtant ce livre,
> Pour estre de charge delivre,
> A ma dame transmet et livre,
> Par qui je puis mourir ou vivre.   3455
>   El le lira
> Et pas ne les escondira,
> Et puis son avis en dira;
> Si sarons comme il en ira.

Therefore, in order to discharge my duty, I transmit and deliver this book to my lady, upon whom my life depends. She will read it and won't refuse them and then will give her opinion; thus we shall know how it will turn out.

The future tense in the last four lines serves to bridge the gap between fiction and "reality"—but in a way that underlines the fictionality of the entire undertaking. Part of the lengthy dedication with which he accompanies the manuscript he gives her—and gives us, as well—again emphasizes both his place as its author and its function as a written record of a "real" debate:

> Il m'est commis que je demande   3475
>   Vostre avis, Belle,
> D'une question bien nouvelle
> Dont en ce livre la querele
> J'ay mise en rime tele quele,
>   Au long escripte;   3480
> Et se si bien ne la recite
> Comment elle m'a esté dicte,
> Ignorance m'en face quicte.
>   Or la lisez
> S'il vous plaist, afin que disez   3485
> De bouche, ou au moins excripsez,
> Laquele plus triste eslisez
>   De quatre amantes,
> Dames belles, bonnes, savantes,
> Qui sont tristes et desplaisantes   3490
> Et de leur debat requerantes
>   Vostre sentence.

I've been charged with asking your opinion, comely lady, on a very recent question, the discussion of which, just as it occurred, written out at length, I've put into rhyme in this book. And if I don't recite it as well as it was told me, let ignorance be my excuse. Now please read it, so that you can announce—or at least write down—which one you choose as the most unhappy of the four lovers, beautiful, good, and learned ladies, who are sad and wretched and are asking for your judgment in their debate.

At the very end of the poem, author's book and lover's heart are identified one with the other: the poet wants his lady to read in his heart as she does in his book; the book has been written for her, inspired by her; she will do with it—and with him—as she will:

Et pourtant il desire bien
Que ce livre pour son grant bien   3515
     Souvent peussiez
Veyr, et que aussi bien leussiez
En son cuer, par quoy vous sceussiez
Quel pouoir dessuz lui eussiez
     Par droit acquis,   3520
Car vostre doulceur m'a conquis
Et je n'y ay remede quis;
Amours l'a bien sceu et enquis.
     En gré soit pris
Ce livret pour vous entrepris,   3525
Car se aucun bien y est compris,
Ce a fait l'amour dont suis espris;
     Et s'ay emprise
Trop haulte ou trop fole entreprise
De moy mectre en vostre servise,   3530
Faictes du vostre a vostre guise.

And therefore he [i.e., the author of the book] is most desir-
ous—for his greater good—that you look often at this book—
and that you also read in his heart, by which you would know
what power you had acquired over him by right. For your
sweetness has conquered me and I've sought no remedy for it;
Love knew and asked for it. May this book, undertaken for
you, be taken in good part, for if there's any good in it, that has
been done by the love with which I am smitten. And if I've
attempted, in putting myself at your service, an enterprise too
ambitious or too mad, do with him who is yours what you will.

This is an obvious and elaborate variation on the convention "J'aime
donc j'ecris."

    Belle Dame is another case of eavesdropping. So is *Herault*,
where Chartier adopts a playful attitude toward this convention: the
Acteur comes in only at stanza XLI and again in stanza XLVIII, where
he claims that he could not quite hear the conversation! He returns
in the last three stanzas (LIII–LV), where he characterizes all that he
has just heard as a farce, played out between the three participants in
the debate: "Me sembloit d'eulx ouyr parler / Qu'entre eux jouassent

une farce" (To hear them speak, I thought they had played out a farce; ll. 425–26). He appears to finish the whole poem as a literary joke, addressed in a spirit of friendly rivalry to his friend Pierre de Nesson, the "vaillant bailly [bailiff] d'Aigueperse" (l. 428).[8]

Although less evident, a high degree of literary consciousness is present as well in the three other poems where the narrator's "I" speaks directly. *Plaisance* begins with an evocation of Chartier's chosen persona: "Tristesce ne se deporte / De moy mener guerre forte; / Pensee m'assault" (Sadness never leaves off waging war against me; Melancholy assaults me; ll. 20–22). He then exhorts his friends directly in the rest of the poem, urging them to be unlike himself and to enjoy *plaisance*:

> Pour ce, amis, je vous enhorte
> Que tousjours tenez la sorte,
>   Sans faire deffault,   25
> De Plaisance qui supporte
> Cil qui en lui se deporte;
> Riens plus ne vous fault.

On that account, friends, I urge you always, without fail, to keep company with Pleasure, which always sustains him who rejoices in it; you need nothing more.

The very title of *Complainte* tells us of its nature as a public literary exercise. And finally, in his *Excusacion*, the poet defends his own book—*Belle Dame*—as a piece of fiction:

> Mon livre, qui peu vault et monte,
> A nesune autre fin ne tent
> Si non a recorder le compte   195
> D'un triste amoureux mal content
> Qui prie et plaint que trop atent,
> Et comme Reffus le reboute;
> Et qui autre chose y entent,
> Il y voit trop ou n'y voit goute.   200

My book, which is of little worth or value, has no other purpose than that of recording the account of a sad, unhappy lover who entreats and complains that he's been waiting too long, and that Refusal rejects him; and whoever sees anything else in it either sees too much or nothing at all.

This evident literary self-consciousness thus relates Chartier to the Guillaume de Machaut of the "Prologue" and to the Christine de Pizan who claims that she is merely doing her duty as a poet and not writing autobiography when she composes love poetry. Its corollary is the poet's persona. We have just seen this mournful figure in the early lines of *Plaisance*, and it will reappear in four more of the first-person poems. "Et je fu loing, pensif, triste et farouche" (And I was far away, pensive, sad, and unsociable; *Deux Fortunés*, l. 9); "Autre par maniere commune / Ont les biens, dont je n'ay que dueil" (Others ordinarily enjoy the benefits of which I have only the pain; *Quatre Dames*, ll. 51–52); "Je muir sur bout, et en ce point me pors / Comme arbre sec qui sur le pié se dresse" (I'm dying though yet erect; I'm like a withered tree that still stands straight; *Complainte*, ll. 23–24); "Je n'ay bouche qui puisse rire / Que les yeulx ne la desmantissent, / Car le cuer l'envoyeroit desdire / Par les larmes qui des yeulx yssent" (My mouth couldn't laugh without my eyes giving it the lie, for my heart would contradict it by the tears coming from my eyes; *Belle Dame*, ll. 21–24). It is possible also that the same persona may be indicated at the beginning of *Reveille Matin*, where the narrator who will overhear and relay the discussion of the Amoureux and the Dormeur describes himself thus: "Apres mynuit . . . / Pensoye ou lit ainsi qu'on veille / Quant on a la puce en l'oreille" (After midnight . . . I was brooding in bed, as one does when one's awake and in travail; ll. 1, 4–5). One of the meanings of "avoir la puce à l'oreille" is to suffer mental anguish or torment. For Poirion, the reiterated despair of this persona—present in over half of the first-person poems—is characteristic of Chartier. He notes a particularly striking expression of it in Chartier's prose as well in the early pages of *Le Livre de l'esperance*:

> En ceste dolente et triste pensee, qui tousjours se presente a mon cueur et m'accompaigne au lever et au couchier, dont les nuys me sont longues, et ma vie ennuieuse, ay ja long temps travaillé et foullé mon petit entendement, qui tant est surprins

et environné de desplaisans frenesies, que je ne le puis ex-
ploicter a chose dont me vienge liesse ne confort.[9]

In this sad and sorry cogitation, which is always present in my
heart and never leaves me waking or sleeping, making my
nights long and my life vexatious, I have long since exercised
and searched my puny wits, which are so overcome and begirt
by anguished frantic fancies that I can't put them to anything
that might bring me happiness or comfort.

But is this despairing character in fact very original? One finds
it frequently, palely loitering, in love poetry, and it affords many
poets a chance for variation. As we saw in Chapter 1, William Calin
has shown that Machaut, by increasing the bumbling, aged aspect of
the personage, makes of it a nearly comic character in *Le Voir-Dit*.
Eustache Deschamps and Froissart offer variants of it. Christine's
original version is that of a lovelorn widow. Charles d'Orléans will
give the figure an interesting profundity through insistence not so
much on its *tristesse* as on its *mélancolie*, coupled with the *nonchaloir*
that is such a well-known feature of his work. Villon combines the
unhappy lover with the cynical ne'er-do-well in a way that has
intrigued and moved readers for centuries. But many years ago
Ernst Curtius reminded us that, given the rhetorical nature of medi-
eval poetry, the important thing is not the "experience" of the poet,
but rather the theme that is to be treated in his poem,[10] and our
reading of Machaut and Christine confirms this principle. It would
surely be a mistake to abandon that principle in the case of Alain
Chartier, who, like them—and like every author—is free to choose
his own mask. In this he hardly differs from a Hugo or a Baudelaire,
for the Saturnian personality was as much a convention in the nine-
teenth century as it was in the fifteenth century, although its har-
monics, from Lamartine to Laforgue, may cover a much richer
range. What constitutes the difference between them, then, is not the
fictionality of the "I," but only the much more limited choice of
masks open to a late medieval poet. The writer's own history, that is,
does not necessarily provide him or her with a persona—although it
may well suggest one. Yet history in a large sense—understood as
the sum of all cultural, intellectual, political, and social manifesta-

tions of any given period—is the inevitable condition of that persona: because no author works in a vacuum, that history furnishes him or her with the repertory from which all available or allowable individual choices must be made.

I do not mean to suggest that the first-person voice in these eight poems and those like them is the same as the generalized, undifferentiated "I" of much of medieval lyric poetry, and in particular of *le grand chant courtois*: far from it, as we shall see in some detail in another essay. It is certainly different, more personalized, closer, perhaps, to its author, to the aged cleric called Guillaume, to the widowed bluestocking called Christine, to the diplomat with literary tastes called Alain Chartier. But can we, even when this persona comes near to what might be the "real" person, draw from it anything in what can be termed a material way that might usefully teach us something of that person's life? Very little, it seems to me—even less, surely, given the conventions of the time, than one can learn from the work of a Lamartine or a Baudelaire or a Proust. The conscious choice of that voice should, rather, put us on our guard, for it is, paradoxically, a means of distancing, of contriving some space between creator and what he (or she) creates. In other words, it is already pointing us toward one facet of how these poems work, and of where the author stands in relation to them.

In three of the five poems where this personality appears without question, the despair and sadness are clearly caused by love and its misfortunes. In a fourth, *Plaisance*, the narrator claims that he has never loved, or at least has never had a faithful lover: "Sans dame suy; onc ne me fut donnee / Loyale amour jusqu'a celle journee, / Car je n'ay pas sens pour y labourer" (I'm without a lady; never to this day has a loyal love been given me, for I've no wit to work on it; ll. 10–12). Yet all the variations on the definition of *plaisance* that make up the poem tie it firmly to the pleasures of love, so that in this poem, too, love—in the form of its lack—may be seen to be the cause of the narrator's melancholy. Although little is said about his own feelings by the eavesdropping narrator in *Reveille Matin*, we have already seen that the same character is probably implied. In *Herault*, however, the "I" does not mention any such feelings, nor do they occur in *Excusacion*, in which the narrator relates the dream that constitutes Chartier's defense of the earlier *Belle Dame*. Despite the fact, then, that it appears in only five or six of the eight first-person poems, the distressed and pensive nature of the authorial "I" remains fairly constant, as does its intervention in the text.

This intervention, however, does not necessarily mean active participation. Hearing or overhearing involves him less, that is, in the ostensible occasion for the text—in those acts or accounts that motivate it—than in its generation or creation. In five of the eight— *Deux Fortunés, Reveille Matin, Quatre Dames, Belle Dame, Herault*— Chartier remains, unlike Machaut in *Le Voir-Dit*,[11] for example, and unlike the Dante of the *Commedia* but more like the Chaucer of the *Canterbury Tales*, almost entirely on the sidelines, offering his pen more than his active presence, rarely giving more than an occasional comment, as when he sees in *Herault* a huge joke, or when, at the end of *Belle Dame*, he addresses lovers and ladies with advice based on the preceding story.

Where is he in the other three poems, in those, that is, where he alone speaks? In *Plaisance*, probably the earliest of them all, he directly addresses his "friends" on New Year's Day; it is implied that his poem is a kind of New Year's present. As a lover sorrowing after having lost his lady, he directs his *Complainte* to Death, as he directs his *Excusacion* to the ladies of the court who had written him expressing their dissatisfaction with *Belle Dame*. There is thus some variation in the way this literary "I" produces its text: in five cases it is through the voices of others, without whose overheard conversations there would presumably be no text. These works, then, are not, at least in any simple way, "narrative poems" or *dits*, convenient as these terms may be to distinguish them from those cast in lyric forms. "Double *dits*" would fit them better as a label, for the authorial first person in each of them quotes what others have said, using not the third person of the *récit* but the first person of the *discours*. In these poems, the author largely replaces his own narrator-persona with other narrators, or speakers, whose speech is relayed in the first person. In the other three poems, there is no such intermediary; they are based directly on the persona's "own experience" (or, in the case of *Plaisance*, lack of experience). The same could be said, of course, of *Paix* and *Breviaire*, the two poems in which no "I" appears: since they are literary works, they do have an author, expressing, we are tempted to say, his own thoughts through the character Paix or through a neutral voice. But we shall steadfastly resist this temptation and posit instead in all five an author expressing thoughts (but not necessarily his thoughts) on a given subject, in poetry: I can call this author "the poet." These thoughts may be made more poignant when a certain "I" expresses them, as, notably, in the *Complainte* to Death. But does the author's use of the "I" without intermediary, or what might be called the direct first person (or, in the case of *Paix* and *Breviaire*, an implied author's voice) give to these poems any larger quality of "narrativity"? One can only answer that it does not; in none of them is there any "story," any recounting of events arranged to amuse, to cause suspense, to please. There is narration, that is, but very little narrative. What this direct first person does bring to them, on the other hand, is a character of didacticism and moral fervor. In these poems, this single "I," not telling a story, relays a confidently—even passionately—held opinion to a public assumed to be in need of the particular lesson. Perhaps the lesson—or what I termed "thoughts" a few lines above—is indeed one in which the man Alain Chartier believed: it is not unusual to fear and hate death, to admire and urge pleasure, or to propose peace as an alternative to war. In any case, the literary personality of Chartier proposes these things directly, unambiguously, man-to-man, as it were.

But the situation is quite different in what I have called the double *dits*, with their multiple "I's." In these, the poet-persona, the first person who introduces the subject, who occasionally comments on it, and who closes the poem, is not the same as the one to be found in the other five poems, those with a single voice. In the latter, to use the somewhat ambiguous terminology of the time, he takes on the role of the Acteur; even if he is not very active, his is at least the voice of a dramatic monologuist. That this actor is also an author is, of course, abundantly clear, for all of these direct first-person poems use, in various ways, highly "literary," conventional forms: the com-

plicated formal structure of the lay in *Plaisance* and *Paix*, the conven-
tion of the *complainte*, in *Complainte*, and that of the dream-vision in
Excusacion. In the five double *dits*, however, the poet hides, in a way,
behind the characters who speak and whose discourse he quotes—
the Dame and the Amant, the four Dames, the Thin and Fat
Knights in *Deux Fortunés*. He assumes, in other words, in a much
less incidental way, as it were, the role of the Aucteur.

What this Aucteur presents is discussions, debates, in which his
own active role is minimized but in which his function as scribe,
however self-effacing, is paramount: without the characters, there
would be no occasion or excuse for the text, but without the scribe,
we would not even have the text. Paradoxically, however, it is in
these very poems where he functions more as author than as actor
that the poet's own opinion on the subject central to the poem is the
most difficult to define—although, at least in the case of *Belle Dame*,
scholars have made the attempt.[12] Despite their efforts, I should say,
rather, that the essential characteristic of these poems, what distin-
guishes them from the others, is that the "real" opinion of the poet is
in fact not expressed, that the very point of these double *dits* is their
doubleness (their duplicity, perhaps, in all but an artist), in their
quite neutral presentation of several—or of at least two—points of
view, with some truth to be found in all of them. Is this not the case,
after all, in the prose *Quadrilogue invectif*, in which the allegorical
figure of France bemoans her fate, following which other figures
representing each of the three estates defends his own part in that
fate and condemns the role played by the other two? The conclusion
is that all are at fault because all are responsible. That this conclusion
also represents the author's point of view is patent; he seems, that
is, to be an astute political realist rather than a passionate partisan:
his is an enlightened patriotism that refuses *le parti pris* in favor of
the complexity of political reality and a larger view of the national
interest.

Can we find in the debate poetry with which we are concerned
this same general attitude—one that explores questions, then refuses
to side with any one answer? The subjects of these poems seem at
first glance to present a fair variety. One of them recalls, indeed, the

Quadrilogue; although only three persons debate in *Herault*, their argument concerns the present state of France, those responsible for it, and their own respective roles in its affairs. The debates in the other four center on various questions of love. In *Deux Fortunés*, two knights argue about the good and bad effects of love and which outweighs which. In *Reveille Matin*, the author "overhears" two men, "qui gisoient en une couche" (who were sleeping in one bed; l. 9); one, the Amoureux, is sleepless and engages his companion, the Dormeur, in a dialogue, some 300 lines long, on the nature of love and the respective roles of the man and the woman. *Belle Dame* gives a voice to this woman who, again following an introduction in which the poet's persona appears, confronts her suitor in a witty verbal battle of some length, refuting with much irony every argument he can muster in favor of her according him the *mercy* that, as we know from the title, she is without. Finally, the viewpoint shifts, in *Quatre Dames*, from one to another of the four women; after an introduction by the narrator, each presents a case claiming that she is the most to be pitied because she is the most unfortunate. One's lover has been killed in battle, another's has been taken prisoner of war, the third's is missing in action, and the fourth's has fled the field. In a way, this poem combines the courtly love conventions with the patriotic themes of *Herault*.

Beneath this apparent variety of subject, however, lie certain central concerns and poetic strategies that lend, as we shall see, a quite remarkable unity to this part of the poet's work. It should by now be apparent that one of these strategies is exactly the fact that in all of these poems the subject or problem on which each turns is left unresolved; the authorial "I" makes no pronouncement at all to conclude the debate: no side wins. It is, it seems to me, therefore a less than useful exercise to try to define Chartier's "real" ("his own") position in them, for it is precisely one of nonintervention. It is not that these poems have no meaning, but rather that part of the whole import of the poem is the question or problem, part of it the various answers, and part of it the Aucteur's noncommitted redaction of these answers and the forwarding of them to another authority: the reader, or public. For even in the *Quatre Dames*, where ostensibly he submits the matter, in the traditional manner of the Courts of Love,[13] to the judgment of a highborn lady, it is of course we, his readers (or listeners), who are invited to judge. I suggest that this teasing of the reader's discriminatory wit by proposing a problem with several solutions is a rhetorical strategy, designed *en toute connaissance de cause* to give pleasure, and thereby to increase acceptance of the work. The author is deliberately leaving a certain ambiguity in the text, but it is not the ambiguity that we think of as "modern" (but that can in fact be found in such works as the *Délie* of Sceve or the narrations of Rabelais)—that is, an ambiguity in the author's attitude. The attitude of the presumed author in these works of Chartier is never in doubt, for he never opts for one or the other of the proposed arguments. If one takes "ambiguity" to mean "susceptible of multiple interpretations" (as in the *American Heritage Dictionary*), then the ambiguity lies, rather, in the subject itself, in *le sujet de l'énoncé*, to use a convenient term. And it is just this, the presenting of the several facets of these subjects, that constitutes one of the distinctive features of the double *dits*.

In the eight "nonlyric" poems of Chartier with which we are presently concerned, we have seen so far that the "I," the grammatical first person, is a common feature. We have also observed that this common first person is not, in any of these poems, a real narrator or storyteller—it is not the Guillaume de Machaut, for example, of *Le Voir-Dit*—but rather an enunciator of truths, of truisms, of diverse points of view on a moral problem. Further, it is this same first-person enunciator, as we have just found, who allows us to see an important difference between two kinds of first-person, nonnarrative *dits*, to distinguish, within the eight poems, two groups: one in which the speaker (whom I have called the Acteur) assertively presents "his own" point of view on the subject of the poem, and one in which the speaker is, rather, a reporter (the Aucteur), is nonassertive, and presents largely other people's points of view, underscoring and hiding behind his own role as a scribe or recorder of other people's arguments, darting out occasionally to give us a glimpse of what may be his own self. We find once more, in other words, as so often in the earlier chapters, the poet at play—at a game of hide-and-seek.

These points can best be illustrated by looking briefly at the poems in each of the two groups. I should like to start with those I have called double *dits*, or games of hide-and-seek, and go on later to those in which a single speaker figures. Within the first group is to be found the one poem of Chartier's that is very well known; it is, of course, *La Belle Dame sans mercy*, and although it is certainly not the first of Chartier's poems, it can serve as a convenient starting point for our discussion. Its fame is partly due to its standing as the most celebrated of Chartier's poems in the fifteenth century; it has survived in forty-four manuscripts.[14] Although two of his other poems, *Breviaire* and *Paix*, are found in a greater number, it is by far the one mentioned most by contemporaries and clearly figured as an important event in the literary consciousness of the time. Its present fame is doubtless also due to its being until recently the only poem of Chartier's to be found in a modern, accessible edition.[15]

From the moment it appeared, the text produced other texts that recreated it or commented on it—castigating it, refuting it, or diluting it.[16] Nor have twentieth-century views of it shown much unanimity: Arthur Piaget finds it "a poem full of amorous trivialities," with little originality, and E. J. Hoffman sees it as a "conventional piece of late-medieval *courtois* poetry [that] reflects the indifference of the author to external events."[17] Robert Garapon, on the other hand, praises the work, applauding not only its "delicacy of poetic expression," but also its dramatic expression of profound human truth.[18] In an interesting and provocative essay, one of the best analyses of the poem to date, C. S. Shapley, placing it firmly in the context of Chartier's other works, identifies in it the same moral concerns he finds in them and presents it as a personal reaction to the perceived situation of the nobility, a comedy of alienation, "in spite of its wit and verve, . . . the poem of a defeat, occasioned by moral decline and the poisoning of the springs of trust, and issuing in despair and death."[19] For Poirion, its importance and its fascination come from Chartier's originality in combining in the single person of the Belle Dame, in a kind of prefiguration of Baudelaire, both beauty and cruelty, with all that that implies for the poet, as well as the lover.[20] Finally, in an almost complete reversal of Piaget's and Hoffman's opinions, William Kibler agrees with Shapley that the poem was greatly influenced by contemporary events but believes that it "takes a staunchly conservative political stand in the face of a pleasure-seeking, debauched courtly circle."[21] Given the richness and ambiguity of the text (if not the narrator's attitude) it is doubtful that this will be the last word on *Belle Dame*.

Indeed, I should like to look at it in my turn, both as the first example of a nonlyric text we shall have considered and as a model of others of the same nature. Most readers of these pages will know that the poem is a lengthy debate between the Amant, passionately but woefully—because hopelessly—in love, and the Dame, cool, witty and, finally, indifferent to his arguments. Their dialogue, made up of alternating stanzas, is introduced by some twenty-four stanzas in which a first-person speaker, who describes himself as being pensive and joyless, as in much the same state, that is, as the Amant (see ll. 119–20), tells us that his depression comes from the recent death of his mistress ("Ma maistresse," l. 6, could be either a woman beloved by Chartier or his persona, or a patron of Chartier's, or, of course, a fiction) and will surely cause him to give up song-writing.[22] Riding to meet some friends for a festive repast, he is forced somewhat against his will to join the crowd of men and women, "toutes . . . bonnes et belles" (l. 68). He soon descries among them the one who reminds him of himself, who, even while dancing after dinner with other women, makes it obvious that he has eyes for only one. Tired of the feast, the speaker leaves the crowd and, hidden behind a trellis, is able to overhear—and to repeat word for word, presumably—the lengthy (some seventy stanzas!) conversation of this couple, ill-assorted as it turns out: the woman remains quite unmoved by the young man's arguments and insensitive to his pleas throughout the poem. In his closing remarks, the speaker tells us he later learned that this unyielding attitude caused the erstwhile lover's death, and he concludes with a few words of advice to both sexes.

Though Shapley is surely right in his *Studies in Fifteenth-*

Century Poetry to insist on the individuality of each text, we have seen in our analysis of short works by Machaut, Christine de Pizan, and others that this "individuality" is not the same as the individuality of a modern text, that while on one level every rondeau differs from every other—and often in subtle ways—on another, it resembles every other rondeau, too. Can this, or something like this, be true for the much lengthier *dits?* There are many elements in *Belle Dame* that clearly derive from the courtly tradition, although they are not, perhaps, the elements that earlier commentators seized on. It is now obvious, for instance, that the Belle Dame's character is not, as Piaget would have had it, merely another copy of the character of all the unyielding ladies in courtly poetry.[23] Although I shall certainly have occasion to refer to recent interpretations of the poem's meaning, what I shall be essentially concerned with here is not so much what the poem means as how it means what it does.

As a first step toward discovering the ways in which *Belle Dame* is both like and unlike other poems of its type, it will be useful to see what it has in common with the shorter lyric forms we already know. What is immediately noticeable is that, because of its very length (it comprises 100 strophes; Laidlaw, pp. 332–60) its formal structure is, apparently, quite different. But each strophe is, in fact, an octosyllabic huitain, rhyming a b a b b c b c—and this is the commonest stanza form of the ballade in the period.[24] Deschamps alone appears to have used it in nearly 500 ballades. Chartier, then, extends the use of a very familiar lyric strophe in his nonlyric poem. There is, further, another prosodic feature familiar from the shorter works, and that is the deliberate cultivation of variety in rhyme, which here becomes vast indeed. Of the three rhymes in each strophe, very few are repeated twice in the course of the 800 lines of the poem. The rhymes are often rich; there is frequent play with rhymes coming from the same root word. Stanza xxvii is a good example:

> Ja soit ce que pas ne desserve
> Voustre grace par mon servir,   210
> Souffrez au moins que je vous serve
> Sans voustre mal gré desservir.

Je serviray sans desservir
En ma loiauté observant,
Car pour ce me fist asservir   215
Amours d'estre voustre servant.

Even though I don't deserve your favor through my service, at
least allow me to serve you without deserving your ill-favor. I
shall serve without ill-service, serviceable in my faithfulness,
because for that Love subjected me to being your servant.

It is likely that Chartier is also using this kind of play with
rhyme—which manuals and histories of literature often charac-
terize as typical of the Rhétoriqueur poets later in the century—in
another, more complicated game, for the strophe is the last one
spoken by the Amant before the Dame answers and begins the
dialogue in alternating strophes that constitutes the largest part of
the poem. Before her first response, which takes up only half a
strophe, the Acteur—as the speaker is called in the text—acknowl-
edges the peculiarity of the Amant's last speech: "Quant la dame oy
ce langage, / Elle respondy bassement" (When the lady heard *this
kind of language*, she replied in a low voice; ll. 217–18; my emphasis).
The term "langage" can refer both to the style and to the content of
the Amant's preceding protestations. In her first full-stanza reply,
the Dame shows that she can play at the same (word-)game, and she
demonstrates as well the robust good sense that will be her most
powerful arm against the Amant's amorous entreaties:

Il a grant fain de vivre en dueil
Et fait de son cuer lasche garde,
Qui contre un tout seul regard d'ueil   235
Sa paix et sa joye ne garde.
Se moy ou aultre vous regarde,
Les yeulx sont faiz pour regarder.
Je n'y prent point aultrement garde;
Qui y sent mal s'en doit garder.   240

He who doesn't protect his peace and joy from one little look
has much appetite for living in sorrow and is a poor protector
of his heart. If I or another look at you—the eyes are made for

looking. I take no other notice of it; the one who suffers from it must protect himself.

The richness and variety of rhyme in these two stanzas are doubtless particularly apparent because of the play on rhymes coming from the same stem—but they are present throughout *Belle Dame*, where they are often wittily continued through two corresponding strophes and, indeed, account for part of the text's charm. This close attention to the effects of rhyme is to be found, in fact, in nearly all of Chartier's *dits*, often allied to a "lyric" stanza concatenated into a long poem, as in *Belle Dame*. But the care and variety accorded to rhyme are in general subordinated to the meaning of the text. It is, finally, not its formal structure so much as the clash of wits between the Amant, endlessly varying the lessons of the old-fashioned code he has learned, and the Dame, ever parrying his elegant paradoxes, and the flash of wit playing on the page that characterize *Belle Dame* and make it the poem it is. Two other poems offer the identical stanza form: *Excusacion* (not surprising, since it is in a way an extension of *Belle Dame*) and *Reveille Matin*. The latter poem is, moreover, similar in overall conception, although not in length (it is only 368 lines long; Laidlaw, pp. 306–19). In a four-stanza introduction the Acteur sets the scene and then reports an overheard discussion on the nature of love in octosyllabic huitains alternating between the first-person voices of the Dormeur and the Amoureux, the former somewhat grudgingly giving up his sleep to listen to his friend's complaints about his ladylove. The Acteur reappears in the forty-sixth and last stanza to end the poem, again on a very consciously literary note, as we saw earlier.

Its identical stanzaic form and general structural resemblance to *Belle Dame* invite a comparison between the two poems. In both, the lover complains of a beauty who, although she has every desirable quality, is unyielding (*Reveille Matin*, ll. 117–20):

J'ay de longtemps une servie,
A mon gré sage, bonne et belle,
Et de tous biens tresassuvie
Fors que pitié n'est pas en elle.

I have for long served a lady discreet, good, and lovely accord-
ing to my fancy, replete with every virtue—except that she has
no pity.

This is the same Belle Dame that the Acteur describes (ll. 149–52):

Jeune, gente, fresche et entiere;
Maintien rassis et sans changier;
Doulce parolle et grant maniere,
Dessoubz l'estendart de Danger.

Young, pleasing, fresh, and true, composed and constant in
conduct, gentle in speech, noble in manner—under the banner
of Danger.

In the one poem, the lover's complaints are addressed to the lady in
person; in the other, the lover seeks counsel by pouring them into the
ear of a friend and confidant (*Reveille Matin*, ll. 101–4):

. . . s'a vous comme amy sans blame
Je di ce qui m'estraint et charge,
En descouvrant ma dure flame,
J'en avray le cuer plus au large.

. . . if I tell you—as to a blameless friend—what besets and
burdens me, revealing my fierce flame, my heart will be the
easier for it.

The psychological situation in both cases is a familiar and realistic
one. In *Belle Dame*, we witness (with the author) a "scene," in which
a lover has finally decided to confront the person he loves and reveal
his passion to her; in *Reveille Matin*, a lover seeks the benefit of
confession to a friend both of his passion and of the treatment he
receives from his beloved. He finds, in other words, the kind of
sympathetic listener of whom we all occasionally avail ourselves.

Shapley sees in the Amoureux of *Reveille Matin* "a first sketch
of the Amant of the Belle dame."[25] I agree with him that the situation
of the two lovers is clearly similar, but it seems to me impossible to
tell whether *Reveille Matin* was written before *Belle Dame* or not.[26]
Rather than considering *Reveille Matin* a sketch for the longer poem,
it makes more literary sense, given our entire lack of chronological

certainty about the date of composition, to see it as another act in the same emotional drama; on that view, it may take place either before or after the "scene" presented in *Belle Dame*, the lover either seeking advice from his friend on the course of action to be taken or informing him of what had taken place after his declaration of love. Stanzas XXXI and XXXII exemplify their exchanges; in his reply to the lover, the Dormeur points to the relationship with *Belle Dame* by his use of the very term "merci," as well as by his reference to danger, whose standard, as we have just seen, flies over the beauty of the Belle Dame:

L'AMOUREUX
Se m'aist ores Dieu que je sens
Mons cuer si hors de mon bandon
Que, quoy que soit, folie ou sens,
Puis que je le donnay en don—
Et n'eusse jamais guerredon—   245
Il me convient en ce point vivre.
Se j'en meur, Dieu me doint pardon;
Si seray de tous maulx delivre.

LE DORMEUR
Merci de dame est un tresor
Pour enrichir amans sur terre,   250
Si ne l'a pas chascun tresor
Qui a voulenté de l'aquerre;
Ains le fault a dangier conquerre
Et en souffrir doleur amere,
Car pour prier ne pour requerre   255
Nul n'a bien s'il ne le compere.

So help me God, I feel my heart so out of my control that, whether it be folly or good sense, since I've given it away as a gift (and even though I may never get the reward), I know I must live on in this condition. If I die from it, God grant me pardon; that way I'll be free from all ills.

A lady's favor is a treasure house that enriches lovers in this world, but not everyone who seeks to acquire it gets a treasure; rather must it be gained dangerously and by bitter suffering,

for through begging and entreating no one gets wealth unless
he buys it.

The statement of the Amoureux in this passage even suggests the
possibility of his own death through unrequited love; this, it will be
remembered, is what the author tells us was the fate of the lover in
Belle Dame.

Whether written before or after *Belle Dame*, *Reveille Matin*
has, then, an evident relationship with it, in its stanza form (its
microform, to adapt a term introduced earlier), in its general presen-
tation (macroform), and in its subject; but it differs from *Belle Dame*
in the perspective it affords its reader on that subject, and this
variation is what makes it a *nouveau dit*, just as each of Machaut's
variations on the theme of Fortune becomes a new poem. Here, the
wit of the traditional Lover, with his courtly code, must confront not
that of a woman but that of a reasonable, objective friend. The stakes
may be the same, but the game is different.

On the formal level, a very similar though not identical micro-
structure gives its shape to *Herault*, at 440 lines somewhat longer
than *Reveille Matin* (Laidlaw, pp. 421–35). Again, we find the eight-
line octosyllabic strophe, but with a slightly different rhyme scheme.
And again, after a brief introduction by the Acteur, strophes tend to
alternate regularly between the Herault and the Vassault, with an
interruption at two points by the Villain (stanzas XLII–XLVII, L–LII).
But the rhymes throughout are much less dazzlingly varied than in
Reveille Matin and *Belle Dame*: could this be because of the subject
matter, which is not love but the seriously deteriorating condition of
the country? One critic, J. E. White, Jr., considers this work (known
from its discovery in 1914 until Laidlaw's edition as the *Débat pa-
triotique*) "the best of Alain Chartier's poems" precisely because it
eschews most of "the poetic conventions (except the debate form)"
and "contains all the best qualities of that prose which is the source
of . . . Chartier's reputation."[27] Aside from its central contradiction
(how can a poem be a very good poem if it resembles prose?), this
statement appears to me to represent an opinion difficult indeed to
uphold, and a radical misunderstanding of fifteenth-century verse to

boot. The rhyme scheme, a b a b c d c d, effectively breaks the stanza into two parts that are repetitive yet have no satisfying aural connection one with the other, and it thus seems much less interesting poetically than the a b a b b c b c common to *Belle Dame*, *Excusacion*, and *Reveille Matin*. Although the scheme used in *Herault* was known to the lyric poets, they used it only infrequently.[28] This more pedestrian rhyme scheme, combined with the relative lack of rich rhyme play, surely makes *Herault* a less successful poem, at least in fifteenth-century terms, than White suggests. It is, if one wishes, "vigorous and bold,"[29] but its poetic quality is surely not superior to that of any of the *dits* we have so far discussed. Further, White appears to count for little the importance of convention, which in this poem allows Chartier to use the debate tradition in a poem of a political nature, distinct from its use in all his other debate poems (with one exception, as we shall see) but at the same time relating it to them, though its subject relates it to his prose *Quadrilogue*. Like the other *dits*, it has its playful aspects. The Acteur, only introduced as such in stanza XLI, in order to present the Villain, claims in stanza XLVIII, in an obvious send-up of the eavesdropping convention, that he cannot quite hear the words spoken by the Herault, an old man:

> . . . le saige vieillart
> Se print lors a parler moult bas
> Et tirer le vassault a part;   380
> Et sembloit qu'il eust grant desir
> De blasonner ne sçay lesqueulx.
> Qu'il dit, je n'en peuz riens oir,
> Fors qu'il dit: "Croyés, ilz sont teulx."

> . . . the wise old man then very quietly started to speak, drawing the vassal aside; and it seemed that he greatly desired to go on at length about some of them. I couldn't hear anything of what he said, except that he said: "Believe me, they're like that."

And at the end of the poem, he presents the whole discussion—perhaps ironically—as a farce, played out by the three participants in the debate:

Me sembloit d'eulx ouyr parler   425
Qu'antr'eulx jouassent une farce,
Et lors il me va remambrer
Du vaillant bailly d'Aigueperse
Qui me dist une foys: "Alain,
J'ayme trop mieulx paier la taille   430
Et vivre longuement villain,
Que noble mourir en bataille."

To hear them speak, I thought that they had played out a
farce together—and then I remembered the valiant bailiff of
Aigueperse, who once said to me, "Alain, I much prefer paying
taxes and living long as a commoner to dying in battle as a
nobleman."

In the next (and last) strophe of the poem, the Acteur invites his "bon
compaignon Neczon" (Pierre de Nesson, "vaillant bailly d'Aigue-
perse" and poet) to write something in reply to what seems to be a
jovial literary attack. True, the love convention makes no appear-
ance in it, but that does not necessarily have anything to do with its
quality as a poem, unless one is of the opinion that politics is a
necessary ingredient of good literature.

The debate form, the poet-scribe of neutral opinion, and the
love commonplaces: all of these conventions are present in *Le Debat
des deux Fortunés d'amour*, which is nonetheless, it seems to me,
a highly successful poem. With its 1,246 lines a fairly long text
(Laidlaw, pp. 158–95), it differs in one striking formal way from the
double *dits* I have so far discussed: it is written not in stanzas, but
rather in mixed meters, through-rhymed. Its rhyme scheme can be
represented as follows, with the superscript indicating the number of
syllables in the line: $a^{10} a^{10} a^{10} b^4 b^{10} b^{10} b^{10} c^4 c^{10} c^{10} c^{10} d^4$ etc. The short
line is often used to great effect—to mark the end of a sentence, to
underscore a point, to emphasize the beginning of a thought, to
introduce a parenthetical thought. Here is one example, from the
speech of the Fat Knight, who speaks for the good effects of love, as
the Thin Knight will speak for the bad:

A festoier jusqu'a soleil levant
    Amours le porte.

> Desir le maine et Espoir le conforte,
> Et Plaisance le soustient et supporte;
> Et le desir de sa dame l'enhorte   420
>   A s'esjouyr,
> A chacer Deuil et Tristese fouyr.

Love inclines him to make merry until dawn. Desire leads
him, Hope comforts him, and Pleasure sustains and supports
him; and desire for his lady exhorts him to rejoice, to chase
away Sorrow and flee Sadness.

This rhythmical play goes a certain way toward compensating for
the somewhat monotonous rhyme scheme, which does not appear to
have inspired the display of virtuosity to be found in other poems.

There is another important difference between this text and
the other Chartier poems that we have looked at: this one presents a
real, formal debate, whereas the others are more in the nature of
discussions or repartee formalized by their being set down as poems.
Long sections of *Belle Dame*, for example, can be characterized as
marivaudage avant la lettre, a word or expression or image in one
character's speech being used in some witty way in another charac-
ter's reply. When the Fat Knight and the Thin Knight speak in *Deux
Fortunés*, however, it is because one of the ladies in the courtly
company of which the author is a part and which has been discussing
the contradictory nature of love, asks specifically for a debate on the
topic of whether the pleasure or the pain of love is greater:

>   Une y avoit
> Belle et bonne, qui bien parler savoit   190
> Comme il affiert et quant elle devoit,
> Qui leurs vouloirs assez appercevoit;
>   Et pour esbatre
> S'ala un peu en leur parler embatre
> Et demanda a trois d'eulx ou a quatre,   195
> Pour les faire joyeusement debatre
>   Entre les dames,
> Que lui deissent verité. . . .

There was one lady, good and beautiful, who knew how to
speak appropriately and when she should; she discerned their

humors well enough, and for fun broke in a bit upon their discussion and—to engage them in an amusing debate amongst the ladies—enjoined three or four of them to tell her the truth.

Instead of alternating brief speeches, the two knights give lengthy declamations, and these are described in legalistic terms. Regarding the Fat Knight's speech in defense of love, the recorder-author writes of "*l'opinion* qu'apres lui je recite, / Et *sa raison* bien longuement deduite" (the *opinion* that I recite according to him, and his lengthy *argumentation*; ll. 672–73; my emphasis). The Thin Knight uses the same kind of language at the beginning of his speech—which can be seen as the case for the prosecution: "Ne je ne sçay comme vous entendez / L'*opinion* que de *ce cas rendez*, / Ne *les raisons* dont vous la *deffendez*" (Nor can I understand the *opinion* that you're *rendering* in *this case*, nor the *arguments* with which you're *defending* it; ll. 692–94; my emphasis). Their two main speeches are of almost equal length; each is allowed a brief rebuttal of the other's opinion, where legal language again comes into play.[30] And play it is, not in the same way as the farce of *Herault* or the nocturnal conversation between a lover and his sleepy friend, or yet the witty exchange between a knight and his unwilling lady. Here the debate form is used directly by the company, in the tradition of the Courts of Love and the cases presented, for example, in the treatise of Andreas Capellanus. But it is used to amuse, as the lady who instigates the whole thing reminds them (and us); we have seen that she proposes the debate as a pastime: "Pour les faire joyeusement debatre." The result of this mock debate is inconclusive:[31]

> Lors quant chascun leur debat entendi
> Et ce qu'un dist et autre deffendi
> Et que nulz d'eulx pour mat ne se rendi,
>   Les ungs en dirent
> A leur plaisir, les autres contredirent,   1160
> Mais les dames le parler deffendirent
> Ne plus alors enquerir n'en souffrirent,
>   Fors qui seroit
> Cellui qui bien du debat jugeroit
> Et a tous deulx loyal droit en feroit.   1165

Then when everyone had heard their debate and what the one said and the other defended, and when neither one admitted being beaten, some spoke at their own sweet will, and others contradicted them. But the ladies forbade discussion and didn't allow any further examination of the question, except for the matter of who would be the one who would judge the debate and give equal justice to them both.

Is this text not clearly, then, a fiction, set within a frame? The artist, or author, tells us much in the quatrain that concludes the work (ll. 1243–46):

Ce livret voult ditter et faire escripre,
Pour passer temps sans courage vilain,
Un simple clerc que l'en appelle Alain
Qui parle ainsi d'amours par ouir dire.

To pass the time in no mean spirit, a simple cleric called Alain wants to compose and indite this little book; he speaks thus of love by hearsay.

Attempts to identify the Fat or the Thin Knight are thus best made, it seems to me, on the basis of their literary rather than their historical character. We already know, in fact, who the Thin Knight is, and why he is so thin, "pensif et pale" (l. 679): he is, or might as well be, the Amoureux of *Herault* or the Amant of *Belle Dame*—or the poet of the lyric poems. The originality here is to have placed him this time beside a lover "qui n'estoit pas mourne ne songeux, / Maigre, palle ne melencolieux, / Mais en bon point, sain, alegre et joyeulx" (who was neither mournful nor pensive, thin, pale or melancholy, but in good shape, healthy, happy, and joyous; ll. 210–12). His point of view is as sanguine as his complexion, and both are in distinct contrast to those of his opponent. Unique in the Chartier canon, he is one of only a handful of happy courtly lovers in late medieval French poetry.

One last poem in the double *dit* series remains: *Le Livre des quatre dames*, with 3,531 lines Chartier's longest poem (Laidlaw, pp. 198–304). As in the others, the poet, as Aucteur, is again on the sidelines, although the character of his persona is here relatively well developed, more in the manner of *Belle Dame* than in the manner of *Reveille Matin*, *Herault*, or *Deux Fortunés*. The beginning is particularly "literary," with its Petrarchan evocation of a May morning contrasted with the poet's melancholy as he wanders *solo e pensoso* through the flowery fields:

> Pour oublïer melencolie
> Et pour faire chere plus lie,
> Un doulz matin es champs yssy,
> Ou premier jour qu'Amours ralie
> Les cuers et la saison jolie   5
> Fait cesser ennuy et soulcy.
> Si alay tout seulet, ainsy
> Que l'ay de coustume, et aussy
> Marchay l'erbe poignant menue
> Qui toute la terre tissy   10
> Des estranges couleurs dont sy
> Long temps l'yver ot esté nue.

To forget melancholy and be more cheerful, I went out into the countryside one morning, on the first day that Love reunites hearts [i.e., the first of May] and the pleasant season causes anguish and sorrow to cease. All alone I went, as is my wont, walking through the fragrant tender grass that wreathed all the earth in the unaccustomed colors of which throughout the long winter it had been bare.

The poignancy of this traditional contrast is increased by a lengthy description of the spring countryside, with its flora and fauna, the *locus amoenus* for the debate to come. The poet is here resolutely—and at some length—a thin rather than a fat lover: "Autres par maniere commune / Ont les biens, dont je n'ay que dueil" (Others ordinarily enjoy the benefits from which I have only pain; l. 52):

> Car de riens ne m'appartenist
>   Tant amoureuse   300
> Pensee ne si gracïeuse,

> Tant haulte ne si eüreuse,
> Ne de joie tant planteureuse,
>   Veu que je suis
> Cellui qui a moy mesmes nuys   305
> Par mon mal eur; n'oncques depuis
> Mon enfance n'eu fors ennuis,
>   Et en amours
> Courte joie et longues doulours.

> For in no way did a thought so amorous or so gracious, so high
> or happy or full of joy, belong to me, seeing that I am the one
> who harms himself, through my bad luck. I've had nothing but
> troubles since my childhood, and in love only short joys and
> long sorrows.

This is the same poet who says of himself in a ballade that "Je ne fu
nez fors pour tout mal avoir / Et soustenir les assaulz de Fortune"
(I was born only to have every displeasure and to experience the
assaults of Fortune).[32] The only unusual thing about this born loser-
in-love is that his self-pitying interior monologue goes on in *Quatre
Dames* for nearly 350 lines at the beginning of the poem.

The *complaintes* of the four Dames, all of substantial length,
constitute the body of the poem. Each is divided from the next by
comments by the poet, and after the main speeches are over, there
follows a recapitulation, as in a formal debate, of her story and state
of mind by each Dame. The poet returns in the last 171 lines of the
text; he refuses to judge the controversy, suggests his own lady as
judge, writes the poetic account of the debate, and takes it to Paris to
present to his "Belle."

It is thus apparent that the basic structure of this work is that of
Belle Dame, but its main elements are more developed—if I may use
that word with no chronological implication, since most scholars
agree that it was written before *Belle Dame*.[33] The greatly increased
presence of the Aucteur signals the larger complexity of his role. At
the beginning of *Belle Dame*, it is obvious that the poet's mood
matches to a certain degree the Amant's; having lost his love, he can
sympathize with his character: "'Si m'aist Dieux, / Autel fumes
commes vous estes'" (So help me God, I used to be like you are now;

ll. 119–20), he says to himself. The same holds true in *Quatre Dames*, where Chartier establishes carefully and at length, as we have seen, the sympathy of spirit between the poet-scribe and the four woebegone Dames: despite the difference in sex and in situation between him and them, their common experience of love creates a bond. The relationship between the Aucteur and the text that we read and that he writes is also more complex. Near the end of the poem, his desire to remain neutral in the debate is made explicit (ll. 3361–63, 3367–70):

> . . . me fut adoncques advis
> Que ne me sceusse estre chevis
> D'en jugier, et le feisse envis.
> · · ·
> Autre juge leur acointay
>   Et diz en hault:
> D'oüyr mon advis ne vous chault,
> Car mon savoir trop petit vault.

> . . . then I thought that I couldn't cope with such a judgment and would do it reluctantly. . . . I made another judge known to them and said clearly: "My opinion doesn't matter, because my wisdom is worth so little."

It is then that he proposes his own lady as arbiter; they accept, and after parting ways with them, he already envisages presenting his book to her, and he tells her (and reminds us), in its inscription, of his commission:

> Il m'est commis que je demande   3475
>   Vostre avis, Belle,
> D'une question bien nouvelle
> Dont en ce livre la querele
> J'ay mise en rime tele quele,
>   Au long escripte;   3480
> Et se si bien ne la recite
> Comment elle m'a este dicte,
> Ignorance m'en face quicte.

> I've been charged with asking your opinion, comely lady, on a very recent question, the discussion of which, just as it oc-

curred, written out at length, I've put into rhyme in this book.
And if I don't recite it as well as it was told to me, let ignorance
be my excuse.

For the reader, the narrator is made altogether a more interesting
and attractive figure than in any other of the poems we are discuss-
ing. The main participants in the debate receive a high degree of
individualization as well, and they are of course more numerous
than in any of the other poems; four distinct points of view other
than the poet's are presented.

   This increased complexity is reflected in the thematic content
itself, for it combines the love conventions of *Belle Dame* and *Reveille
Matin* with the political or moral concerns of *Herault* (and, inciden-
tally, of *Le Breviaire des Nobles*), with each Dame either praising her
lover's courage in battle or, in one case, castigating his cowardice and
that of other members of the nobility. Whereas in *Belle Dame* Char-
tier gives a voice to only one woman, here he increases the number to
a quartet, not in dialogue with a present and would-be lover, but
with four absent lovers, and with each other and the poet. What
Chartier offers us in this poem, to continue the musical analogy, is
a theme with variations. The theme—the unhappiness caused by
love—is presented through the figure of the poet as unhappy lover,
with the evocation of the spring landscape providing harmonic
richness. Interest is added by the introduction of another motif, that
of the battle and its consequences, the event that turns the joy of love
to sadness. In Wagnerian style, this theme of war will weave in and
out of the theme of love throughout the poem. The first Dame has
lost all hope because her lover has been killed, and her threnody is a
kind of *Liebestod*. Captured by the enemy, the second Dame's lover
gives her the opportunity for the kind of variation on the theme of
Fortune and its vagaries we have already encountered in the poetry
of Machaut. The fact that the lover is in prison across the sea in
England renders the theme particularly moving, and Chartier
makes exceptionally effective use of the situation in some of the
poem's most touching lines. I shall quote them at some length, partly
to show their extraordinarily affective character, and partly as an

example of the poet's craft: notice the skill with which he movingly manipulates the contrast between geographic distance and emotional closeness, and his delicate introduction of the image of two branches from one stem and of the idea of the reciprocity of true love. In the preceding lines, the Dame claims that even though her lover is a captive far beyond the sea, her heart is with him in his prison:

> Si suis alee,
> En toute joie tresalee,
> De cuer dela la mer salee;
> Maiz, quoy que la grandeur a lee
> Si qu'esgarer   1305
> S'y puet on sans terre apparer,
> Jamaiz ne pourra separer
> Noz cuers qu'Amours fait reparer
> Ensemble et joindre
> En un seul vouloir que conjoindre   1310
> Les fait, et comme egaulx adjoindre
> Sans qu'il y ait greignieur ne maindre.
> Amours oblige
> Noz deux cuers en un, ainsi di ge
> Comme deux raims en une tige.   1315
> Il se dit mon vray servant lige
> Et je suy sienne;
> Mot n'y a si non "tien" et "tienne."
> Se maistrise y a, elle est mienne
> Par la loy d'Amours ancïenne.   1320

Thus I went in heart, consumed by every joy, across the salty sea. But although it is wide enough that one can get lost out of sight of land, never will it be able to separate our hearts, which Love brings together and joins in a single purpose that causes them to conjoin, and to unite as equals without there being a greater or a lesser. Love binds our two hearts in one, I say, just like two branches in one stem. He calls himself my true liege-man, and I am his: no word is spoken save "I'm yours" and "I'm yours." If any authority exists, it's mine, according to the old law of Love.

Skillfully summarizing and contrasting the sorrow of her two companions, the third Dame shows that she understands their claims to pity:

> . . . Son ami mort plaint l'une;
> L'autre la prise et la fortune   2060
> Du sien que Adversité fortune,
>   Et sans deserte.
> La premiere ploure la perte
> D'Espoir, comme a tousjours deserte.
> L'autre dit: "Desir m'a deserte   2065
>   Et recreue,
> Sans Desperance mescreüe,
> Plus l'ay par mon desir creüe,
> Plus m'est doubte et douleur creüe.[34]

The one bewails her dead friend, the other the capture and misfortune of hers, ill-used by Adversity, without deserving to be. The first weeps for the loss of Hope, forsaken as she is. The other says, "Desire has ravaged and exhausted me, not to mention faithless Despair; the more my desire made me believe in it, the more have my doubt and sorrow increased."

But she insists that hers is the greatest grief, since her lover is missing in action, and she can therefore neither be certain of his death nor have sure hope of his return. Her tragedy is thus uncertainty, in the face of her consuming love:

>   Las! congnoissance
> N'ay se m'amour et ma fiance
> Est mort, prins ou mis a finance.
> Entre espoir et desesperance
>   Ainsi chancelle,   2070
> Plaine de doubtes, comme celle
> Qui a douleur et ne scet quele.
> Je ne scay quel nom je m'appelle:
>   Ou d'amours veufve,
> Ou prisonniere. . . .   2075

Alas! I have no knowledge of whether my love and my trust is dead, captured, or put up for ransom. Thus between hope and

hopelessness I waver, full of doubts, like one who suffers pain
and knows not its cause. I know not by what name to call
myself; whether the widow of love or its prisoner.

Death and its despair, captivity with its flickering hope, unex-
plained absence with its cruel uncertainty: all of these are tied to love
and war. And so is the fourth Dame's tragedy, yet it seems to her to
surpass all the others, for is not shame worse than despair, hope, or
uncertainty? Her lover has proved to be a coward, and she, unlike
the others, has only herself to blame for having believed in his virtue:
". . . j'ay quis ma male aventure; / Si n'en blasme Fortune obscure, /
La mort ne la bataille dure" (I asked for my own misfortune, so I
don't blame dark Fortune, death, or the fierce fight; ll. 2628–30). She
was fooled by a false lover, whose perfidy was revealed only by his
ignominious flight in battle, a perfidy that her love for him was
powerless to change. The alliteration insists on the outrage she feels
at his cowardice: "Or fuÿt quant ferir falu; / L'amour de moy riens
n'y valu / Et son honneur fut nonchalu" (Then he fled when he
should have fought; my love meant nothing, and his honor was of no
account; ll. 3005–7).

Even from this brief analysis, it should be clear that though all
their unhappiness has been in some way the result of love and war,
each Dame's case is different, and each is argued in a different way.
The poetic sum is here greater than the parts, for the relationship of
one lament to the other adds to the effect of each, as does the presence
of the poet-scribe and of an eventual judge—in reality the reader, of
course, upon whose emotions Chartier plays in so complicated a way,
using elements found in all the other poems. The prosodic structure
of the text itself also presents a combination of features from other
dits. The poet's introductory monologue (ll. 1–164) is made up of
octosyllabic stanzas of twelve or sixteen lines, each one with a com-
mon rhyme scheme, which resemble the ballade-like stanzas of *Belle
Dame*, *Reveille Matin*, and *Herault*.[35] The rest of the poem is
through-rhymed, with three octosyllabic lines followed by one short
line of four syllables, followed by three more octosyllabic lines, and
so on. With the change of the ten-syllable to the eight-syllable line,

this is the same meter that is used in *Deux Fortunés*. The work thus has a richness of texture, both thematic and structural, that makes of it one of Chartier's most successful poems.[36]

Starting from *Belle Dame*, we have passed in review all of the poems in which the poet as Aucteur stays, more or less resolutely, on the sidelines. We have seen that though their shapes and subjects may at first appear quite different, there is in fact a good deal of similarity between them, as there is in their presentation as unresolved debates or discussions. In each case, Chartier-the-author presents a first-person poet whose own opinion on the subjects put up for debate is unspecified and cannot be the center of interest of the poem. Thematically, with its lovers' complaints and its political and moral overtones, and structurally, with its ballade-like stanzas and its mixed-meter lines, *Quatre Dames* incorporates elements from all of the poems in which the poet plays this passive role of recorder or reporter of a debate. But the role is made more active in *Quatre Dames*, as we have just seen, by his introductory soliloquy and by his taking the case to be judged by his lady in Paris. Put another way, his role slips slightly from that of Aucteur to that of Acteur. By thus enlarging the place of the poet, Chartier makes him more moving, at least for modern sensibilities, and renders his voice more independent, in the manner of the lyric pieces. He thus approaches the tone and stance of the voice in the three other poems in which a first person appears, *Excusacion*, *Plaisance*, and *Complainte*.

Of the five nonlyric poems we have so far considered, only in the last have we found that this poetic first-person is allowed much degree of autonomy, and even there his personal opinion on the subject of the debate is not given. The opinions of the *participants* in all the debates, on the other hand, whether they be the four Dames, the Belle Dame, or the Herault, are expressed vigorously and with conviction. In the three poems we shall now consider, this situation changes radically. The poet—by which, let me remind the reader, I mean the "je" expressing himself within the poem (and as a fictional being created by Chartier-the-author, only perhaps representing his own opinions or state of mind)—now leaves the sidelines, becomes himself the main speaker, the Acteur, as I have termed him, communicating, vigorously and with conviction, his own views to his public.

L'Excusacion aux dames (Laidlaw, pp. 362–70) can in fact be considered a work falling somewhere between the two groups I have distinguished, for although the Acteur expresses himself directly therein—after a twelve-stanza intervention by the Dieu d'Amours— he does so in response to a request by some court ladies that he defend his own *Belle Dame* against the accusations of some of their courtier-friends, who see it as proposing a subversive message to women. So the debaters, although they are extratextual, nonetheless make their presence felt; they constitute, in fact, the occasion for the poem. And, as part of his defense, Chartier, all innocence, claims again that, in writing *Belle Dame*, the responsibility is not his, for he has been but a recorder; it is the impatiently suffering Amant who is to blame:

> Puis que son mal lui a fait dire,
> Et apres lui pour temps passer   210
> J'ay voulu ses plaintes escrire
> Sans un seul mot en trespasser,
> S'en doit tout le monde amasser
> Contre moy a tort et en vain,
> Pour le chestif livre casser   215
> Dont je ne suis que l'escripvain?

> Since it was his lovesickness that made him speak, and, following him, I wanted as a pastime to write down his complaint, without omitting a single word, should everybody join against me, wrongly and in vain, to suppress the wretched book—of which I'm only the inditer?

A passage like this demonstrates, it seems to me, that this poem— written in the same octosyllabic eight-line stanzas as *Belle Dame*, ending as it does with a quatrain naming the author—constitutes with that poem and the letters of the courtiers (copied with most of the manuscripts of *Belle Dame*[37]) a literary game not to be taken too seriously, except in a literary context. The numerous spin-offs from the poem lead one to the same conclusion: a fine occasion for poetical fireworks but hardly a real war—a literary "event," if one wishes, like the earlier so-called "Querelle du Roman de la rose" or the later "Querelle des Amies," precipitated in the 1540's by the *Amye de court* of Bertrand de la Borderie.[38]

Chartier puts a rather specious attack against himself as author in the mouth of the Dieu d'Amours, who is in fact only repeating what the poem's detractors have said; the god speaks constantly of *Belle Dame* as a text aiming to teach "*Les Dames* a geter au loing / Pitié la debonnaire et tendre" (*Ladies* to reject Pity, so mild and gentle; ll. 30–31; my emphasis). Since Chartier's poem is only concerned with one particular lady, and since at the end the Acteur counsels all "dames et damoiselles" not to be so cruel as the Belle Dame, this is not a difficult argument to counter—and it affords, incidentally, another indication of the nonserious, playful nature of the attack. In the perspective of this chapter, the whole poem, with its attendant prose documents, its mock attack and defense, provides, too, a further example of a literary artist highly conscious of his role and of the possibilities it affords for an ironic stance in relation to his own creation. The author knows that we know that he is indeed the creator of the fiction he is pretending to present as a true tale, and the entire poem is a kind of *clin d'oeil* or a snook cocked at his (female) audience, upon whose mercy—that very quality at least one of them, according to his earlier poem, is without—the Acteur throws himself at the beginning of the poem:

> Mes Dames et mes damoiselles,
> Se Dieu vous doint joye prouchaine,
> Escoutés les durez nouvelles
> Que j'ouÿ le jour de l'estraine.
> Et entendez ce qui me maine,   5
> Car je n'ay fors a vous recours;
> Et me donnez par grace plaine
> Conseil, confort, aide et secours.

Dear ladies all, if so be that God soon grant you joy, harken to the cruel news that I heard on New Year's Day. And under-

stand my motivations, for my only help lies with you. And by
your ample favor give me counsel, comfort, help, and succour.

The following highly conventional beginning, a dream-vision in
which the Dieu d'Amours appears to him and propounds his spe-
cious case against him, is another sign that we are firmly placed in an
entirely literary context that presupposes a willing suspension of
disbelief. We remain, in other words, in the world of make-believe, a
world that is the domain of poetry.

At the beginning of *Excusacion*, Chartier claims that the Dieu
d'Amours appeared to him on New Year's Day, when it was custom-
ary for lovers to exchange gifts—"le jour de l'estraine." Since the
year was then counted as beginning at Easter, that could mean, of
course, a day in the spring. In the first stanza of *Le Lay de plaisance*
(Laidlaw, pp. 148–54), which all scholars agree is his earliest poem,[39]
the poet evokes the same day (ll. 1–4):

> Pour commencer joyeusement l'annee
> Et en signe de bien perseverer,
> Est au jour d'uy mainte dame estrenee
> De son amant qui la veult honnourer.

> In order to begin the year joyously, and as a sign of continuing
> on together, today is the day that many a lady receives a gift
> from her lover, who wants to honor her.

And he goes on to say that though all lovers are giving and getting
gifts, he is not, for "onc ne me fut donnee / Loyale amour jusqu'a
celle journee" (Never to this day has a loyal love been given me;
ll. 10–11). Already in this early poem, then, the author has chosen
the persona that is to be his throughout his work (ll. 18, 20–22):

> Car Plaisance est en moy morte,
> . . .
> Tristesce ne se deporte
> De moy mener guerre forte;
>   Pensee m'assault.

> Because Pleasure is dead in me, . . . Sadness never leaves off
> waging war against me; Melancholy assaults me.

This fundamental sadness of character is emphasized by its contrast with the happy New Year, the spring of love. The rest of the poem, however, is not centered on the first-person speaker, who instead gives to his friends a long definition—or, better, a series of variations on the definition—of Plaisance, which he proposes as the central and motive quality of life and which he ties closely to the pleasures of love despite his own ignorance in the matter.

The title of a lai generally names its subject,[40] and this one is no exception. With its intricate formal structure, based on the principle of progressive repetition (the expression is Poirion's), it also provides the poet with a chance to show off his skills at rhyme and meter, and the young Chartier meets this challenge with some brio.[41] The 196 lines of *Plaisance* are divided into twelve sections, of which only the first and last are, as is traditional in the lai, identical. In each of the resulting eleven different sections, made up of from twelve to twenty lines each, the poet varies not only the rhymes (of which there are two in every section but one), but also their arrangement, as well as the meter of the lines they cap. In no section (always excepting sections 1 and 12) is the metrical scheme the same; although each section has four stanzas, these vary from three to five lines in length, and the line lengths themselves vary from three to five to seven to ten syllables, the last being reserved for the first and last sections. The lai is, strictly speaking, a lyric—that is, a musical—form, and it adheres to that principle of variety-in-sameness that we have found in our analyses in earlier chapters. And it is, at least in this case, a lyric form (though now without music) expressing directly the opinion of the person who enunciates its lines—even though this opinion has little to do, as we are told, with that person's own experience. If, then, it is clearly a game on the formal level, it is also one on the thematic level, a game of bluff played by a man who is not blinded by love but blinded to it.

The case would seem to be quite different in the poem I have left to the last, *La Complainte* (Laidlaw, pp. 321–27), also known in various manuscripts and editions by such titles as *Complainte contre la mort, Complainte que fist lacteur contre la mort, Complainte maistre alain de la mort de sa dame*, and *Complainte piteuse*.[42] Here, at last, as in the rondeaux and ballades, we find a *je* who seems less an *autre*, a first person who stands center stage, alone, and in a direct and moving lament reproaches Death for having taken his lady.

It seems to me surprising, given that it is the only poem in Chartier's canon—outside the group of rondeaux and ballades—entirely made up of the voice of the poet expressing what is asserted to be a personal experience, that very little critical attention has been given to this complainte.[43] That it is in addition an extremely successful poem only deepens the mystery. But this mystery is, after all, one that surrounds much of late medieval literature and should not, perhaps, be unexpected. It is doubtless explained by radical nonreading. Let us, then, pointing toward the conclusion of this chapter, attempt to read *La Complainte* in the light of what we have learned about the poetry of the time and particularly the works of its author that we have already surveyed.

In my attempt in the first two essays in this book to see this poetry on its own terms, I have gone from the outside in, as it were. Beginning with the various aspects of form (in which I include topical conventions, "theme," and so on) and their permutations, I have tried to arrive at meaning and its larger or smaller domain, and eventually at the "I" of the poet and its place. The reader will have noticed that the movement in the present chapter has been the inverse, that is, we have started with the "I," gone on to the subject of the poem and its meaning, finally to reach form. The goal in both of these approaches has been to show how, in an apparently rigid and highly conventionalized art, the artist can still create a work uniquely his own and can do this because of a stance toward his materials—words and their sounds, their meaning (or lack of meaning), their pretended provenance, their presumed effect—that I have constantly described as consciously playful, in several domains and to one or another degree. Can we see in *Complainte* another game, albeit serious?

It will be both amusing and instructive, I think, to begin our reading with Pierre Champion's opinion of the text, in the first volume of his *Histoire poétique du quinzième siècle*, published in 1923: "This piece, much admired in its time, which a Charles d'Orléans and a Villon knew by heart, fatigues us today with its mass of epithets; but we have no right to doubt the sincerity of the feelings it expresses."[44] He is right about one thing: the poem was indeed well known in the fifteenth century; Laidlaw lists thirty-seven extant manuscripts (compared, for example, with thirty-two for *Quatre Dames* and forty-four for *Belle Dame*), and it is found in all the early printed editions, as well as in a separate edition printed around 1485.[45] That Charles d'Orléans and Villon knew it by heart would be hard to prove, although Champion probably means to imply that its affective quality, together with some similarity of expression, is to be found—improved on, we are to believe—in their works. The rest of the quotation amuses by its tranquil assurance of knowledge of the poet's "true" feelings, and instructs us on the criteria of aesthetic judgment used. Assuming that "fatigue" may not be all it can hold for us, our entire attempt in the foregoing pages has been to find a reasonable and fruitful critical path through this kind of poetry, without applying foreign artistic expectations to it. And we now assume, of course, the right to question an author's sincerity, that quality so important to critics of literature from Rousseau to Cocteau and beyond. Villon's reputation was made on it (though not, perhaps, by him); Champion and many another critic would like Chartier's to be, too. If only there were more poems like *Complainte*!

Which brings us face to face with the (first) person of this poem, the one who appeals the harsh judgment of Death. He is the scribe this time only of his own words; he assumes full responsibility for them; there is no hide-and-seek with other characters, no debate, no irresolution. Even the melancholy that characterizes his favorite persona in the other poems is here entirely in its place: what more natural state for someone who has lost his "dame et . . . maistresse" (l. 13)? We have no reason, then, to believe that it is anyone other than Chartier who speaks—Chartier-the-Acteur, of course, as one of the manuscript titles reminds us. But whoever says "author" implies someone who makes conscious creative choices, who transmutes emotion into artistic form. What choices does Chartier make?

At first this question seems easy to answer. As in most of his other long poems, Chartier chooses a relatively unconstraining mold for his apostrophe of Death, that of the complainte, of which *Quatre Dames* offers, in a way, four examples—each longer, in fact, than the 184 lines of *Complainte*. Like *Belle Dame* and *Reveille Matin*, it is composed in stanzas, though they are longer here: there are twelve of them, the first two of twelve lines each, the rest of sixteen (the same mix we find in the introduction to *Quatre Dames*). His choice of a rhyme scheme, by contrast, is a fairly restrictive one, frequent in the complainte tradition, a a b a a b b b a b b a, to which the sixteen-line stanza adds one line in each of the four groups, a a a b a a a b b b b a b b b a. Only two rhymes, then, in each strophe, necessitating the finding of a good many words for each. But when one looks at all twelve strophes, another choice becomes apparent, for no rhyme is repeated twice within the poem. This variety of rhyme is itself a characteristic of the complainte.[46] We shall see how effectively Chartier uses this self-imposed obligation.

It is at this point that the answer to our question about the author's choices becomes more complicated—much more complicated, for example, than any similar answer to the same question concerning a sixteenth-century poem. For we cannot forget that this text predates the printing press, and that its earliest versions are known to us from manuscripts. J. C. Laidlaw, the most recent editor of Chartier's poetical works, distinguishes four manuscript traditions for the text, all of which present the same twelve stanzas.[47] But in no one of the groups of manuscripts is the order of the stanzas exactly the same; it is therefore impossible to speak of any overall structure of the poem in the way one might do, for example, of Ronsard's *Hymne de la mort*, or Musset's *Nuit de mai*, or one of Claudel's *Cinq grandes odes*. This is an example of what Paul Zumthor has termed the *mouvance* of medieval texts, that is, their instability (or, in a more positive sense, their dynamism) compared with most modern texts.[48] The result is that we simply cannot be entirely sure of the order in which the poet wanted us to read, or to hear, the stanzas.[49]

It is clear from the information provided by Laidlaw, however, that certain parts of the poem were stable, occurring at the same spot in all versions. The accompanying table pictures the poem in the

Stanza Order in the Various Manuscript Traditions of La Complainte

	1	2	3	4	5	6	7	8	9	10	11	12
Mss Nf, Nj	I	II	III	V	VI	VII	IV	VIII	IX	X	XI	XII
Mss Pc, Ql	I	II	III	IV	VII	V	VI	VIII	X	IX	XI	XII
Ms Ph	I	II	III	V	VI	VII	IV	VIII	X	IX	XI	XII
Mss Oa, Qd	I	II	III	IV	V	VI	VII	VIII	IX	X	XI	XII

SOURCE: Chartier, *Poetical Works*, pp. 320–21.

four manuscript traditions as made up of twelve slots (1–12) into
which twelve different strophes (I–XII) can be fitted. As we can see,
the first three slots are always filled by the same three stanzas, and in
the same order—it is therefore legitimate to call them stanzas I, II,
and III. In the eighth slot, there is always to be found, again, an
identical stanza, and it can thus be called VIII, just as XI and XII are in
the same position in all versions. Two stanzas, however, demonstrate
more instability, for although the one always follows the other, their
position relative to the other stanzas (their place in the slots, in other
words) is different in the several traditions: they are found at slots 4
and 5 in two, at 5 and 6 in another (Oa, Qd, that followed by Laidlaw
in his printed text, which is the one I shall follow in my discussion of
the poem), and at 6 and 7 in a fourth. The whole middle section of
the poem—slots 4–7, that is—is thus unstable, the same in only two
versions and different in each of the other two. Finally, between the
fixed points of stanzas VIII and XI, two stanzas—obviously IX and
X—are in that order in two versions (but not the same two with the
same middle section) and reversed in the others.

    This shuffling of strophes from one place to another should
alert us to the danger of applying any general structural principles or
ideas of "unity" to the poem, although it is evident that certain
stanzas, at the beginning and at the end in particular, were conceived
of as units.[50] It is further evident, as we shall see, that some organiz-
ing principle is at work, though in a way different from that in texts
of a later age. Seen as twelve separate stanzas, and from the point of
view we adopted earlier, what Chartier gives us in *Complainte* is a
series of variations on the subject of his grief over the death of his
lady; the individual place of these variations in the overall economy

of the poem is not as important as their total effect. Let us now turn to the text itself to see what that effect might be.

We can begin with the first three stanzas:

Contre toy, Mort doloreuse et despite,
Angoisseuse, maleureuse, maudite,
Et en tes fais merveilleuse et soudaine,
Ceste complainte ay fourmee et escripte
De cuer courcié, ou nul plaisir n'abite,   5
Noircy de dueil et aggrevé de peine.
Je t'appelle de traïson vilaine;
De toy me plaing de toute riguer plaine,
Quant ta durté a tort me desherite
Du riche don de joye souverainne,   10
Et que ton dart a piteuse fin maine
Le chois d'onneur et des dames l'eslite.

Tu m'as tolu ma dame et ma maistresse,
Et as murtry mon cuer et ma lëesse
Par un seul cop, dont ilz sont tous deux mors.   15
Du cuer n'est rien puis que plaisir le laisse
Et que je pers la joye de jennesse;
Ainsi n'ay plus fors la voix et le corps.
Mes yeulx pleurent ens et rïent dehors,
Et tousjours ay le doloreux remors   20
Du hault plaisir qui de tous poins me cesse.
Las! Or n'est plus ce que j'avoye, Amors.
Je muir sur bout, et en ce point me pors
Comme arbre sec qui sur le pié se dresse.

Si suis desert, despointé et deffait   25
De pensee, de parolle et de fait,
De los, de joye et de tout ce qui fait
Cuer en jennesse a hault honneur venir,
Quant a celle qui ne t'a riens meffait
Tu as osté ce qu'el n'a pas forfait   30
Et qui jamais ne puet estre reffait.
C'est sa vie que tu a fait fenir,
Dont la mienne se souloit soustenir
Pour mieulx valoir et plus hault avenir

Et mectre peine a meilleur devenir.   35
Or as tu tout mon penser contrefait;
Si ne say plus a quoy me doy tenir,
Et ne me puet de confort souvenir,
Quant j'ay perdu sans jamais revenir
De tous les biens ce qu'estoit plus parfait.   40

Against you, Death—doleful and evil, fraught with anguish, disastrous, accursed, terrible and sudden in your actions—have I conceived and written this complaint, with a heart distressed, abandoned by pleasure, black with mourning, burdened with travail. I accuse you of evil treason; I make complaint against you with utmost severity, now that your cruelty wrongly despoils me of the rich donation of supreme joy, and your dart brings to a piteous end honor's elect, the very flower of ladies.

You have taken away my lady and my mistress; you have slain my heart and my happiness with a single stroke that killed them both. Nothing remains of my heart, since pleasure is deserting it and I am losing the joy of youth; thus I've nothing left save my voice and my body. My eyes weep within and laugh without, and I suffer constant remorse for my great pleasure, now wholly coming to an end. Alas! Now, Love, what I had before exists no more. I'm dying though yet erect; I'm like a withered tree that still stands straight.

I am despoiled, destitute and deprived of thought, word, and deed, of esteem, of joy, and of everything that brings the youthful heart to great honor. As for her who in no way did you wrong, you have taken away what she did not forfeit and what can never be renewed. You have brought to an end her life, which used to give its sustenance to mine, so that it could become more worthy and more seemly and work at becoming better. Now you have disfigured all my thinking; I no longer know what to believe and have no more thought of solace, for I have irrevocably lost what was of all riches the most perfect.

"Apostrophe is the figure which expresses grief or indignation by means of an address to some man or city or place, or object. . . . If we use Apostrophe in its proper place, sparingly, and when the importance of the subject seems to demand it, we shall instill in the hearer as much indignation as we desire." This quotation from the rhetorical treatise known as the *Rhetorica ad Herennium*, popular throughout the Middle Ages,[51] defines exactly what the poet does, for he uses the apostrophe to Death with which the poem opens to underline his own grief and to indicate the reaction he expects from his audience. The piling-up of adjectives describing Death ensures that reaction, as do the repetition in lines 1–3 of the interior rhyme in *-euse* and the extraordinarily obsessive quality of the end rhymes, each repeated six times. Throughout this first stanza all of the sound effects are in fact carefully combined to contribute to the desired impression: alliteration is discreetly used (ll. 5, 7) and in line 9 it is combined with the hard initial [k] of "Quant" and the harsh vowel sound in "tort" to characterize strikingly Death's criminal action, much in the way (and, I suggest, for the same reason) that Ronsard uses these same sorts of sounds in a line from his well-known sonnet on the death of Marie: "Quand la terre & le ciel honoroient ta beauté, / *La Parque t'a tuée.*"[52] The stanza itself is beautifully organized, from the opening attack on Death, with the word "Mort" at the accented fourth syllable (it would be possible to add a comma after "Mort," to emphasize its place), to the withholding until the last line of the subject of Death's deed. The author subtly gives the title and nature of his work in line 4, reminding us that he is indeed an author, albeit a grief-stricken one ("Ceste complainte ay . . . escripte"). The partial reprise of the poem's title in the verb "plaing" (l. 8) delicately insists on the poet's place at the center of the poem, since it is he whom Death has despoiled of his heritage, which as we finally learn in the last line is a well-born lady, the Chosen One.

Continuing to address Death, the opening line of the second strophe makes the loss more personal to the poet by the repetition of the word "dame" and the use of the pronoun and the possessive adjective, enhanced once more by Chartier's subtle play with sound, this time [t] and [m] in the interior of the verse. The rest of the lines explain that her death has in turn caused his, for his heart and his happiness are both dead (ll. 14–15); joyless, he has only the appearance of life, having lost his very heart. The striking image of the last two lines show him as a dead tree, divested of the green leaves of youth and pleasure.

The third stanza explicates the image, emphasizing with the three adjectives "desert," "despointé," and "deffait" the poet's desperate, disinherited state. The contrast between the life that has been ended by death and the one that, now disoriented, he must lead is poignantly restated in the middle section (ll. 32–35); the last line reminds us of the lady's unique quality, reiterating what the last line of stanza 1 has already claimed.

It seems evident that the first three strophes make up a unit: not only does the apostrophe to Death end after the third stanza (not to return until the eleventh), but also the first stanza presents the (written) Plaint, the next gives the Reason for it, and the last insists on the two participants in the drama—"Elle," who has disappeared but who is nonetheless ever-present, with all the enthusiasm and encouragement that love for her superlative nature could instill, and "Lui" (or better, perhaps, "Moi"), with all his capacity for suffering. Other stanzas, less closely related one to the other, are organized around this "Moi" and this "Elle," emphasizing now the sorrow of the former (e.g., IV, VIII), now the merits of the latter (V, VII). In stanza VI, the poet continues his praise of her and goes on to say that, although he is aware that other ladies may be praiseworthy, and although he is a great defender of their sex (ll. 77–80; is there a reminiscence here of *Excusacion?*), he finds it hard to believe that he will ever meet her equal:

> Je ne di pas—ne l'entente n'est telle—
> Qu'il n'ait des biens en mainte dame belle,
> Et qu'il n'en soit de tresbonnes sans elle,   75
> Ou faulte n'a de rien que dame amende.
> Ainçois maintien des dames la querrelle,
> Pour leur bonté qui croist et renouvelle;
> Et se je fail en rien, je m'en rappelle
> Et cry mercy et engage l'amende.   80
> Mais c'est trop fort que jamais je m'actende
> A mieulx trouver, quelque part que je tende

N'en quelque lieu que mon las cuer se rende;
Et y faillir seroit douleur mortelle.
En ce point veult Amours que je l'entende   85
Et qu'a tousjours Loyauté m'en deffende,
Qui tant l'ayma et tant fu de sa bende
Que peu s'en fault qu'el n'est morte avec elle.

I don't say—nor is it my understanding—that there are not
virtues in many a lovely lady or that, without her, there are not
excellent women who lack nothing worthy of ladies. I support,
rather, the ladies' cause, because of their goodness that thrives
and revives; and if I fail in anything, I retract it and beg for
mercy and pledge to make amends. But it's too much for me
ever to expect to find better, wherever I may look or wherever
my weary heart may go—to err in that would be a mortal
sorrow. That's how Love wants me to understand it, that my
looking be forever forbidden by Faithfulness, who loved her so
and kept her such close company that it almost died with her.

In other stanzas, the lament is varied by combining his sorrow
or her praise with the evocation of Fortune and its vagaries (VII, VIII,
IX). Stanza x (which as we have seen occupies the ninth place in two
groups of manuscripts) provides a particularly fine variation on his
chosen theme: his personal and inner sorrow is made more pathetic
by being contrasted with the happiness of others and by his express
desire to enjoy his sorrow in solitude.

Mes semblans sont de joye contrefaiz,
Tout au rebours du penser et des faiz,
Et ne me plaist riens de ce que je faiz
S'il ne sortist a doulours et a plains.   140
Estre tout seul est ma joye et ma paix;
Je chemine sans savoir ou je vais.
Qui parle a moy, je l'escoute et me tais
Et pense ailleurs s'a force ne me vains.
J'oy les autres chanter, et je me plains;   145
Ilz vont dançant, et je detors mes mains;
Ilz festoient, et je tout seul remains;
J'ay fait leurs tours: maintenant les deffais.
Plus voy jouer, et tant m'esjouÿs moins;

Tous mes plaisirs sont de lermes estains.   150
Le noir me plaist, car mon cuer en est tains
De tainture qui ne fauldra jamais.

I put on the appearance of joy, exactly the opposite of my
thought and my deeds; nothing I do gives me pleasure unless it
result in sorrow and lamentation. Being alone is my joy and my
repose; I trudge along not knowing whither I go. I listen in
silence to whoever speaks to me, distracted unless I consciously
force myself. Others I hear singing, and I make moan; they go
dancing, and I wring my hands; they make merry, and I stay
alone; I've done those tricks: now I undo them. The more
goings-on I see, the less fun I have; tears extinguish my every
pleasure. Black is my color, for my heart is dyed with it, with
an everlasting dye.

We have seen Christine de Pizan use the same contrast; we find
it in other poems by Chartier,[53] and even in this poem: "Mes yeulx
pleurent ens et rïent dehors" (l. 19). Charles d'Orléans will bend it to
his own poetic designs in a somewhat different register. And Pe-
trarch had long before given moving expression to the contrast and
the predilection that, following him, was to become a commonplace
of sixteenth-century love poetry. Nothing original, then; just a set of
conventions. But if we stop with that, we have learned nothing about
late medieval poetry, where "originality" is something quite differ-
ent. From the opening evocation of the social hypocrisy in which he
feels obliged to indulge to the ending in which the black of mourn-
ing becomes the eternal blackness of his heart, the lines paint a
powerful portrait of the preoccupation—of the self-centeredness—
of one who mourns. No mention of love and the lady, only the bald
desire to be alone with his sorrow. Distracted, he can think only of
his own grief, seen here in opposition to the careless gladness of the
world about him. The solace he seeks in solitude is denied him;
society presses about him, oblivious to his private feelings. Here a
particularly Chartier-like series of ordered antitheses expresses
beautifully this opposition between "je" and "les autres" (ll. 145–
47),[54] with the former in one hemistich of the line and the latter in the
other. The opposition is bitterly summarized in line 148—"J'ay fait

leurs tours: maintenant les deffais"—and the compound verb at the
end of the line, with its somber play on the root verb at the beginning
emphasizes the poet's moral *defeat*, at the same time that it reminds
us of the *counterfeit* joy of line 137 and the subsequent denial of all
motivations except sorrow. The dark ending of the strophe, termi-
nated by the uncompromising and ominous ring of "jamais," subtly
recalls the "cuer courcié, ou nul plaisir n'abite, / Noircy de dueil et
aggrevé de peine" of stanza 1 and is an example of the kind of unity
the poem possesses. This unity is not, obviously, structural; it is
rather a unity of tone and of overall effect.

It is indeed to gain this effect that the "mass of epithets" of
which Champion wrote so slightingly is of such importance—rather
than fatiguing, they are meant to be heartbreaking, and they con-
tinue unrelentingly nearly to the end of the poem. The penultimate
stanza gathers up all the elements of the complainte in an almost
unbearably intense summation. Obsessed with his own loss and his
own sorrow, the poet translates the fullness of that obsession through
the use of *-party* as the only rhyme in the *a* position of the scheme. Its
sixfold repetition is not puerile rhyme-play, and if we laugh at it we
are not understanding its seriousness. It is, in fact, exactly at mo-
ments of greatest intensity that we often find such play, which is
designed to increase that very intensity:

> Trop dur espart est sur moy esparty,
> Quant esgaré me treuve et departy
> D'un per sans per, qui oncques ne party   155
> En faintise n'en legier pensement.
> Oncq ensemble n'avions riens parti
> Mais un desir, un vouloir, un parti,
> Un cuer entier de deux cuers miparti,
> Pareil plaisir et commun sentement.   160
> Mort, or as tu fait le departement
> Dont j'ay pardu mon bien entierement;
> Si appelle de ton faulx jugement
> Car tout ce mal m'est avenu par ti,
> Dont je renonce a tout esbatement,   165
> Chacié d'Espoir, banny d'Alegement,

Et souhaite la mort tant seulement
Disant: "Mon cuer, pourquoy ne se part y?"

Too cruel a separation has been allotted me, for I find myself
lost and separated from a paragon without peer who never
took part in pretense or fickle thought. Never shared we any-
thing together save one desire, one will, one resolve, one whole
heart divided into two hearts, equal pleasure and mutual feel-
ing. Now, Death, you have caused the separation by which I've
wholly lost my treasure; thus I appeal your false judgment, for
through you has come to me all this evil, because of which I
renounce all amusement, driven out by Hope, banished by
Solace, and I long only for death, saying "Why does my heart
not break?"

The poet again addresses Death—but we all know that his appeal,
however pitiful, will not change the inflexible judge. Ironically,
instead, it brings him in the last line to wish for his own death: "Why
does my heart not break?"[55]

After this literally heartrending question, the last lines of the
poem bring some appeasement, with the poet's resignation before
life and its pleasures. "No more *lais de Plaisance*, no more songs and
verses; life is too much with me, and I aspire only to die." Beginning
with his angry refusal to accept the death of his lady, the poem ends,
then, with the evocation of his own death, which will reunite him
with her in Paradise:

Si prens congié et d'Amours et de Joye
Pour vivre seul a tant que mourir doye,   170
Sans moy trouver jamays en lieu n'en voye
Ou Liece ne Plaisance demeure.
Les compaignons laise que je hantoie.
Adieu, chancons que voulentiers chantoye
Et joyeux diz ou je me delitoye;   175
Tel rit joyeux qui apres dolent pleure.
Le cuer m'estraint; angoisse me queurt seure.
Ma vie fait en moy longue demeure;
Je n'ay membre qu'a mourir ne labeure,
Et me tarde que ja mort de dueil soye.   180

Autre bien n'ay, n'autre bien n'assaveure
Fors seulement l'actente que je meure;
Et desire que briefment vieigne l'eure,
Qu'apres ma mort en paradis la voye.

Thus I take leave of Love and Joy, to live alone until I die, never to be in the place or way where Gladness or Pleasure dwell. I leave behind the friends I frequented. Farewell, songs I gladly sang and happy ditties in which I took delight: many are glad who after are sad. My heart pains me; anguish overcomes me. My life stays too much with me; I have no part but strives to die, and I long to die of grief. I have no other good, nor do I savor any other, save only the expectation of my death; and I wish my hour to come shortly, so that after my death I might see her in paradise.

There is nothing in the text to give us any inkling of the lady's identity, and thus we cannot even know whether she existed outside the author's imagination. We have noted that a dead lady is mentioned in other poems, notably in some of the rondeaux and ballades and in the opening lines of *Belle Dame*, where the poet again claims that he must renounce poetry and its pleasures for tears:

La mort me tolly ma maistresse
Et me laissa seul, langoreux
En la conduite de Tristesse.
Si disoye: "Il fault que je cesse
De dicter et de rimoyer,   10
Et que j'abandonne et delaisse
Le rire pour le lermoyer."

Death took my mistress from me and left me alone, languishing under the guidance of Sadness. And I said, "I must stop writing and rhyming and abandon and forsake laughter for tears."

This is as it should be—and it is where we must distinguish, once more, the author Chartier from the poet (or Acteur) who appears in the poem; the latter, doubtless, does give up writing poems, but the author obviously does not. It strikes me that *Complainte* very much resembles a *déploration funèbre*—the kind of official lament and eulogy caricatured by Jean Lemaire de Belges in the first *Epître de l'amant vert*—with its characterization of the nameless lady as "le chois d'onneur et des dames l'eslite" (l. 12), "ma dame et ma maistresse" (l. 13), who spurs youth on to high honors (l. 28). This would posit some sort of official relationship between the man Chartier and the lady, perhaps a relation like that between Guillaume de Machaut and the king of Bohemia, for example, or between Christine de Pizan and the queen of France or the duke of Burgundy. I have already suggested the connection between Christine's art and socioeconomic reality: not only does she seek material support, she is also keenly aware of the travails of her adopted country, as such works as *La Mutacion de Fortune* and *La Lamentacion sur les maux de la France* testify. Chartier's case is no different; although unlike Christine he held paid positions at court, both were witness to a time of great political turmoil in France: the disastrous defeat at Agincourt in 1415, the insecurity of the Dauphin, economic depression. The sorry state of the country finds forceful expression in his prose *Quadrilogue invectif*, with its opening allegorical presentation of the figure of France as a distressed lady, blond hair unbound, crown askew, dressed in a mantle representing the three Estates, now all tattered and torn.[56] But one must admit that if *Complainte* was inspired by a real woman's death, it does so without such direct references to historical reality as those found in the prose treatise. The woman remains nameless throughout, and the expressions that describe her are ambiguous indeed. In their hyperbole, they could in fact be applied as much to a queen or other noble patroness as to any "queen" of the poet's heart. But that is doubtless part of the point: when, as it inevitably must, the poem loses whatever historical contingency it may have had, its author knows that the very absence of precision regarding the identity of the woman is what will ensure its value as a poetic lament, the emotions of which are timeless and universal. The relationship between poet and lady is one of respect and love, perhaps even a certain kind of intimacy, but even the impassioned evocation in stanza XI of hearts with but a single desire need not be more than a way of saying that he always agreed with her, as one is well advised to do with a patroness of any sort. While it is hard to deny to the text some sort of historical relevance, autobiographical, perhaps, be it in the private or in the public sense, it is equally hard to identify that relevance absolutely, for the poet has removed every sure signpost and left only teasing traces to guide the reader. He thus ensures that the poem can function transhistorically, as it were. This is a feature of many of the texts we are considering, and I shall return to it at the end of this chapter and again in the next.

Supposing that the poem is a more or less official *déploration*, can we then claim it—remembering Champion—to be "insincere" because the lady is not the poet's beloved, and therefore "bad" (that is, artificial and unfelt)? I propose that we cannot call it "bad" on grounds of insincerity—even if we were certain that Chartier was only hired to write it. The poem is quite clearly artistically "true," in the way that Ronsard's sonnets on the death of Marie are "true," true and moving expressions of grief caused by the premature death of a beautiful lady. It does not matter whether Ronsard pretends that the Marie of these sonnets is the same—as she almost certainly was not—as the Marie of his earlier love poems (of whose very existence we have absolutely no proof outside of the poems). Chartier's poem was celebrated and influential in its time, and deservedly so, I think, not as a historical document, but as the masterly expression of a poet's feelings in a given and known situation.

But Champion does not blame it for insincerity of any sort. He does, however, censure it on aesthetic grounds, the "mass of epithets." One could also claim that the poem is "bad" or unsuccessful because of its "typical fifteenth-century use of allegory" or its "typical late medieval abuse of *rimes riches*, *équivoques*, etc." But Death is hardly present as an allegory in the poem at all; its presence is there, menacing, as it should be, but I do not think that presence strikes us as being any more artificial or foreign to our way of thinking than the presence of Time and his winged Chariot in Marvell's "To His Coy Mistress." And if we accept the fact that rhyme and its intensive use carries, within this poetry and its canons, an important expressive function, then we can hardly condemn a poet for using it; we must, rather, try to see how he uses it and with what skill. But one does not, it seems to me, need to excuse this poem or explain it away on the basis of the contemporary particularities of rhyme, for it can stand on its own as a poetic text giving much aesthetic pleasure. What causes this pleasure? A number of lines offer memorable images: "Je muir sur bout, et en ce point me pors / Comme arbre sec qui sur le pié se dresse" (ll. 23–24); "Tous mes plaisirs sont de lermes estains" (l. 150); "Trop dur espart est sur moy esparty" (l. 153); "Le cuer m'estraint; angoisse me queurt seure" (l. 177). Others are especially striking because of particularly harmonious combinations of sound: "Qui me pourroit de ce dueil conforter? / Je n'ay pas cuer a tel doleur porter, / Car adoulcir ne puis ne supporter / Les durs acces de mon dolent mesaise" (Who could comfort me for this grief? I have no heart to bear such sorrow, for I cannot soften or support the cruel attacks of my woeful affliction; ll. 41–44); "Je faiz tresor de regrez que j'amasse" (I make my treasure-store of the griefs I am piling up; l. 109); "Je chemine sans savoir ou je vais" (l. 142). Throughout, one finds clearly articulated rhythms supporting vigorous expression. All of these features combine to produce a total effect of poignant beauty, a superb use by Chartier of the conventions of the genre.

It is exactly in their differing relation to convention, I have suggested, that we can often see the originality of late medieval poets, and Chartier's relation to it can lead us to an assessment of his accomplishment as one of them. All of these poets received conventions of form, of narration, of topos and theme or idea, furnished by the historical moment at which the poet lived, and they thus represent the relationship of the poet qua poet to his or her whole tradition. What is Chartier's use of this tradition? For all that his narrative persona is arresting because of its consistency, it is hardly new; he does not, like Machaut, create a new kind of narrator, with a new character and a larger and larger role, ever more active in his text. Indeed, even when his "I" is at the center, as it is in *Complainte*, except for its keening, it withdraws, on its fictional level, from all activity. Although he demonstrates with apparent ease great skill with rhyme and rhythm, he does not, like Christine de Pizan, seem very interested in exploring forms, in elaborating or varying them; his versifying, smooth, elegant, often beautifully made, does not usually call attention to itself.

Working, then, well within the limits of narrativity and form they helped to set, he plays rather with meaning itself—that is, on the very upper limits of that poetic game board I outlined in the last chapter. Thus we have the ambiguity of the debates, thus, the tug-of-war of wit involving the courtly love tradition itself in *Belle Dame*, *Excusacion*, *Reveille Matin*, *Deux Fortunés*, and even *Quatre Dames* to a certain extent, as well as the political tug-of-war of *Herault*. I do not mean to suggest that there is not in the other two authors something of the same thing—one has only to think of *Le Voir-Dit* or *Cent Ballades d'amant et de dame* to realize that all of them do this to a certain degree. And both Chartier and Christine, like Machaut—we have had ample demonstration of it—play with the narrative voice in different ways. What seems to me evident, however, is that Chartier goes further than either of the other two in playing with the conventions of thought or behavior—with, it could be said, the codes of his time.

I should like to put this another way. In a sense, it can be said that all the poems we have talked about so far preexist, like Platonic essences, before their particular incarnation by one or another poet in a particular written text. They can preexist in two ways, either through their form (all rondeaux resemble the Rondeau; all ballades resemble the Ballade, and so on), or through their theme or subject ("Lament over Death of a Lady," "Unhappy Suitor and Unyielding Lady," "Lady in Love with Knight," and so on). Sometimes—often, in fact—these two modes of preexistence occur at once, and we then have the shorter lyric poems, where the poet can, if he wishes, ring all sorts of changes both on the proto-Form and on the proto-Idea. In other cases, such as the poems of Chartier with which we have been concerned in this chapter, form is secondary, and the poet chooses to elaborate the idea.

We have seen how Chartier has done this by adding a first-person presence, other speakers, particular circumstances. One could even suggest formulas for such texts. For *Complainte*, for example: (Lament-over-dead-lady) + "I." Or for *Reveille Matin*: (Love, unrequited) + (Suitor, unhappy) + (Friend, objective) + "I." The formula for *Belle Dame* would be similar: (Love, unrequited) + (Suitor, unhappy) + (Lady, unyielding) + "I." That for *Quatre Dames* would be more complicated, something like (Lady in love with knight) × 4 + (War: defeat) × 4 + "I." Truly to represent each poem, of course, all these formulas would necessarily have a given, that is, "poetry"—i.e., the subjects are not embodied in prose, although they could be. In each case, therefore, the formula would have to be completed by another formula made up of the rhyme scheme plus indications of line length, number of lines to a stanza, number of stanzas, and so on. Such a formula for the lays, for example, would be quite lengthy, since each of the eleven different stanza forms would have to be indicated. The result for a fairly simple poem like *Herault* could look something like this (the rhyme scheme is indicated in the usual way, the superscripts show the number of syllables in a line, and 55 is the total number of stanzas):

$$[(\text{France, present state of}) \times (3 \text{ persons}) + \text{"I"}]$$
$$+ [(a^8\, b^8\, a^8\, b^8\, c^8\, d^8\, c^8\, d^8) \times 55]$$
$$= \textit{Le Debat du herault, du vassault et du villain}$$

But would this pseudo-mathematical formula really represent *Herault*? Obviously not, because *Herault* is *Alain Chartier's* version of all the factors in the formula, factors that you or I could combine to come up with our own version, which would not be his. That is why poetry is not mathematics. What is missing in each case is what is essential to the particular poet. We have seen that in the case of Chartier, that quality is not a highly "personal" point of view or a striking display of prosodic technique. Rather, that essential quality seems to me to be what can be called his wit, in both senses of the word: his understanding and good sense, and the ability to perceive relationships between sometimes incongruous things, and to express them ingeniously, that has been seen as the characteristic of English metaphysical poetry, for example, but that could also be applied to such a poet as Maurice Scève. It is, to my mind, the latter, the play of wit, that makes *Belle Dame* (or *Reveille Matin* or *Herault*) such a fascinating poem, as it is the former, the highly intelligent use of topic and idea and their skillful combination with sound, rhythm, and image, the elements of poetic utterance, that make something more of *Complainte* than its formula, however elaborated, can express.

Whether this wit embodies or not a certain *Weltanschauung* of a sentimental or a personal nature is open to question, to say the least, given what little we know of the man and what little the poems tell us that is directly contingent to "the world." *Herault* probably does refer to the social conditions in France caused by the bloody rivalry between the Burgundian and Armagnac factions and the continuing war with the English in the early decades of the fifteenth century; the battle that causes the four Dames' distress may well be the catastrophe of Agincourt, as *Complainte* may have been occasioned by the untimely death of a great lady or by that of the poet's love. We simply cannot know with certainty if these possibilities are true or not—and this can only be because the poet does not want us to know. Historical fact, biographical fact, may be there, but is deliberately occulted: the poet removes, to a greater or lesser degree, the signs of historical contingency. The Dames' sorrow, detached from dates and places, thus transcends the sorrow caused by any particular war and becomes the grief of all women whose lovers have disappeared in war; and the lament on the death of a particular mistress becomes for us, since it contains no proper names, a threnody on the death of a beautiful woman dear to the poet. "History," then, is important, because it may generate the text and, in the form of the tradition of literary conventions of the time, it certainly shapes it, both ideologically and formally. But at the same time poets may choose to allow their text to function transhistorically as well, by eliminating obvious references to their own life and times. Just as in the debate poems of Chartier we have seen that the author's own opinion on the question is purposefully concealed, so must we recognize this other concealment. We are free to propose, if we wish, a number—limited, I think, by all that we can know of the probabilities inherent in such a world—of interpretations or intentions for the poems. Yet it seems to me of major importance to be very cautious in this domain, the more so since the relevant documents at our disposal are so few. Is it really so little to try to see Chartier as a poet, rather than as a man, or a patriot, or a thinker? Can we not find such works as *Belle Dame* or *Complainte* successful even though they "fail to reflect the events of their time," as if every poem today had to "reflect" the dropping of the atom bomb at Hiroshima or the fighting in the Middle East? This is not to deny the importance of historical events in the lives of poets; it is, rather, to insist on the larger importance of the historically determined tradition in which they work.

We are tempted today to find in every deviation or variation from a historical code—behavioral, aesthetic, religious—a criticism of it or, indeed, an attempted subversion of it. Thus, for some scholars, the Belle Dame saps the foundations of the courtly code with her wit and her realism, just as the bourgeoisie sapped the feudal power of the aristocracy. Rather than a weapon aimed at the Ancien Régime, however, or a conservative defense of the old traditions and values, it seems to me less hazardous—and just as exciting—to discover in *Belle Dame*, as in Chartier's other poems, a *literary* text, and in this light I propose to see it as a witty playing with the conventions of courtly love, an elegant, somewhat satirical literary game. This does not mean that the text does not, in a large sense, reflect its time; what text can really do otherwise? It may, in fact, be a measure of its time that the game is, perhaps, pushed further in it than it had been before: Chartier is constituting his own voice, his own creative space, as Guillaume de Machaut and Christine de Pizan had in other ways established theirs.

4 ⚛ The Play of Rhyme with *Raison*: Jean Meschinot and the "I" of Everyman

t is evident that, in many of their works, the authors whom we have considered so far are trying to teach a lesson, even though occasionally, as we have seen, they appear to play in various ways with that very idea itself—by making of the Acteur a nonprivileged witness, by presenting divergent points of view, by some distortion of convention. This is not so in the type of poem with which we shall be occupied in this chapter: on the contrary, the lesson, pushed to the fore, is made clear and unambiguous, often by the Acteur himself.

Indeed, in many of these texts, the Acteur is so present, and his authenticity seemingly so guaranteed by the references made to historical figures and events, that one tends to identify him unwittingly with the poet. This was, at least, my own reaction when first I began to read Saint-Gelais's *Séjour d'honneur* (ca. 1490–93), or Pierre Michault's *Doctrinal du temps présent* (1466), or Jean Meschinot's *Lunettes des Princes* (ca. 1461–65). It seemed to me that I had at last found, with some relief and in the most unlikely place, that autobiographical "I" of which, in so much modern poetry, we are so aware, and which we so prize. Who, in these heavily allegorized—and allegorizing—texts, with their relentless drumming-in of lessons for moral living and their inevitably dismal depiction of the dangers of this world, would expect the appearance of what seems to be an individual poetic persona, confessing, in some detail, the sins of his youth, as does the Acteur of *Le Séjour*, or a nearly fatal temptation to suicide, like the poet in *Les Lunettes*? I was delighted to discover what I thought was a significant paradox in late medieval literature: contrary to modern usage, it was not in the lyric genres that the real "I" displayed itself (or, at any rate, its real emotions), but, rather, in certain passages of these lengthy, often ponderous poems, whose ostensible end is the moral elevation of the reader.

Some early critics seemed to have realized this before, it is true, but in perspectives that were not exactly mine. Thus, Arthur de La Borderie, until recently the standard authority on Meschinot: the beginning of *Les Lunettes*, he writes, is a real autobiographical fragment, "where the note of personal poetry is sounded, giving a verve, a loftiness, a truly original character to the style." Thus, Henry Guy, claiming that in *Le Séjour d'honneur* Saint-Gelais recounts his own life, even if it is with the intention of making of his autobiography a life exemplary for Everyman.[1] Thus too, of course, innumerable commentators on *Le Testament* of François Villon, for whom Villon's "spontaneity" and "sincerity" are what most distinguish his moral poetry from that of other fifteenth-century poets. Joseph Alston James, for example, compares some strophes from Saint-Gelais's *Séjour* with Villon's ballade of the "Dames du temps jadis" and concludes that, although many of the same elements are present in both, "there is something missing from Saint-Gelais's ballad [sic]. It is the spontaneity of Villon. . . . Where Villon's ballad is the sincere expression of a poet's profound anguish at the temporal quality of life, Saint-Gelais's is, unfortunately, little more than an exercise in rhetoric."[2] But in other parts of the poem, it seemed to me that I could detect "anguish" even in Saint-Gelais. Did not the "I" in these poems afford, then, for someone sensitive enough to interpret it, a superb occasion for analyzing such works as something like psychological autobiography? The idea was dizzying.

Sober reflection, however, obliged me to reconsider my discovery, from several points of view. Why should a Villon and a Saint-Gelais (or Christine de Pizan, or Alain Chartier, or Jean Molinet) be so different? Is it enough to say that one is a real poet and one a hack? Could they not both be "sincere"? Could both, on the other hand, be

engaging in an "exercise in rhetoric"? If I was to have the courage of
my convictions, based on the arguments in the foregoing essays, I
must at least admit that it is possible to look at both Villon's ballade
and the strophes from Saint-Gelais as exercises in rhetoric (although
one may be more successful than the other), for we have seen that
such "exercises" can at the same time be extraordinarily effective
poems. Perhaps, too, it was more reasonable to remember, once
more, in Nancy Regalado's words, that "the reliance on a poetic
personality appropriate to the theme rather than to the man writing
the work is a useful key to much of medieval literature written in a
subjective mode." [3]

Somewhat dashed, I decided that the kind of poem with this
first-person voice, often telling of "its-own-experience" in a dream
or on a pilgrimage, referring to contemporary events, and inculcat-
ing a moral lesson, was worth investigating, nonetheless, both for its
similarities and for its differences with those works whose nature we
have been studying.

Moreover, these long didactic and moral poems seem charac-
teristic of the Middle Ages, early and late, in the vernacular as well as
in Latin. Whether called "speculum," "doctrinal," or "pilgrimage,"
or by any of the other titles that provide Rabelais with so much
fodder for satire in his catalogue of the books in the library of the
Abbey of Saint-Victor, such poems share, to a greater or lesser
degree, a number of features. Their very length is one of them: they
are always longer than the longest lyric poem, and though certain
narrative poems are fairly long—Guillaume de Machaut's *Prise
d'Alexandrie* (1369–71), for example, has nearly 9,000 lines—these
didactic and moral treatises in verse often outrun them. *Le Mirour de
l'omme* (1376–79) of Chaucer's friend John Gower has some 30,000
verses; Christine de Pizan's *Livre de la mutacion de fortune* runs to
more than 23,000, with a short passage in prose; Martin Lefranc's
Champion des dames (ca. 1440) exceeds 24,000. And one must not
forget that *Le Roman de la rose*, a kind of model for many of them,
has almost 18,000 lines in the second part alone. From the formal
point of view, another characteristic is that, like the *Mutacion*, these
works often include prose passages: this combination, the *prosi-*

metrum of the Rhétoriqueurs, constitutes the *opus magnum* of the period. As the modern editor of *Les Lunettes des Princes* remarks, this genre allowed authors to show their skill in both kinds of "rhetoric," prose and poetry.[4]

Their goal was the teaching of a lesson, often moral, but not always: the *Doctrinale puerorum* of Alexandre de Villedieu, of the thirteenth century, was the handbook of Latin syntax used in schools, for example. *Le Mirour de l'omme*, though, treats the vices and virtues; *Le Séjour d'honneur* describes man's way through life, fraught with false hopes but brought eventually to contentment under the guidance of reason. Other poems use politics or accounts of life at court to make their point. But all of them teach—which is why the title "doctrinal" has become something of a generic label for them. The lesson is not infrequently underlined by the use of satire, sometimes general, sometimes pointed and particular, sometimes both. It is the combination of the general with the particular, for example, that makes Michault's *Doctrinal du temps présent* the lively text it is; other authors, like Lefranc and Saint-Gelais, use the same mixture to great effect.

A further characteristic is that, to some degree, these can be called narrative poems, for all of them contain some narrative elements. Some narration is inevitable in satire, of course, and it is implicit in allegory, as well. Frequent, also, is the recounting of a dream, with its attendant revelations; so too is the tale of a journey undertaken by the narrator, in the course of which he always confronts various allegorical entities.[5] Speeches, dialogue, descriptions abound. Despite this, the kind of work I am describing is not the narrative *dit* of a Guillaume de Machaut or a Christine de Pizan, nor what I have called the nonnarrative *dit* of an Alain Chartier, for narration and exposition are always carried out within a framework that might best be described as "emblematical." This is often indicated by the title: *Le Pèlerinage de la vie humaine*, *Le Pèlerinage de l'âme* (Guillaume de Digulleville; 1330–32, 1357), *La Danse macabre* (Jean Le Fèvre de Ressons; 1376), *Le Temple d'honneur* (Froissart; ca. 1363), *Le Chemin de longue estude* (Christine de Pizan; 1403), *La Forest de tristesse* (Jacques Milet; 1459), *Le Specule des pecheurs* (Jean

Castel; 1469). It is this kind of title, exactly, that Rabelais caricatures at such length in the seventh chapter of *Pantagruel*, with a catalogue that includes, among a multitude of others, *Bragueta Juris*, *La Couillebarrine des preux*, *Le Pacquet de mariage*, *Les Lunettes des Romipètes*.[6] These are very close indeed to such titles as *Le Bréviaire des nobles* by Chartier, *Le Psautier des villains* by Michaut Taillevent, and *L'Eperon de discipline* by Rabelais's friend Antoine du Saix.

Such titles obviously seemed humorous to a humanist in the 1530's, when their vogue was on the decline; the plethora of modern titles for thrillers like *The Andromeda Strain*, *The Odessa File*, and *The Anodyne Necklace* is surely beginning to seem silly to us, too. But while both practices may be modish, there is a profound difference between them. Behind that medieval combination of concrete symbol—the emblem, if you will—and class (Princes, Nobles) or abstraction (Honneur, Noblesse) lies a habit of the mind that any reader of medieval literature must try to understand: that is, of course, the habit of thinking allegorically. For seeing in an everyday object or action or category—a mirror, eyeglasses, a journey, grammar—a sign of abstract truth, if it is not, in itself, an allegory, can surely still be included in the allegorical cast of mind. And it is a cast of mind that, despite Rabelais, we cannot dismiss lightly if we wish to understand the kind of poetry with which this chapter is concerned. It provided, for some centuries, a dramatic way for authors to present to their public not only abstract thought but also psychological notions that had not as yet conquered, entirely, their own vocabulary. Henry Guy's refusal to recognize this is one of the reasons his 1910 study of the Rhétoriqueur poets seems today not only biased but downright wrongheaded.[7]

The presence of continuous allegory, then, is still another distinguishing feature of this kind of poetry. Let us briefly review its other characteristics, as I have already listed them. One finds (1) the presence of a narrator who speaks in the first person, with (2) the clear purpose of (3) proposing a lesson, (4) often moral or political in nature (and sometimes both), but (5) never amorous. It may (6) take the form of satire and is (7) transmitted in a relatively lengthy and continuous form, (8) compounded of both prose and poetry (the *opus magnum*). The whole, with its (9) narrative elements, is (10) presented within the allegorical framework just defined.

None of the other poems studied so far entirely resembles this type. It is obviously far from the lyric genres with which we began. Although it may look a bit like the *Enseignemens moraux*, for example, of Christine de Pizan, her pieces are not allegorical, nor do they form a continuous text. And though *Le Livre des quatre dames* or *La Belle Dame sans mercy*, say, offer some narrative elements and perhaps include a moral lesson, and even were one to grant that the four ladies or the Belle Dame are allegorical figures of a sort, the lesson is far from clear and obviously comprises erotic elements. Nor do any of these poems include prose passages. This leaves us with the problem of what to call this genre, if genre it is. Henry Guy simply gave up trying to name it, although he recognized it as a genre: "But this genre has never, to my knowledge, been baptized, and it does not seem easy to assign a name to it, given its numerous and contradictory characteristics."[8] He nonetheless goes on to use the designation *opus magnum*, which can nowadays, it seems to me, be considered a perfectly valid baptismal name—its only fault being that it was never accepted into the consecrated codification of genres in French. Guy even entitles the section of his study in which he discusses such poems "Le Grand Genre"—this is an excellent French equivalent for the Latin name, which we may prefer to use in English.

I think we can go further than this, however, in the useful taxonomy of this "grand genre." Certain of its characteristics ally it very closely to what Northrup Frye has called the "anatomy," which he proposes as a modern replacement for the classical "Menippean satire."[9] Important in the Menippean satire is the clash of ideas, often represented by classes of people; in a medieval context, these could be such figures as Noblesse or Tempérance. As Frye formulates it, these ideas constitute what he calls "a vision of the world in terms of a single intellectual pattern."[10] The allegorical framework in our texts represents this pattern not only by accentuating but also by actualizing it, as we shall soon see. The other elements Frye finds in Menippean satire are also present in the *opus magnum*: fantasy or morality (or both); dialogue; intellectual exuberance shown through a large display of erudition. Although he claims that it is now known only as a prose genre, Frye reminds us that the Menippean satire probably originated in verse satire to which prose interludes were added, and this appears to correspond singularly to the mixed prose and poetry of the *opus magnum*, too. Given the concordance of the rest of the definition with other medieval poems, I am tempted respectfully to disagree with Frye and to suggest that despite the absence of prose passages, the second part of such a work as *Le Roman de la rose*, for example, is very like an anatomy or a Menippean satire. I suggest, further, that an understanding of the tradition of the anatomy goes far toward sharpening our perception of a considerable amount of medieval verse. This notion seems even more reasonable when one finds Boethius's *Consolation of Philosophy*—signally influential, of course, in medieval literature—given as an example of "a pure anatomy."[11]

The case for using this category to refer to the *opus magnum* is further strengthened by Frye's comment that "the anatomy in particular . . . has baffled critics, and there is hardly any fiction writer deeply influenced by it who has not been accused of disorderly conduct."[12] The same is true of certain medieval writers in verse: Jean de Meung has constantly been taxed for his seeming disorderliness, and it is clear that it was something very like it that Henry Guy perceived in "le grand genre," and that, as a traditional French literary historian, he could not like.

But so far we have only a general and perhaps rather vague picture of these works; it is high time to focus on a precise example. *Les Lunettes des Princes* by Jean Meschinot has much to recommend it for this role. First of all, it displays, as we shall shortly discover, all of the traits we have listed as being typical of the genre as a whole. Second, it is a work that enjoyed extraordinarily wide favor in its own day. Written in all likelihood around the same time as *Le Testament*, but probably nearer to 1465 than to 1461,[13] it had at least as much popularity as Villon's work, if the number of editions is any indication: there were at least thirty of them in the fifty years follow-ing its first appearance in print in 1493, making Meschinot the most frequently printed poet of the time.[14] Finally, the text exists in the excellent modern edition to which I have already referred, with careful annotation and a judicious introduction by its editor, Chris-tine Martineau-Génieys. I am not aware of any other work of the same type that brings together these three advantages: eminently characteristic of the genre, it can serve as an excellent example; its popularity assures us of its being, at least in a historical sense, a central literary text; and its accessibility makes it an ideal point of reference for the reader.[15] And it presents us with another intriguing question: why was it so popular? This question may be particularly significant in view of its contemporaneity with *Le Testament*.

Jean Meschinot, born about 1420 near Nantes, spent most of his adult life in the service of five successive dukes of Brittany, not primarily as a poet but as a soldier—"écuyer de corps," "lance," "gentilhomme de la garde." When the last duke, François II, died in 1488, Meschinot became the head chamberlain for the young Anne de Bretagne, who was to bring her province to the French crown as part of her dowry when she married Charles VIII in 1491, in all probability the year of the soldier-poet's death.[16] Although his output is considerably less copious than that of any of the other authors we have considered heretofore, he seems to have had, during his life-time, a certain fame as a poet. The official historiographer of Bur-gundy, for instance, George Chastellain, "le grand George," engaged in a literary exchange with him: in his *Vingt-cinq Ballades*, Mes-chinot uses the last line of each of the twenty-five strophes of Chas-tellain's poem *Le Prince* (or *Les Princes*) for the refrain lines.[17] A few poems deploring internal strife in Brittany; a number of religious poems (prayers, ballades bemoaning man's wicked ways and pro-nouncing the inevitability of death); some "official" verse; a handful of poems, probably early, on conventional love themes: this is largely the extent of Meschinot's versifying outside of his one major work.[18]

It is, of course, this work, with its picturesquely curious title, which has caused his name to be more than a footnote in French literary history. Even so, one cannot claim that it is a very well-known text, even among specialists of medieval literature. A very brief account of what it looks like and what it says may therefore not be amiss. The work is clearly divided into three parts: the first is made up of 86 twelve-line stanzas of decasyllables; the second, in the modern edition, of 125 lines of prose; and the last of 2,039 lines of verse, subdivided by their rhyme and metric schemes into four sections.* Beginning with a meditation on the difficulties of this life—our "miserable et tresdolente vie" (miserable and most sorrowful life; stanza IV, l. 1)—the poet goes on to recount his own grief and distress, and to give the reasons for them: four of the dukes he has served have died successively, either at a tragically young age or after an all too brief reign. He is, therefore, a prey to Desespoir and his followers—among them Penser, Foiblesse, Desplaisir, Peine, and Soucy—to the point of thinking of suicide (stanza XLI). But after a prayer to God, he is visited by Raison and her suite; she preaches for his benefit a lengthy sermon on the vagaries of fortune, the certainty of death, and the consequent necessity of keeping faith not only in God but in Raison herself. To this end, she promises to give him when he wakes from a refreshing sleep a pair of glasses with which to read clearly in a book called *Conscience*, and she explains that the glasses are composed of prudence, justice, fortitude (*force* in the text), and temperance. The first part ends with Raison's recommending that he pray to God for his forgiveness.

The poet's orison once finished, he tries to sleep but cannot, and in a kind of dream state—"par une maniere d'illusion, resverie ou songe" (in a sort of illusion, reverie, or dream; *Lunettes*, p. 33, l. 64)—he sees Raison again; she appears in splendor, bringing him the promised spectacles and the "petit livret." She explains how they will be helpful to him: through them he will learn what is necessary for spiritual salvation, profitable for daily conduct, and useful for commerce with others of every estate (p. 34, ll. 94–98). She goes on to tell him why they are called the "spectacles of princes." Raison then vanishes; the poet comes to full consciousness; all that is left of

---

*All citations are from the Martineau-Génieys edition. In referring to the first part, I cite by strophes and their line numbers; for the prose of the second part, I give pages and line numbers; and for the third part, I cite line numbers alone.

his dream or vision is the little book. It is this book that constitutes the last part of the work, with its allegories of the four cardinal virtues, each of which—prudence, justice, fortitude, temperance—is presented by a first-person narrator who is presumably the author of the book. But from the vigorous address that begins this last part—"Homme miserable et labille, / Qui vas contrefaissant l'abille, / Menant estat desordonné" (Miserable and wayward man, you go on pretending to be clever, leading an unruly life; ll. 1–2)—to the evocation, at the very end, of "Celluy qui vit et regne / Eternellement en son hault siege et regne" (Him who lives and reigns eternally from his glorious throne and kingdom; ll. 2038–39), the question of the exact identity of this "I," as we shall see, is more problematical than it at first appears. The counsels given in the name of each virtue are those expected in any such moralising treatise based on the medieval Christian tradition. Yet their "originality" is ensured by the emblematic allegorical device of the eyeglasses through which they are presented. The right lens is prudence, the left justice. The frame is made of fortitude, and the whole is held together by the pin ("clou") of temperance. That death and its menacing presence are frequently evoked is hardly surprising for the time, nor is the presentation of the seven deadly sins, the folly of war, or the need for following a path of moderation through life. In the verses devoted to justice, the conscious and repeated use of proverbs brings with it a lightly ironic note; one finds there, too, some mild satire of *les gens de justice* and of others in the verses that evoke the seven sins, prayers, digressions—and an almost constantly sermonizing tone. Another prayer forms the conclusion of the whole work.

Even this very summary presentation of *Les Lunettes* makes evident its exemplary character as an *opus magnum*. From the first-person narrator who gives a clear moral lesson that includes narrative elements and some satire (although this is admittedly not a principal ingredient here) in a fairly long text of mixed poetry and prose, enclosed in an allegorical frame, nothing is missing. And one can discover in it, as well, the characteristics of the anatomy, almost as Northrup Frye lists them for the *Consolation of Philosophy*, "with its dialogue form, its verse interludes and its pervading tone of contemplative irony."[19] The tone of irony may not be exactly all-pervading, but it is there. The display of erudition, while hardly as exuberantly evident as in *Le Roman de la rose*, for example, can be discerned, especially in the third part, with its lengthy exposition of the lessons to be learned from the four cardinal virtues. Still, if the *Consolation* is a "pure anatomy," then *Les Lunettes* is certainly an "impure" one, for its first part—which La Borderie called "a true autobiographical fragment"—seemed to that scholar so different from the rest of the work that he considered it a separate poem: "there are in reality two works here, two compositions that are entirely distinct and of a very different character."[20] Despite this opinion, the logical connection between the first part and the rest is not difficult to discover—the so-called autobiographical elements explain the poet's despair, which, in turn, can only be overcome through a prayerful and reasoned meditation on life and death and the obligation for the Christian to live it virtuously. Even so, the first part of the work does seem distinctly different from the last. Meschinot's modern editor, countering La Borderie's arguments, reminds us that, as an *opus magnum*, *Les Lunettes* has its own kind of unity, that it constitutes, in fact, "a vast architectural ensemble."[21]

This formal unity is enhanced, she further maintains, by the fact that its author was consciously and closely following the model of the *Consolation*, and she claims that the plan of the two works is exactly the same. The notion of some relationship between the two seems to me helpful indeed, and it is certainly true that Boethius's work, with its admixture of prose and poetry, its narrator who thinks himself overcome by Fortune and her unjust ways, and its allegorical visitor who reasons with the narrator and finally persuades him to change his thinking, is a model for Meschinot's. But I do not think that one can call *Les Lunettes* "exactly modeled on the *De Consolatione*,"[22] and in consequence put its unity beyond question. There are a number of striking differences between the two. First, of course, the *Consolation* is much longer and the mix of prose and poetry is entirely different, the prose passages constituting a much larger proportion of the whole than the single prose interlude of *Les Lunettes* does. Although the Dame Raison of the latter is certainly a close relative of the Philosophia of the *Consolation*, they are not quite one and the same, for Philosophia is not connected specifically with the Christian faith, whereas *ratio* and *fides*, as one might expect, clearly support one another in the later work. Further, the arduous philosophical questions discussed in Socratic manner at such length by the narrator and Philosophia find little place in Meschinot's treatise, although their shadow, I suppose, hovers over the sections devoted to the four virtues. The beginnings of the two works differ, too, that of the *Consolation* centered squarely and immediately on the woes of its narrator, and that of *Les Lunettes* reaching the narrator's personal sorrows only after a dozen or so stanzas devoted to a general complaint concerning the woes of the world. Lastly, beyond the presence, similar in both, of the personifications of Philosophy and Reason, nothing in Boethius corresponds to Meschinot's central symbolical and allegorical devices of the eyeglasses or the "petit livret." In other words, there is a very general similarity between the two works, together with many important differences of detail. Put another way, one could say without much exaggeration that *Les Lunettes des Princes* is as different from the *Consolation of Philosophy* as a modern philosophico-literary text like Sartre's *La Nausée* (with a symbolic title and a protagonist who suffers from an acute sense of the ills of this world) is from *Les Lunettes*.[23]

Yet the work cannot be seen as a mere heterogeneous juxtaposition of distinct parts, and Martineau-Génieys is surely right to insist on its unity. We have already seen that there is an obvious thematic connection between the first and last sections, despite the "autobiographical" nature of the one and the "impersonal," doctrinaire character of the other. May the parts be related in any other, more formal way? Here, another notion from the discussion of rhetorical criticism in *Anatomy of Criticism* can help us. Northrup Frye's classification of various kinds of specific continuous fictional forms includes not only the novel, the romance, and the anatomy, but a fourth kind, which he calls the "confession."[24] Examples include Saint Augustine, Montaigne, and Rousseau, of course, with such modern descendants as Newman's *Apologia* and Joyce's *Portrait*

of the Artist as a Young Man. Although these categories are intended
for prose, there appears to me no reason why, if one can use the idea
of the anatomy to describe certain medieval works in verse, one
cannot also use the confession. It suits particularly well a consider-
able number of the many dream-vision poems and pilgrimage
poems that often make up what Zumthor has called the "type-
cadre" of the allegorical narrative.[25] And it fits even such an appar-
ently maverick text as Machaut's *Voir-Dit* surprisingly well. Its use-
fulness in the context of late medieval poetry becomes particularly
apparent in the light of another of Frye's observations: "Nearly
always some theoretical and intellectual interest in religion, politics,
or art plays a leading role in the confession." This, he maintains, is
what unifies the author's life and his point of view.[26] For the author of
a doctrinal, we know that this overriding interest is often moral, and
the moral frame is a Christian one. Politics, too—particularly royal
politics, or the clash of feudal interests with royal politics—may play
a central role. Thus the category of the confession helps us consider-
ably in understanding a text like Saint-Gelais's *Séjour d'honneur*,
with its apparently autobiographical elements and its allegorical
recounting of its author's "way" through life. And this "way" is
related to the court (which is the "séjour d'honneur") and therefore
to politics, as it is to an essentially Christian scheme of life. Although
the confession is, again in Frye's words, "introverted," it is also,
therefore, "intellectualized in content."[27]

Just as one finds in Book 1 of the *Consolation* an abbreviated
confession, with details of the author's life (is it, then, such a "pure
anatomy"?), so one finds an "autobiographical" confession in the
first part of *Les Lunettes*. What we have, in fact, much more clearly
in the later and less lengthy work, is a combination of the confession
with the anatomy—both are intellectualized forms, the former in-
troverted, the latter extroverted. One could imagine, too, the com-
bination of the confession with the romance: remember the "per-
sonal" beginning of *La Belle Dame sans mercy*. Or with the novel
—to which, of course, in modern times, we have no difficulty assimi-
lating it: *A la recherche du temps perdu* is an obvious example. Noth-
ing says that confessions must be true, not even their titles; in *True*

Confessions as in *Le Voir-Dit* it is the "true" that is false. What we have seen of both lyric and narrative poetry so far would incline us to believe, in fact, that the confession may already be a fictional or partly fictional form in the fourteenth century. As the anatomy is a form apt for treating certain subjects, so the confession is an apt form for others; nor should the combination of the two, with the particular (confession) leading to the general (anatomy), surprise us, for it is widespread indeed at the time. This notion might well prove useful, for example, in understanding the text of Villon; and its application to such a prose work as the *Mémoires* of Commynes would allow us to bring that work solidly into the realm of "literature," where it belongs as much as it does to "history." [28] The idea of a false "true confession" as a practical literary strategy deriving from the subject being treated accounts, too, for the pseudo-autobiographical "I" that abounds in late medieval moral treatises, and that gave me, when first I descried it, so premature a sense of discovery. This approaches once more, and from a slightly different angle, the relationship of these works to what I termed in the preceding chapter the larger historical context. Although they may refer to events, real or imagined, in the life of their authors, they are in fact entirely conditioned by more overarching concerns (the Christian religion, for example, in the period that interests us, or the role and rule of princes). This is where the "reality" or historical contingency of such works lies.

The preceding remarks, though they may define the constituent parts of *Les Lunettes* as the example of an *opus magnum*, still hold this example at arm's length. They show little, as yet, of the way in which the author has worked out his own particular version of a doctrinal on moral problems. As we have seen in earlier chapters, however, it is exactly the variations each poet executes on given material that make up his or her creative personality, despite what we perceive as the severe constraints of convention in both idea and form. Let us put this principle into practice in looking more closely at Meschinot's text. Our exercise in taxonomy has already shown it as a work much different from the others we have considered: it is a mixture of prose and poetry; it is a combination of confession and anatomy; and it presents a clearly didactic—in contrast to a fictional or lyrical—character. But in its details, it is even more complex. Let us try, nonetheless, in the way we have done before, to penetrate the poem from the outside in, starting this time with the title itself.

Les Lunettes des Princes: it seems clear that this kind of title in general and this title in particular were meant to startle and to intrigue the reader. The startling aspect comes, obviously, from the juxtaposition of an everyday object with so exalted a class as princes, and the combination of them increases the enigma of the title's meaning.[29] The author, quite consciously, enhances this enigmatic quality through the device of suspense: the first mention of "lunettes" occurs only in the seventy-eighth strophe, more than 900 lines after the beginning of the poem. And even then the spectacles are introduced not on their own, as it were, but rather as the result, or the necessary accompaniment, of another allegorical object, the book called *Conscience*. After reminding the author to hold fast to her lessons and admonishing him to lead a holy life, Dame Raison promises to give him a guide book for that life (LXXVIII, ll. 1–3, 7–8):

> Pour parvenir doncques a grant science,
> Un livre auras qui a nom conscience,
> Ou tu liras choses villes et nectes:
> · · ·
> Mais pour plus cler les voir te fault lunettes
> Qui discernent les blanches des brunettes.

> Thus, to reach great knowledge, you will have a book called *Conscience*, in which you will read things both base and fair. . . . But to see them clearly, you will need spectacles that distinguish the white from the dark.

There are two descriptions of the glasses themselves, one given by Raison in verse (LXXIX–LXXX), the second by the author, in prose (p. 34, ll. 69–79) and in his dreamlike state, as if to guarantee the authenticity of the first. There is no enigma, no ambiguity in the allegory of the spectacles, for what the author seeks is not, as in so much symbolism since the nineteenth century, to be hazily suggestive, but to be vividly clear and significatory. This does not mean, however, that the symbolism of the glasses is simple; it is, on the contrary, fairly complex and very carefully worked out. In both descriptions, the eyeglasses are made up of four parts—the two lenses, the frame, and the "clou" or pin—each of which has a specific function. Once put together, these four parts, formerly separate, acquire a new name and a new quality: they become a pair of eyeglasses, which will enable the author to see, or to read, clearly. Without temples, they resemble what we now call pince-nez, doubtless much like the pair with the single pin holding them together found in the well-known picture of Saint Jerome in his study painted by Ghirlandaio only some twenty years after the composition of the text.[30] The reader is told at least twice that these four parts correspond to the four cardinal virtues, each of which, in the same way, has a specific allegorical function both by itself and in the whole. Once assembled, they will enable the author clearly to see his way through life—clearly to read, that is, the symbolic book *Conscience*. Prudence and justice are each necessary as ways of looking at life, but they cannot be used to their best effect without the encircling frame of fortitude, which, itself of value, increases that value in conjunction with them, just as all three virtues are strengthened when they are assembled, or tempered, by temperance. The allegory of the glasses is thus, from its introduction, double, and its force is increased through its always being presented in conjunction with the book, itself an allegory.

The third part of the poem adds still another allegorical layer when the virtues are seen not as parts of a pair of glasses, but as qualities (and in the case of Temperance as a personification) whose characteristics will be described and defined by Dame Raison. Thus the inanimate object, the emblem, is animated by allegorical figures and by the author in the exegesis of the object itself. Nor does the symbolic strength of the glasses end there, for their peculiar appropriateness is underlined even more when we realize that we are, in fact, reading the very book, *Conscience*, the author himself is reading (and, in truth, has written), and that we could not do so in the right—that is, the "clear"—way without the four cardinal virtues, since they are, in fact, the subject or substance of the book itself. Awakening from his vision, the author, at the very end of the prose passage, introduces us to the book, which he takes and reads (as do we with him); it contains, he assures us "formellement et en effet ce qu'aprés cest histoire ensuyt" (formally and effectively what follows after this story; p. 35, l. 125).

"We" are reading, but are "we" really the readers of the book? *Les Lunettes des Princes*: are not the spectacles intended for rulers? The second part of the title would seem to indicate that they are, but in an explanation almost Protestant in cast, Meschinot lets his readers know—but only in the prose interlude, well after the glasses have been introduced—that all men can be called princes.[31] Raison is speaking to the author:

> Saches aussi que je leur ay donné a nom les *Lunettes des Princes*, non pas pource que tu soyes prince ne grant seigneur temporel—car trop plus que bien loing es tu de tel estat, valeur ou dignité—mais leur ay principalement ce nom imposé, pource que tout homme peult estre dict prince, en tant qu'il a receu de Dieu gouvernement d'ame. Et ceste principaulté prefere toutes aultres, d'autant que le bien spirituel et de l'ame, qui jamais n'aura fin, vault mieulx que celluy qui en brief temps passe et perist. (*Lunettes*, p. 35, ll. 100–108)

> Know also that I have called them *The Spectacles of Princes* not because you are a prince or a great temporal lord—for you are very far indeed from such a condition, worthiness, or dignity—but I gave them this name chiefly because every man can be called a prince, insofar as he has received from God the government of his own soul. And this princedom surpasses all others, inasmuch as that good which is spiritual and of the soul, and which is neverending, is better than any good that passes away and perishes in a short time.

Thus the "princes" of the title are an allegory, too, for they signify not only the *principes* among men, rulers and leaders, but all humanity, all Christians, all who, through free will, must have the governance of their own souls. At a period in which the widespread

symbolism of the Danse Macabré insisted on the equality of all, high
and low, before death, this idea surely seemed less surprising than it
may appear to modern eyes to have been.

The title amuses one, startles perhaps, intrigues, in much the
way that the title *Le Testament*, contemporary to it, was in proba-
bility meant to do. There can be no doubt about its element of play.
Yet this play is designed with a serious end—it is, in twentieth-
century terms, an educational toy. Its goal is not to teach us to count
or spell, but to teach us to think seriously about our own lives and
those of others, unlike us, perhaps, in social station, but like us in the
eyes of God. The title captures one's attention for the game; and it
can provide us, too, as modern readers—distinct, that is, from medie-
val Christians—a way of understanding how Meschinot works out
his game. In the following pages, I shall try to show, then, how the
two parts of the title find their full expression in the body of the work
itself.

It will be easier to do this, I think, if we look first at what has
often been treated as the surface of texts like this and is without
doubt one of their most salient features: their rhymes. Let us listen to
stanza 1:

> Aprés Beau-Temps vient la pluye et tempeste,
> Plaings, pleurs, souspirs viennent aprés grant feste,
> Car departir de plaisance fort griefve;
> Aprés esté profitable et honneste,
> L'iver hideux froidure nous apreste;   5
> Se nous avons liesse, elle est bien briefve;
> Aprés temps coy le bien grant vent se lieve;
> Guerres, debatz viennent aprés la trieve;
> Aprés santé vient mal en corps et teste;
> Quant l'ung descend, tantost l'autre s'eslieve,   10
> Povres sommes se Dieu ne nous relieve,
> Car a tout mal nostre nature est preste.

After good weather comes rain and storm; lamentation, tears,
sighs come after great rejoicing, for parting from pleasure
causes great sorrow; after a gainful and seemly summer, grim
winter readies cold for us; happiness, if we have it, is of short
duration; after calm weather a great wind rises; after health

comes illness of body and mind; when one man sinks, then the
other rises; we are wretched unless God helps us, for our
nature is prompt to all evil.

Although the rhymes used are far from common, it is perhaps not
these rhymes in themselves that, among all the elements brought
together in the first strophe, strike us most on a first reading. The
very first line continues the title's effect of surprise on the reader by
boldly presenting the inversion of a proverb; it is not, writes Mes-
chinot in effect, that every cloud has a silver lining, but rather that
every silver lining has its cloud. Even in its inverted form, this
proverb at the beginning of the strophe serves as what Zumthor has
called a "thematic globalization," [32] and the following lines are varia-
tions on what is, from its proverbial nature, implied as a general
truth applicable to all of "us." These variations, in the form of
pseudo-proverbs, drive home that truth, with their repetition of the
initial "Aprés" in succeeding lines (ll. 4, 7, 9). The resolutely pessi-
mistic tone is emphasized as much by the alliteration in the second
and third lines ("Plaings, Pleurs, souspirs" / "Car departir de plai-
sance"), and by the rhythmic effect created partly by the elimination
of definite articles, as it is by the omission of autumn in the poet's
couplet using a seasonal metaphor (ll. 4–5): we go directly from
summertime to the winter of our discontent. Behind the whole
stanza looms the menacing figure of Fortuna, her wheel just discern-
ible in line 10, whose unstabilizing effect on man's corrupt nature,
the poet reminds us, can only be countered by God. The opening of
the poem is thus a strong one, with its calculated alternation of
syntactical order, its careful rhythmic control, its series of antitheses,
and its relentless reiteration of its foreboding point of view.

Then one realizes that all of this is framed by a rhyme scheme
admirably embodying the principle of repetition with variation that,
as we have seen, informs so much of late medieval poetry. Each of
the 86 twelve-line strophes has the same scheme, in which the second
half of each strophe—b b a b b a—is the mirror image of the first six
lines—a a b a a b. By "mirror image" I mean that though the
repetitive sequence of the rhymes remains the same, their place is
reversed, the *b* rhyme taking the place of the *a* rhyme and vice versa.

Repetition of the rhyme scheme, then, but variation of the rhymes. As one reads on, one recognizes that the same principle works, in a different way, in the section as a whole, for although every strophe repeats each of its two rhymes within itself six times, hardly any rhyme used in one strophe is repeated in another. Out of 172 possibilities for different rhymes (i.e., 86 × 2), 164 are different, and the eight repeated rhymes are each repeated only once. In other words, over the entire first part, rhyme is varied to very nearly the greatest extent possible, while within each strophe, its reduction to two means that, to follow his scheme, the poet must find half a dozen rhyming words for each, no mean task when one finds him using such rare endings as *-erme* (xxxi), *-cheu* (xxxvii), *-erche* (xxxviii), or *pieça* (lvi), to say nothing of *-icque* (xiii), *-oc* (xxxiv), and *-acque* and *-ocque* (xli)!

Nor does Meschinot's play with rhyme stop with the use of such unusual sounds. There is throughout both the first and the third part of *Les Lunettes des Princes* a constant search for rhymes enriched beyond the simple identity of three phonemes. Thus, in the first part, one can find not only the rhyme *-tion* (lxii; repeated in lxx), but also richer rhymes that include the same ending: in *-nation* (v), in *-tations* (xxvi), and in *-lation* (xxxiv).[33] Moreover, the "simple"—for Meschinot—rhyme in *-tion* is in all but one line of lxii a rhyme in *-diction*; only the *-duction* of the ninth line prevents its being an entirely new rhyme. And in lxx, the same phenomenon occurs: all the *-tion* lines with the exception of the sixth line (*-eption*) end with *-ration*. Other examples of such rhyming games are not hard to find. In lxviii and lxxx, for example, the poet plays on rhymes based on similar word forms; the first half of each will be enough to give the flavor:

> Tu as ton cueur sy bas mis et posé,
> Et entreprins, conclut et proposé
> D'y trouver paix, santé, ayse et repos:
> Faulte de sens t'a ainsi disposé.
> De ton plaisir es souvent deposé.
> Propose bien: Dieu juge des propos.

> You've put and placed your affection so low, you've undertaken, concluded, and proposed to find there peace, health,

happiness, and repose: foolishness has thus disposed you. Your pleasure is often taken from you. "Man proposes; God disposes."

Bien est raison que ton corps se repose
Et de te mettre a dormir une pose,
Car long temps a que tu ne reposas.
A bon repos doncques bien te dispose
Et tout ennuy soubz ton oreiller pose.
De sept heures assez pour repos as.

Now it's right that you rest and go to sleep for a while, for it's been a long time since you rested. Dispose yourself therefore for a good rest, and put all care under your pillow. Seven hours will give you enough time to rest.

We are far indeed from the unobtrusively smooth rhyming of an Alain Chartier.

But we have seen this kind of prosodic pyrotechnics before, in Molinet's poems to the Virgin, for example, or in Meschinot's own astoundingly polymorphous litany (Chap. 2, p. 97), and we know that it cannot be written off as mere bad taste.[34] We have learned that it must be understood, on the one hand, as being part and parcel of the poetic craft of the time, one of the most precious ways for the writer to distinguish the rhetoric of poetry from the other rhetoric, that of prose. This is why the poetical treatises are called *arts de seconde rhétorique*, with their elaborate lists of different sorts of rhyme: *équivoque, enchaînée, rétrograde, battelée, à double queue*, and so on.[35] It thus provides him with one way of showing his mettle, of operating freely, to a degree, within self-imposed bounds.

On the other hand, we have realized that in late medieval poetry rhyme and meaning (both more and less) are inevitably intertwined, and so it is in *Les Lunettes*. Martineau-Génieys notes that each of the three strophes in the first part that employ the prosodic technique known as *rimes enchaînées* is devoted to one of the major allegorical figures of that part, Mort (xxvii), Fortune (lv), and Raison (lxxxiv), and that they are distributed evenly within the section's 86 strophes.[36]

That at least one of them was considered to be of particular importance is evident from one of the manuscripts, the particularly

sumptuous vellum volume BN fr. 24.314, in which, on folio 16, the
lines corresponding to LV in the modern edition are singled out for
special treatment. The border of the folio is beautifully illuminated
with gold leaf, with gaily colored birds and flowers, and a space is left
for a miniature, which unfortunately was never painted. The stanza
comes near the opening of the argument of Dame Raison, whom
God has sent in response to the poet's prayer and who has just
"entered [his] understanding" (LI, l. 1) with her followers Sens,
Gouvernement, Providence, and the others. Beginning to speak—to
"reason"—with him, she develops, like so many of her allegorical
ancestors, the theme of the instability of Fortune (stanza LV):

> Fortune fait ces presens incertains,
> Tainctz de douleur, environnez de plaings,
> Plains de regrets, de larmes et meschance;
> Mais chance y ont joyeuse souvent maints;
> Ains congnoistre ses doulens faictz est vains: 5
> Vaincs la doncques par cautelle et savance,
> Avance toy, monstre ton exellance,
> Lance te fault ou n'ayt oultrecuidance,
> Dance en la main des plus petis compaings,
> Paings en ton cueur la vertu de constance,   10
> Tance a toy seul contre folle plaisance,
> Aysance nuyst aux dissoluz mondains.

Fortune renders these gifts uncertain, tinged with sorrow,
ringed with lamentation, full of grief, of tears and ill luck; yet
to many she often gives good luck. Thus it is vain to know her
grievous works: overcome her, then, by craft and knowledge,
press forward, show your excellence; you must wield modestly
your lance, treat the meanest fellows familiarly, paint in your
heart the virtue of constancy, rebuke yourself for idle pleasure;
leisure is harmful for dissolute worldlings.

Although each end rhyme is phonetically "chained" to the beginning
of the verse that follows it, the meaning is always changed; the part
of speech frequently changes as well, adjectives or nouns becoming
verbs, for example. Our attention is caught; at one and the same time
we must make an extra intellectual effort to understand what is
being said, and we must marvel at the capacity of the language—and

the poet—for ringing such changes. This is Jean Meschinot's varia-
tion on the well-worn theme of Fortune with which we watched
Guillaume de Machaut playing so subtly, in so many ways. The
efforts of both poets produce a reaction of what might be termed
intellectual wonder in the reader: "Ah yes, here's 'Fortune' . . . I
follow the argument; how beautifully he puts it!" Nor is this reac-
tion allowed to flag in the following strophe (LVI), in which another
kind of prosodic prowess continues to force our attention; on the
difficult original rhyme *pieça*, the poet makes five *rimes équivoquées*,
which I emphasize here:

> Fortune doibs congnoistre de *pieça*,
> Car s'aujourd'hui tu luy vois le *piet ça*,
> Soubdainement autre part le remue:
> Aulcunefois les biens grans des*pieça*
> Et les deffaictz mist hault et ra*pieça*.　　　　　5
> Son mouvement en peu d'heure se mue,
> Des saiges gens n'est pas ferme tenue,
> Mais en tous cas est de fermeté nue;
> De loyaulté trop petite *piece a*:
> Tantost s'en va aussitost est venue,　　　　　10
> Son service est douteuse revenue,
> Et sa doulceur d'amertume ap*pieça*.

You've surely known Fortune for a long time—because if
today you see her foot planted on this side, suddenly she's
shaking it on the other: at times she's destroyed great riches,
and she elevated and mended those who had been undone.
Her movements change within the hour; she's not considered
stable by wise men, rather is she in every case devoid of sta-
bility; she owns but the tiniest bit of trustworthiness: as soon as
she goes, she's back again. Her service is of doubtful profit, and
her sweetness is conjoined with bitterness.

As in the preceding stanza, meaning is again underscored by the
intensity of the rhyme, though this time it is an intensity produced by
a different technique.

Very rich rhyme is a given of Meschinot's verse in *Les Lu-
nettes*—as it is, of course, of that of many of his contemporaries—but
if one examines carefully the moments of the greatest intensification

of rhyme in this part of the work, like the one we have just seen, it is apparent that these are moments of great emotional intensity as well. Let us look at the others, beginning with stanza xxvii, the first that displays *rimes enchaînées*. In it the author poignantly sums up the death of the four dukes whom he has served and its effect on him: "Par ceste Mort je sens guerre mortelle: / Mort telle fut, desoncques tresrebelle, / Belle n'est pas, gente ne advenante" (Through that Death I know deadly war: Death was ever thus, most willful, un-lovely, unkind, uncomely; ll. 1–3).

The following strophe introduces Desespoir and his depressive followers. Obviously another important juncture in the text, the allegorical account of the author's depression and its consequences begins here. The allegory is illustrated in the superb miniature found on the second folio of the Paris manuscript mentioned above, where the poet is shown seated at his desk; Langueur, Fureur, and Cour-roux crowd around him, and on another plane, closer to the ob-server, Le Fourrier, or Quartermaster, shows Desespoir, Peine, and Soucy their new lodgings. This illustration suggests to me that one must add Desespoir to Martineau-Génieys's list of Mort, Fortune, and Raison as one of the primary allegorical figures of the first part of the text, and the extraordinary rhyme in the succeeding strophes comes to strengthen this claim. Following xxvii, we witness a grad-ual buildup of intensity: Desespoir comes to dwell within the poet ("logier dedans ma fantasie"; xxix, l. 3), and Le Fourrier finds "tout ouvert." There follows some sign of a psychological struggle be-tween the poet and despair ("Desespoir, maulvais hoste, / Eslogne toy et aussi tes gens oste"; Despair, you unpleasant guest, go away— and take your followers with you; xxxii, ll. 1–2), but since he is entirely bereft of reason (xxxiii, l. 1), he has little hope of winning. The variety and difficulty of the rhymes underline this despair, beginning with the pair *-oste* and *-illé* in xxxii, increasing with the *-ouche* and *-erme* of xxxiii. The next stanzas contain even rarer rhymes: *-oc* and *-lation* in xxxiv, *-aulme* and *-endus* (except for *-ondus* in l. 3) in xxxv, *-ievre* and *-ongne* in xxxvi, *-cheu* and *-ueille* in xxxvii, *-erche* and *-uche* in xxxviii. There can be no doubt that the intensity of rhymes like these has a progressive affective purpose, and these stanzas lead in xxxix and xl to a kind of crisis of grief and despair on the part of the poet, expressed in two series of pathetic confessions, which are both a culmination of what has gone before and a presage of what is to come:

Je suis garny de santé langoureuse;
J'ay liesse penible et douloureuse
Et doulx repos plain de melencolie;
Je ne vy plus fors en seurté paoureuse:
La clarté m'est obscure et tenebreuse;   5
Mon sentement est devenu folie.
Comblé de dueil, pour faire chiere lie
De tous ebas je ne donne une alye,
Mais treuve paix grandement encombreuse;
Plus ay de maulx et moins je me humilie;   10
Avisez donc se ma vie est jolye:
Mais que la Mort fust de moy amoureuse.

L'arbre sec suis, pourtant d'ennuis verdure,
Vivant en mort, trouvant plaisance dure,
Noyant de soif en la mer assechee:
Tremblant je sue et si ars en froidure;
En dueil passé ay mal qui sans fin dure,   5
Et ma santé d'infeccion tachee;
En plaings et pleurs ma liesse atachee,
J'ay corps entier dont la chair est hachee
Et ma beauté toute paincte en laidure;
Au descouvert s'est ma joye cachee   10
Et en mon ris est tristesse embuchee,
Que doulcement, en grand yre, j'endure.

I am provided with faint health; my happiness is painful and grievous, my sweet repose full of melancholy; I no longer live save in frightened security: light is for me dark and shadowy; my feelings have become folly. Overcome with grief, in making merry I care not a fig for any pastime, yet I find inactivity greatly vexatious; the more ills I have, the less humble I become; judge then how fine my life must be: if only Death would love me!

I am a dry tree, bearing leaves of discontent, living in death, finding pleasure harsh, drowning of thirst in the arid sea. Trembling I sweat, and yet I burn with cold; my constant pain comes from past sorrow, and my health is stained with infec-

tion, my happiness fastened to lamentation and tears. My body
is whole, though my flesh is cut to pieces and my comeliness all
limned with ugliness. My joy hides in the open; within my
smile sadness lies in wait; I suffer it gently—with great rage.

With their violent oxymora and vivid imagery—the Corneillian
note of xxxix, l. 5; the echoes of Charles d'Orléans; the dry tree
bearing leaves of sorrow of xl, l. 1—these are some of the strongest
and most beautiful lines in all of fifteenth-century poetry. And they
move us even more, it seems to me, because of what we perceive
as their "sincerity," until we remember the poetic "Concours de
Blois"—"Je meurs de soif auprès de la fontaine"—and realize that
this is yet another version of that type of antinomic ballade. Al-
though the form is different, Meschinot's lines seem in no way
inferior to those of Charles d'Orléans or François Villon in the same
vein. After this apparent high point, we tend, then, to dismiss stanza
xli simply as a particularly good (or bad) example of the Rhétori-
queurs' inordinate love of difficult rhyme:

> Des biens mondains n'ay vaillant une plaque,
> Mais des douleurs plus de plain une cacque
> Sens en mon cueur: de ce, point ne me mocque.
> Je vois aux champs sur ma petite hacque:
> La conviendra que la dague je sacque,   5
> A celle fin que ma vie je defroque,
> Car la cause qui a ce me provocque
> Trop cruel est. Helas! je me revoque
> D'avoir ce dict; par monseigneur sainct Jacque
> Je m'en repens; la grace Dieu invoque   10
> A deux genoulx, ostant bonnet et toque,
> Luy suppliant qu'a mon adresse vacque.

Of worldly goods I've nothing worth a cent, but of sorrows I
feel a barrelful in my heart: this is no laughing matter. I ride
my little mare into the fields: there it would be right for me to
draw my dagger to put an end to my life, so cruel is the cause
that incites me to it.—Alas! I retract what I said; by my lord
Saint James, I repent of it; kneeling bareheaded, I call on the
grace of God, begging him to attend to my amendment.

Can the rhyme scheme of xli seem anything but trivial to the modern reader? That its effect on readers of the time was meant to be anything but that must surely be proved, however, not only because of its place as the climax of a progression of strophes expressing the poet's despair, but also because of its subject, which is his temptation to suicide (ll. 5–8). These "playful" rhymes, then, were deliberately associated with the idea of suicide, hardly playful in itself, and served to increase the pathos of the lines. These verses, moreover, constitute a significant turning point in the whole poem, for in the very next stanza, the poet turns to God and, in a kind of *De profundis*, prays fervently that he may be delivered from "tant de maulx" (XLII, l. 3).

The final example of the intensification of rhyme shows in the same way a concomitant intensification of emotion. We have already seen that the poet's prayer will be answered through the agency of divinely sent Raison, whose arguments promise him, with the book and the glasses, a renewed way of looking at life. Late in the first part, she further assures him that this will permit him to write the work "that [he] never wrote": "Et l'ouvrage qu'oncques ne composas / N'a le savoir tes espriz ne posas, / Mon sens fera que le tien le compose" (And the work you never wrote nor set your mind to, *my* wit will ensure that *yours* compose it; LXXX, ll. 10–12). There follow two stanzas in which the poet expresses his extreme joy at his conversion to reason (in a series of rhymes in *-joye*, LXXXII), and his conviction that nothing can equal the good that reason confers (rare rhymes in *-eille* and *-ache*, LXXXIII). Finally, he murmurs his last supplication in her ear, expressing himself for the third and last time in *rimes enchaînées* (LXXXIV, ll. 1–5):

> Noble dame Raison, haulte princesse,
> (Prins cesse n'as de moy donner adresse)
> Dresse mon cueur vers Dieu et l'y maintien.
> Maintien mauvais ay eu en ma jeunesse:
> Jeu n'est ce pas . . .

> Noble lady Reason, great princess (you have never stopped working to my betterment), turn my heart toward God and keep it there. My youthful behavior was bad: this is no game.

If we are by now readers sympathetic to this kind of poetry, we have discovered in ourselves at each point of the intensification of rhyme both increased intellectual effort and increased aesthetic response. In light of the foregoing examples, to these we must add, I think, increased emotion as well, for each of these points are critical psychological moments in the author's narrative: the obsession with death and the consequent arrival of despair (xxvii–xli); the return of reason (liv–lvi); the result of this return, which is the author's return to literary creation—and to God (lxxx–lxxxvi).

While it is true to say, as I have been doing, that the *reader's* attention is solicited by the extravagant expense of rhyme, it is just as true to maintain that, within the fiction of the text, it is the *author's* reaction that counts at each of these critical moments. It is, at the first of them, his own meditation on death that brings Desespoir and his attendant ills. After Raison arrives and hammers home her lesson on Fortune's vagaries, there is no doubt that it is the author whom she wishes to persuade, for in the strophe immediately following the one with *rimes équivoquées* quoted earlier, she invites him to draw the consequences: "Veulx tu *doncques* sembler a beste brute" (lvii, l. 1; my emphasis). Finally, as we have just seen, it is the author's prayer to Raison to continue to guide him that, after lxxxiv, will allow the conclusion of the first part, as well as that of the rest of the book. Put another way, this means that the author must be present as a first person and that his reactions, in fact, guide those of the rest of us, his readers: this is the relatively celebrated "autobiographical" aspect of *Les Lunettes*, which has so appealed to its modern readers, from La Borderie to Champion to Martineau-Génieys.

Let us look at it more closely now, this "I" whom we have so often seen designated as the Acteur in narrative poems.[37] This "I" is not present at the beginning of the work—or, rather, it is as yet undifferentiated from the "we" of the general observations on the human condition with which it opens: "L'iver hideux froidure nous apreste" (Grim winter readies cold for us; i, l. 5); "Boire, manger et dormir nous convient" (Drinking, eating, and sleeping are our occupations; ii, l. 1); "Gens aveuglez, gens sourdz, mutz, insensibles, / Gens sans amour, a nous mesme nuysibles" (Blind, deaf, mute, unfeeling folk, folk loveless, hurtful to ourselves; v, ll. 1–2); "La mort nous rend trespuans et horribles" (Death makes us stinking and horrible; v, l. 12), and so on. This first-person plural implies, of course, a first-person singular, and we are not surprised when a "je" soon appears, rather timidly, in the sixth, seventh, and eighth stanzas, to state its own reasons for the plaintive tone of the preceding verses and to ask the reader's forgiveness for it (the examples are from vi, ll. 1–6, and vii, ll. 1–3):

C'est assez mal pour yssir hors du sens;
Car j'aperçoy clerement, voy et sens
Tous les plusgrans, les moyens et menus
Que chacun jour, voire a millier et cens,
Mort tire a soy violentement, sans
En avoir eu oncques pitié de nulz.

Se ma langue de trop parler s'avance,
Pardonnez moy, pour Dieu, ma nonsavance,
Car desplaisir me contrainct de le faire.

It's enough to drive you crazy; for I clearly perceive, see and am conscious of all those—the great ones, the lesser, and the least—whom every day Death draws violently to itself, indeed by thousands and by hundreds, without ever having pity on any of them.

If my tongue goes too far in speaking, forgive me my ignorance, for God's sake, for displeasure constrains me to do it.

Then, in some of Meschinot's most powerful lines, the "I" momentarily melts once more into the crowd of all mortal flesh in ix (ll. 1–6):

La guerre avons, mortalité, famine;
Le froit, le chault, le jour, la nuyct nous mine;
Quoy que façons, tousjours nostre temps court;
Pulces, cyrons et tant d'aultre vermine
Nous guerroyent: bref, misere domine   5
Noz meschans corps dont le vivre est trescourt.

We have war, plague, famine; heat and cold consume us night and day; whatever we do, our time runs always on; fleas and mites and so many other vermin make war on us: in short, misery rules our wretched, short-lived bodies.

Nonetheless, there are compelling personal reasons for the author, as distinct from the rest of us, to weep; these he approaches some lines later, in XII (ll. 1–5):

> Tant d'aultres cas nous procurent ennuis
> Et la moictié de nostre temps en nuitz
> Est employé: dont je meurs ou bien pres.
> En y pensant je me tourmente et nuys;
> Pour en yssir ne trouve porte ne huys.

> So many other things bring us anguish, and half of our time is spent in darkness—that kills me, or nearly so. Thinking of it, I torture and harm myself; I find no way out of it.

After a strophe devoted to the fate of heroes of the past—Meschinot's version of "Mais où est le preux Charlemaigne?"—he thinks of his own heroes of the present, and just as Alexander, David, and Solomon can exemplify the power of death over the great princes of the past (XIII), so does the demise of Jean V, François I, Pierre II, and Artus III of Brittany serve as an example of death's hold over those of his own time. In the *déplorations* of their deaths that follow in some dozen strophes (XIV–XXV), Meschinot's tears find verbal expression: "J'ay beau plourer, aultre chose n'y puis" (I weep in vain; I can do nothing else; XII, l. 12). Through these lamentations, the singular "je" has emerged from the "nous" of the opening—but the Breton dukes are still exemplary, still instances of that mortality "we" all face, be we rulers of this world or rulers only of our own soul. "Qui pourroit veoir tant de mutations / Sans en faire grans lamentations?" (Who could see so many changes without greatly lamenting them?; XXVI, ll. 1–2).

It is exactly then, at the first occurrence of what I have called the intensification of the rhyme, that the "I" becomes less public, less the official indicter of death and writer of funeral laments than the faithful servant saddened by the individual deaths of his masters. A careful presage of this development has earlier been inserted in the text—". . . je perdy de Raison le compas, / Tant que ne sceu que je fis ou disoye" (I lost the compass of Reason, so that I knew not what I did or said; xv, ll. 11–12)—and the actual arrival of despair signifies the effect on the poet's mind of his personal experience of grief over the passing of his own princely heroes. It is he—rather than the dead princes—who has now become our example, the example of one man's momentary madness, incarnate in "je, Jean Meschinot." Yet the "nous" is still there, and this one man is still Everyman, an Everyman whose prayer to God for deliverance from the demon of despair begins the same way that the prayer Villon puts in his mother's mouth ends: "Ha! Dieu, par qui je vueil mourir et vivre" (Ah, God, in whom I wish to live and die; xlii, l. 1). That this "je" is both personal and public, so to speak, is clear from the double role of Dame Raison, whose arguments in answer to the poet's prayer serve not only to counter his own unreason (and therefore that of all of us), but also to explain and justify the human condition in general. The "I," with its "personal" experiences, is thus a necessary part of the strategy of the text.

Raison's lengthy *consolatio*, occupying nearly forty strophes (xliv–lxxxi), is essentially a sermon, and she naturally addresses her audience of one as "mon enfant," "tu": "Mon enfant, or entens" (xliv, l. 1); "Or, mon enfant, que la main Dieu te seigne" (lxxvii, l. 1); "Va donc dormir" (lxxxi, l. 10). But the conclusion of the first part of *Les Lunettes* returns us to the author, narrating "his own" actions and promising his readers the rest of the book (lxxxvi, ll. 2–3, 11–12):

> . . . [je] me vins mectre
> Incontinant vers ma petite couche.
>   . . .
> Si priay Dieu que sa grace m'approche,
> Comme orrez apres en ceste lettre.

> I went forth to bed. . . . And I prayed God to bring me his grace, as you will hear in the following text.

Thus, from the "we" of the beginning we have observed the emergence of the "I" of the author, and then the "I" of everyone, which becomes for a time the singular and familiar "you," the "child" of

Raison, listening to her lesson, before reverting to its role of author. Rich prosodic patterns, now insistent, now receding into counterpoint, everywhere accompany and punctuate this itinerary, a kind of dark night of the soul through which the "I" passes successfully, following, as we have done in the foregoing pages, the double path of rhyme and reason. This "I" is about to take on another role; it will become, in its turn, our teacher. To see how that is accomplished, we must go with this first person into the second and third parts of the text.

A simple man with literary leanings analyzes for us the reasons for a kind of midlife crisis,[38] brought on one day when the realization of the misery of life and the inevitability of death, his own and that of all those he most admires, becomes almost unbearable. But because he is a Christian, he turns to God; his prayer is answered, and from the brink of unreasoning despair and doubt he is brought back to the knowledge that, whatever the state of the world, it is in God's hands and he has, through his Son, provided a way for men to cope with it. Stripped of its allegorical expression, that summary of the first part of *Les Lunettes* would be a plausible outline for a modern "Catholic" novel, à la Bernanos or Julian Green, or even Graham Greene or Evelyn Waugh. Each of those authors would enrich or complicate that basic schema with his own particular interpretation or slant—sexual guilt, politics, class consciousness, or what have you, in a twentieth-century way. Meschinot does it in a medieval way, using a medieval form: despite, it must be admitted, some slight reference to political figures and to class, it is essentially through allegory (not, to be sure, absent from the twentieth-century novelists I have mentioned) and through the addition to his narrative of what I am tempted to call straight moralizing; this will constitute the third part of the work.

We have just traced the affective impact of the "second rhetoric" Meschinot uses in the first section of the work.[39] Like many of his contemporaries, he is not afraid, in order to embellish and give greater weight to that work, to combine with it the first rhetoric, that

prose in which is written the interlude between the two verse sec-
tions of this *opus magnum*. Martineau-Génieys has pointed out the
perfect equivalence between the two prose styles used and the two
subjects treated.[40] The first portion of the prose passage is another
prayer, and its "grave" matter is couched in a style using all the
resources of oratory. The second is a description of the author's
dream; it is less elevated and therefore uses a "middle" style, clearly
less oratorical. These two styles emphasize, it seems to me, the two
poles of the Christian life (and of the work itself), God and man, as
they present a prose prayer to God followed by a prose presenta-
tion to man.

   Addressing the "glorious Trinity," the author begins his prayer
in a language heavily reminiscent of Latin vocabulary and syntax,
ornate with balanced periods, parallel terms, rhetorical questions,
exclamation, apostrophe. The prayer follows a traditional pattern of
invocation, adoration, confession, and supplication. It is undeniably
a demonstration of the author's skill, a bravura passage, a *morceau
d'éloquence*—but it is more than that, for it functions in a critical way
in the economy of the entire work. After we have heard in the
preceding poetic text repeated reminders of the four cardinal virtues,
for example, the prayer sets before us, at the end of its first long
sentence, the three theological virtues as well, as the climax of a
paragraph invoking the triune nature of the godhead. The next
sentence addresses God in a different way, as the friend of reasonable
souls ("O amy des ames raisonnables"), and this recalls the author's
recent desperate loss and fortunate recovery of the God-given faculty
of reason. That his conversion is complete is clear from the following
sentence, with its reminder of the "beste brute" that Dame Raison, in
LVII, persuaded him he must not become; both it and the succeeding
lengthy period that I quote are at the same time particularly im-
pressive examples of the grave style. Both contain a remarkable
series of five substantives, followed by five infinitives, each one of
which corresponds, in the same order, to one of the substantives.
With these carefully balanced phrases Meschinot combines various
double and triple sets of nouns and adjectives, all of which go toward
producing a richness of effect, a copiousness, entirely characteristic

of French writers of the late Middle Ages. Compared with the prose of some of them, Meschinot's is in fact relatively sober, if not entirely plain.[41] An influence of Latin, certainly—and what more appropriate, at the time, in such a context?—but no abuse of Latinizing terms or syntax. Christine de Pizan's "artistic" prose is often more difficult to digest, and we are still very distant indeed from the *écolier limousin*. Given the difference in period and in subject, the style is closer to that of Gargantua's letter to his son.

> Que diray je a ce qu'il vous a pleu de vostre amoureuse grace me creer tant dignement a vostre image et semblance, en me donnant sens, raison, memoire, entendement et voulenté, pour vous congnoistre, aymer, servir, doubter et honorer, qui pouvez, si tel eust esté vostre plaisir me faire beste brute ou aultre moindre et insensible creature? Ha! tresdoulx Jesus, glorieulx Redempteur, qui tant humblement avez voulu des benoist cieulx descendre ou precieulx ventre virginel, pour devenir nostre semblable en prenant vraye humanité, laquelle pour moy et les aultres povres pecheurs a tant souffert de maulx, opprobres, peines, douleurs et ennuys, que toute humaine raison deffault a les penser, estimer, concevoir, exprimer et dire, et finablement, par vostre tresangoisseuse, amere et doloreuse mort, m'avez vertueusement de damnation rachaté, ô souveraine bonté, ô inextinguible lumiere, ô richesse essentielle, dont tout aultre bien vient, procede et descend, tant d'aultres avantageux dons m'avez faict et faictes, chacun jour et heure, qu'en y pensant mon cueur default a les nombrer, mon entendement est par insuffisance aveugle et de feblesse offusqué, dont au reciter trouve ma langue mutte, qu'estoit ce, est ou sera de moy sans vous?   (*Lunettes*, p. 32, ll. 15–34)

What can I say about its having pleased you, in your loving grace, to create me so worthily in your image and semblance, in giving me sense, reason, memory, understanding, and will, to know you, love, serve, fear, and honor you, who could—if such had been your pleasure—have made me a brutish beast or any other lesser and senseless creature? Ah! most gentle Jesus, glorious Redeemer, who deigned so humbly to descend from blessed heaven into the precious virginal womb, to become like us by taking on that true human form, which, for me and other poor sinners, suffered so much evil, vilification, travail, pain, and anguish that no human thought can imagine, judge, conceive, express, or tell it; and finally, by your death fraught with sorrow, bitter and painful, you virtuously redeemed me from damnation: O sovereign goodness, O inextinguishable light, O essential richness, whence comes, proceeds, and descends all other good, so many other beneficial gifts did you (and do you still) bestow upon me that when I think of them my heart cannot count them, my understanding is blinded by inadequacy and dimmed by weakness, so that my tongue is mute to tell them out: what was I, what am I, what will I be, without you?

Once the "Amen" has sounded and the matter changes, the style changes, too. Polysyllabic words and swelling magniloquent periods diminish considerably—although, in the manner of the time, doublets of nouns, adjectives, and verbs do not.[42] The vision of "celle belle et tresnobles dame Raison" (p. 33, l. 65) is presented as coming to the author in a reverie or dream, that receptive state in which the narrator in medieval texts spends so much time.[43] Just as the allegorical language of the first part translates the varying psychological states of the author, so it is easy here to substitute a modern vocabulary. The emotional events of the day just passed press in on his mind; he cannot help going over them and remembering the new role of reason in his life, and the new vision it will bring. Thus Raison brings back, when she appears in his dream, the little book and the eyeglasses, and the eyeglasses' four constituent parts are recalled—and it is at this point that the noble Dame explains who the "princes" of the title really are. The revelation, given in this prose interlude, illumines both the poetic section that precedes and the one that is to follow. It shows us retrospectively another connection between the dukes of Brittany and the particular example of the author himself ("tout homme puelt estre dict prince, en tant qu'il a receu de Dieu gouvernement d'ame"): both they and he are princes. At the same time it prepares us for the final section because it puts in a more general light the "definitions" (p. 35, l. 114) of the virtues that will be found there. Especially apt for leaders of men, these virtues, we are to understand, are yet necessary for all men. Once the vision of Raison vanishes, the author wakes up, "comme celluy qui tresgrandement desira voir materiellement et de regard corporel ce qu'en songe et fantaisie m'estoit apparu" (like one who much desired to see materially and with physical sight what had appeared to me in dream and fantasy; p. 35, ll. 119–21). All he finds is the book, *Conscience*, left behind by Raison. "And here," he says in effect, "it is." A perfect introduction to the concluding—and by far the longest—section of the work.

Yet a certain question nags. Who is the author of this book, and who its audience? The question is perhaps not so simple as it sounds. The answer seems obvious, at least to the first query: Raison is, of course, the author of the treatise called *Conscience*. But what does this allegory mean? In the Christian context, it means that God, the source of all knowledge, working through moral reason, informs one's conscience, that is, one's own awareness and judgment of one's own thoughts and acts. To enable conscience rightly to judge in all the varying circumstances of life in the world, the cardinal virtues must be understood and put into practice. This is the theory of Christian living allegorized by *Les Lunettes*.[44] In terms of its fiction, Dame Raison, the author of *Conscience*, then gives her book to another author. We know that the recipient is an author because he has already written a work in poetry and prose, in which he figures as a first-person narrator, a work we have just read. This other author (whose name, although it is never mentioned in the text, we know to be Jean Meschinot) is to be the reader of Raison's book— and his only role (or nearly his only role, as we shall see) in the third part is to read it, but "out loud," as it were, for other envisaged readers; it is in this way that he takes on the function of a teacher. Yet it is evident that the first person, the "I," of the first section wants us to know that it is itself the author of that very book. I have already referred to those lines in which Raison tells the writer that her wit ("sens") will allow him to compose the work of which he could not formerly even conceive (LXXX, ll. 10–12).

Just as there are two authors, then, and two books, there are two levels on which the reader must understand this text. On the level of the fiction, wrapped in its allegory, Raison is the author and "je, Meschinot" the reader of the "most beautiful little book" (p. 34, l. 80), while on the level of the reader's reality, "je, Meschinot" is the author of the same book (as well as of what precedes it in the whole work) and "nous" (which is also the "vous" designated by the real author) are its readers. The relationship between the two authors, the one fictional and the other real, is already clear: Meschinot, becoming "reasonable," and having "learned reason," becomes, in a way, Raison—and can therefore write the book. The relationship between the two putative audiences remains yet to be entirely spelled out. What is evident is that there is here the same highly self-conscious sense of authorship that we found in *Le Livre des quatre dames*, for example, when Alain Chartier takes a book made of the very discourses he has just been hearing to be judged by his lady in Paris. The level of fiction and the level of reality are both kept before us: we know (nor are we allowed to forget) that Meschinot is really the author—and how could a real book fall out of a dream, anyway? The author is playing with his statute as author, as he is with our statute as readers. The play is not nearly so developed as it will become some seventy years later in Rabelais,[45] for example, but it is there, nonetheless, and it shows an already subtle awareness of the shifting line between "fiction" and "reality." It should warn us, once more, that any plain autobiographical interpretation of such works must be subject to caution.

   It is doubtless the third and final section of *Les Lunettes des Princes* that seems at once the strangest and the least interesting to a modern reader, both on account of what it lacks and on account of what it includes. No poetic persona bewailing his fate; no historical references; strange concatenations of rhymes ending hundreds of lines (2,039 in all) of banal moral pronouncement and dire warnings of what lies in store for sinful man. "Nothing would be drearier than his book," writes Henry Guy, "if the blunt outspokenness of the admonitions addressed to the great ones of this world didn't occasionally catch one's attention."[46] Slight praise indeed. Pierre Champion is more sympathetic to the man; he admires the same "outspokenness" as Guy and mentions further the real interest of a few other passages: one on the equality of all humankind, another on the miseries of war experienced by the peasant, a third on the ideal prince. But he refers nonetheless severely to "the author's bizarre taste, and also the tedium that emanates from this part of the *Lunettes*."[47] Given its vast success in its day, these criticisms of the work obviously do not reflect the opinions of the public in the late fifteenth and early sixteenth centuries. As we have done for the first two parts, let us try to discover in the last part what, within the poetic conventions of the time, may have accounted for its popularity.

All of our readings of late medieval poetry in the previous chapters have made us aware that the contemporary audience did not expect thematic originality; no more can we. What could attract them was an ingenious presentation of the traditional, accepted themes: love, death, Fortune, the Virgin, sin, poverty, and the rest. One way this ingeniousness is expressed in the kind of didactic work with which we are concerned is in the allegorical emblem or idea— mirror, journey, breviary, battle (I think in the last connection of *Le Champion des dames*)—around which its many lessons are organized and which serves to unify it. We have seen how cleverly Meschinot uses the striking figure of the eyeglasses for this purpose. In the prose segment, we observed that the tension of the enigma created by the first part ("Where are the eyeglasses?") is at last released, and the full energy of the emblem and its pairing with the "princes" of the title, in the expanded meaning of that word, is ready to be used for the moral, didactic ends of the last part. There, the allegory will be fully worked out. Each of the four times in the preceding sections that the spectacles have been mentioned by either Raison or the author (stanzas LXIX and LXXXI; pp. 34, ll. 74–77, and 35, ll. 115–17), their four parts are given in the same order, and this will be the order of the exposition of the allegory. Near the beginning of the section devoted to each virtue, we are reminded of its status as part of the central allegory of the spectacles and of its relationship to the others. Thus prudence "est de tes lunettes l'une," Raison tells her reader (l. 13); "Justice, verrine tresclere, / Par ou les princes doibvent lire" (Justice, pellucid lens through which princes should read) begins the next section (ll. 565–66). The reciprocity between the parts becomes clearer as more of them are defined, as the example of fortitude shows:

> En Force est Prudence mise
> > Et assise;
> Justice y est bien comprinse
> > Et submise:
> Dont les lunettes se font,
> Qui sont de belle devise.
> > Or les vise.

1140

1145

Prudence is put in place and stabilized by Fortitude, which also includes and undersets Justice: thus are the glasses made, and they are well devised. Now look at them.

And the whole allegory is summarized when Raison presents the last of the four virtues, temperance. I shall quote at length because the text demonstrates the very careful way in which Meschinot has composed his treatise:

> Toutes vertus en elle [temperance] se conservent
> Et les berilles de repture preservent
> > Qu'elle conjoint;
> Composeement en estat tient et joinct
> Les lunettes et les mect a droit point,
> Qui aultrement certes ne seroyent point
> > Assez entieres.
> Ainsi se sont ycy quatre matieres,
> Car Prudence et Justice premieres
> Les deux verrines rendent nettes et cleres,
> > Force ensement,
> Comme j'ay dict des le commencement.
> > · · ·
> Pour parfaire donc cestes lunettes,
> Dame Atrempance, je maintien que l'une estes
> Qui les tendrez tousjours clerres et nettes,
> > Sans separer.

1590

1595

1610

All virtues are preserved in Temperance, and they keep the lenses that she conjoins from breaking; she holds and joins the spectacles carefully in the right shape and keeps them there; indeed, otherwise they wouldn't be complete. Thus there are here four matters, for Prudence and Justice first make the two lenses clean and clear, Fortitude too, as I've said from the first. . . . To complete, then, these spectacles, Lady Temperance, I claim that you are the one who will always keep them clear and perfect, unbreakable.

More explicitly than the opening lines of the sections devoted to the first three virtues, these verses insist not only on the individual role of the virtue in question but also on its place in the whole. While temperance, like the pin of the eyeglasses, aligns all the others and holds them together (ll. 1588–92), the wordplay in lines 1597 and 1609—"nettes et cleres," "clerres et nettes"—shows that all of them, prudence and justice, fortitude and temperance too, tend toward the same end of clarity and integrity.

The same passage is useful in another way as well, for it reminds us of the identity of the speaker throughout the entire third part of *Les Lunettes*. All the commentators on the work imply that the personification of each virtue speaks in turn directly to Meschinot. One finds in Champion's account casual references to the "speeches that the cardinal virtues are going to give to Meschinot," for example, or a phrase like "Meschinot . . . has put in the mouth of Temperance."[48] Zumthor writes of "Justice's monologue," and even the careful Martineau-Génieys seems to think that the four sections of this part are composed of the speeches given by each of the virtues.[49] But it is not the virtues who do the talking; as line 1599 in the quotation above recalls, it is, rather, Raison—the author of the book. It is clear, for instance, that she addresses Dame Attrempance: "je maintien que l'une estes" (l. 1608), as she does all the other virtues. When first she speaks of justice, for example, she claims that "je, Raison, toujours la guyde" (I, Reason, always guide her; l. 577), and she concludes the section with "Mes parolles cy finiront / De Justice" (I'll stop speaking here of Justice; ll. 1132–33). I insist on this identification of the "I" here because it seems to me important for an understanding of Meschinot's art to realize that he does not simply present a series of abstract allegorical entities—the cardinal virtues—who each speak in turn. A portion of his "originality" consists, instead, in the presentation by Raison of these virtues as parts of a pair of glasses. Surely this goes some way toward explaining the contemporary appeal of the text.

So it is Raison who tells the reader of the qualities of each virtue in turn and of why each is necessary in the Christian conduct of human affairs, which leads in each case to that major affair of each believer, his or her own death and salvation. This general schema is followed for each virtue, but with a varying emphasis. In her first lesson, on prudence, Raison begins in a general way, reminding us of our ultimate end and of the necessity for each of us—and even for popes, emperors, kings, dukes, and counts (l. 123)—of being able to render a good account of our life at the last day:

> Ainsi te souviengne tousdis   125
> Que des faictz, vouloirs et tous dictz
> Te fauldra compter a ce jour:
> Pource n'ayme tant le sejour
> Du brief temps que dure ce monde
> Que ne faces ton ame monde.   130

So always remember that you must make an account of all your deeds, intentions, and words on that day: thus love not so much your brief stay in this world that you don't have time to purify your soul.

The idea of damnation ensuing because of an impure soul leads into the exposition of the seven capital sins that occupies the largest part of the section. In the next section, devoted to justice, Raison emphasizes the literal meaning of princes, always present along with the figurative meaning that has been explained to us; this is natural in explaining what should be the preeminent virtue of a ruler—"Royal virtue," Montaigne will write, after so many others, "seems to consist most of all in justice."[50] These considerations preface a double development. The first treats unjust rulers, who cause the misery of their people but who are, from the eschatological point of view, no different from them. The second castigates more particularly the corruption of justice at every level.

Although Raison again addresses both kinds of "princes" when she speaks, in the following section, on fortitude, it is not surprising that a considerable part of it is directed toward those who "hold high places" (l. 1419). "Fuiez injustes querelles" (Flee unjust disputes; l. 1439), she implores these rulers: the consequences of war are catastrophic. Moreover, "le povre peuple en est las" (the poor people are weary of it; l. 1464). Finally, in the last section, Raison lets Dame Attrempance speak for herself, or to be exact, she quotes her at length. This is the shortest of the four presentations, but at 380 lines, it still affords time for the kind of lesson of moderation that belongs typically to the traditional notion of the French character, and that neither the seventeenth nor the eighteenth century would gainsay:

> Conduy tes sens   1810
> En telle forme que Raison ne soyes sans
> Et a Folie jamais ne te consens,
> Ne monte hault ne trop bas ne descends,
>   Le moyen garde,
> De toutes pars mect en toy seure garde: 1815
> L'on oyt tes dicts, tes gestes on regarde,
> Bien sera dyct sy aulcun ne te larde.

> Direct your senses so that you are never without Reason, and
> never give in to Folly; don't rise too high or descend too low,
> keep the middle way; watch carefully on all sides: people hear
> your words, they watch your deeds; it will be well if nobody
> can mock you.

It is the very tone of certain morals of La Fontaine or of Orgon's reasonable brother-in-law.

From the very first line and throughout the four sections, Raison addresses the reader in the singular, that stern singular of Biblical and preacherly admonition: "Homme miserable et labille, / Qui vas contrefaissant l'abille" (Miserable and wayward man, you go on pretending to be clever; ll. 1–2). Since Meschinot is reading the book, he can take this as being aimed at himself—but so can any other reader. The pages of *Conscience* are not pointed at any particular "person," but at all. That this "tu" is exemplary is even clearer

than it was in the first part because Meschinot is no longer an Acteur
here—that is, on the level of the fiction, neither actor nor author.
The Acteur has become the Lecteur, and all *lecteurs*. And the other
name for these readers, we must remember, is "princes." Yet distinc-
tions will be made in this implied group of readers, for Raison passes
at will between the two kinds of princes, between the "tu" of Every-
man and the "vous" of the ruling class: "Seigneurs, servez vous des
loyaulx!" (My lords, be served by loyal men!; l. 332). In the section
devoted to justice (and therefore, we have noted, more especially to
the literal kind of prince), this collective "vous" is frequently re-
duced to the singular, with a consequent increase in its affective
value: "Seigneur, qui as souverain regne, / Gouverne tes subgectz en
paix, / Fais que Justice sur eulx regne" (My lord, as sovereign ruler
govern your subjects in peace, let Justice reign over them; ll. 593–
95); "Seigneur, tu es de Dieu bergier" (My lord, you are a shepherd
of God; l. 663). When Raison admonishes in turn those who, under
the ruler, administer justice, she speaks to them both as a class and as
individuals: "Juges, vous en [i.e., de justice] avez la garde" (Judges,
you stand guard over justice; l. 915); "Juge, qui es sans equité"
(Judge without equity; l. 964); "Ne cuidez jamais, advocas, / Que
Dieu vous deigne pardonner, / Si bien n'avisez a voz cas" (Lawyers,
never believe that God will deign to pardon you if you don't attend
well to your cases; ll. 1034–36); "Par haine, don, craincte ou faveur, /
Ne varie en ton temoignage" (Do not shift your testimony through
hatred, bribe, fear, or favor; ll. 1104–5); "Toy, clerc, qui les procés
escrips" (You, clerk, who transcribe the trials; l. 1125). This variation
in address continues to the end, thus insisting on the double mean-
ing of "princes" and ensuring at the same time the widest possible
audience for the work.

The interest of this audience in what appears to us to be the
banalities enunciated by Dame Raison regarding each of the virtues
was doubtless increased by the variations in presentation and address
we have just reviewed. But even more than in the first part, Raison's
discourse here is enhanced by all the resources of prosody. In each

section, Meschinot varies the meter, influenced perhaps by the variety of the meters in the *Consolation of Philosophy*, as well as by the poetic fashion of the time. And in each section, this change in meter is accompanied both by astonishing rhyme-play and by a distinct tone created by the interaction of all of these elements. The use of rhyme in the last part of *Les Lunettes* can only strike the modern reader as excessive—or what I prefer to call intense. We saw some examples of this intensification in rhyme in the first part, used at those moments of strongest emotional intensity to underline the author's psychological states. Its display is greater in the last part of the work, although here, since the author is Reason herself, it is not psychological states that predominate, but rather argument and admonition.

The reader will remember in the early part of *Les Lunettes* the occurrence of rare and difficult rhymes (e.g., *-ouche*, *-erme*, *-acque*, *-ocque*) and at three important junctures, of *rimes enchaînées*. Before we look at how rhyme functions in Raison's discourse, it will be useful first to distinguish these rhymes—and rhyme in late medieval poetry in general—as being of two sorts, which I shall call vertical and horizontal. All rhyme is in one sense vertical: for it to exist at all, the significant phonic element at the end of an initial line must be followed at some point in the poem by a line ending with an identical phonic element. Put another way, although we usually write out rhyme schemes linearly, they represent in fact a succession of sounds in a text printed vertically. The poet can emphasize this verticality by choosing rhymes that are odd or rare and by using end-stopped lines. But one can speak also, in French poetry, of horizontal rhyme, in which the axis is created by sounds repeating themselves lengthwise along the line. The origin of this may well be the notion in French prosody of the "richness" of rhyme depending on the number of repeated phonemic elements. The linear or horizontal quality of the rhyme is emphasized as this "richness" is increased. Logically, it is easy to go from the repetition of an entire syllable with its vowel and consonant or consonants to the repetition of two or more entire syllables. Examples of various forms of this kind of horizontal duplication (or, in some cases, triplication) of the basic phonetic repetition necessary for rhyme abound in the poetry of the time, particularly in that of the Rhétoriqueur poets, but one finds it still in Clément Marot in the sixteenth century. One of his chansons includes a charming example of two kinds of horizontal rhyme, the first stanza being in *rimes enchaînées*, the second in *rimes couronnées*:[51]

Dieu gard ma Maistresse et regente,
Gente de corps et de façon.
Son cuer tient le mien en sa tente
Tant et plus d'ung ardant frisson.
S'on m'oyt poulser sur ma chanson   5
Son de lucz ou harpes doulcettes,
C'est espoir qui sans marrisson
Songer me faict en amourettes.

La blanche colombelle belle
Souvent je voys priant criant: 10
Mais dessoubz la cordelle d'elle
Me jecte ung oeil friant, riant,
En me consommant et sommant
A douleur qui ma face efface,
Dont suis le reclamant amant   15
Qui pour l'outrepasse trespasse.

God keep my Mistress and Ruler handsome in body and manner. Her heart keeps mine mightily in her power with an ardent thrill. If you hear me play my song with sound of lutes or sweet harps, it comes from hope that gaily makes me think of dalliance.

I often entreat the pretty white dove: but under her sway she throws me a saucy, laughing glance, fulfilling me—and summoning me to a pain that will deface my countenance; whereby I am the lover earnestly begging, who dies for her who is unsurpassed (*or*: for his transgression).

Poems with single or double rhymes at the hemistich, or with three consonant syllables at the end of lines—these and others are listed in those compendia of prosodic technique of the time, the *arts de seconde rhétorique*. It is entirely possible, of course, to combine vertical and horizontal rhyme; pushed to an extreme, this results in so-called "holorime" verses, in which all syllables of two successive lines rhyme with each other. Examples can be found long before Hugo's celebrated couplet ("Gall, amant de la Reine, alla, tour magnanime / Galamment de l'Arène à la Tour Magne à Nîmes"), although doubtless because of their extreme difficulty they are rare even in the verbal fireworks of the Rhétoriqueurs. The example below is the work of Guillaume Crétin (d. 1525), who might be called a specialist in *rimes équivoquées*. It comes from a decasyllabic poem of seventytwo verses in *rimes plates*; the first four syllables of the second line of every couplet rhyme, in *équivoque*, with the first four syllables of the preceding line, and the last two or three syllables of the couplet's lines rhyme as well. At one point, Crétin pushes these six or seven identical phonemes even further and makes one entire line echo exactly the preceding verse: "Tournay en tour sa folle outrecuidance / Tournoye en tour, se affolle oultre qui dance" (Tournai in turn turned all about its foolish presumption, and thus is undone the more the one who "dances").[52] Rhyme can reach no further (except in an alexandrine).

For many late medieval poets, any adequate schematic representation of the rhyme scheme of their verse is thus not easy to devise. It might seem to be relatively simple for Dame Raison's presentation of the virtue of prudence, for the entire section of 564 octosyllabic lines is in couplets, which produce, in principle, the simplest rhyme scheme of all: a a b b c c , and so on. But this leaves out entirely the fact that a large majority of the verses end in leonine rhymes, with two completely homophonic syllables, or in *rimes équivoquées*, which add a play on words, often of a punning sort, to the lateral intensity of the rhyme.[53] The first six lines of the section illustrate in turn, for example, *rimes équivoquées* of two (not counting the feminine ending), four, and three syllables (I italicize the rhyme words):

Homme miserable et *labille*,
Qui vas contrefaissant *l'abille*,
Menant estat *desordonné*,

Croy qu'enfer est *desor donné*
A qui ne vivra *sainctement*,
Ou l'Escripture *saincte ment*.

Miserable and wayward man, you go on pretending to be clever, leading an unruly life; you must believe that hell is the reward of him who will not live devoutly, or the Holy Scripture lies.

Occasionally rhymes of even one syllable (again discounting the final *-e*) present the same character, as in lines 13 and 14: "Elle est de tes lunettes l'une: / Tel berille n'a soubz la lune" (She is one of your lenses: there's not another such lens under the moon [i.e., under the sun]. Infrequently, in this section, Meschinot uses "ordinary" rich rhyme: "Pape, empereur, roy, duc, et conte, / Se tu n'en sceiz rendre bon conte" (Pope, emperor, king, duke, and count, if you cannot render a good account of them; ll. 123–24). Inventing a shorthand notation for this rhyming diversity, even assuming as the basis for rhyme the complete syllable and not a single vowel phoneme, would yield a complex formula in which the extent of rhyme along every line would have to be indicated by showing the number of syllables involved in the rhyme at the end of the line. For the first six lines of the section cited above this might look something like a(2) a(2) b(4) b(4) c(3) c(3). But even this, obviously impractical for a text of over 500 lines, would not convey the equivocal—or what might be termed the intellectual—side of the *rimes équivoquées*.

It is here that we touch the difference in function between vertical and horizontal rhyme, for it is evident that in such lines the poet combines phonetic play with intellectual—or at least mental—play, in the very rhyme itself. Readers of French poetry are not much used to this, for since the development of the Classic canon the ludic and even ludicrous side has been emphasized at the expense of poetic effect. Such punning play with intense rhyme continued to exist, however, despite the Classical strictures. *Rimes équivoquées* can be found in the twentieth century in the work of Louis Aragon and Tristan Derème, and Mallarmé can use it to considerable effect in his *Prose (pour Des Esseintes)* (emphasis mine):

Gloire du long *désir, Idées*
Tout en moi s'exaltait *de voir*
La famille *des iridées*
Surgir à ce nouveau *devoir*.

Glory of the long desire, Ideas—everything in me grew ex-
cited to see the family of the Irideae rise up at this new duty.

It might be claimed that Meschinot's almost constant use of
rimes équivoquées in the first section of Raison's book has as much
poetic justification as Mallarmé's display of it in *Prose* does. Raison,
after all, is speaking—and the slight increase in intellectual effort
required to understand such phonetic recombinations is entirely
justified: this is reason's play with rhyme. Yet even here the fifteenth-
century poet is careful to vary his effects; not every line presents the
same *jeu*. Some passages are made particularly striking by the cease-
less abundance of horizontal rhyme. In the following example it
relentlessly drives home the lesson of human death and putrefaction.
The effect becomes even more terrifying as much through the insis-
tence in every line on the [r] sound—not, it must be remembered,
the modern uvular—and the run-on lines (ll. 101–2, 102–3, 104–5,
105–6) as through the sinister evocation of the Last Judgment:

Quant morte sera ta charongne
Puante, quier qui ta char ongne
D'aulcune odorante liqueur:
Homme ne vouldra, car ly cueur
Ne pourroit durer a sentir   105
Tel odeur, ne s'y assentir.
Aprés, au jugement yras:
Croy tu qu'au Juge mentira,
Qui sest tout? Ne t'y attens point.
Sa rigueur en cestuy temps poingt: 110
Plus n'y aura misericorde.
Davantaige, misere y corde
Dur cordaige pour les damnez
De la lignee d'Adam nez:

When you're just a stinking corpse, try to find someone to
annoint your flesh with fragrant balm: no one will want to, for

the heart could not bear to smell such an odor or to agree to do it. Afterward, you'll go to judgment: do you think you will lie to the Judge, who knows everything? Don't expect to! His severity will appear at that time: there will be no more pity. Moreover, misery there twists cruel ropes for the damned, born of the line of Adam.

Prudence, says Raison, consists in thinking on such things and in reflecting also on the consequences of lying and of yielding to the temptations of the seven deadly sins.[54] Time after time, Raison's lessons and warnings will be underscored by the horizontal replication of rhyme. Throughout the section the reader's attention will be solicited by the effort needed to understand—one could say "to figure out"—the meaning of these densely rhymed couplets. I think this figuring-out, this series of small decodings, is meant also to give pleasure to the reader (here again one is surprisingly close to Mallarmé); even while teaching, the poet does not forget to ensure the delectation of his public: "[mixing] the useful with the agreeable," as the *Ars poetica* recommends. This is how such moral poetry avoided appearing for its public "morose" or "dismal" or "tedious," or any of the other adjectives applied to it by so many modern critics. This is how it adheres to the principle of poetic joy enunciated by Guillaume de Machaut: "Et s'on fait de triste matiere, / Si est joieuse la maniere / Dou fait . . ." (Chap. 1, p. 30). And the function of such intense rhyme goes even further, for it works in the poet's favor as well, affording him another way of showing his own skill at rhyming—that is, at what was then thought to be the essential and distinctive quality of poetry. Our pleasure and instruction are ensured by the poet's joyful and skillful exercise of his art: "pleasing and instructing the reader at the same time," to complete the Horatian tag.

Meschinot never loses sight of this goal, and in each of the following sections he exercises his art in a different way in order to attain it. In the second, the discourse on justice, Raison begins by addressing, once more, Everyman (l. 570) and by recalling his status as a prince (l. 566), but as a prince with duties, emphasizing them by her use of *devoir* in both verbal and substantive forms (ll. 566, 568, 571):

> Justice, verrine tresclere,   565
> Par ou les princes doibvent lire,
> Qui aux bons et maulvais esclere
> Quel chemin ils doibvent eslire,
> Fait assavoir a tous que l'ire
> De Dieu viendra, saches de voir,   570
> Sur ceulx qui ne feront debvoir.

> Justice—that pellucid lens through which princes should read, which shows to good and bad alike the pathway they should choose—makes known to all that the wrath of God will come down (understand this truly) on those who do not do their duty.

But she soon turns (l. 593) to those ruling princes whose special charge it is to ensure justice for all the others, and the rest of the section, as we have seen, is devoted more particularly to their instruction. Although Meschinot continues to use a fairly high percentage of *rimes équivoquées*, and although this sermon on justice of 574 lines is about the same length as that on prudence, with its 564 lines, he differentiates between them in a number of ways. To begin with, its overall shape is different, for it is structured in strophes made up of seven octosyllabic verses rhyming a b a b b c c, not an unusual stanza in the fifteenth century.[55] These *septains* were thought to be particularly appropriate for the enunciation of "an authority or a common proverb or [a line] of other serious substance," according to Pierre Fabri in *Le Grand et Vrai Art de pleine rhétorique* (1521).[56] Meschinot follows this tradition in almost three-quarters of the eighty-two strophes devoted to justice.

The rhetorical term for the appearance of such brief sententious matter in a text is "epiphonema"; the presence of epiphonemas in literary texts—and especially the proverb—has been of much interest to medievalists.[57] We have seen it briefly before in a ballade of Alain Chartier, and we shall find a variation of it again in licentious verse in the next essay. We need not here enter into the linguistic and literary issues raised by the author's inscription of a proverb or maxim or some such authoritative statement in his text. It is clear that such insertions relate the text to a social tradition and bring the weight of authority to it. It seems peculiarly appropriate to use such received truths in a presentation of justice, concerned as it is with the proper functioning of law: these lines act like so many affirmations of the law. Often, even when the final line of the strophe is not a proverb, it resembles one in its categorical brevity: "Povres gens ont trop de destresse" (The poor are too much straitened; l. 760); "On doibt aymer sa nation" (One should love one's country; l. 802); "Chacun son ame a garder a" (Every man should keep watch over his own soul; l. 816). At one point in Raison's address to princes and prelates, Meschinot piles up three proverbial sayings at the end of a single strophe; even *rime équivoquée* appears pale, reduced as it is to one example (ll. 890–91), in the face of such insistence:

> Pensez pourquoy Dieu vous a faitz
> Et vers luy ne soyez ingratz.
> Mettez rayson dans tous vos faictz,
> Combien que soyez gros et gras.   890
> Sçachez que moust vault mieulx qu'esgras.
> Bonté est plus que mal propice.
> Truye ne scet que vault espice.

> Think why God has made you and do not be ungrateful toward him. Make reason a part of all your deeds, however much a bigwig you may be. Know that new wine is better than sour grape juice. Goodness is more meet than evil. Sows don't know what spices are.

The effect of the strong iteration of these truths throughout the section is considerable, and it combines with the relatively short stanzaic form to produce some particularly vigorous passages. One thinks inevitably of Villon when Meschinot evokes, for the same reason, the Cemetery of the Saints Innocents in Paris: all, prince and pauper alike, are indistinguishable in death, their bodies gone the way of all flesh, as he assures us in the last line of the strophe, with its oracular ring. The septain that follows is equally affective in its contrast between the proud who think the earth is made for them and the peasant who tills that same earth; the last line, again, sums up the preceding six and points the moral:

> Si tu vas a Saint Innocent
> Ou il y a d'ossement grant tas,
> Ja ne congnoistras entre cent   735
> Les os des gens des grans estas
> D'avec ceulx qu'au monde notas
> En leur vivant, povres et nus:
> Les corps vont dont ilz sont venuz.

> Hommes ont doncques tous ensemble   740
> Povre entrée et dolent yssue,
> Combien qu'aucuns sont a qui semble
> Que la terre est pour eulx tissue
> Et que le bon homme qui sue
> Au labeur, n'est riens envers eulx: 745
> Aveugle est tel qui a vers yeulx.

If you go to the Cemetery of the Holy Innocents, where there are great heaps of bones, you'll never recognize in a hundred the bones of people of high estate from those you saw, in life, poor and naked: the bodies disappear whence came those bones.

All men have thus together a wretched entrance and a painful exit, even though there are some to whom it seems that the earth has been made for them and that the laborer who sweats at his toil is nothing compared with them: some are blind whose eyes are bright.

The next strophes continue the comparison between the powerful and the weak—"Or visons l'entree et la fin / De l'empereur et d'ung porchier" (Now let us look at the beginning and the end of the emperor and of a swineherd; ll. 747–48)—and emotion mounts, to the point where, in an effective return to the first person of the author, the poet appears to forget for an instant that it is Raison and not he who is supposed to be speaking:

> Si j'ay maison pour ma demeure,
> Bon lict, cheval, vivres, vesture,   755

Le roy n'a vaillant une meure
En plus que moy, selon nature.
On luy faict honneur: c'est droiture;
Mais il meurt sans emporter rien.
Peu vaut le tresor terrien.   760

If I have a house to live in, a good bed, a horse, food, clothing,
the king has nothing worth a fig more than I, by nature. Honor
is done to him; that's only right; but he dies without taking
anything with him. Earthly treasure is little worth.

But this "je," never really personalized, is soon reabsorbed into the
"nous" of all of us, which reappears in the epiphonema, preceded by
a discreet reminder of the deaths of the dukes deplored in the first
part of *Les Lunettes*:

Quant au corps gueres d'avantage   775
Ne voy d'un prince aux plus petis.
Les aulcuns s'en vont devant aage
A la mort, povres et chetifz;
Aultres suyvent leurs appetiz
Pour aulcun temps, et puis se meurent.   780
Noz oeuvres sans plus nous demeurent.

As for the body, I see little advantage in the prince over the
least of men. Some go off to death before their time, poor and
wretched; others follow their appetites for a time, and then
they die. Only our works remain to us.

Although most of the rhymes of the foregoing stanza are
leonine, in the other lines of this section the pleasure of rhyme is
generally of a different degree than that in the preceding section, for
it comes more from the constant presence of simple rich rhyme than
from the intense use of lengthier horizontal rhyme, so remarkable in
the discourse on prudence. To it is added, however, another kind of
pleasure for the reader: that of discovering a known proverb (or
something resembling one) aptly adapted to the arguments concern-
ing justice—and adapted also to an octosyllabic line with an obliga-
tory rhyme at the end. Thus does Meschinot combine for his reader
the pleasure of recognition with the pleasure of innovation.

Raison ends her lesson on justice with a reminder of the final accounting everyone must make before the judgment seat of God. Earlier she had told her readers of the four evils of the judicial system—fear, favor, hatred (that is, of the criminal and not the crime), and bribery. And she had devoted a number of verses to the exposition of these evils (ll. 929–95, 1104–10), which "trouble justice in many places" and are both forbidden by law and condemned by God (ll. 920–25). Now, in her conclusion, which provides a further instance of Meschinot's careful structuring of his text, Raison reasserts that none of them will be of any use before the last Judge:[58]

> Mes parolles cy fineront
> De Justice, quant a present,
> Mais a la fin trestous yront
> Au siege ou Dieu sera present.   1135
> Là, paour, faveur, crainte ou present,
> Riens n'y vauldra faire des faulx.
> Chacun congnoistra ses desfaulx.

I shall stop speaking here of Justice, for the present, but at the end, all will go to the seat where God will be present. There, fear, favor, awe, or bribe—nothing there will serve to bear false witness. Everyone will acknowledge his faults.

A striking shift in metrical form distinguishes the next presentation, that of the virtue of fortitude. Instead of the isometric octosyllabic lines to which we have been accustomed since the beginning of Raison's book, we find a series of twenty-two heterometric strophes, each of twenty lines. Twelve of them are heptasyllabic; eight are trisyllabic, arranged in a pattern of two rhymes in the following fashion (the superscript indicates the number of syllables in the line): a^7 a^3 a^7 a^3 b^7 a^7 a^3 a^7 a^3 b^7 a^7 a^3 a^7 a^3 b^7 a^7 a^3 a^7 a^3 b^7—that is, a cinquain repeated four times. Meschinot needs therefore, for each stanza, sixteen rhymes in *a* and four in *b*. As in each of the preceding sections, he has not set himself an easy task, but the difficulty here is of a different sort. The poet is not obliged to find rare rhymes or to invent combinations of words resulting in striking horizontal rhyme, nor is he constrained to adapt sententious sayings to fit an octosyllabic line. His task, rather, is to choose rhymes susceptible of sixteen variations, in two meters; this in fact precludes any very rare rhyme in the *a* lines, since sixteen versions of a rhyme like -*uc* would be impossible to find. And even for the *b* rhymes, Meschinot does not choose very difficult endings (with the exception of -*erme* in ll. 1323ff). Clearly the play is elsewhere. There is great variation in the rhymes used in the entire section, for example, only one of them being repeated.[59] The structure of the stanza itself is rare,[60] but its real originality in Meschinot's hands comes from the combination of the two rhymes, in the proportion of four to one, with the heterometric verses. The short lines are often used with particular effectiveness to emphasize a point just made, by means of another verb or a second adjective: "En Force est Prudence mise / Et assise" (By Fortitude is Prudence put in place and stabilized; ll. 1139–40); "Force donc le feix soustient / Porte et tient" (Fortitude thus upholds the weight, bears and holds it; ll. 1159–60). The apposition of sixteen adjectives rhyming in -*able* followed by sixteen in -*euse* is especially striking in the prayer to the Creator that forms the twentieth and twenty-first stanzas of the section (and in one important manuscript ends it). I shall quote only the first of the two, as an example of the way Meschinot employs to great effect both the rhythm and the rhyme he has chosen to give to Raison in her presentation of fortitude. As befits the subject, the poet's technique is here both forceful and resourceful:

Hault createur pardurable,
    Treslouable,   1520
A tes servans secourable,
    Piteable,
De tous biens source et racine,
Tant est ce monde damnable,
    Detestable,   1525
Incertain et decevable,
    Variable,
Ou n'a de bonté nul signe,
Des humains trop guerroyable,
    Peu durable,   1530

Meschant et abhominable,
  Miserable,
Car de tous maulx les assigne,
Mais t'amour incomparable,
  Veritable,   1535
Ta passion cheritable,
  Amyable,
Leur donnes pour medicine.

Great creator—eternal, praiseworthy, helpful to those who
serve you, compassionate, the source and origin of all good—
this world is so damnable, detestable, uncertain, deceptive, and
changeable, unmarked by goodness, fit for war by men, short-
lived, evil and abominable, miserable, because it allots them
every woe. But your love, incomparable, true, your merciful
and gracious passion, you give them as a remedy.

Implicit in these lines, as throughout the work, is the importance of
the abundance of language. And one sees here with particular clar-
ity, too, that this same abundance is—must be—a sign of artistry as
well. This effect of copiousness seems in fact to be one of the distinc-
tive marks of the medieval moral treatise.

We have already remarked that the final section begins with
a resumé of the relationship between the four parts of the pair of
spectacles as a prelude to the presentation of the last virtue, tem-
perance. It also inaugurates a very interesting rhythmic change, in
which the principle of heterometric lines is kept but within a struc-
ture entirely different from that of the preceding section. Instead
of strophes, Meschinot chains four-line units one to the other by
making the phonemes at the end of every fourth line—a four-
syllable line—become the rhyming sound (or sounds) for the follow-
ing three decasyllabic lines. The scheme can be represented like this:
$a^{10} a^{10} a^{10} b^4 b^{10} b^{10} b^{10} c^4 c^{10} c^{10} c^{10} d^4$, and so on for 460 lines to the end of
the work. There is a subtle rhythmical relation between the ten-
syllable line of this section and the insistent repetition of the seven-
and three-syllable couplets in the preceding part, a relation that

seems particularly appropriate to "Temperance, dame bien mesu-
ree" (l. 1579). Raison goes on to ascribe other qualities to Tem-
perance at the beginning of her lesson: she is also "sobre, paisible,
constante et asseuree" (l. 1581). These adjectives describe aptly the
meter itself, with the weight of the three decasyllabic lines pulling it
constantly forward, relieved and given a tap ahead by the recurrent
fillip of the lighter fourth line, which provides the phonetic impetus
for the next unit of longer verses.

This fourth metrical variation in Raison's book brings with it
another change: for the first time, one of the virtues is personified
and her words are quoted at length by Raison. This personification is
adumbrated in the very first line of the section—"Temperance,
dame bien mesuree"—and it is recalled when Raison addresses
"Dame Atrempance" in line 1608. It actually begins, however,
with the emphasis provided by a *rime équivoquée*, 140 lines later:
". . . quant bien presseras / Dame Attrempance, / El te dira: 'Mon
amy, aprens ce'" (when you rightly urge Lady Temperance, she will
tell you: "My friend, learn this"; ll. 1717–19). There follows, not
surprisingly from the mouth of Temperance herself, the series of
admonitions and counsel of moderation mentioned earlier, which
represent the traditional *aurea mediocritas* of the moralist. "Tiens toy
plus bas / Suffise toy de petit" (Stay lower down: be content with
little; ll. 1726–27); "Ayez [= aies] vergongne si villains sont tez dictz /
Soyes courtois, non lourd ni estourdis" (Be ashamed if your words
are base; be civil, not rude or heedless; ll. 1771–72). In lines 1826–29,
one hears an echo of Christine de Pizan's *Enseignemens moraux* for
her son:

> Mais t'applique
> A Dieu aymer, parens et bien publicque.
> Viles parolles ne mensonges n'explique
> Et au jangleur ne contens ne replicque.

> But apply yourself to loving God, parents, and the public weal.
> Use neither base words nor lies, and give no reply to prattlers
> or wranglers.

Very occasionally in this section, Meschinot employs *rime équivo-*

quée; its use in the following lines (ll. 1834–39) is all the more evidently effective (and affective) by its rarity:

> Contre prudence,
> Doulcettement l'un passe oultre qui dance;
> L'autre ne bruyt que par oultre cuydance;
> L'un a l'aultre desplaist, non cuydant ce,
>   Et, pour ce, brigue
> S'ensuyt entr'eulx et chascun faict sa ligue.

Imprudently, the one skips quietly too far; the other is noisily presumptuous; each displeases the other, not imagining the thing, and thus contention ensues between them, and each one forms his party.

As in all the other sections, both kinds of "princes" are firmly addressed; through his mouthpiece Dame Attrempance, it is clear that Meschinot has no illusions about the intemperate temptations to which rulers are subject and no qualms about telling them what they should do about it (ll. 1871–76, 1882–85):

> Si Dieu t'a mis en hault estat de prince,
> Il desire que tu ays aprins ce
> Pour gouverner mainte grande province.
>   Il te convient
> Plus avoir soing que cil qui dessoubz vient
> En bas estat.
>   · · ·
>   Mais ta plaisance,
> Ta liberté, ton eureuse naissance,
> Ta jeunesse, ta fortune et puissance
> Te seduysent et portent grant nuysance.

If God has placed you in the lofty position of a prince, he wants you to have learned this in order to govern many a great province. It is fitting that you take more care than he of low estate who comes under you. . . .
But your pleasure, your freedom, your favorable birth, your youth, your fortune and power seduce you and do you harm.

Follow sage counselors; avoid drunkenness and other vices; profit from the examples of ancient history; leave theology to the preachers; find exercise in "honest games" (l. 1943) and sport; remember that even those who have scaled worldly heights can in an instant fall to the depths. Such are the lessons of Temperance—traditional, banal, if you will, but renewed by their poetic expression.

This cautionary tone and the same metrical arrangement continue in the conclusion, which occupies the last seventy-seven lines of the work, but the speaker changes. The "je" of the narrator returns, with his disabused view of the world and references to his personal woes (ll. 1963–66):

> Voy [= Je vois] qu'en ce monde n'a que confusion.
> Ceulx qui le suyvent n'auront infusion
> D'aulcune grace, ains toute illusion
>   Rappourteront.

> I see that in this world there is but confusion. Those who follow it will get no in-pouring of any grace; rather will they bring back only illusion.

There follow final admonitions to the reader, as Everyman, to abide by the counsels of Reason; to the reader, as prince, to avoid war; and to all to direct their hearts and minds heavenward. *Les Lunettes* thus comes full circle: the authorial voice reminds the reader at the end, as it did at the very beginning, of the vagaries of Fortune, of the miseries of this life, and of the author's own bitter experience of them—"C'est la saison que par maintes fois j'eus" (That's the time I often had; l. 2029). But the prayer of the last five verses shows that moral progress will be made if "we all"—"je, Meschinot," "tu," "hommes," "vous, les princes"—stay on the right track, which is that of the virtues to which the treatise has been devoted. God's grace will come to redeem the sins of man (ll. 2034–39):

> Dieu part sa grace
> A tous nous aultres qui maintenons la trace
> De ces vertus; prions qu'on nous efface
> Tous nos pechéz, pour le veoir face a face.
> Ainsi l'outtroye Celluy qui vit et regne
> Eternellement en son hault siege et regne.

> God gives his grace to all of us who follow the pathway of these virtues; let us pray that all our sins be wiped away, so we can see

him face to face. May it thus be granted by him who lives and reigns eternally in his glorious throne and kingdom.

Thus the "nous" of the beginning returns at the end; it embraces, as does the work itself, all of mankind, and its return and repetition underscore the unity of *Les Lunettes*, realized both thematically and structurally. Like the other fifteenth-century poets whose works we have considered, Meschinot is eager to bring to his *opus magnum*, within this unity, all the variety of which he is capable, the more so in that the genre he has chosen demands it—at the very least the differing rhythms of verse and of artistic prose. We have seen that this variety is both one of voice (which alternates in the first and second parts between the author and the allegorical figure of Raison and becomes almost entirely that of Raison in the final part) and of the language in which this varied voice speaks. The strong strophic structure backed by the formidable diversity of vertical rhyme with which the work opens gives way to a prose that itself demonstrates both the high and the middle style. This is followed in turn by the quadruple display of prosodic variation in the book of Raison, which gives us another example of Meschinot's careful balancing of disparate elements within the text.

A rapid summary of the results of our prosodic investigation will make clear the manner in which he plays them off one against the other. Of the four subsections, the first and last are both non-strophic, with through-rhyme, but the first (on prudence) is made up entirely of octosyllabic couplets and the last (on temperance) of ten- and four-line units tied phonetically one to the next. The section on prudence is further distinguished from the others by its extraordinarily high percentage of horizontal rhyme. The two middle sections are both strophic, but the short septains of octosyllabic lines on justice, built on three rhymes, contrast strongly with the long twenty-line strophes on fortitude, with the astonishing tour de force of their two rhymes. The striking number of proverbs metamorphosed into poetry also gives the second part a character of its own. We have noted before the rhythmical relationship between the heterometric lines of sections 3 and 4. And the sententious nature of many of the dicta of Dame Attrempance recalls the *dictons* in section 2. Thus each section is different (and, it must be remembered, peculiarly appropriate in some way to its subject), yet related to the others. The poetic structure in this way mirrors the four parts of the spectacles; it is, in other words, a symbol of the symbol. Far from being "added" to the thought, form becomes here the image of that thought.

We are not used to thinking in just that way of Rhétoriqueur poetry, in which rhyme has often been seen as the particularly thick icing on a fairly flat cake. And so it may sometimes be. But the example of *Les Lunettes* should make us at least reconsider that judgment, for it has revealed that, once we accept the premises of this kind of poetry, rhyme and its manipulations can be potent agents indeed of what the poet wishes to say. That Meschinot was recognized as an effective communicator of certain great truths of the Christian religion by a large Francophone public for three-quarters of a century is clear from the popularity of his work. The foregoing pages have sought to demonstrate that that popularity was due not only to what he was communicating but also to how he communicated it.

This communication, as in many of the works we have considered in earlier chapters, is effected by means of a first-person narrator, the presumed author of the text, the "poète figure," the "global identity" behind the oeuvre, as Kevin Brownlee calls it in his study of Machaut.[61] But we have seen that this figure, stemming no doubt from Machaut's highly original development of his artistic self-consciousness, finds different manifestations in Christine de Pizan and Alain Chartier (and in other poets as well), according to differing emphases in the works themselves, both structural and thematic. Yet it still gives to the works of each poet, however different those works may be one from the other, a certain unity. It has been interesting to observe what happens to this poet-narrator, represented by an "I," in a moral treatise like *Les Lunettes*. Where the Acteur in such *dits* as *Le Debat des deux fortunés d'amours*, *Le Livre des quatre dames*, and *La Belle Dame sans mercy*, after an initial appearance, stands aside from (or hides behind) the actors, in this other kind of work he becomes both a protagonist and an exem-plum—as in the first part of Meschinot's text or in *Le Séjour d'hon-*

neur, for example—and then may also disappear completely, absorbed by the sinner(s), the "tu" and the "vous," to whom the work's moral lesson is addressed. Moral and didactic works are thus irresistibly drawn from the first person to the second, and back again: we (sinners all: examples) → I (a sinner: an example) → you (sinner[s]: the lesson) → I/we (examples of the lesson learned). This is the movement we have discovered in *Les Lunettes*, and its general direction is characteristic of many other *doctrinaux*, whether their form is that of the *opus magnum* or not. It may be surprising to remember that it is also very nearly the movement of "Au lecteur" at the beginning of Baudelaire's *Les Fleurs du mal*, in which the poet includes himself with all of us from the outset and then identifies himself at the end with "Tu . . . lecteur . . . / —Hypocrite lecteur, —mon semblable, —mon frère!" We modern readers, in our search for the individual poetic voice, tend often to overlook the exemplary nature of this "je," the "tu," that is, which it so easily becomes. But Baudelaire did not, nor did Meschinot or other writers like him. Brownlee's expansion of his claim that *Le Testament* "may be viewed as a kind of culmination of the entire tradition of lyric-based poets originating with Machaut, but with its roots in the *Roman de la rose* and Rutebeuf" is insightful and richly suggestive,[62] but it neglects, it seems to me, the (occasionally ironic) moralizing aspect of *Le Testament* that relates it to works like Meschinot's. With either Meschinot or Villon in mind, one can agree with Pierre-Yves Badel when he writes that "medieval didactic poetry tends to be confessional. The poet can there reveal himself in his singularity, with his opinions, his wrath, his doubts, and his distress."[63] Yet earlier in his excellent introduction to medieval French literature, the same scholar emphasizes the fact that in the Middle Ages the poet inevitably shared all the values of his society ("he exists only for the collectivity that gives him a living"[64]); with this one must, I think, concur. How does one bridge the gap, then, between the poet "revealing himself in his singularity" and the poet as the voice of the community? Meschinot (and Villon) give us, perhaps, an answer, the necessary nuance: part of being, again in Badel's words, "interdependent with a given culture and a [certain] history" is, exactly, in the case of poets operating in the moral didactic mode, showing up the ills of that society (which in a Christian context are equivalent to the sins of humankind), of which the poet, the "I," is a part. The orientation of the text, in other words, is exactly the opposite from what is found in Romantic and post-Romantic literature, where it is the individual in his distance from society that is emphasized. Baudelaire ("—mon semblable, —mon frère!"), in a curious way, is closer to Villon ("Frères humains qui après nous vivez") and to the Middle Ages—and to Meschinot—when he reasserts the fraternity of the artist and his public.[65] In *Les Lunettes des Princes*, as in so many other texts of that Christian time, one may start with an individual—but the end (that is, both where the text stops and why the text is written) is Everyman.

This apparent obliteration of the personality seems paradoxical only in a world in which the tenets of Christianity—which insist both on the value of the individual life and on the brotherhood of man—do not form the very fabric of everyday life, both public and private. As a Christian, Jean Meschinot in *Les Lunettes des Princes* asserts these truths as he and his society perceived them.[66] But he asserts as well his literary personality. Less elegant than the lyrics of a Guillaume de Machaut, less gracefully playful than the verses of a Christine de Pizan, his poetry lacks the ambiguous charm and the wit of an Alain Chartier. Music is to a degree replaced by meter, ambiguity by conviction. His subject demands it. Yet he, like many another Rhétoriqueur writer, meets those demands with inventive craftsmanship, enlivening his certitudes—his reasons, if you will— with all the resources of verbal play at his command, in both rhyme and prose.

Buried among the hundreds of lines of earnest moral entreaty in Jean Meschinot's oeuvre is another kind of entreaty that may seem curious coming from his pen. No anguished Acteur; no allegory; no Christian doctrine. We hear, instead, the straightforward, even crude demand by a man of a woman whose virginity he has taken to accord him once more those favors he has been the first to enjoy. In at least one of the early printed editions, this little rondeau follows only one page after Meschinot's prayer to the Virgin in which each line begins with one of the letters of the *Ave Maria*.[67] Far from being an anomaly, we shall see in the final essay how the existence of such "free" verse—and even its juxtaposition with poetry of an entirely different character—constitute, in the very liberty of its language, another means for the poet of asserting his artistic status.

5 ⚡ Playing Dirty: Jean Molinet and Bawdy Verse

n the preceding chapter we noted, almost in passing, Jean Meschinot's effective use of proverbs to give weight to his expression of the virtue of justice. In Chapter 3, I gave short shrift to the ballade of Alain Chartier made up of proverbial sayings, the only one in which a melancholic first-person lover does not appear. Despite my relative neglect of it, the popularity of this kind of poem, consisting partly or entirely of proverbs or maxims, was considerable in the fifteenth century. Here is Chartier's first stanza, the model for the other two:[1]

> Il n'est danger que de villain,
> N'orgueil que de povre enrichi,
> Ne si seur chemin que le plain,
> Ne secours que de vray ami,
> Ne desespoir que jalousie,
> Ne hault vouloir que d'amoureux,
> Ne paistre qu'en grant seignorie,
> Ne chere que d'omme joieux.

There is no danger like that from a churl, nor any pride like that of an enriched beggar, nor any road as sure as the high road, nor any succour like that of a true friend, no real despair except jealousy, no great purpose like a lover's, no battening like that in great lordliness, no welcome like that of a joyous man.

Villon, one recalls, gives a backhanded version of this ("Il n'est soing que quant on a fain"; There's no care like being hungry) in one of the *ballades à proverbes* found in his works, the so-called "Ballade des contrevérités."[2] But there is another parodic version of Chartier's ballade that, instead of listing proverbs turned wrong-side-to, as Villon does, plays with the idea in a different way. We find the same three eight-line strophes and four-line envoy of octosyllabic one-liners as in the Chartier poem—but in the later ballade the anonymous poet achieves an entirely different tone when he offers as the refrain the line "Ne jeu que de cul et de pointe." We are somewhat prepared for the shock of this straightforward assertion by the determinedly sensual—indeed, sexual—"verities" of the entire first stanza:*

> Il n'est aise qu'avoir argent,
> Ne menger que bonnes viandes,
> Ne vesture que draps changeant,
> Ne corps traictis que de Flamandes,
> Ne mamelles que de Normandes,   5
> Ne plaisir que de femme ensainte,
> Ne passe temps qu'entre truandes,
> Ne jeu que de cul et de pointe.[3]

> There's no pleasure like being rich, no eating like good victuals, no better covering than clean sheets, no bodies as shapely as those of Flemish women, no breasts like those of Normans, no pleasure like that from a pregnant woman, no pastime like that among trollops, no better game than tail and tool.

The other two stanzas are not quite so singleminded, but the refrain at the end of each brings us back to the *jeu*, of which the envoy reminds us one last time:

> Prince qui avez froit aux plantes,
> N'espairgnez ne salle ne cointe:
> Il n'est challeur que de deux ventres,
> Ne jeu que de cul et de pointe.

> Prince, you who have cold feet, spare neither the nasty nor the

---

*BN MS fr. 24.442, fol. 98; reprinted in Schwob, *Le Parnasse satyrique*, pp. 177–78; cited hereafter as "Schwob."

nice girl: there's no warmth like that of two bellies, no better
game than tail and tool.

When one is used to the kind of love poetry we have examined,
generally pervaded as it is by the notion of unrequited passion,
expressed with considerable decorum, or to the solemn expression in
didactic verse of some sober (though often banal) moral dictum, the
sentiments set forth with such vigor here seem at first out of place—
if refreshing—in a ballade. It is as if the author, adopting the elegant
form of the ballade, with its obligatory repetitions, set out deliber-
ately to use it to increase the shock value of his text, in much the same
way, for example—although to a different degree—that the elegant
pluperfect subjunctives and the precious turns of phrase in Sade's
Cent-vingt Journées de Sodome increase the obscenity of what is being
recounted. The same phenomenon of contrast can be found in non-
lyric form as well. In a poem with the explicit title "Comment ung
povre amoureux qui estoit en la compaignie des dames estant au
jardin de plaisance s'enhardit de deprier l'une des dames. Et les
responces de ladicte dame a ycelluy amant" (How a poor lover who
was in the company of the ladies, being in the garden of pleasure,
was bold enough to entreat one of the ladies. And the reply of the
said lady to that lover), reproduced in *Le Jardin de plaisance* (fols. 126ʳ–
29ᵛ),⁴ we find an amorous debate like the one popularized by *La
Belle Dame sans mercy*, with the same octosyllabic huitains alternat-
ing between the Amoureux, still trying to persuade his lady to love
him, and the Dame, still refusing. But she bases her refusal, this time,
not on any levelheaded objection to what she perceives as the hypoc-
risy of the courtly code, but rather on the levelheaded though per-
haps more cynical notion that money makes the world go round,
especially the world of love (fol. 127ᵛ):

> Donc vous povez facilement sçavoir
> Que grant amour commence par pecune
> Parquoy je diz qu'il en fait bon avoir
> Car par ce point aucun contente aucune.

Thus you can easily see that great love begins with money;
that's why I say it's good to have it, for by that argument any
man contents any woman.

The lover, moreover, agrees with her. But he claims that he has other virtues and only wishes to serve her, body and soul. It is the body, however, that is emphasized in the numerous sexual allusions contained in his speech, just beneath the veneer of the chivalric vocabulary (fol. 126ᵛ):

> Recevez moy s'il vous plaist à hommage
> Comme le vostre feal et sans vice,
> Pour eviter d'avoir aucun dommage,
> Car ie vous offre le courtault de service.
> Et du surplus aiez ceste notice
> Que tout est vostre, et le corps et les biens,
> Le corps pour tout—esprouvez la à la lice;
> Je vous supplie que vous n'espargnez riens.

> Please let me pay you homage as your own, faithful and fault-less, to avoid any harm, for I offer you the dray horse on duty. And moreover understand this, that everything is yours, both my body and my fortune: my body above all—try it out in the lists; I beg you to spare nothing.

The lady's speech is no less filled with erotic metaphor; she ironically admits his attraction but regrets his poverty (fol. 127ʳ):

> Vous estes beau, pas ne diz le contraire,
> Jeune, puissant, et homme de courage,
> Chief que nature a bien voulu pourtraire
> Pour congnoissance de son parfait ouvrage,
> Homme pour faire impetueuse rage,
> Fendre, briser, rompre à puissance d'armes.
> Mais quant à moy, ie crains tant ce fourrage
> Que ie ne prens nulz si povres gensdarmes.

> You are handsome, I don't deny it, young, strong, a man of courage, a head that nature has willingly drawn as evidence of her perfect work, a man adept at raging around, at cleaving, at smashing, at breaking by force of arms. But as for me, I am so afraid of this ravaging that I'll take on no man-at-arms so poor.

The poet here obviously goes much further in his play with the courtly conventions than Alain Chartier, whose language in *Belle Dame*, as in his other works, though often metaphoric, is entirely free from double entendre of this kind, just as the dialogue is free from any such sordid consideration as money.

The more one reads late medieval literature, however, especially outside the usual anthologies or manuals, the more one realizes that a considerable part of it speaks openly not only of such topics as money but of sexual matters as well. In this, as in much else, it is the inheritor of a rich earlier tradition, exemplified most notably by the *fabliaux*. These tales in verse, which transgress in both subject and diction what has usually been thought of as the "courtly" mode, were a well-developed genre by the beginning of the thirteenth century. Although the fabliau has often been dubbed "bourgeois" or "realistic" by literary historians, both its audience and its relation to its subjects have occasioned much critical discussion and reassessment of late. Per Nykrog, for instance, in a substantial study first published in 1957, almost completely reverses received scholarly opinion by maintaining that, read and appreciated at court, the fabliaux constitute a kind of courtly genre.[5] Although they seem to have fallen somewhat from favor by the fifteenth century, the same mixture of unambiguous sexual antic and unblushingly direct sexual language can be found, in prose, in the well-known *Cent Nouvelles nouvelles*, supposedly recounted by Philip of Burgundy and his circle. Many of the tales in that fascinating collection treat amorous adventure in a fashion that hardly fits with the traditional notion of what is "courtly." And the same jocose sexual frankness can be found, as we have just seen, in poetry as well. Doubtless it was found in much more of it than has come down to us. It is that kind of poetry I shall look at in this chapter, partly because so little attention has been paid to it, and partly because, as what seems to be a significant part of the poetic production of the time, some account of it may help us in our reading of late medieval poetry.

Much of this poetry is anonymous and has reached us in manuscript texts, a number of which have been published. The collection known as the Cardinal de Rohan Manuscript, for example, brings together 663 poems, many of them bawdy, probably compiled between 1470 and 1475.* Parts of ten different manuscripts of the same nature were published by Marcel Schwob in 1905 as *Le Parnasse satyrique du quinzième siècle*.[6] These are heterogeneous compilations grouping poems of many kinds, from delicate to indelicate, and by many authors, from the very well known to the anonymous. *Le Jardin de plaisance*, with its 672 pieces, shows the same heterogeneity, beginning with a rhetorical treatise and including lengthy narrative poems, debates, and many rondeaux and ballades, some anonymous, some written by authors ranging from Machaut and Deschamps to François Villon. Although it was not published until ca. 1501, it thus constitutes an extraordinary anthology of the literary production of the preceding 150 years.

We have seen that a certain mixture of genre, and of form, is not untypical of poets like Machaut, Christine de Pizan, and Chartier, who also, within certain limits, can be said to vary tone as well, although Machaut's disciple Eustache Deschamps goes much farther than any of them in this regard. In this he is followed by one of the least-known but most interesting poets of the fifteenth century, Jean Molinet, author of the acrostic to the Virgin discussed in Chapter 2. I there also quoted from a laudatory "dictier" by him that could be addressed with equal plausibility by a devout Christian to the Virgin Mary or by a passionate lover to his lady. The poem, Janus-like, thus looks toward both the religious and the secular tradition, much as does the work of Molinet as a whole. Typical of the writers who have been known for some time, for better or for worse, as the Rhétoriqueurs, he is little read nowadays, although he was one of the most admired of French poets from the mid-fifteenth to the mid-sixteenth century. He was a literary disciple of the great historian of Burgundy George Chastellain, and he became in his turn "indiciaire," in his *Chroniques*, of the reigns of Charles the Rash, Maxmilian of Austria, and Philip the Fair. His nonhistorical works are numerous, including an *Art de rhétorique*, *Le Roman de la rose moralisé*, and a considerable corpus of religious, occasional, satiric, and even dramatic verse. Born in 1435, he is of the same generation as Villon, but unlike him,

---

*Löpelmann, *Die Liederhandschrift des Cardinals de Rohan*; cited hereafter as *Rohan*.

Molinet spent his life as a frequenter of princely courts. He died in 1507, after more than forty years of intense literary activity.[7] His career, then, was that of many poets of his time, and even in the domain of ribaldry, although one thinks inevitably of Villon and "la grosse Margot," Molinet's work, it seems to me, in its variety and abundance, offers more typical—and perhaps more telling— examples.

But which entry should one choose into an oeuvre that contains—like the work of Deschamps, in whose lineage he obviously stands—samples of nearly every kind of poetry produced in the fifteenth century? I have already used one of them, that of poems to the Virgin. I shall here open another door, already familiar to us from elsewhere, that of the poetical debate. Amorous or moral, often serious, occasionally humorous, it is one of the genres typical of the poets we have been considering. With Alain Chartier, we have been able to use it to uncover some of the ways his poetry seems to work. How can it give us access to what earlier French scholars might elegantly but prudishly have termed *le jardin secret* of late medieval poetry?

There is by Molinet a debate that appears, from its title, to fall into the same category of poems whose center is defined by that motto of "Armes, Amours, Dames, Chevalerie" to which most of the contemporary poets subscribed. *Le Debat du viel gendarme et du viel amoureux,** with its 281 lines divided into seven-line stanzas alternating between the Homme Armé and the Amoureux, may remind one, as it is perhaps meant to do, of some poem like Chartier's *Debat de reveille matin* or *Debat du herault, du vassault et du villain*. The Acteur begins by presenting a discussion we seem to have heard before:

> En ung gent et joieux pourpris,
> Deux hommes firent grant debat:
> L'ung en armes queroit le pris,
> Et l'aultre estoit d'amours espris,
> S'en prisoit le joieux esbat;   5

---

*Molinet, *Les Faictz et dictz*, ed. Noël Dupire, 2: 616–27; cited hereafter as *Faictz*.

L'homme armé juoit du rabat,
Qui exaulchoit dars et espieux.

In a pretty, gladsome garden, two men had a great debate: one
sought honor in arms, and the other was smitten with love and
prized its joyful sport; the man of arms played that down; he
extolled spikes and spears.

But then the tone of the verse changes, invaded by the broad innu-
endo and sexual metaphors that will continue throughout. Even
though one finds in this piece none of the subtle play between the
author, the characters, and the audience that we have analyzed in
earlier poets, it deserves a closer look than its apparent simplicity
would warrant.[8] Superficially, it is indeed very close to the tradi-
tional debate poem as it is found, for example, in Chartier. The
Acteur introduces the debaters and their subject, the resolution of
which is left, as usual, to an outside agency. The personages who
argue the two sides of the question represent love and chivalry, those
two great axes on which so much of late medieval literature turns,
with their concomitant commonplaces on the lady's beauty and
character and the lover's prowess. But like the refrain of the ballade
we looked at a few pages earlier, the second stanza turns all of this
upside down. As the Acteur continues his introduction of the debate,
we are brought up short by his leap in reference from a conventional
lady to a lover whose riding gear seems unfit for either war or love:

Gente de corps, belle aux beaux yeux
Fust celle dont l'amant s'approche,
Mais pour chevaulcher es bas lieux,   10
Il n'avoit point trop bons hostieux,
Son harnas fault, son ronchin cloche
Et ne sonnoit que a une cloche.

The woman whom the lover approached had a fine figure and
was beautiful, with lovely eyes—but for riding in the lowlands
he wasn't too well fitted out: his equipment was faulty, his nag
limped, and he could only ring with one bell.

Although the subject of the debate—what is the better occupation
for a man, love or war?—is one Chartier's Quatre Dames, for

example, might well have argued, they would certainly not have done it in the terms used by the two old combatants in the games of love and war who argue it here. The Homme Armé turns out early on to be a kind of Matamore, the *fanfaron* of farce—"Mais tousjours chantoit le vassal: / 'A cheval, tout homme, à cheval!'" (But the vassal was always singing out: "To horse, everybody to horse!"; ll. 14–15)—not, perhaps, the best beginning for a serious debate. He insists, but too much, that all honor comes from arms, while the Amoureux seems to be a *vieux beau* interested only in the pleasure of luxurious living:

> Mon oeul est de tenre temprure
> Et mon corps envys se traveille;
> Je ne puis sentir chose dure,
> Ne grand challeur, ne grand froidure,
> Ne court disner, ne longue veille;
> Je loe amours, qui me resveille   40
> En mon beau lict engourdiné.

My eye is of the tender sort, and my body exerts itself unwillingly; I cannot bear hard things, nor great heat, nor great cold, nor a short dinner, nor staying up late. I praise love, which wakes me in my pretty curtained bed.

This seems straightforward enough—but we are never allowed to forget the essentially parodic nature of the discussion. Even when he is praising soldiering, the Homme Armé's language is filled with double entendre:

> L'homme armé doibt on redoubter.
> Il n'est riens qui tant plaise aux dames   30
> Que le behourt et le jouster,
> Et qui voeult en glore monter,
> C'est l'eschielle a sauver les ames;
> Rompre bois et quasser hëalmes
> Est ung cler bruyt qui tousjours dure.   35

The man of arms is to be feared. There's nothing that pleases ladies so much as tilting and jousting, and whoever wants to gain glory, that's the ladder for saving souls: breaking lances

and sundering helmets makes a shining reputation that lasts
forever.

And even in these early verses there appears some agreement be-
tween the two on the real interest of women in men: it is venal and
venereal. After evoking the doleful heart and tearful eye, the "rose
doulce" of the courtly tradition (ll. 64–70, 78–84), the Amoureux
claims that he enjoys a lady's favors nearly every night (ll. 92–93).
Both then use obscene musical metaphors to speak wittily of their
relative copulative prowess (ll. 99–119), and they go on to talk of the
"ladies" they have known; the soldier is here particularly cynical
(ll. 129–33).

> L'une se dit entiere et france,
> Et elle a veu cent rois en France
> Et bien autant de curratieres;
> Ce sont gauppes, ce sont ratieres
> A prendre les gens par l'oreille.

One of them says she's honest and open, and she's seen a
hundred kings in France and just as many madames; they're
bawds, they're thieves out to fool people.

The Amoureux tries to defend his lady from this attack, but
after a line that could be taken from any one of hundreds of love
poems, his praise of her virtue becomes quickly concrete in the
precise listing of her physical attributes:

> De tous biens plaine est ma maistresse,
> Je ne sçay que requipoller,
> Elle a court tallon, dure fesse   150
> Et con assés, je le confesse,
> Mais riens ne scet du bas voller;
> Tatter, baisier et accoller
> Luy sont en oultre et de bien loing.

My lady is full of every virtue—I don't know what to reply—
she has round heels, a solid rump, and a big enough cunt, I
admit; but she knows nothing about low-flying; petting, kiss-
ing, and cuddling are far beyond her.

This is a curious way indeed to defend a lady's chastity. And the lover's opponent is quick to point out that some young court dandy with plenty of money in hand would soon fix her up (ll. 155–59):

> A deux genoux, l'argent au poing,
> Ung gentil gorgias de court
> Secourroit elle a son besoing,
> Qui luy frapperoit sus son coing
> D'ung gros martel pesant et lourt.

> On his knees, money in hand, a gallant dandy would fill her needs; he would drive in her wedge with a big weighty heavy hammer.

In the face of the lover's insistence that his lady remains *sans mercy*, the old soldier, in the best macho style, is ready with his reply: "We know what women really want, and if you haven't got it, you won't get her."

> Nostre amy, vous vous abusés;
> Ung gallant portant grosse mache,   170
> Josne et radde, sans estre usés,
> Jamais ne seroit refusés,
> Il luy fourbiroit se cuirache;
> Se vous avés molle vitache,
> James ne luy ferés cela.   175

> My friend, you're wrong; a swain carrying a big club, young and erect, not worn out, would never be refused; he would polish up her breastplate. If you have a flabby old prick, you'll never do it to her.

The argument then takes what seems to be a curious turn, until we remember that this is a debate between two old men. The Amoureux appears to admit the rightness of his opponent's analysis. Alas, he confesses, I *am* a bit frigid and underendowed ("Je suis froit et mal avité"; l. 180). "Never reveal that to a woman!" advises the Homme Armé, whose own "arms," we assume, are in better shape. But no; when the Amoureux asks him if, indeed, he can boast of bigger and better things, he can only reply—with a richness of proper names applied to the male organ that leaves the "John Thomas" of Lady Chatterley's lover far behind—that, even if he was at one time a paragon of virility, he is now all used up:

> Il est mort, le singe Lottart,
> Il ne voeult plus lever le teste;
> J'ay tant jousté sus mon Baiart
> Que j'ay trouvé Collin Ploiart,
> Qui luy a deffendu le feste,   215
> Et si n'ay rescout de le beste
> Que la pel vellue et riddee.

> He's dead, my little monkey Lottart; he won't even raise his head anymore. I've used my stallion in so many jousts that I've finally found Colin Bender, who's forbidden him all flings, and all I have left of the beast is the hairy, wrinkled skin.

Both indulge in senile reminiscence, both lament the former state of members now sadly impotent—but this does not lead them to change their initial position, the one finding pleasure only in combat, the other ever loyal to love. Even in their final summing-up, however, lewd allusions abound in the speech of both:

> L'HOMME ARMÉ
> Mon seul plaisir, ma douce joye
> Gist en lances et en escus;
> Il vault mieux qu'on s'y esbanoie,   255
> Combien que a le foys on s'y noye,
> Qu'il ne fait muser en ces culz;
> Ils sont lés et ors et cocquus,
> Je n'y perchoy chose nouvelle.

> L'AMOUREUX
> De plus en plus se renouvelle   260
> Amours, qui tient son puissant dart;
> Sans aïde de macquerelle,
> Son leal droit et ma querelle
> Soustenray comme bon saudart;
> Vive qui tient son estandart,   265
> Et recule qui se desvoye!

> My only pleasure, my sweet joy, lies in lances and in shields;

it's better to amuse yourself with those (even though sometimes you founder) than it is to think of those fannies; they're ugly and dirty and misshapen; I can't see anything new in them.

Love, holding his strong spear, revives more and more; without the help of any bawd, like a good soldier I'll uphold his trusty law and my contention. Long live the one who holds his banner; let him withdraw who goes another way!

And the final decision on whether war or love is better is left to the public, "gentles all." The Amoureux concludes: "Jugiés, seigneurs, de nos contens; / Se proesse a plus de vertu, / Je ne seray plus vert vestu" (You be the judges, my lords, of our dispute; if valor is more virtuous, I'll no longer put on green [i.e., the color symbolizing new love]; ll. 279–81).[9]

I have quoted at some length from this joyfully licentious poem not only to show how it takes its ingredients from the courtly and chivalric traditions and turns them on their head in a variety of ways, some obvious, some more subtle, but also to present it as a kind of paradigm of the many facets of a poetic tradition that is often the reverse of the other. Let us now, through this text, look at that tradition.

We have already seen that the piece is, quite obviously, a send-up of the debate poem. Such parodic versions of "regular" genres are not rare in the medieval tradition, beginning with the verse of Guillaume d'Aquitaine in the eleventh century. *Aucassin et Nicolette* (13th century) stands in the same line, as does *Le Roman de Renart* (12th–13th century), and it can easily be traced through Rabelais and the seventeenth century to the *Ode à Priape* of Piron ("Foutre des neuf garces du Pinde!") in the eighteenth and such Surrealist spoofs in the twentieth as Louis Aragon's *Le Con d'Irène* or Benjamin Péret's *Les Rouilles encagées*. Nor are other examples lacking in the fifteenth century. One of Molinet's coarsest works, for instance, is the parody of a sermon. The *Sermon de Billouart* (*Faictz*, 2: 558–66), like any sermon, is the explication of a text, stated at the outset, in this case in Latin: "Introivit in tabernaculo, / Lacrimante recessit oculo"

(He entered into the tabernacle, he withdrew with weeping eye; ll. 1–2). In an almost Joycean display of wordplay, all of the obscene implications in French of these Latin phrases are developed by Molinet in the course of his exposition, which purports to be "la vie, legende et histoire / Du devot frere Billouart" (ll. 25–26). Since "Billouart" (cf. "billard" and modern French "queue de billard") is a term for the penis, the *-vit* of "introivit" comes to preside over the whole; and the repetition of *-culo* at the end of each of the verses presages the development within the poem, at some length, of two of the meanings of the word *cul*, anus and vagina. The tone throughout is that of the *taberna*, as in "taberna-culo."[10]

The same tone pervades the Molinet parody of another solemn contemporary genre, the epitaph (*Faictz*, 2: 762–65). This is not surprising, of course, when it is the epitaph of Hotin Bonnelle, a court fool, who, apparently, was not even dead (ll. 1–4):[11]

> Chy couche pour chose nouvelle,
> Sans estre mort, Hottin Bonnelle,
> Qui fit mains tours de le boielle,
> Sans rompre nez, col ne cervelle.

> Here sleeps, for something new—without being dead—Hotin Bonnelle, who performed many feats of gluttony without breaking his nose, his neck, or his skull.

Bonnelle's exploits as "des sots patron" are enumerated but, as in the preceding poem, it is the exploits of his *vit* and his *cul* that are emphasized:

> Hotin avoit et a, s'il vit,   45
> En ce monde grand audivit;
> Oncques homme ruer ne vit
> Sy loingz qu'il pichoit de sen vit.

> Son vit estoit droit comme broche
> Et maintenant il est a croche;   50
> Il cline en bas et se desloche,
> Et ne sonne qu'a une cloche.
>   · · ·
> S'on encassoit cul en relicque,
> Comme chief de sainct angelicque,

Son cul, qui haultement desclique,
Seroit en fiertre magnificque.   60

Hotin had—and has, if he's alive—a great reputation in
this world; there never was a man who could jump as far as he
could piss with his cock.

His cock used to be straight as a skewer, and now it's all
bent over; it bows down, it's out of joint, it only rings with one
bell.

If asses were enshrined as relics, like the head of an angelic
saint, *his* ass, which rings out loudly, would be in a magnificent
reliquary.

From "Plourés, petis enfans, plourés" (l. 73) to "Prions à Dieu
misericors" (l. 77) at the end, none of the elements of a serious
epitaph (such as the two Molinet wrote for the death of the composer
Johannes Ockeghem [*Faictz,* 2: 831–33]) are missing, but they are
played with in a way calculated quite clearly to amuse, both by the
parody of a genre and by the use of a linguistic register sharply
different from the one used in the "serious" epitaph. A milder form
of this kind of parody of what are essentially religious genres can be
seen in such poems as *Le Breviaire des nobles* of Chartier and its spin-
off, *Le Psaultier des vilains,* by Michault Taillevent, or, in another
way, in the anonymous *Amant rendu cordelier à l'observance d'amours.*[12]
In prose, *Les Quinze Joyes de mariage* provides a doubly ironic version
of it, since the title refers to the traditional fifteen joys of the Virgin
and the text is a violent indictment of the married state.[13]

These are only a few of numerous possible examples. What
they all seem to establish—and what Molinet's humorous debate
seems to exemplify, too—is a tradition of the parodic use of both
secular and religious genres, often by the same hands who regularly
use them in a nonparodic fashion. One can call them, with Paul
Zumthor,[14] "anti-structures," if one wishes, since as with any parody
it is true that much of their meaning, as well as their humor, appears
only against—or at least in relation to—the genres they caricature.
Yet the form of their structure remains the same as in those genres, of
which they are thus, in fact, a formal duplication.

But the constituent parts—in the case of *Le Debat du viel
gendarme,* the debaters and the subject of their debate—really are

reversals, to some degree, of traditional elements, and they invite us to look further at this "other" tradition, one to which I have stead-fastly refused to give a qualifying adjective that establishes anything beyond its alterity, but which literary historians have often called "bourgeois." Let us turn once more to Molinet's poem. One notices immediately that both speakers are old, unlike the vast majority of participants in medieval erotic poetry, where not only the year is usually at the spring, but the lovers are, too. The change in such verse from May to December seems to be a constant source of comedy, then as now; one remembers particularly the bumbling old lover—purportedly the poet himself—in Machaut's *Voir-Dit*. But it is his admirer Eustache Deschamps who gives the situation the twist that it will have in much of the fescennine verse of the time, and that is so evident in *Le Debat du viel gendarme et du viel amoureux*: the regret for lost youth becomes the regret for lost sexual vigor, a *complainte* on impotence. It will be instructive, I think, to read the entire ballade in which Deschamps tells, as the title has it, "De la demande d'une vielle a un vieillart par maniere de moquerie et la response sur ce" (Of the question asked mockingly of an old man by an old woman, and its answer):*

> *O domine, respondeas michi*:
> Que te semble il du noble temps passé?
> *Qualiter te habes de presenti?*
> As tu encor en armes poësté?
> —Queles armes?—Ton bourdon aceré,   5
> Dont je t'ay veu jouster au talevas?
> —Nenil, par Dieu, il est tristes et mas,
> Car puis .x. ans ne m'en aiday en rien;
> L'en me puet bien clamer frere Thomas:
> Onques mais homs n'ot si foible merrien.   10
>
> —*Que de causa?*—*Nonne tu vidisti*,
> Que j'ay tousjours aux armes labouré
> *Juventute, sumptu dampnabili*,
> Tant que je suy de viellesce attrapé

---

*Deschamps, *Œuvres complètes*, ed. A. de Queux de Saint-Hilaire and Gaston Raynaud, 6: 244; cited hereafter as *Œuvres*.

Gouteux, fruileux, es armes reboute,   15
De jeusne temps que tu me gouvernas?
S'en est usez et destruis mes harnas,
Et je te voy encor ou vert lien,
Qui du mestier et de jouster suy las:
Onques mais homs n'ot si foible merrien.   20

—*Ad hec autem confiteor tibi*
Que vielle suy, mais riens n'est qui me blesse,
Nisi tantum quod omnes amici,
Et chascun d'eulx, ma poursuite delesse;
J'ay ventre emflé, grant cul et plate fesse,   25
Con estendu, large comme un cabas,
Pour herbergier tout le charroy d'Arras:
C'est droictement hostel saint Julien,
Tout s'i reçoit. —Aler n'y puis, helas!
Onques mais homs n'ot si foible merrien.   30

O vetula, tot sunt inimici
Tunc tempore mee senectuti,
A toy aussi, pour ton aage ancien!
Va t'en, vielle, loing de moy, je t'en pri:
J'ay grant paour quant je te voy icy;   35
Onques mais homs n'ot si foible merrien.

O domine, respondeas michi: what do you think of the noble
time gone by? *Qualiter te habes de presenti*? Are you still power-
ful in arms? —What arms? —Your sharp staff with which
I've seen you joust against the shield? —No way, by God, it's
sad and defeated; for ten years now I've not been able to use it
for anything; I can really be called Brother Thomas: never had
a man so feeble a pole.

   —*Que de causa*? —*Nonne tu vidisti*, that I always worked at
arms, *juventute, sumptu dampnabili*, until old age caught me
up, gouty, chilly, rejected in arms, compared with the young
days when you commanded me? That wore out and ruined my
equipment. And I, tired of the job and of jousting, see you still
in your prime; never had a man so feeble a pole.

   —*Ad hec autem confiteor tibi* that I am old, but there's
nothing that wounds me. *Nisi tantum quod omnes amici*, and
each of them gives up chasing after me; I've a swollen stomach,

a large bum, and flat buttocks, a widespread cunt, as broad as a
fruit basket, so all the wagons of Arras could lodge inside: it's
really Saint Julian's hospice, everything's at home there. —*I
can't go in, alas; never had a man so feeble a pole.*

O vetula, tot sunt inimici tunc tempore mee senectuti, for you,
too, in your old age! Go on, old woman, get away from me, I
beg you: I'm very frightened when I see you here; never had a
man so feeble a pole.

One finds here not a debate but a dialogue, not the polished and
gallant conversation between the Amant and the Dame that occurs,
to cite only one instance among many, in the *Cent Ballades d'amant et
de dame* of a Christine de Pizan, but the mocking questions of an old
woman who, with a wink, asks an old man how his weapon is (l. 4),
and, when he pretends not to understand, makes it very clear which
weapon she means (l. 5). Like Molinet's Homme Armé, the gaffer
here boasts of his past vigor (ll. 12–13) but admits his present sorry
state, reiterated metaphorically, and piteously, in the refrain: "On-
ques mais homs n'ot si foible merrien."[15] In the third stanza, the
woman confesses that she too is old, although she admits to no
decline in libido (ll. 21–23). She repeats, in other words, the tradi-
tional masculine idea of woman's sexual nature—unsurprisingly,
since the author of her words is a man. But her appetite—which has
doubtless been at least part of the cause of her initial question to her
old lover (cf. l. 16)—finds no satisfaction, since no man lusts after her
any more. Her physical charms have fled, leaving behind, as she
acknowledges in terms that in their crudity recall the Homme
Armé's unsavory thoughts of women's genitalia,[16] only the unap-
petizing attractions of an ancient harlot (ll. 25–29). At the end, they
both agree: "Nobody loves you when you're old and gray."

It is easy to recognize here the principal elements of "Les
regrets de la belle hëaulmiere" and of the ballade that follows it in *Le
Testament*: the contrast between youth and beauty and old age and
ugliness, and a more or less poignant regret for what has gone before.
Now these are elegiac themes, yet they are found in profusion in the
bawdy verse of the fifteenth century; but their poignancy is much
reduced, if not eliminated, by their being centered quite precisely, as

we have seen in Molinet and in Deschamps's ballade, on the sexual organs. In the case of the woman, it is not her carnal appetite that subsides, only her carnal allure: in this originate any number of the so-called "sottes chansons" that paint burlesque portraits of ugly, lustful old harridans (one thinks of the paintings of Hieronymus Bosch or of the caricatures of Leonardo da Vinci). With the man, what is ridiculed is, rather, the subsiding of sexual power, emblematized by the subsiding of the penis, often burlesqued as well by military, musical, or even culinary metaphors. A look at each sex will demonstrate how far we are from the Belle Dame and her suitor.

La grosse Margot is hardly alone in the poetry of her time. Her fellow creatures may be old or young, ugly or attractive; all are unrepentently lecherous. One of the most extraordinarily lively— and obscene—caricatures of a woman is found in an anonymous ballade in *Le Parnasse satyrique* (Schwob, p. 123). The linguistic verve of the opening address to the woman is already Rabelaisian: "Marque loffue, gauppe, vieille paillarde, / Refus de ceulx qui gisent en clappier" (Crazy broad, trollop, old whore, the reject of those who sleep in brothels).[17] The third stanza begins no less truculently, with references to two ways that the woman emits unpleasantness, top and bottom: "Vostre langue picque comme laisarde, / Et sault ung vent de vostre cul broudier / Qui put plus fort que pouldre de bonbarde" (Your tongue stings like a lizard, and the draft from your fat ass stinks more than cannon powder).[18] The "Prince" of the envoy is, as often, called as a witness, but not to the lady's beauty or the lover's sorrow:

> Prince, duquel, infame dissolute,
> Nommee serés par nom plus pute,
> (Car vous avez sur toutes clicqueté
> Vostre vieil trou qui ne vault une prune,)
> Savoir le doit qui nouveau l'a hurté,
> Se soubz les draps vous estes blanche ou brune.

> Prince, by whom, scandalous slut, you'll be called by a more whorish name, for you've clattered your worthless old hole

around more than all the others; the next one who knocks into it should know whether, between the sheets, you're white or brown.

Another anonymous ballade (*Rohan*, pp. 60–61) draws the same sort of sketch, made even more grotesquely amusing by its use of rhymes in *-ac*, *-ec*, *-ic*, *-oc*, and *-uc* (in that order) in each stanza, and by the poet's claim in the first that "j'ame et sers la belle ric a ric" (I love and serve my beauty wholly; l. 7). This does not stop him from going on to begin the following strophe with a description we are beginning to recognize: "Elle a le ventre aussi uny qu'ung sac, / Elle a le cul aussi plat comme un hec [defined in the manuscript as 'une claie'], / Dedans son saing a de trippes plain bac" (Her stomach is as smooth as a sack, her ass is as flat as wattle, there's a pan-full of guts in her lap; ll. 13–15). Nor does he spare us the usual vivid description of the vulva, this time in the envoy: "Prince, rouge comme creste de coc / Elle a le treu et espés comme un soc" (Prince, red as a coxcomb is her hole, and thick as a plowshare; ll. 37–38).

Not all references in this kind of poetry to women's physical attributes are quite so scurrilous. In Deschamps, for instance, one can find a witty and fairly lighthanded plea to women not to bind up their breasts too tightly (*Œuvres*, 8: 169–70); the refrain: "Dame, aiez pité de tettine!" (Lady, take pity on your titty). And Molinet's rondeau of advice to a fifteenth-century Lolita-lover (*Faictz*, 2: 875) evokes the girl's figure with comparative delicacy, at least before it becomes disturbingly ironic and cynical:

Ceste fillette a qui le tetin point,
Qui est tant gente et a les yeux si vers,
Ne luy soyez ne rude ne parvers,
Mais traictez la doulcement et a point.

Despouillez vous et chemise et pourpoint,   5
Et la gectez sur un lit a l'envers,
Ceste fillette . . .

Apres cela, si vous estes en point,
Accollez la de long et de travers,
Et si elle a les deux genoux ouvers,   10

Donnés dedens et ne l'espargnez point,
Ceste fillette . . .

This little wench whose breasts are beginning to show, who's so nice and whose eyes are so green—don't be rough or forward with her, but treat her gently and properly.

Take off your shirt and your doublet and tumble her backward onto a bed, this little wench . . .

Then, if you're up to it, kiss her all over, and if both her knees are open, rush right in and don't spare her, this little wench . . .

Nonetheless, many of the physical descriptions of women—more particularly, of old women—are unequivocally coarse; the foregoing quotations are but a small sample. In "courtly" verse, there is some account of the lady's (or, at times, the man's) corporeal charms, to be sure; the poet often describes, or at least mentions, the lady's hair, her eyes, her face, even occasionally—and in a decorous way—her breast (I am tempted here to write "bust"), or her *maintien*. But this is all done in generally abstract terms: "Douce dame, plaisant et gracieuse, / Bonne et bele, delitable a veoir" (Sweet lady, pleasant and gracious, good and lovely, delightful to see), writes Machaut typically in *La Louange des Dames*, or "Douce dame, vo maniere jolie / Lie en amours mon cuer et mon desir" (Sweet lady, your pretty ways bind in love my heart and my desire), or again, with slightly more detail, "D'uns dous yex vairs, rians, fendus, / Et d'un dous ris, fait par mesure, / Sui je par mi le cuer ferus" (By a pair of gentle gray eyes, laughing and open, and by laughter gentle and moderate, am I struck within my heart).[19] Based on this kind of description, however, it would be very difficult indeed to distinguish one *doulce dame* from another, and even Chartier's Belle Dame, so controversially individual in her ideas, outwardly resembles countless other damsels of medieval love poetry:[20]

C'estoit garnison de tous biens
Pour faire a cuer d'amant frontiere:
Jeune, gente, fresche et entiere;
Maintien rassis et sans changier;
Doulce parolle et grant maniere.

> She was the very garrison of all virtues for attacking a lover's
> heart: young, pretty, fresh, and honest; composed and steady;
> gentle in speech and stately in appearance.

It is easy enough to assert that these chaste ladies are the inversion of
the women in the poems we have just been reading. Yet this is not
entirely true, for those "ladies" all resemble one another, too—and
for exactly the same reason. They are all reduced, like their sweeter
sisters, to a few traits, although these traits are not hair, eyes, or
complexion, but *tétins*, *con*, and *cul*, and they are described not in
abstract but in brutally concrete terms. A perfect example of this
kind of reduction is found in an anonymous rondeau in which the
masculine first person makes no bones about his only interest in his
ladylove, and the refrain drives it home: "Je n'ayme de vous que le
con" (All I love in you is your cunt; Schwob, p. 87). These women
make up, in other words, another type, reversed, turned upside
down, one might say, but nevertheless a poetic type. For a reversed
type, reversed diction: where "courtly" diction is all generality, here
all is particularity—but the particularities are always the same ones.

Lest any reader have the idea that late medieval licentious
verse is particularly antifeminine, I must hasten to add two remarks.
The first is simply that, certainly in the case of the known authors
(and in all likelihood in that of the anonymous authors as well), the
poets who wrote in such unflattering terms about women also wrote
about them in the most unfeignedly adulatory, indeed sycophantic,
way as well. Further, in their less decorous verse they did not spare
the other sex either, as we shall now see.

Eustache Deschamps can once again provide a good starting
point. In the refrain of one ballade, he designates himself, for in-
stance, king of the Uglies and justifies this amply in the first stanza,
which is the equal, as are the other two, of any female grotesque in a
sotte chanson (*Œuvres*, 4: 273–74):

> Se nulz homs doit estre roy de Laidure,
> Pour plus laideur c'on ne porroit trouver,

Estre le doy par raison et droiture,
Car j'ay le groing con hure de sangler,
Et aux singes puis assés ressambler;   5
    J'ay grans dens et nez camus,
Les cheveulx noirs, par les joes barbus
Suy et mes yeux resgardant de byays,
Par le front sui et par le corps velus:
Sur tous autres doy estre roy des Lays.   10

If any man should be king of Ugliness, for being uglier than
any you could find, I should duly and by rights be it, because I
have a snout like a wild boar's, and I look rather like a monkey.
I have big teeth and a pug nose, black hair, with whiskery
cheeks, and I'm cross-eyed. My forehead and my body are
hairy: above all others I should be king of the Uglies.

In another ballade, a worthy predecessor of Molinet's *Sermon
de Billouart*, addressed to an unnamed enemy (*Œuvres*, 4: 277), Des-
champs piles coprological insult on carminative injury, with no *holes*
barred; the second stanza and part of the third give a colorful
example, with a trooper-like vocabulary:[21]

Li vins es narines te flote;
Tu poiz, tu boiz, tu es estoux,   10
Ton ventre joue a la pelote
Et bruit; maudit soit il de tous!
La froideur, la rume et la toux
En reuppant par ta bouche advis,
Et en dy comme merveilloux: 15
Estront, par la! g'iray par huis.

Va chier, laisse tel riote,
Euvre le conduit de dessoubz,
Cy faiz venir au bout la crote,
Le remonter est trop prilleux.   20

Wine runs out of your nostrils, you fart, you drink, you're
stupid, your stomach tosses up and down and rumbles; cursed
be it by all! Belching, your mouth sends colds and coughs on
their way—it's really wonderful: turd, this way! I'll go out the
door.

Go shit, leave off your brabbling, open up the lower chan-
nel, let the dung come out that end; sending it back up is too
dangerous.

But the poets often define the whole man, however ugly, by a
metaphor for the male member: swords, lances, hammers, and mal-
lets abound, as do musical instruments, especially the flageolet, a
kind of flute. One characteristic example of the last is found in the
Homme Armé's admission that "Son flaiollet ne vault plus riens"
(His flageolet is worthless; *Faictz*, 2: 620). Less noble than these
"instruments," even when they are rusty or out of tune, is another
metaphorical equivalent, the *andouille*, or chitterling sausage. As
often, Deschamps can furnish an early example in our period, in a
series of facetious questions and answers—the parody, really, of a *jeu
de société* like the *Jeux à vendre* of Christine de Pizan—the last of
which asks a "sire preudoms" what a lady would most want to be
served to her after Christmas. He answers readily (*Œuvres*, 8: 125):

DEMANDE
Dont veult dame, sire preudoms,
Apres Nouel estre servie
Et dont a elle grant envie?
Respondez, nous le demandons.

RESPONSE
Voulentiers. Puisqu'il fault que die,
Ce mangier ci lui est tresbons,
D'une andoille entre deux jambons,
Qui soit roide et non pas rostie.

With what, honest sir, does a lady like to be served after
Christmas, and what is her great desire? We ask you to reply.

Willingly. Since I must say it, this is what she really likes to
eat: between two gammons, a sausage that's stiff and not
roasted.

A particularly free rondeau in manuscript (Schwob, p. 58) advises
women to lay hold of such a sausage:

Prenés en gré du manche de ma couille
Si n'est si gros comme vous vousissés.

Il est tout fait en faczon d'une andouille
Prenés en gré du manche de ma couille,

Puys que souvent ainsi il vous fretouille   5
En vostre trou large par ou pissés
   Prenés en gré.

    Take gratefully the handle of my balls, even though it's not
as big as you'd like.
    It looks just like a sausage; take gratefully the handle of my
balls.
    Since it's often itchy in that wide hole through which you
piss, take gratefully the handle of my balls.

Women demand the same dish so often from a cook, in another
ballade in the same manuscript (Schwob, p. 122), that he must give
up his profession, as he tells the prince and us in the envoy:

Prince, du tout je renonce a l'office,
Et vous voyez apparentes raisons:
Car trop souvent fauldroit que je fournisse
Ung pié d'andouille entre les deux jambons.

    Prince, I'm giving up my functions, and you can easily see the
reasons why: too often must I supply a foot-long sausage be-
tween two gammons.

A servant—"fillete jolie"—asks for "une andouille a faire bon pois"
(a sausage of good weight) in a poem in *Le Jardin de plaisance* (fol. 64ʳ),[22]
and "ung galant" is glad to furnish her with it. Even given the
gourmandise, implicit or explicit, of the women in these verses, a
chitterling sausage hardly appears to confer much phallocratic dig-
nity on the male. The very pronunciation of the word suggests
humor (as it does notably in the famous battle with the Andouilles in
Rabelais's *Quart Livre*, and as it still does in popular French), even
though its shape may designate it as an apt comparison. Is there,
then, much to choose from when both sexes are reduced to their
sexual organs, and these organs to objects?
    But there is, perhaps, even less to choose from when this object
itself, in the case of the man, is reduced to nothing. Very frequent
indeed are the poems in which the penis—*vit, vitache, martel, mache,*

lanche, lanchette, poussoir, Collin Mollet or Collin Ployart[23]—is not what it used to be. We have already seen an instance of this in Deschamps's dialogue between the pair of old people. He follows that, in the manuscript, with three other ballades, each presenting a male first person who laments in this particular way the passing of his youth; the refrains of each indicate the subject and the tone: "Je ne puis la queue mouvoir" (I can't wag my tail); "Par deffault de bon vit avoir" (Through lack of a good cock); "Je ne puis mais fors que baisier" (All I can do now is kiss; *Œuvres*, 6: 225–29). We have observed also that both the old soldier and the old lover in Molinet's mock debate are honest enough to admit not only their age but their failing—or failed—sexual powers, and in intimate detail. Their regrets for youthful vigor are echoed in many ballades and rondeaux, in which they are symbolized by the woeful inadequacy of an organ no longer able to do its duty. Such lamentations are frank and, it may be said, to the point: "Et mon pauvre v.i.t. ay perdu aux / Deduis d'amours, en faisant un duo" (And I lost my poor cock in the pleasures of love, playing duets; *Faictz*, 2: 778); "il est perdu le povre vit, / Qu'on souloit nommer rigordaines" (It's lost, my poor cock, that they used to call Good-time Charley[?]; *Rohan*, p. 377); "Je n'ay flaiau qui vaille, ne gros ploustre, / Pour embranler ces josnes lavendiers" (I have no worthy flageolet, nor any big hoe, to shake up those young washerwomen; *Faictz*, 2: 798); "Et tant au bas mestier je me suis occupé / Qu'en la fin de mes jours je me trouve pippé" (And I was so busy doing the dirty that at the end of my days I find myself caught out; ibid., p. 777).

Such quotations make it obvious that these laments for a dead member constitute the ribald version of the regrets for lost youth, with its strength and beauty, that form so characteristic a part of the poetry of a Charles d'Orléans or a François Villon. Eustache Deschamps, too, wrote many poems on old age, his own as well as that of others, some humorous, some more bitter.[24] And some of them, as we have seen, center that plaint on absent sexual power, as another ballade shows (*Œuvres*, 6: 11). Each of its stanzas lists a series of misfortunes—poverty, debt, prison, lack of love—all brought about by phallic failure. The third stanza evokes the proud past appearance of a formidable implement, "Gros et nervus . . . / Bien venuz et bien hostelez / En mains lieux" (Big and veiny, welcomed and well-housed in many places) now, alas, "muez de rouge en noir, / Pale et destaint" (changed from red to black, pale and wan). Every ill, every misfortune, so the envoy tells us, would be cured if only he could . . .

> Prince, de mes maulx confortez
> Fusse du tout et depportez,
> Riches, jolis, gais et riens,
> Bien venuz et bien honourez
> Et entre les dames louez,
> Se j'eusse mon vit d'Orliens.

> Prince, I would be wholly eased and exempt of my woes, rich, handsome, gay, and everything, welcomed, honored, and praised by the ladies—if only I had my Orleans cock [i.e., that of my youth].

Nor is he alone among late medieval poets in such wishful thinking.[25]

It is, of course, natural for old age to lead poets to thoughts of lost youth. Some of the variations on this traditional theme elaborated by Charles d'Orléans are doubtless among the poems of the time best known to readers today, with their characteristic evocation of ennui, and those tonalities of *nonchaloir* and *merencolie*, often personified, so particular to him. A few lines will suffice to remind us of the style: "Le monde est ennuyé de moy, / Et moy pareillement de lui" (The world is tired of me, and I likewise of it).[26] His young vigor is gone, too, like that of Molinet's debaters, but in a different register:

> Se le Medecin Espoir,
> Qui est le meilleur de France,
> N'y met briefment pourveance,
> Viellesse extainct mon povoir,
> Assourdy de Non Chaloir.

> If Doctor Hope, who's the best in France, doesn't take care of it soon, Old Age will quench my strength, deafened by Unconcern.

In one well-known rondeau, Old Age obliges the poet to take leave of the joyous company in which he spent his youth; he has given up the game of love and the company of those who still play it: [27]

> Amoureus fus, or ne le suy ge mye,
> Et en Paris menoye bonne vie;
> Adieu bon temps, ravoir ne vous saroye!
> Bien sanglé fus d'une estrete courroye,
> Que, par Age, convient que la deslie:
> Salués moy toute la compagnie!

> I was a lover—now I'm not at all—and I led the good life in Paris; farewell good times, I can't get you back again! Girt was I with a tight strap, which now Age makes it meet for me to loosen: greet all the crowd for me!

If the vocabulary is not the same, the sentiments are those of all the sad old men we have heard bewailing their shriveled potency. Nor is Charles d'Orléans, in fact, a stranger to their language of obscene allusion. A ballade thanking the Duke of Bourbon for a gift of rabbits proves that he could work in the same register when he chose. Although his diction is not quite as direct as that of a Deschamps or a Molinet, with the play on the word for rabbit, *connin*, which is as frequent in fifteenth-century France as it is, with *cony*, in sixteenth-century England, he comes up with an elegantly indecorous version of the same "Good-bye-to-all-that" theme with which we are familiar in the explicit terms of Deschamps, Molinet, and the others, but he gives it a twist typically his own when he personifies his "instrument" as a hermit. [28] Here is the first strophe:

> Mon cheir cousin, de bon cueur vous mercie
> Des blans connins que vous m'avez donnez;
> Et oultre plus, pour vray vous certiffie,
> Quant aux connins que dittes qu'ay amez,
> Ilz sont pour moy, plusieurs ans a passez,   5
> Mis en oubly; aussi mon instrument
> Qui les servoit a fait son testament
> Et est retrait et devenu hermite;
> Il dort tousjours, a parler vrayement,
> Comme celui qui en riens ne prouffite.   10

My dear cousin, I thank you heartily for the white coneys you
gave me; and moreover, I can truly guarantee you that, as for
the coneys you say I loved, it's been several years since I've put
them out of mind. Likewise my instrument, which served
them, has made its will and retired and become a hermit; it
sleeps all the time, to tell the truth, like one who doesn't profit
from anything.

The rest of the ballade continues in the same allusive style to admit
that "his heart no longer delights in raw flesh" (l. 18), so that he is
ready to "resign his office" (l. 33). This is a particularly striking
example of the same poet treating the same theme, ostensibly elegiac,
in two different tones—or according to two different conventions,
the one traditionally called "courtly," and the other "bourgeois."
Whether or not a duke—indubitably a courtly writer—can at the
same time follow a bourgeois tradition is a problem that I shall for
the moment reserve.

Along with the giving up of youthful pleasure, be it sexual or
otherwise, the lament over the passing of youth brings with it an-
other medieval thematic complex about which much has been writ-
ten, and to which the Latin tag "Ubi sunt?" has been affixed.
"Where are the beauties of yesteryear?" "Where have all the heroes
gone?" Johan Huizinga gives the history of the poignant question in
a few brilliant pages,[29] noting its appearance in a number of late
medieval authors and, of course, its most haunting expression in the
"neiges d'antan" of Villon's celebrated ballade. What he does not
bring to the attention of his readers is that even this motif, which he
characterizes as "a graceful and elegiac sigh,"[30] has, like that of the
decay of youth and beauty, its bawdy versions as well. Although the
aged jade in Deschamps's dialogue does not phrase her question to
her former and equally aged lover exactly as "ubi sunt?," she does
use Latin in her interrogations and her second line—"Que te semble
il du noble temps passé?"is clearly another way of putting the same
query.

The most obvious instance of this obscene version of the motif
that I am aware of comes from a manuscript collection containing
other licentious verse (Schwob, pp. 139–60). However disguised by

the coarseness of its language, this rondeau poses forcefully, in its fashion, the same question as Villon does in one of the huitains of *Le Testament*. It precedes the full orchestration of the theme in the well-known later ballades, one evoking bygone beauties, another, dead heroes, and another, with even greater resonance, the "regrets de la belle hëaulmiere." It may be instructive to look at them both at the same time.

Testament, huitain 29:

> Où sont les gracieux gallans   225
> Que je suivoye ou temps jadis,
> Si bien chantans, si bien parlans,
> Si plaisans en faiz et en dis?
> Les aucuns sont morts et roidis,
> D'eulx n'est il plus riens maintenant: 230
> Repos aient en paradis,
> Et dieu saulve le remenant!

Where are those noble fellows that I was with in former days, who sang so well, talked so well and were so merry in word and deed? Some are dead and stiff—of them nothing now remains; may they find peace in Paradise, and may God save the rest!

Schwob, p. 148:

> Les gros vis qui sont de plain poing,
> Plains de vaines roides charnues
> Où sont-il? Il n'en est plus nulz:
> Il sont allez ailleurs au gaing,
> Veu qui frapoient si bon coing,   5
> Sçavoir faut qu'ilz sont devenus,
>   Les gros vis.
> Dames qui en avés besoing,
> Se ne les avés retenus,
> Passer vous faulra des menus   10
> Car je pense qu'il sont bien loing
>   Les gros vis.

Those big pricks that are a handful, full of stiff meaty veins—where are they? There aren't any more of them; they've gone elsewhere to make a profit. Seeing as how they were so good at driving a wedge, we should know what's become of them, those big pricks. Ladies who need them, if you haven't kept them, you'll have to put up with small ones, 'cause I think they're far away, those big pricks.

It is obvious that the writer of the anonymous rondeau sets out to make a very different effect from the one attempted by Villon, who puts the painful question first, the subject of the verb as those elegant and sociable young blades whom he frequented, so he tells us earlier, "ou temps de [sa] jeunesse folle" (in the days of his foolish youth; l. 202). The answer comes all too soon: some are dead and gone; may God help the others, those others among whom he implicitly includes himself. The final precatory exclamation is effective indeed in arresting the reader's sympathy, upon which no irony intrudes.

The author of the lewd little rondeau seeks to touch no such sympathetic chord. He chooses another interrogatory form, which puts the subjects up front, as it were, and insists, partly through the repetition of sounds in "plain poing / Plains" (ll. 1–2) and partly through the physical detail, on their fleshly attributes of size and solidity. And the answer to the question, posed only in the third line, is much more cynical than affective, heavy with the irony that continues throughout the rest of the verses. We know we are in the humorous register when in the last part of the text the poet addresses himself with equal—and traditionally masculine—cynicism to the ladies. The very choice of an expression like "Les gros vis qui sont de plain poing" as the first line, which becomes necessarily in the rondeau the center and the end of the poem,[31] assures us of the author's desire perhaps to shock or titillate, certainly to amuse, through the playful reference to another tradition and the irreverent treatment of it. We are here, then, in the presence of a fascinating reversal, in which we find Villon using the language of a "courtly" poet, and the anonymous author of the rondeau displaying the cynicism and ribaldry often thought to be typical of Villon.

Starting with a mock debate, we have seen so far that its two characters typify, in their age and in the broadness of the language with which they bemoan it, those personae, both masculine and feminine, who do the same thing in many of the poems of the sort we are here trying to define. It has become evident, also, that their lament and its corollaries, centered singlemindedly on the loss of sexual vigor, are also a feature of this poetry. After having looked at the debaters, it is now time to turn to the subject of their debate, the relative value of love and war. Can we, through it, arrive at some further characterization of the nature of this poetry?

When one begins to look for a debate, one finds that there is, in fact, none at all in *Le Debat du viel gendarme et du viel amoureux*. We have already remarked that neither debater leaves his initial position: the Homme Armé continues to prefer war; the Amoureux will wear the green of lovers until the debate is judged—and this means forever, since the resolution of it is left up to the reader. But it is not this that makes it a false debate: we have seen in a previous chapter that the lack of resolution is typical of the genre. It is, rather, that the two sides of the debate are reduced by the author to one. Although the soldier and the lover continue to state their preferences, they do so throughout, as I have already suggested, in terms that reveal their real preoccupation as a single one: neither love nor war, but lust—or, more precisely, the sexual act. This is sometimes directly expressed, as in the numerous stanzas devoted to the inadequacy of their organs; we have already seen some characteristic examples. But even in the others, in which the subject is ostensibly some aspect of love or arms—like the second stanza describing the lover and his lady, or the strophes summing up the two "arguments," for example—sexual references abound and provide, indeed, the humor that salts these verses. One final illustration will suffice, drawn from the passage near the beginning of the poem that still forms part of the obligatory exposition of the subject (I have already quoted the Homme Armé's speech in another context):

L'AMOUREUX
J'ay prins amour a ma devise,
Il ne m'est d'escut ni de lanche:
Car j'ay mon esperance mise
En Venus, en vent de chemise,   25

En bon vin qui au coeur me lanche;
C'est mon deduyt, c'est ma vaillance:
Aultre bruyt ne voeul contester.

L'HOMME ARMÉ
L'homme armé doibt on redoubter.
Il n'est riens qui tant plaise aux dames   30
Que le behourt et le jouster,
Et qui voeult en glore monter,
C'est l'eschielle a sauver les ames;
Rompre bois et quasser hëalmes
Est ung cler bruyt qui tousjours dure.   35

    I've taken Love as my motto; I care nothing for shield or
lance, for I've put my hope in Venus, in wanton sport, in good
wine which strikes my heart; that's my pleasure, that's my
valor: I seek no other reputation.

    The man of arms is to be feared. There's nothing that
pleases ladies so much as tilting and jousting, and whoever
wants to gain glory, that's the ladder for saving souls: breaking
lances and sundering helmets makes a shining reputation that
lasts forever.

The "Venus, en vent de chemise" of line 25 shows where the lover's
thoughts really are, as do the double meanings in lines 30–31 for his
opponent.[32] There is but one game in this text, then, and it is the *jeu
de cul et de pointe* celebrated in the refrain of the ballade that opened
this chapter.

    That the sexual act is indeed a game in this sort of poetry is
made evident in a short poetic joke based on the *jeu de paume*, found
in slightly different versions in two published manuscripts (Schwob,
pp. 194, 301–2).[33] "In the game with a woman, when you reach
intercourse, you win!"

Si vous la baisés, comptés quinze;
Si vous touchés le tetin, trente;
Si vous avez la motte prinse,
Quarante-cinq lors se presente.
Mais si vous metés en la fente   5
Ce de quoy la dame a mestier,

—Notés bien ce que je vous chante—
Vous gaignes le jeu tout entier.

If you kiss her, count fifteen; if you touch her tit, thirty; if you
take her mound, then you get forty-five. But if you thrust into
the slit what the lady really needs—mark well what I'm telling
you—you win the whole game.

That the game of love—and its playing out—should be one of
the centers of late medieval poetry, in both lyric and nonlyric forms,
will hardly surprise any reader of these pages. Guillaume de Ma-
chaut dedicates himself to it explicitly in *La Louange des Dames*, as
does Christine de Pizan in many of her works. And even so se-
rious—or so chaste—an author as Alain Chartier demonstrates how
the profession of arms really depends on the profession of love. In *Le
Livre des quatre dames*, for instance, the fourth Dame (the one whose
lover has fled the field) expresses what is held to be a general truth,
that virtue in love assures virtue in war, and vice versa (ll. 2746–51).
There is in her speech a constant passage from love to war to love,
because, as she reminds the Acteur (following a long European
literary tradition), "Vraie amours fait les cuers vaillans, / Entrepre-
neurs et assaillans / Semblablement!" (True love makes hearts val-
iant, enterprising and aggressive, too!; ll. 2926–28). Yet, even in her
noble utterance, lust, the other version of the game—its "adult"
version, to use the current ironic euphemism—is not far off, and sex
can rear its ugly head. In the context of the poems with which we are
mainly concerned in this chapter, the lady's adjectives "entrepre-
neurs" and "assaillans" could easily sound equivocal. And so they
are, to a certain degree, even in the context in which they stand, for
the lady goes on to explain that he who is a bad soldier is also
necessarily a lover who seeks to betray his lady's trust, who wishes, in
other words, to seduce her (ll. 2934ff.): "Quant envayr / Veult l'on-
neur sa dame et trayr" (When he wants to invade and betray the
honor of his lady; ll. 2940–41). We should remember here, too, the
countless literary occasions when military metaphors are used for
the battle of the sexes, in which the woman is often seen as a fortress
to be conquered, or, from the other perspective, as a position to be
defended.

The poetry at which we are now looking, however, goes much further than this age-old metaphorical identification of love with war, for it reduces, more or less explicitly, both love and war to sex, which is the single preoccupation, it claims, of both men and women, just as it is the single preoccupation of old soldiers and old lovers in Molinet's debate. The "service" that love demands, in the Western tradition of *fin'amours* stemming from troubadour poetry, the service that ladies insist on, that true lovers are willing to give—and behind which it is so easy to discern sublimated desire—becomes here a precise service indeed. To the lover willing to pine forever to prove his love, an anonymous poet opposes his version of "All or nothing at all," in response to the high-sounding mottoes of his courtly counterparts (*Rohan*, p. 282). Lines 6–9 refer explicitly to the erotic tradition, only to insist on its true end:

> Cela ou riens! est ma devise.
> Sans cela c'est une bestise,
> De cela tout premier me chault;
> Car avoir de cela deffault
> Est une mort, quoy qu'on me dise.   5
>
> Je confesse que l'entreprise
> D'amours est haulte et fort la prise;
> Maiz, par Dieu, en la fin il fault
>   Cela.

> *That*—or nothing! is my motto. Without *that*, it's stupid; my first care is *that*, because the lack of *that* is death, whatever they say.
>   I admit that the adventure of love is lofty, and I prize it greatly; but, by God, at the end, you've got to get *that*.

Another anonymous masculine voice in the same manuscript (*Rohan*, p. 282) is less peremptory but just as insistent, with a sly play on words in line 6 (*con-fort*):

> Je vous pry, faictes moy cela
> Que savés! soiés en d'acort!
> Car, par dieu, vous avés grant tort
> Tant me pourmener ça et la.

Ma bouche mieulx oncq ne parla   5
Qui dit querant votre confort:
Je vous pry, faictes moy cela!

    I beg you, do *that* (you know!) with me; won't you agree?
Because, by God, you're really wrong to tease me so much.
    My mouth never spoke better than when it says, seeking
your comfort: I beg you, do *that* with me!

A third, more crudely, simply gives advice to girls, telling them what
their true profession really is (*Rohan*, p. 363):

De user votre con a pisser
N'est pas grant sens, joesnes fillettes;
Souvent faire jeu d'amourettes,
Si est le votre droit mestier.

Faictes vous bien le bas froter,   5
Toutes; autrement perdues estes
De user votre con a pisser.

Bon corps avez pour endurer,
Ventre plat et fesses durettes.
Trop seriez nommez follettes,   10
Si non tantost vueillez quitter
De user votre con a pisser.

    Using your cunt for pissing doesn't make much sense,
young girls; instead, frequently playing the game of love is
your true occupation. All of you, get your downstairs well
polished, otherwise you'll be lost, using your cunt for pissing.
    You've got bodies that can take it, flat stomachs and firm
buttocks. You'll be known as too crazy if you won't soon stop
using your cunt for pissing.

A rondeau in another manuscript (Schwob, p. 101) maintains that
even "Femme[s] de bien, s'il en est point au monde" (Honorable
women—if there are any in the world; l. 1), want the same thing,
and it goes on to "quote" one (ll. 6–9):

Je vueil tres bien que mon grant con on sonde
D'un grant vit d'asne, affin que tousjours fonde
Foultre en mon corps; car c'est ce que demande
    Femme de bien.

I really want my big cunt sounded by a donkey-prick, so that there's always come melting in my body; for that's what's wanted by an honorable woman.

Nor is there any paucity of women's voices in this concupiscent chorus. We have noticed before, in the poets we have looked at, considerable play with voice, a Machaut or a Deschamps assuming occasionally the voice of a woman, or a Christine taking on that of a man. So it is here; although one suspects that the anonymous poets are men, they can adopt the female voice, in which they express in other ways the universal obsession. In a bawdy version of the plaint for an absent lover or husband, one "woman" admits that, unless a husband is found for her immediately, she will "give it away" (*Rohan*, pp. 289–90). Another claims she is so burning with desire that she is in desperate need of "ung refreschiseur / Qui medecine [sa] chaleur" (a refrigerator-man, to doctor her heat; *Rohan*, p. 297). The modesty and decorum that characterize so many *douces dames* are the antithesis of the bluntness displayed by other women, exemplified by the voice in this rondeau (*Rohan*, pp. 364–65):

Le plaisir qui tous autres passe
Et dont jamaiz je ne fus lasse,
Vous le m'avez fait, mon mignon!
Helas, je l'ay trouvé si bon
Que voulentiers g'y retournasse.   5

Sain Jehan, si je vous rencontrasse,
Je vous disse a voix bien basse:
Alon le faire, allon, allon!
Le plaisir qui tous autres passe.

Compaignie n'est que n'en laissasse,   10
Ne honneur que je n'abandonnasse
Pour ung si tresfriant boucon.
Je meurs, se brief n'y retournoy.
Nous l'arons fait en peu d'espace,
Le plaisir qui tous autres passe.   15

The pleasure that surpasses all others, and of which I've never tired, you've given it to me, my dear! Alas, I found it so good that I'd willingly do it again.

Saint John, if ever I met you, I'd whisper to you: Let's go, let's go do it, the pleasure that surpasses all others.

There's no company I wouldn't leave, no honor I wouldn't give up for such a tasty tidbit. I'll die if I don't do it again soon. It won't take us long to do it, the pleasure that surpasses all others.

Others are even more brazen and admit not only their pleasure in doing "that"—a common term, as we have seen, for the sexual act, which may be euphemistic but is entirely unambiguous (and which, of course, still exists in this sense in French)—but also a venal motive (Schwob, p. 56, ll. 1–4):[34]

Je vouldroye bien faire cela
Mais que mon amy me le fist,
Car j'en feroye mieulx mon prouffit
Que quant on me despucela.

I'd be willing to do that—but let my friend do it with me, because I'll make more than when I lost my maidenhead.

Even old age, as examples from Deschamps and others have already shown us, does not distract women from their pursuit (Schwob, p. 100, ll. 1–4):

Mon mignon, mon gentil varlet,
Gressez moy bien ma vielle bote
Et secouez ma vielle cotte
Et le tour ne sera pas let.

My dear, my gracious youth, grease up my old chute and shake up that old skirt—and the trick won't be so shabby!

If, for both men and women, both love and valor are thus subsumed in lust, the latter is yet not the reverse of either of them. It is, rather, the words and actions caused by lust that result in making the conventions of this kind of poetry a reversal of those in the courtly love tradition. In other words, *fin'amors* itself is reversed to *fol'amors*, in every particular, against a background of love and valor reduced to the sexual act, and man and woman reduced, concretely, to their sexual parts. This poetry pushes further, that is, the reduction of all of life, in much of late medieval lyric, to "Armes, Amours,

Dames, Chevalerie," and of lover and lady to their abstract qualities. Against such a reduction, then, beginning with Molinet's false debate and looking through it to a large body of obscene texts, we have been able to find many examples of neat inversions of the courtly love code, in which the chastity of the lady becomes nymphomania, just as the patient service of her suitor changes to a frenzied search for sexual satisfaction: "Cela ou riens! est ma devise." Since all life is lust, military prowess reverses not into cowardice but into sexual impotency. Beauty turns to ugliness; compliment becomes insult; that necessary secrecy traditionally so much a part of courtly love becomes confession, avowal, public proclamation. Another anonymous rondeau illustrates this particularly well (*Rohan*, p. 356):

> Puisqu'a chaqu'un ris et quaquectes,
> Sans craindre en riens les mesdisans,
> Tu branleras devant dix ans
> Les fers de maintes esguillettes.
>
> Et deviendras des godinettes   5
> Qui tiennent rencs a tous venans,
> Puis qu'a chaqu'un ris et quaquectes.
>
> Par quoy ton ventre et belles tettes,
> Fesses dures comme aymans,
> Certes, deviendront en brief temps   10
> Ridees, pandens, deshonnestes,
> Puis, qu'a chaqu'un ris et quaquectes.

Since you laugh and prattle away with everybody, without fear of the gossips, before ten years are up, you'll swing the strings of many a codpiece.

And you'll become one of those lasses who stand around waiting for anybody, since you laugh and prattle away with everybody.

That way, your stomach and your pretty tits, your buttocks firm as iron, will doubtless in short order become wrinkled, sagging, shameful—since you laugh and prattle away with everybody.

The murmured invitation becomes a strident demand, the promise of silence, a threat of exposure, as in the following rondeau (*Rohan*, p. 387; see especially line 10):

Ne peu ne point je ne vous ame.
Aussi point n'y suis attenu;
Car vous m'avez termes tenu,
Les plus mauvais que fit oncq femme.

Se ne vous pourchasse aucun blasme,   5
De brief je vueil estre tondu:
Ne peu ne point je ne vous ame.

Et se pis ne puis, sur mon ame,
Comme s'il estoit cler congneu,
Je publieray qu'avez foutu;   10
Car, si m'aist dieux et notre dame,
Ne peu ne point je ne vous ame.

    I don't love you either a little or at all, so I'm not beholden to
you, because you showed me the worst countenance a woman
ever did.
    I'll be confounded (in short order) if I don't keep on blam-
ing you: I don't love you either a little or at all.
    And if I can't do worse, upon my soul, I'll spread it
abroad—as if it were well known—that you've fucked, be-
cause—so help me God and Our Lady—I don't love you
either a little or at all.

Much of this is summarized in a particularly telling way in a
manuscript ballade in which a man deplores having fallen in love
with a *belle* who turns out later, as he tells us with no reticence, to
have been no virgin, to have haunted whorehouses left and right, to
have lied to her lover, to be so hot-blooded that "il luy convient tous
les jours char nouvelle / Pour reffreschir le cul qu'elle a sy chault"
(she needs fresh flesh every day to refresh that hot box of hers;
Schwob, pp. 119–20, ll. 25–26). But unlike the legions of poetic
lovers who become jealous merely when their lady looks at another
man, he no longer cares, and the refrain, disillusioned, cynical, re-
signed, is the exact antithesis of the adoring, pitiable, or hopeful
refrain of so many courtly swains: "Le cul est sien: face en a sa guise"
(Her ass is hers: she can do with it what she wants). As one reads
such verses, one realizes, finally, that it is at this level, the level of
convention and topos, that the reversal occurs, and not at the level of
genre or form or—as we shall see—of language. Whereas in one

erotic mode (or tradition, or set of conventions) the man desires the woman, and his desire must be sublimated, in the other he desires her but does not need to sublimate that desire. The woman, in the former mode, while she may delicately express her own desire, is bound at first—and, often, even at last—to put off her suitor, at least physically if not sentimentally. But in the latter mode, she clearly states that her carnal desire is the equal of the male's, if not superior to it. Both modes, that is, treat sexual relationships between men and women, with all their attendant problems and frustrations; these can of course be made into tragedy or comedy. As the reader will have realized, the authors of the texts that interest us in this chapter invariably choose the latter.

A brief recapitulation of what we have learned so far through our extrapolation of significant features of *Le Debat du viel gendarme et du viel amoureux* will help us to go further, I think. First of all, just as that poem is a traditional debate, albeit a parody debate, all the other poems that we have seen also fall into traditional genres. Clearly, many can be placed within the general area of the love lyric (parodies of the encomium addressed to the lady, of the plaint of coldness on her part, of the lament for an absent lover, and so on), while others caricature other genres such as the epitaph, the sermon, or, in the lyric mode, various versions of the *complainte* on lost youth and glory. All of these depend, for at least part of their effect, on the recognition of the original genre.

It is, perhaps, partly because of this that they stay very close to what can be called the standard form of these genres: there is little play with form itself, for example, in *Le Debat du viel gendarme*, which resembles formally many other debates. True, the rhyme scheme of its seven-line stanzas is a bit unusual, with the last line of each stanza introducing a new rhyme, which is then repeated in the first, third, and fourth lines of the succeeding stanza. But even this modest attempt at strophic originality is characteristic of this type of poem. The reader will have noticed, too, that the ballades and rondeaux I have quoted display little if any formal originality; despite their content, their shape is that of the most decorous poems of a

Froissart, a Christine de Pizan, or a Charles d'Orléans. If one accepts, then, that the authors of bawdy verse follow, as do those of its opposite, a set of conventions, both topical and formal, one must ask of them the same question we have asked of the others: where is the space within which the artist can operate? A large part of the answer will be the same: it is in the variation, however slight, that the poet impresses on topos, convention, idea, on voice, rhyme, and meter, that we can find his originality, or, to use Machaut's term, his "nouveauté."

But there is, I suggest, a further freedom in obscene poetry, and that is in the language itself, independent of the form, independent of the genre. It is now generally accepted that the notion of what is obscene is related closely to a specific culture, that it has both a historic and a sociological dimension.[35] It is therefore hard for us to estimate the shock value at the time of words like *vit* or *con*, the extent to which they constitute a transgression of a linguistic taboo. If the prevalence of *con* in current French is any indication, the term did not have the impact that its direct equivalent in English would have had in the same period. Of *vit*, quite rare in modern French, we cannot even be sure which of the many words for the male member really translates it best; that is, which one would cause the same reaction in a reader today as *vit* did in its fifteenth-century public. That there *were* linguistic taboos at the time is clear from the Querelle du Roman de la rose, for Christine de Pizan specifically took Jean de Meung to task for using offensive language to designate body parts.[36] But even though in literature as in law it is difficult to reach agreement on what constitutes obscenity in language or subject matter, surely most readers will agree that much in the verse we are now considering is what has traditionally been perceived in Western culture as "obscene." Further, it seems reasonably clear that much if not all of this is the sort of obscenity that has been termed "Dionysian." The same philosopher who proposes this useful term, writing of obscenity as an aesthetic category, goes on to define it as consisting "in what society regards as 'excessive' sexualism." "As a quality of a work of art," he writes, "it is an expression of an exuberant delight in life."[37] In French cultural and literary history, the adjective "Rabelaisian" implies much the same thing. The artistic and comic use of verbal freedom, as in Rabelais, can often be effective indeed, and the laughter it produces, salutary for the reader (and perhaps for the writer). The very use of "forbidden" words, of lewd allusion, even—or especially—poured into the mold of conventional form, was surely as liberating for the artist in the late Middle Ages as it has always been, at least until the very recent abolition of all restraint, official or social, changed what was formerly exciting transgression, in all senses of both of those words, into mere modish exhibitionism or self-indulgence. One senses, however, in the unabashedly coarse language of these fifteenth-century verses, the kind of pleasure in verbal daring that children experience when they use "dirty" words. The pleasure may be mild enough, it is true, but it represents a certain exhilarating liberation from restraint. It is in part the laughter, of course, that generally keeps this kind of writing from being pornographic. Even so, at times the poets appear to be intoxicated by this freedom and to indulge in a kind of paroxysm of verbal lewdness. The following rondeau is a good illustration of such heady linguistic excess (Schwob, p. 130): [38]

> De bren, de foutre et de sang
> J'ay ma chemise gatée
> Y en ay honny no banc
> De bren de foutre et de sang.
>
> Il (me) semble voir ung chanc   5
> De mon crapault con quant il baye.
> De bren, de foutre et de sang
> J'ay ma chemise gatée.

> I've soiled my smock with shit, come, and blood, and so I've disgraced our banns with shit, come, and blood.
> I think I see a chancre in my ugly cunt when it gapes open.
> I've soiled my smock with shit, come, and blood.

Here, as in other poems occasionally, the laughter may be less, appear darker, the obscenity less jovial. But this is rare.

Free—and freeing—language, without any sexual connotation, can also be found. The following poem (*Jardin*, fol. 124ʳ) is a particularly interesting example, for, along with its insistent coarse directness, it makes facetious use of the rondeau form itself, by vividly comparing its "roundness" to that of the anus.[39]

> Le trou du cul d'une nourrice,
> C'est le plus beau rondeau qui soit:
> En quelque maniere que soit
> Il n'y croist saffren ne espice.
>
> Fors aucuneffois la jaunice   5
> Que elle mesme elle conçoit,
> C'est le plus beau rondeau qui soit.
>
> Son trou luy est tousjours propice
> Et ne fut-ce que pour pisser.
> Cella n'est point tenu pour vice: 10
> Ung chascun ne s'en peult passer.
> Devant qu'el se voise coucher
> Son trou lave d'eau de melice
> Et au matin, quant elle pisse,
> On n'a gard' de l'ouyr tousser,   15
> Tant va roide le jus de tisse
> Qui le trou rond lave au passer.
>
> Puis va sa chemise amasser
> Et en essuye les crevices.
> Puis le trou couvre de sa pellice.   20
> Que le feu saint puisse embraser
> Le trou du cul d'une nourrice!

The ass-hole of a wet nurse is the prettiest little round there is: in no way do saffron or spice grow there.

But sometimes jaundice, which she herself conceives: it's the prettiest little round there is.

Her hole is always well inclined, were it only for pissing. That's not considered a vice: no one can do without it. Before she goes to bed, she washes her hole with melissa cordial, and in the morning, when she pisses, you can't hear her cough, so loud is the juice that washes the round hole in passing.

Then she always gathers her smock and wipes out the crannies. Then she covers the hole with her pelisse. May holy fire burn up the ass-hole of a wet nurse!

Much as we have seen in examples in earlier chapters, *forme* and *fond*, if you will, are here combined in an obviously ludic fashion, the further importance of which will soon become apparent. Villon's ballade for la grosse Margot gives a version, somewhat paler, perhaps, of this kind of exuberant crudeness, as do some of the poems of Molinet I have cited, in which obscene allusion is replaced by the direct use of scurrilous language.[40] In one of these, "Le Mandement de froidure," the word *con* is introduced almost gratuitously in the course of the poem, the rest of which is not notably obscene, and is repeated thirty-eight times in a "catalogue de cons" of nineteen verses: "Cons à detail avons et cons en gros, / Cons à ung blanc et cons à demy gros, / Cons à deux rengs, cons à doubles foeulles" (We have retail cunts and wholesale cunts, cheap cunts and dear cunts, cunts in two rows, cunts with double leaves; *Faictz*, 2: 734–35, ll. 91–93).[41] In such texts, the poetical element—that is, what gives them the force, or character, of poetry rather than of prose—comes from the very violence and obscenity, often repetitive, of the terms used, rather than from such elements as rhyme or meter.

Nevertheless, given our experience so far of late medieval poetics, we should expect some other treatment of such terms, something more playful—and this can be found. Puns are rife—this is still traditional, of course, in the immense para-literature of the dirty joke or the folktale—and their use is often combined with more directly coarse expression to obtain a humorous effect.[42] I quote to demonstrate this the first stanza of an anonymous ballade (found in a manuscript also containing a translation from Petrarch by the seneschal of Anjou, Louis de Beauvau), which gaily relates the adventures of "ung petit con." The poet cleverly uses the refrain of the ballade to repeat the familiar term twice more, as part of other words (Schwob, p. 173):

> Ung petit con apopiné
> Vis l'autre jour, par ung matin,
> Qui estoit tres bien attourné
> Et marchoit joint sur le patin.
> Bien me sembloit estre guoudin,   5
> Sur mon ame, quant l'aparceu.

Et si ne vis onc taint si fin
De tous ceulx la c'onques congneu.

A dolled-up little cunt I saw not long ago, one morning, which
was well decked-out and walking along all closed up on its
clog. It seemed very comely, 'pon my soul, when I espied it, and
I never saw a finer complexion in all the ones I ever knew.

Molinet plays much more than this with such words, three-
letter ones in French instead of four-letter. His "Ballade figurée"
(*Faictz*, 2: 866–67[43]), although it adheres strictly to the ballade form,
uses as rhymes only the three potentially ribald syllables *-cons*, *-vis*,
and *-cus*, in all sorts of word formations (e.g. "faucons," "Gascons,"
"seconds"; "je vis," "ravis," "advis"; "cocus," "escus," "tappecus");
the surface meaning of the poem is not necessarily licentious, but its
rhymes point to the double meanings with which its author has filled
it. The result is a poem that reduces rhyme, if not life, to sex and its
physical expression; image and theme must of necessity be touched
by the obsessiveness of the rhyme—their contrast with it, or, put
another way, their struggle against it, constitutes a large part of the
interest of the poem.

The "Lettres de Molinet à de Fenin" is an even clearer example
of the same phenomenon, since it is hard to find any indelicate
double meanings at all in the poem's message. It is, according to
Dupire, a "very friendly letter"—but the rhymes are only two, *-roie*
and *-point*, and both of them are equivocal, *roie* being an equivalent
at the time of *cul* (cf. modern French *raie culière*), and *point* that of
penis.[44] As Paul Zumthor remarks, regarding this and similar poems,
"the endings *-roie*, *-roit*, and *-roient* sound their joyful drumbeat in
the underpinning of the verse, while the visible surface is not, as it
were, penetrated by them."[45]

The reduction of rhyme to sexual syllables may, of course, be
combined with an entirely equivocal meaning, play with rhyme thus
joining play with meaning to produce another kind of game, of the
sort we saw in another context in Chapter 2. This is what happens,
for example, in the following rondeau (*Faictz*, 2: 872), in which
point, *con*, and *roie* are all brought into a broad play on words about a
currier, or leather-dresser, and a lady:[46]

Madame, vous plairoit il point
Me prester (ja) vostre conroie,
Si vous voulez que je conroie
Vostre cuyr, qui si fort vous point.

Je mettray bas robe et pourpoint   5
Pour acteindre jusqu'a la roie,
Madame . . .

Et pour le faire a juste point
Il n'y fauldra que peu de croie,
Afin que personne ne croie   10
Qu'on ait frayé que bien a point,
Madame . . .

Madame, why don't you give me your leather gear, if you
want me to dress your leather, which pricks you so much.

I'll take off coat and doublet, to get down to ass-level,
Madame . . .

And in order to do it right, it will only take a little chalk, so
that no one will believe that we've consorted save in a proper
manner, Madame . . .

But the most successful and striking example by far of this
combination of play with rhyme and meaning can be seen in a
curious poem by Molinet that from the very first syllable of its title
demonstrates an unusual degree of reductive obsessiveness. The
"Complainte d'ung gentilhomme à sa dame" (*Faictz*, 2: 731) makes
even the word *complainte* into an indecorous allusion, for the text
under the title is made up of seventy-six verses, rhyming in couplets,
in which every other rhyme, beginning with the first, is a compound
word with *con(-m)*-as the first syllable, and every second verse ends
in a *rime équivoque* using the word *con* plus the other word necessary
to complete the rhyme. This tour de force is, for once, particularly
appropriate because what the "I" of the poem is complaining about is
the venereal disease he has contracted from "la belle" (l. 1) to whom
he reproaches, indignantly and at length, his condition. The last
verses, in which he advises all youths to heed his example, are
particularly amusing in their straight-faced use of a typically medi-
eval didactic ending:

> Josnes gens, escoutés de quoy je me complains,
> Regardés le dangier de quoy est ung con plains;
> Les gouttes et bouttons sont en moy congellés,
> Tous mes membres et sens sont par ung con gellés;
> Aiés l'oeul a mon cas et point ne consentés   75
> D'endurer que telz maux par aucun con sentés.

Young men, hear my complaint; behold the danger with which a cunt is filled; gout and pox have congealed in me, all my limbs and senses have been frozen by a cunt. Cast an eye on my case and don't consent to tolerate bearing such ills by way of any cunt.

Here, where the very subject of the poem is so obviously venereal, the combination of equivocal rhyme with equivocal meaning, produced by the contrast in each couplet between a line that is clearly obscene and one that is not, seems particularly appropriate.[47] That is, it is in no sense gratuitous, like so much of the poetic wordplay we have seen. Viewed in this way, it reminds one of Christine de Pizan's extraordinary one-syllable rondeau on the existence of God, reflecting both trinity and unity, or of Molinet's own acrostic to the Virgin. Although the comparison of Molinet's litany of Marian praise with his litany of venereal woes may be surprising, I do not mean it to be frivolous, for it can show us, it seems to me, that poetic language is working in the same way in the licentious poem as it is in the religious one.

What I have just proposed can be brought more clearly into the perspective of our previous discussions of the poet in relation to the text by stating it another way. Instead of "language working in the same way" in these poems, one could say, with less emphasis on the autonomy of the text than on the role of its maker, that the same kind of poetic wit is at play in both. This seems a more comprehensive way of asserting the same thing, for wit implies the combination by the poet of language with topos, convention, and image. Although wit in a text addressed to the Virgin and in one addressed to a syphilitic woman obviously produces quite different poems, in a sense it issues in poems that are the same, poems in which the poet has the same place, is the same "I," acts—or plays—in the same way.

The fervent prayer may become a perfervid complaint—or does the parody precede the prayer? Is *fin'amors* reversed to *fol'amors*, or is it, perhaps, the other way around? In the present context, the answer to these questions does not matter, for the important thing, surely, is to recognize that we are here in the presence of a single poetic tradition containing within it two—at least two—sets of conventions.

It is important, I think, carefully to spell out the consequences of the contention to which my analysis of fifteenth-century fescennine verse in the foregoing pages has led us. We have noticed, first of all, that although many such poems are anonymous, a substantial number are not, and that Molinet, Charles d'Orléans, and Villon, for example, are capable of writing in both the "obscene" and the "courtly" registers. Is there any reason to believe that the anonymous authors were any different? That they were not is strongly suggested, if not proved, by the collections of texts I have cited so frequently in these pages. All of them mingle works by known and unknown authors and of wide diversity. In making up *Le Parnasse satyrique*, his anthology of late medieval bawdy, Schwob worked mostly with manuscripts that contain a mixture of poems, some edifying, some "courtly," some ribald. The same mélange is found both in manuscript "anthologies" of the time, such as the Cardinal Rohan manuscript edited by Martin Löpelmann, and in an early printed anthology like *Le Jardin de plaisance*, which reflects manuscript practice. It exists also, of course, in the work of an author like Molinet. As far as I know, no extant manuscript is composed in its entirety of obscene verse. From the point of view of their time, then, what would seem to define these poems is not so much their content as their intended audience, for it is only logical that all poems in any particular manuscript or book were destined for the same audience, be it a group or an individual reader. Stephen Minta has summed up the situation handily. Speaking of *Le Jardin de plaisance*, he remarks: "The contrast between courtly decorum and traditional obscenity, between the praise of women and the vulgar abuse of women, seems to have been accepted quite naturally. Apparently the same people read both kinds of poetry."[48] The point is made in another way by Robert Guiette, who reminds us that recent studies have shown that the sharp distinctions between social classes traditionally seen as characteristic of the Middle Ages were not, in fact, so sharp.[49] What he writes of a somewhat earlier era seems to me even more characteristic, in its general meaning, of the fifteenth century: "If they read romances in the châteaux, if they sang of love there according to certain modes and certain conventions, they nevertheless were not unaware of the *chansons de gestes* or the *fabliaux*. That there were coarse habits, or violence, did not escape the gentlemen or the Ladies!"[50]

The careful formulation of this remark is worth some explication, for it implies a distinction that is sometimes overlooked in discussions of medieval literature. The problem comes with the adjective we translate in English as "courtly" (Old French *cortois*, *corteis*; Old Provençal *cortes*), because it carries several related connotations under its general meaning of "what is characteristic of the court," "proper to a court."[51] One of them is that of a social milieu ("in the châteaux," in Guiette's words): this is fairly easy to define (setting aside important nuances necessitated by the evolution of the bourgeoisie and of the *noblesse de robe*) as the aristocratic class attached to the court of a magnate. In this social sense, it is often opposed in the Middle Ages to *vilain*, "that which characterizes a peasant or commoner." It follows that in medieval usage the adjective thus implies not only a class but also a certain behavior—whether this behavior on the part of "the gentlemen" and "the Ladies" (even with a capital letter) was real or rather ideal or imagined is a point of some contention;[52] we need not join the debate here. What is important to note is that the courtly *ideal* of behavior, whatever its relation to reality, was embodied from the twelfth century on in a large number of literary texts, especially in the romance and in lyric poetry, and that this code, with its literary conventions, carried with it its own diction: courtly literature embraces, that is, both the characteristic subjects of "courtoisie," centered on the relationship between the sexes,[53] and a courtly linguistic code, the language "proper" to such subjects.

In medievalist circles, the waters are further muddied by the still lively controversy over the use—and usefulness—of the expression "amour courtois," introduced by the scholar Gaston Paris in 1883 to characterize the love of Lancelot and Guinevere in the novel of Chrétien de Troyes. Scholarly tempers flare at the mere mention of the term. Like God, it cannot be ignored even if you don't believe in it; and even though I am of the opinion that, again like God, the term would have to be invented if it did not exist, my argument in these pages concerning the use of "courtly" plainly has only a tangential relationship to the debate, which I am thus happily able largely to avoid.[54]

It would be foolish to contest the existence of the adjective "courtly" as a medieval term with multiple meanings, social, ethical, and linguistic, just as it would be inappropriately contentious in this study to question its usefulness as a designation for a recognizable complex of traits in the literary expression of love. It is, rather, its application as a sociological category by modern literary historians to certain kinds of literature, with the implication that this literature is thereby sufficiently defined, that I question. Our readings of the authors treated in this book make such a claim untenable, in my view. It is hard to believe that the audience for Molinet's poetry, or for that of Charles d'Orléans—or of Alain Chartier, for that matter—changed much according to the subject of any individual piece. Their audience has traditionally been labeled by literary historians as "courtly," in contradistinction to a "bourgeois" audience, and their literary production has been labeled accordingly. Must we not then so define the entirety of their literary production? Does Molinet aim at the bourgeoisie in his "Complainte d'un gentilhomme à sa dame," with its relentlessly risqué rhymes, and at the court in his "Complainte des trespassés" or his *Hault Siege d'amours*, with its allegory and its dialogue between the Amant and Espoir? Is the "courtly" form of the rondeau less courtly when it describes "le trou du cul d'une nourrice" than when Charles d'Orléans uses it to speak of "les malades cueurs amoureux" or Chartier to emphasize "triste plaisir et doloreuse joye"?[55] I suggest that the answer can only be "no." We have seen that not only the works of individual authors like Molinet but also the manuscript collections of poems of various authors contain a mixture of pieces of differing inspiration—or, one could say, of pieces following different conventions (including those of diction)—but sharing largely those traditions of form, of repetition and variation, with which we have been concerned. If this is true, with the same or similar authors using the same forms to express the same sets of conventions—and their conventional reversals—to the same audience, must we not question a certain use of the word "courtly" as a modern literary category? We all know what such expressions as "courtly manners" and "a courtly turn of phrase" mean: used in this way, the adjective suggests stateliness, elegance, refinement, and no one could quarrel with the usage. If, in reference to literature, it means only the same thing, then this is a convention and can be accepted as such. But unless, when we use it, we are very careful to distinguish its legitimate medieval meaning as a designation for certain types of behavior, in a certain setting, described with a certain linguistic code, from its modern sociologically descriptive sense, I see two important difficulties with applying the adjective to a class or category of literature. First, if when it is attached to literature it means reflecting the habits of life and thought (and not merely the aspirations or ideals) of the court, then obscene poetry is courtly, too, since it was at least read by, if not produced for, those at court. Second, if indeed the term courtly reflects the literary taste of the court, and thus rightly embraces all the literature courtiers wanted to hear or read (and for which they were thus the "market"), then its traditional usefulness as discriminating between two kinds of texts aimed at two different publics is much reduced, for it must include both "idealistic" texts, such as those expressing certain tenets of courtly love, for example, and their opposites, be they called "burlesque," "grotesque," or—with much less reason—"realistic."

But "the notion of two kinds of audience and two kinds of medieval mind is one that dies hard," as Minta reminds us.[56] One cannot disagree with Daniel Poirion when he states that the princely court was what gave life in the fourteenth and fifteenth centuries its particular character,[57] but one must include in that court, and in that character, as well as in any "aristocratic" view of life, not only the values of the chivalric code—of "courtoisie"—expressed in "official" literature, but also the elements that are their parodies or opposites, low-sounding rather than high-sounding. Although Poirion does not much agree with him, he cites Italo Siciliano, who as early as 1934, in his well-known study of Villon, wrote of the factitious nature of the division between popular and aristocratic poetry.[58] Texts like those we have been reading in this chapter tend to give credence to Siciliano's contention. They do so all the more in view of the very free morals of the Valois courts. One of the noblewomen who signed the letter protesting Alain Chartier's alleged disrespect to women in *La Belle Dame sans mercy* was a notorious libertine, for example, at the court of Charles VII,[59] the monarch, it must be remembered, who first installed an officially recognized royal mistress. Duke Philip of Burgundy, "the Good," was well known as a profligate, with numerous mistresses; one of his biographers, Guillaume Fillastre, a bishop and chancellor of the Order of the Golden Fleece, wrote that the duke suffered from "the weakness of the flesh." And the bishop himself was the son of an abbot and a nun. Even George Chastellain, Duke Philip's official historian, claims that the duke was "durement lubrique" (extremely lubricious).[60]

Such evidence, along with texts like *Les Cent Nouvelles nouvelles*, produced in Philip's circle, and the poems of a Molinet, seem to undermine the notion that assigns to an aristocratic public a literature uniquely attached to the exposition of the moral values of the chivalric code. Paradoxically, such a view appears to have been elaborated with the development of medieval studies in France by the savants—themselves largely of bourgeois origin—of the Third Republic, the inheritors of a Romantic disdain for the bourgeoisie. But it is a mistake—or a misunderstanding of human nature—to imagine that even in the Middle Ages, it was only the bourgeois who engaged in adultery, who expressed lecherous desire, or who liked a ribald tale. One may speak with justice of an age still based essentially on an aristocratic society,[61] as long as one includes as part of that society, among others, the element of what I shall call "courtly obscenity."

This is not the place to argue whether such obscenity is the result of the displacement of chivalric values by the values of the bourgeoisie. For Charles Camproux, the disappearance of a noble— a morally noble—concept of love, already in the thirteenth century, was undeniably due to "the bourgeois conception of the cuckold and the deceitful wife," based on an "instinctive mistrust of human nature."[62] Yet recent studies of the history of the bourgeoisie show that it expanded as a class alongside the coeval expansion of the aristocratic feudal regime.[63] And Camproux himself points out that many troubadour poets—all "chevaliers"—came from bourgeois origins.[64] The example of the historian and poet Chastellain, who although born in a bourgeois family became a knight in the Order of the Golden Fleece, or of Pierre de Nesson, secretary of the Duke of Berry, bailiff of Aigueperse, and poet, who was the son and grandson of drapers, leads one to wonder whether this were not possible some two centuries later in the northern courts, as well. And that leads one, again, to question the appropriateness of social labels for literature.

Two further consequences emerge, it seems to me, from this identification of courtly obscenity; I shall state them briefly despite their obvious importance for literary history and theory. The first concerns an objection to the characterization of the elements of licentiousness as "bourgeois." Seeking to give value to such features rather than to denigrate them, some critics dub them "carnival-esque," admire them for their vitality, and ascribe them to the "popular" spirit.[65] This view appears to me to be as untenable as the other, and for largely the same reasons. The "people" have no more exclusive right to ribaldry than does the bourgeoisie (or the aristoc-racy). Such epithets as "popular," "bourgeois," and "courtly" are best kept, I repeat, as sociological terms, unless their use is historical or carefully circumscribed and conventional. In literary history or analysis, they can at best serve as a shorthand way of referring to various complexes of values or traditions characteristic of each of these three classes. And even here much care must be taken in their use: any text may express "popular" ideas, whether it originates or not in a popular milieu. Any bourgeois poet in the fifteenth century could write a ballade instinct with "courtly" values and couched in "courtly" diction—hundreds of examples prove it.

Does this mean that writers who parody such values do so in order to subvert or contest "the chivalric code," "the courtly system"? Again—and this is the last consequence I shall enumerate—if such values, as they are expressed in the written word, at any rate, can include their opposites, or parodies of themselves, as the corpus of poems we have been considering demonstrates, then obviously the answer to this question is, again, negative. When Charles d'Orléans parodies his own poems on old age in the lament on impotence we saw earlier, it is highly unlikely that he is at the same time sapping the foundations of the aristocracy by underlining in a subtle way its powerlessness. Nor does every unfaithful or lustful knight necessarily symbolize the decadence of chivalry, any more than every lecherous lady means that all ladies are lecherous (as Christine de Pizan was quick to point out in her defense of women). Zumthor, in his extraordinarily interesting reevaluation of the Rhétoriqueur poets, extends the view of poet-as-subverter to an entire body of late medieval literature.[66] His case is a good one, made partly on the basis of the *équivoques*—obscene and otherwise—he discovers in their writing. The notion is seductive in the current critical climate. It results in a thoroughly contemporary vision of Huizinga's "autumn of the Middle Ages." Is it entirely satisfactory, however, even given the subtle nuances with which it is presented? It would not be appropriate here to summarize his argument, only a small part of which concerns bawdy texts. Yet one wonders, when this bawdy is so much a part of the very tradition against which Zumthor claims the Rhétoriqueurs were in revolt, whether their obviously extravagant use of language was designed to subvert language, in a tradition that seems to have allowed—indeed, to have led to—that use, at least for a certain period in its history.

If obscenity in thought and language are not necessarily the appanage of any one class, and its expression in literature a sign of subversion, the opposite is also true: every pure, unyielding or devoted *dame* found therein does not mean that all ladies should be like

that. Nor even that all aristocratic ladies *are* like that. The presence
of courtly coarseness alongside courtly delicacy and refinement, of
obscenity next to purity, suggests, rather, both the human reality and
the unreality of the literary text. The situation—the juxtaposed
composition of both kinds of writing for the same audience—surely
reflects human complexity, no less in the fifteenth century than
now.[67] Neither extreme, however, reflects, in any simplistic way,
"reality," if by that we mean the picture of the life of ordinary people
doing ordinary things, any more than the ideal state proposed in a
political campaign speech or that other ideal presented in a por-
nographic film really represents "life-in-the-United States." More
than a slice of life, what courtly literature—understood as including
all its aspects—really gives us is both the transgression and the
transcendence of reality, of values as they were lived out, with that
reality being somewhere in the middle. Somewhere between *fin'amors*
and *fol'amors* lies ordinary, everyday, unliterary love.

It has always been the artist's prerogative to play with what he
or she perceives as reality, to imagine variations of it or evasions from
it. That play, like the play of Christine de Pizan or Alain Chartier,
may be decorous, though lively, or, like that of Molinet in certain
poems, wilder and more fantastic. A very good example of this, in
another domain, can be found on the pages of medieval manuscripts,
the illuminations of which often present a double aspect: that of
miniatures illustrating the text, and that of the marginal ornamenta-
tions. The latter, often called *drôleries*, present a profusion of hybrid
and fantastic flora and fauna. The contrast is complete, as Jurgis
Baltrušaitis notes in his fascinating study of Gothic fantasy in art,
between such extravagances and what he calls "the affectation of the
lyric and the serenely epic pseudo-historical cycles," even though
both exist on the same page—and thus, like the text, address the
same audience. "The decorated margins," he goes on to show, "com-
bine in different ways unnatural artifice and artificial nature. They
run along beside the manuscript's text and illustrations like a diver-
tissement."[68] The unfettered and feisty literary licentiousness with
which the last pages have been strewn seems designed to perform

much the same salubrious function, alongside the seriousness of lovers' laments or moralists' dicta.[69]

It should be clear by now that, if I have not analyzed the poems in this chapter in the same way as I did those in earlier chapters, it is not because they are different but rather because I think that they can be read in the same way. When one compares them with poems expressing the concepts of courtly love, one finds, as we have done, many similarities. Both are concerned with relations between the sexes. Although their diction is different, they share the same structures. In both cases these constitute structures of desire, desire that is, on the one hand, entirely explicit and, on the other, often implicit or, indeed, entirely sublimated. Both have their own conventions, and the authors of both—the Acteurs—play with these conventions, which are themselves versions one of the other.

But in order to read these poems in the same way as the others—or, indeed, in the case of most of them, to read them at all— they had to be unveiled, and their robust lineaments measured, as it were, so that they could be recognized as forming part of that same poetic world in which la Belle Dame sans mercy and la Belle Hëaulmiere are really sisters under the skin.

Epilogue: Connections

lbert-Marie Schmidt, writing some twenty-five years ago in the preface to a study of arts and letters in the fourteenth and fifteenth centuries, was not wrong to claim, in his usual truculent style, that the period evoked in general "the disdain, indeed the disgust of scholars." If they are medievalists, he maintained, they refuse to admit that after 1300 and before François I, France was capable of inventing and varying what he terms "the themes of an original civilization, entirely free from decadent formalism."[1] Since then, seminal studies on lyric poetry, on Guillaume de Machaut and Christine de Pizan, on the Rhétoriqueurs, scholarly editions of the works of a number of authors of the time, the establishment of journals, and the meetings of colloquia have changed the picture to a considerable degree, as a glance at the Works Cited section will attest.

Yet it is still true that overall the poetry—and the poets—that have been the subject of the foregoing chapters have had a fairly bad press ever since the middle of the sixteenth century, when Joachim Du Bellay pugnaciously defended the French language by recommending a new poetics based on foreign models. Although the decided oddness of his defense may be explained by his youthful adoption of "Renaissance" habits of mind, his disdain for what he calls "toutes ces vieilles poësies Francoyses . . . comme rondeaux,

ballades, vyrelaiz, chantz royaulx, chansons, & autres telles epis-
series, qui corrumpent le goust de nostre Langue" (all that old
French poetry . . . like rondeaux, ballades, virelais, chants royaux,
chansons, and other such spicery, which corrupts the taste of our
language) has echoed with inordinate resonance down the ages
since.[2] It is echoing still, despite the best attempts of historical and
critical revisionists to bring in a more sympathetic judgment on late
medieval literature and to show that its several modes, including
those with which we have been concerned, did not suddenly disap-
pear at the dawn of the sixteenth century, to be replaced by the
lightheartedness of a Marot or the classically influenced graces of the
poets of the Pléiade. The practice of most fifteenth-century poets still
serves as a whipping boy to prove the superiority now of François
Villon (always seen as exceptional), now of the later Clément Marot,
or again of Ronsard and his band.

The remarks of Luc Hommel in a study of the Burgundian
poet and historian George Chastellain published in 1945 are typical
of what caused Schmidt's *boutade*:

In the fifteenth century the poet is nothing like the "sacred dreamer" of
whom Victor Hugo speaks. He does not let himself get carried away by
inspiration. He does not take himself, in general, as the subject of his poetry
(except in the case of a Charles d'Orléans or a Villon . . .). What pre-
occupies him primarily is the construction [*facture*] of the poem. . . . On
the other hand, what he likes to express, rather than feelings, are ideas. As
for these, it must be admitted that they too frequently represent mere
commonplaces. This poetry is only original when it comments on the affairs
of the time, on political events.[3]

And Robert Griffin, some thirty years later, in his astute study of the
poetry of Marot, still claimed that "the short fixed-form poems, . . .
elaborated and codified by Guillaume de Machaut in the first third
of the fourteenth century, engaged the attention of the meanest
minds of the late fifteenth and early sixteenth century. [Marot's]
contemporaries developed no new forms, and gloried in filling some
of the dustiest bottles with the same old wine."[4] Even though
Stephen Minta in his book on Renaissance love poetry recognizes the
importance of the late medieval tradition in the first half of the

sixteenth century, he claims that anyone passing to Du Bellay's *Olive* (1549) "after reading the love lyrics in a collection such as the *Jardin de Plaisance* (c. 1501) will see that the difference between the two worlds is not in fact one of degree, but of kind."[5]

It has been the aim of the preceding essays to cast some doubt on the certitudes expressed in such statements (to which it would not be difficult to add others of the same tenor by other scholars). To do so, I have put at the center of our reading of certain manifestations of late medieval French poetry the fairly unfettered notion of play, with the poets as players of various games—represented by the poems themselves—in which rules, arbitrary as in all games, govern the form, the content, and the player's own ostensible participation. We have seen, even within such strictly regulated, such seemingly "fixed," games as the rondeau or ballade, for example, an astonishing variety of play, and we have noted as well how the poet, constrained to all appearances by what might seem strangulating conventions of prosody, yet makes room to breathe. This kind of play has thus allowed us to establish connections between the individual poet and his or her work, to define, that is, that space inside which the poetic personality can express itself, not by any Romantic disclosure of the "self" but by play with form and meaning. We have traced the choices made by certain poets in the stock at hand, what they decide to vary, to repeat, to include or eliminate: we have gone from the supremely elegant variations of Guillaume de Machaut, through the always adventurous and frequently masterly permutations of-fered by Christine de Pizan, to the fascinating alterity of the subject found in Alain Chartier's versions of the matter of love and death, to the solemn rhythmical warnings of Meschinot's fantastical rhymes, and on to the licentious and earthy piquancy of the gusty wine with which Molinet sometimes elected to fill those "dustiest bottles," the "courtly" forms. We have, despite Hommel's strictures, often found the presence of an "I," a Doppelgänger that may or may not be close to the often unknowable historical author, who can feign, within the conventions of the time, to be whatever he or she wants to be: a he or a she, like Christine de Pizan, for instance; an observer or a partici-pant in an event or a debate, like Alain Chartier; loved or lost, happy or sad. Like La Fontaine, our authors may not wish to take themselves very often as the subject of their poetry. None of those we have considered choose to be a "sacred dreamer"—although this kind of choice became more available as the century went on.[6] Like Chartier, though, they may wish paradoxically to assure a history for their reputation and their poems by removing the most recognizable historical features or again, like Meschinot (and, incidentally, like Villon) by translating personal experience into that of Everyman.

This central notion of play has made it possible, it seems to me, to look at the texts on their own terms—and not on those of Victor Hugo (or his descendants); if the "facture" of the poem is of greatest concern to the poet, is it not exactly there that the reader's and the critic's task must begin? Certainly reproaching these artists for doing exactly what they set out to do is no way to understand their art. I have thus been led to propose a way of reading the poems that, while showing how the practice they represent connects these late medieval poets one with the other, can also allow us to distinguish one from the other, if we look carefully and closely—more closely than we are used to—at its variety. We have found, for example, that with Guillaume de Machaut they all share a highly developed sense of form; what they do with that sense becomes an essential part of the "inspiration" that seems to Hommel and Griffin and many others to be so lacking.

It is at this point, I think, that the metaphor of play obliges us to make further connections, beyond those between author and text and author and author in the fifteenth century, for it urges a further question. What links this poetry to that of the immediately succeeding poetic generations? Although the space allowed for individual artistic freedom by the kinds of play we have investigated may be small compared with the space given to modern poets, is it really so much more stringent than that allotted to those who follow, not only to a Jean Bouchet, "the longest surviving *rhétoriqueur* poet,"[7] but to a Marot, or even to a Ronsard, to take the poet with the largest breadth in the sixteenth century? I suggest that, in many respects, it is not.

Readers may have noticed that at several points throughout this study I have compared fifteenth-century texts with others of the sixteenth century; this has not been without design. The postlude to a study of late medieval verse is not, of course, the place to undertake any very elaborate investigation of the relation of the earlier poetics to the later. But it seems to me essential nonetheless at least to indicate, in the light of our readings, some paths that appear to connect to those we have already followed. The question is the more compelling in view of the effort of many literary historians not only to delineate but to emphasize what separates late medieval poets from sixteenth-century poets, seen often as the opposite, or nearly so, of their forebears, casting aside old conventions, embodying the new humanism, and responding freely to the new stimuli both Classical and Italian. A few, including such eminent *seizièmistes* as Paul Laumonier and Henri Chamard, have underlined, on the other hand, the undeniable interest of their work for the succeeding generations.[8] I. D. McFarlane appears to me to express this view in an eminently fair-minded and perceptive manner when he underlines the importance in the sixteenth century of the example set by the Rhétoriqueurs; he goes so far as to claim that their dignified concept of poetry was in certain ways close to that of the Pléiade. "The fact that the Pléiade could innovate so much," he contends, "depends on the continuum already provided by the national tradition."[9]

How can this "national tradition," insofar as we have seen it, be useful in reading the poets of the Renaissance, despite the claims to entire novelty that ring along its course and are so often repeated by its present-day chroniclers and exegetes? What is it, in other words, that connects their poetry with the work of their predecessors, that makes them members of the same family of French poets? One link is, of course, their interest, as makers of verse, in prosody and its regulation, in that very "facture" to which Hommel refers. It was in this period, Patterson reminded the readers of his survey of early French poetic theory in 1935, that many rules of classical French versification were formulated: such important features, for example, as the obligatory strict alternation of masculine and feminine rhymes, or the place of the cesura in decasyllabic and alexandrine

lines, or the elimination of the epic and lyric cesura, "and much more
of the ordinary bread and butter of versification."[10] This point is well
documented, and we need not linger over it here.

I should like to approach the question from a different angle,
in the light of our readings in this book. A good starting point is
Minta's claim that the difference between *Le Jardin de plaisance* and
L'Olive is one of kind not of degree, and that anyone going from the
first to the second will recognize that. At first glance, the two do
indeed seem far apart in conception and presentation: the hefty
volume printed in gothic type at the threshold of the century, with
the extreme variety of its nearly 700 poems by both anonymous and
well-known hands not only reflecting the character of earlier manu-
script anthologies but presenting as well a kind of *summa* of poetic
practice of the fourteenth and fifteenth centuries; and the slim vol-
ume of 115 sonnets that appeared in 1550, augmented from a first
edition of 50 sonnets published the year before, a *canzoniere* in the
new style devoted entirely to the love of one poet for one lady. Yet my
experience in teaching French Renaissance literature has been that
students coming to modern editions of texts from each *recueil* for the
first time find them both to be artificial, formally and thematically
repetitive, and far from their own experience either of life or of
poetry: "Ho-hum; another rondeau, another ballade, another sonnet
on unrequited love." They see little to choose from between the
following poem by Chartier, printed in the *Jardin*, and the accom-
panying sonnet from *Olive*:[11]

> Au feu! au feu! qui trestout mon cueur ard
> Par ung brandon tiré d'un doulx regard,
> Tout enflamé d'ardant desir d'amours.
> Grace, mercy, confort et bon secours,
> Ne me laissez brusler, se dieu vous gard.   5
> Flamme, chaleur, ardeur par tout s'espart.
> Estincelles et fumée s'en part;
> Embrasé suis du feu qui croist tousjours.
> Tirez, boutez, chassez tout à l'escart!
> Et dur danger gettez de toute part!   10
> Eaue de pitié, de lermes et de pleurs

A l'aide! las, je n'ay confort d'ailleurs.
Avancez-vous, ou vous viendrez trop tart.

Fire! Fire! it's burning up my heart with the torch of a sweet glance, all enkindled by the burning desire of love. Favor, mercy, solace, and succour, don't let me burn, may God help you. Flame, heat, burning spread everywhere. Sparks and smoke go up. I'm inflamed with ever-growing fire. Pull, push, chase everything out of the way! And throw unkind suspicion out! Help, water of pity, tears and weeping; alas, I've no solace elsewhere. Come forward, or you'll come too late.

Sus, chaulz soupirs, allez à ce froid coeur,
Rompez ce glaz, qui ma poitrine enflamme:
Et vous, mes yeulx, deux tesmoings de ma flamme,
Faictes pluvoir une triste liqueur.

Allez, pensers, flechir cete rigueur,   5
Engravez moy au marbre de cete ame:
Et vous, mes vers, criez devant Madame,
Mort ou mercy soit fin de ma langueur.

Dictes comment ces tenailles d'yvoire
Pour animer l'immortel de sa gloire   10
Ont arraché mon esprit de sa place,

Et que mon coeur rien qu'elle ne respire.
O bien heureux qui void sa belle face!
O plus heureux qui pour elle soupire!

Up, hot sighs, go to that cold heart, break that ice which inflames my breast; and you, my eyes, double witness of my flame, rain down your sad liquor.

Go, thoughts, bend that rigor, carve me in the marble of that soul; and you, my verses, cry out before my lady, Death or mercy be the end of my pining.

Tell how those ivory pincers, in order to give life to her immortal renown, have torn my spirit from its dwelling place, and how my heart breathes nothing but her. How happy he who sees her lovely face! How happier still, who sighs for her!

That there are significant differences between these two poems is undeniable, whether our hypothetical student recognizes them or not. The texture of the fourteen lines of the sonnet is perhaps richer and its organization tighter than those of the thirteen lines of the first text, with the sighs, eyes, and thoughts of the poet all tied to the verses of his poem. The subjects of the two are not entirely identical, although in both a lover speaks in the first person of his inflamed heart and implores mercy, through personified intermediaries, from his lady. The diction is somewhat different; whether one capitalizes them or not, "grace," "mercy," "confort," "bon secours," and "danger" are part of what will seem in the second half of the sixteenth century to be an old-fashioned allegorical vocabulary, although the psychological reality they represent is still there. I am not claiming that one is a better poem than the other. I suggest, rather, that they present similar kinds of problems to a modern reader from the point of view of form and structure, diction and subject or theme, and that no radically different way of reading separates the one from the other, despite Du Bellay's claims. Each one presents a similar though not identical message in a similar though not identical way.

To begin with, despite appearances, both poets have utilized a fixed form, the second of which is instantly recognizable. One must be acquainted with the manuscript tradition of Chartier's works, however, to realize that the first, printed with only thirteen lines, is in fact a rondeau, given in the *Jardin* in its "closed" form, that is, without the usual repetition of the refrain. A well-constructed rondeau must be both closed (making sense without the refrain) and open (making sense with its refrain).[12] Here is the open form as printed in Laidlaw's modern edition, with the refrain in italics:[13]

> *Au feu! Au feu! Au feu, qui mon cuer art*
> *Par un brandon tiré d'un doulx regart,*
> *Tout enflambé d'ardant desir d'amours.*
> *Grace, Mercy, Confort et Bon Secours,*
> *Ne me laissiez bruler, se Dieu vous gart.*   5
>
> Flamme, chaleur, ardeur partout s'espart.
> Estincelles et fumee s'en part;
> Embrasé suis du feu qui croist tousjours.

Au feu! Au feu! Au feu, qui mon cuer art
Par un brandon tiré d'un doulx regart,   10
Tout enflambé d'ardant desir d'amours.

Tirez, boutez, chacez tout a l'escart!
Ce dur dangier getez de toute part!
Eaue, pitié, de lermes et de pleurs!
A l'ayde! Helas, je n'ay confort d'ailleurs   15
Avancez vous ou vous vendrez trop tart!
Au feu! Au feu! Au feu, qui mon cuer art
Par un brandon tiré d'un doulx regart,
Tout enflambé d'ardant desir d'amours.
Grace, Mercy, Confort et Bon Secours,   20
Ne me laissiez bruler, se Dieu vous gart.

I have given both versions of Chartier's poem in order to underline the point that a careful attention to structure is as necessary for the making of a good rondeau as it is for the making of a good sonnet.

Further, one often forgets that the sonnet is also a medieval fixed form, albeit an Italian one; it is in fact the only form to thrive throughout the sixteenth century on French soil (due perhaps in part to its foreignness), although the rondeau and the ballade were to return to favor, the rondeau as early as the seventeenth century.[14] The composition and disposition of the fourteen lines of the sonnet, both individually and as a whole, must then be important in the case of any individual poem, but they acquire even more aesthetic meaning when seen against other examples of the same fixed form, both by the same poet and by others. (The use to which Du Bellay puts the last two verses of the poem quoted above is an example of what I mean by the creative use of the possibilities of disposition of the fourteen lines.) This is one of the essential principles learned through study, for example, of the function of the relatively freer number of lines of the rondeau or of the refrain of the ballade. We have found in those forms variations in *facture*, variations that may appear microscopic to us, yet work toward the constitution of a style. This is no less true in the sixteenth-century sonnet (though it is perhaps more visible)—and it must, I think, be a part of our reading of it. To appreciate the art of the ballade, the rondeau, the chant royal—and the sonnet—we must, in other words, recognize how two given texts, each with the same number of verses and the same rhyme scheme (here the French sonnet becomes more strictly fixed in practice than its Italian model), and treating the same subject, can in fact be two very different poems. In this endeavor I see little essential difference in kind between the lyric forms in vogue in the fifteenth and early sixteenth centuries and the one that was modish some half-century later.

But despite this similarity, not of the forms themselves but of their use by poets of both eras—the careful attention to structure (one thinks particularly of Machaut and Ronsard), the expressive ends to which the obligatory articulations are bent (as in Christine de Pizan, or Du Bellay, or Jean de Sponde, for example), the affective use of different kinds of repetition (the refrain of the ballade, the *sonnet rapporté*)—literary love in the 1420's and in the 1540's, to return to our two examples, must surely have been different. Petrarch and his epigones, Plato and the neo-Platonists have, after all, passed that way. Yet is the difference in fact so great? The heart aflame that figures so prominently in both texts is by no means new in Chartier's day, nor is the "I" whose breast it inhabits and who cries out for help from the lady he loves. Is this "I," this first-person subject to which we have given a certain amount of attention in this study, essentially different in kind from that (or those) found in the *dits* of Chartier or the masculine-voiced ballades of Christine de Pizan? The lesson of the earlier period holds good, I think, for the sixteenth century, with all the playful, almost coquettish, variety we have found. That lesson is what it may not be too forced to call the irreducible alterity of the "I." This too is part of the tradition.[15] Like these despairing subjects, their flames and tears and sighs are entirely traditional elements, as is the death of the lover adumbrated in each text.

Although the sonnet is an excellent example of the Pleiade technique of imitation, using creatively as it does lines from several Petrarchan sonnets (particularly "Ite, caldi sospiri, al freddo core"),[16] and although Tyard, Baïf, Ronsard, and all the rest also imitate the

Italian love tradition, because of the complex nature of that tradition many of its conventions derive in the first place from those found in the earlier poetry of northern and southern France. The genius of Petrarch gave original and striking expression to many of them, and the strength of his poetic personality left its indelible mark on them, too, and these were to be copied and recopied for centuries in the European love lyric. But it is often difficult if not impossible to distinguish in later poetry between a true Petrarchan tag (or one from Serafino or Bembo) and a tag coming from, say, the stock found in troubadour poetry or the French courtly love tradition in general. Minta makes this point in reference to Marot: "the themes which Marot employs are not specifically Italian at all: they belong just as much to the world of traditional French courtly poetry." [17] Even when it is possible to pin down exact sources, however—as in the case of "Sus, chaulx soupirs"—the important thing to recognize, it seems to me, is not so much what that source is as the fact that it is already a kind of commonplace, along with the flames and tears and cries, the *Mercy*, the *Danger*, the sweet cruelty and the happy martyr-dom of so many late medieval love poems. Once its nature as a poetic given is identified, we are free to stop looking for originality in the poet's imagery or psychology and to look for it where it is largely to be found, that is, in the variations impressed on the traditional material. This is how, as we saw in Chapter 1, Machaut made the hoary topos of Fortune and its vagaries into a "nouviau dit"—but this is also how Pierre de Ronsard makes it new in a sonnet like "Comme on voit sur la branche au mois de May la rose" (pp. 54–55). And the same is true in poetic domains other than love, for sixteenth-century poets writing on morality or politics or religion no more eschew commonplaces than do Christine de Pizan, Chartier, Mes-chinot, or Molinet when they treat such subjects.

The very concept of artistic imitation, one of the principal ways, according to Du Bellay's *Deffense et illustration de la langue françoyse*, of improving the quality of French literature, implies quite evidently the reuse, the rewriting, of existing literary material. Machaut's "nouviaus dis" do not, in one sense, say anything new; they are, in a way, old wine put into old bottles. But in another and more important sense it is the label on those bottles—*cru Machaut*—that ensures the quality of the wine. That is the reason that convention, cliché, and commonplace, the very stuff of the poetry of the period that has been at the center of this book (and, I suggest, of the poetry that follows) can in fact be made, through its poetization, to be new, aesthetically, and thus to reveal new truth.

"There is no sudden major breakthrough by the Humanists," writes one scholar about historians in the Renaissance; much as they thought they were returning to the purest springs of Roman history and biography, a comparison will show more similarity to the main medieval tradition than has hitherto been allowed."[18] Something like this may be true, too, for the humanist poets. One caution: I do not in any way mean to leave readers with the impression that late medieval poetry "prepares" for the poetry of the following age, any more than Romantic poetry "prepares" for Baudelaire. That is essentially an ahistoric view, for both must be seen on their own terms. Yet Baudelaire could not have written in the way he did without a Victor Hugo in his literary past. In the same way, the Pléiade did not spring full-grown from the head of Homer or Virgil—or Du Bellay. Though they may have wanted to, the avant-garde of 1550 could not entirely recreate the language—or French poetic habit.

There are undeniable and obvious differences between the way Meschinot in *Les Lunettes des Princes* and Villon in *Le Testament* present "themselves" (and, through the self they choose to represent, the moral lesson they are teaching) and the way Du Bellay, in *Les Antiquitez*, or La Ceppède, in *Les Théorèmes*, for instance, go about reflecting on the ephemeral nature of empires and of man's life or the Christian notion of redemption. What they choose to rewrite is different from the choice of the earlier authors: where Chartier elects to rewrite the drama of courtly love, in *La Belle Dame sans mercy*, Ronsard chooses in his odes to imitate Pindar, singing not the heroes of the Greek games but those of the French court. The artist's option is of course crucial in many ways, for with it come differences in form, in diction, in imagery and tone. But behind these differences, in the very making of the poem (and thus in its reading, too), one can still find the poetic game that their forebears in the French tradition played so well. Perhaps the poet-players of the second half of the sixteenth century, having imbibed more closely to the source the heady neo-Platonic doctrine of the divinity of the poet, or dazzled by the example of Pindar's celebration of heroes and star-struck by Horace's bid for immortality through poetry, take them-selves more seriously than before and carry further the literary self-consciousness that, as we have noted, was part of the stamp of their predecessors. Our exemplary sonnet from Du Bellay, in its self-referential nature, would intimate this. Perhaps the releasing of some of the constraints of the fixed forms (doubtless due in some measure to the example of Classical models) leaves, in the artistic space, more room for the "I." Doubtless the shift from an oral to a printed literary culture brings, with the decline in the repetition of the same rhymes within a poem, new games and new rules. All these may be reasons for the differences; they are fascinating and conjec-tural and must be the subject of another book. The connections I have sketched here suggest, nonetheless, that in a profound sense these poets can be read in the ways that these pages have proposed for the poetry of the preceding age, whose literary legacy they so enthu-siastically rejected. To counter in some measure the irritation such ideas may provoke, perhaps with reason, in both medievalists and *seizièmistes*, I can only remind them that both the poetry of the fifteenth century and the poetry of the sixteenth suffered the same fate in the next: symbolically enough, the last printed edition of the works of Ronsard before the nineteenth century appeared in 1630, only fifteen years or so after the last edition of the works of Alain Chartier.

For many years literary historians have seen sixteenth-century theater only as a "preparation" for the great tragedies and comedies of the Classical period; this is still true to some degree. Perhaps we can avoid such a purgatory for all of fifteenth-century poetry—and not just for Charles d'Orléans and François Villon, or just for the love lyric—for all of it, in its quirky copiousness, its sumptuous and acrobatic rhyming, its frequent moral seriousness, its occasional un-buttoned bawdy, its ego ambiguities, its subtle variety.

Notes

Notes

For complete authors' names, titles, and publishing data on works cited in short form in the Notes, see the Works Cited, pp. 337–47. The abbreviation BN is used for Bibliothèque Nationale.

PROLOGUE

1. The critical debate engendered by Knapp and Michaels, "Against Theory," throws an interesting light on this problem. See the same authors' "Against Theory: A Reply." I need hardly remind readers of the mass of contemporary critical theory that radically questions the possibility of "understanding" texts as they were written.

2. This has been at least the partial endeavor of such important studies in late medieval literature as Olson, *Literature*; Poirion, *Poète*; and Zumthor, *Masque*. I shall have occasion to refer to all of these works.

3. See, for example, the latest book by the distinguished medievalist and literary historian William Calin, *In Defense of French Poetry*.

CHAPTER I

1. The Dutch original, *Herfsttij der Middeleeuwen*, first appeared in 1919.

2. Matthews, "Inherited Impediments." Matthews identifies other obstacles that we shall discuss later. See also his review of R. S. Loomis, *The Development of Arthurian Romance*, in *Speculum* 39 (1964): 719.

3. Meiss, *The Limbourgs*, 1: 5. Meiss claims that Huizinga, as a Dutch republican, "was hostile to all aspects of courtly life."

4. Huizinga, *Waning*, p. 275.

5. See ibid., especially chaps. 1, 2, 11. Consider this, for example: "All things presenting themselves to the mind in violent contrasts and impressive forms, lent a tone of excitement and of passion to everyday life and tended to produce that perpetual oscillation between despair and distracted joy, between cruelty and pious tenderness *which characterizes life in the Middle Ages*" (p. 10; italics mine). Or this (p. 27): "So violent and motley was life, that it bore the mixed smell of blood and of roses. The men of that time almost always oscillate between the fear of hell and the most naive joy, between cruelty and tenderness, between harsh asceticism and insane attachment to the delights of this world, between hatred and goodness."

6. See Lewis, *Recovery of France*. The last essay in this collection is particularly interesting in the context of our discussion: Bernard Guénée, "The History of the State in France at the End of the Middle Ages, as Seen by French Historians in the Last Hundred Years," pp. 324–52.

7. Simone, *French Renaissance*.

8. Guillaume Picot, ed., *Poésie lyrique au Moyen Age* (Paris: Larousse, 1975), 2: 77, 109. Paris's opening lecture at the Collège de France in 1885 was devoted to French poetry of the 15th century. He did not condemn it *en bloc*, to be sure, but after eliminating from consideration the first 40 and the last 20 years of the century, he said of what was left: "Nous ne la [i.e., "la poésie"] verrons, dans l'espace de temps où nous allons l'étudier, que voleter au ras de terre; mais nous l'y trouverons vivace, amusante, variée, nouvelle dans ses formes, parfois déjà presque moderne, et toujours très française" (*Poésie*, p. 261). Cf. his *Esquisse historique*, written in 1901, where the same views are expressed. In Lanson's extremely influential *Histoire de la littérature française*, published in many editions, the section devoted to the 14th and 15th centuries is entitled "Décomposition du Moyen Age," and one of the subtitles for the 15th century is "Décadence générale de la littérature française." See, for example, the 11th ed. (Paris: Hachette, 1909). Henri Guy, in vol. 1 of his *Histoire de la poésie française*, the only general study of the "Rhétoriqueur" poets to appear until 1978, shows a kind of amused condescension toward poets like Crétin, Molinet, and Meschinot, whose work he profoundly misunderstands. His attitude has been widely diffused through manuals and histories of literature.

9. Michaut, *Evolution*, p. 86. Michaut's views are all the more significant because he was not a medieval specialist himself and so, as he confesses in the Preface, had Gustave Cohen, Alfred Jeanroy, and Mario Roques, among the leading French medievalists of the day, read his manuscript and help him to avoid errors.

10. Simone was one of the first scholars after the Second World War to insist on the necessity of re-evaluating the 15th century: see his *French Renaissance* (1961); and *Umanesimo* (1968), pp. 169–99. Schmidt's brief study, *XIVe et XVe Siècles français*, is an attack on Michelet, as well as a passionate defense of the autonomy of the period, written with the author's usual originality and verve. See also his fervent remarks on the Rhétoriqueurs in "L'Age des Rhétoriqueurs." Poirion, *Poète*, dates back to 1965; his *Moyen Age* was published not many years later, in 1971.

11. Badel, *Introduction*, p. 10.

12. This either (medieval)/or (modern) battle is most clearly demonstrated in the difference between Alfred Coville, determined to see "pagan" (i.e., 16th-century) humanism in the early 15th century, and André Combes, who demonstrates—conclusively, I think—a much more intricate relationship between humanism and theology in the same period (see Coville, *Gontier*; and Combes, *Jean de Montreuil*). In one of a series of articles on the controversy, argued largely on scientific grounds, Ernst Cassirer reminds us pertinently that "ideas like Gothic, Renaissance, or Baroque are ideas of historical 'style.' They can be used to *characterize* and *interpret* intellectual movements, but they express no actual historical *facts* that ever existed at any given time. 'Renaissance' and 'Middle Ages' are, strictly speaking, not names for historical periods at all, but they are concepts of 'ideal types,' in Max Weber's sense." ("Some Remarks," p. 55.)

13. In Lewis, *Recovery of France*, Guénée proposes a period stretching from the mid-13th to the mid-16th century, one manifesting considerable historical cohesion, "no longer the era of feudal monarchy and not yet that of absolute monarchy, and whose virtue was . . . not simply to have survived the first and foreshadowed the second. . . . This period has, from a political point of view, a unity, an originality and a character of its own" (p. 339). For a useful rapid survey of economic, social, and political changes, see Johnson and Percy, *Age of Recovery*, especially chaps. 1–3.

14. Cf. Poirion, *Poète*, pp. 55, 57–61. As early as 1405, Christine de Pizan warned merchants' wives not to imitate the classes above them; this of course implies that they did. Cited by Laigle, *Le Livre des trois vertus*, p. 293.

15. Pierre Jodogne, "Les Rhétoriqueurs et l'humanisme: problème d'histoire littéraire," in Levi, *Humanism*, pp. 159–60.

16. Simone, *French Renaissance*, p. 152.

17. BN MS fr. 1584.

18. See Chartier, *Poetical Works*, p. 43.

19. See the interesting pages devoted to this process in Badel, *Intro-*

duction, pp. 96–100 and particularly pp. 224–29. The controversy started by Joseph Bédier's questioning in 1913 of the Lachmann method of establishing an archetypal text by comparing manuscripts seems to have resulted in a combination of that method with the reproduction of the "best" manuscript, as recommended by Bédier. See, for a recent example, the sensible remarks of Eric Hicks in *Débat*, pp. lv–lvii; and Chaytor, *From Script to Print*, pp. 148–52.

20. Charles d'Orléans, *Poésies*, 2: 307–8.

21. Champion, *Manuscrit autographe*, pp. 7, 67. This is reproduced from BN MS fr. 25458.

22. Defaux, "Charles d'Orléans," p. 222. "Qui s'aviserait jamais," he writes, "de ponctuer 'Le Pont Mirabeau' ou 'La Nuit Rhénane'?" He proposes (pp. 218–19) no pause at all between the second and third stanzas of the poem; I do not see how, as he claims, this adds to its charm.

23. The [s] followed by a consonant became silent, in most cases, well before the Middle French period, although it continued frequently to be represented orthographically until the middle of the 18th century (Bourciez, *Précis*, p. 155).

24. All of these changes are found in many modern anthologies. See, for instance, the intelligent selection edited by Alan Boase, *The Poetry of France, 1: 1400–1600* (London: Methuen, 1964), p. 15; the language is also modernized in the following, all with wide dissemination in France: J. Charpier, *Charles d'Orléans* (Paris: Seghers, 1958), pp. 4, 177; André Lagarde and Laurent Michard, *Moyen Age: les grands auteurs français du Programme* (Paris: Bordas, 1960), p. 209 (with a two-line refrain after the second stanza); and Jules Hasselman, *Rutebeuf, Charles d'Orléans, François Villon* (Paris: Hatier, 1964), pp. 34, 129 (at p. 34 one finds "broderie," but "luyant" and "orfaverie" are retained; the punctuation is Champion's).

25. *Le Jardin de plaisance*, a facsimile of the Paris edition of ca. 1501, gives (fol. cxv^v) "Sot oeil raporteur etc." Raynaud, *Rondeaux*, p. 9, prints a two-line refrain after the first section and a four-line refrain after the third, at the end of the poem. In Löpelmann, *Rohan*, p. 408, the first and second refrains consist only of the first verse of the poem, without any indication that any words are substituted for "etc."; Champion also uses only the first verse each time the refrain returns, but he encloses "raporteur de nouvelles" in brackets.

26. Defaux, "Charles d'Orléans," goes into the matter in great detail and summarizes the major theories regarding this problem of evident

importance without offering an entirely convincing solution himself. One of the clearest and most useful accounts of the problem is found in Wilkins, "Structure," p. 343. Wilkins very rightly insists on the necessity, for literary scholars, of understanding the lyric pattern underlying rondeau, ballade, and virelai. It is his opinion that "with Christine de Pisan the shortened refrain is used consistently; that Alain Chartier's Rondeaux should appear with full repetitions of their refrains, that Charles d'Orléans's Rondeaux employ shortened refrains in contrast to full refrain repetitions in his so-called Chansons; that in Villon more than the first one or two words should appear." See also Poirion, *Poète*, pp. 338–39.

27. Chaytor, *From Script to Print*, pp. 5–21. Cf. Reaney, "Guillaume de Machaut," p. 46: "It is possible that half the effect of the fourteenth-century poem depended on the way it was read."

28. Wilkins's attractive and intelligent anthology, *One Hundred Ballades*, includes examples of a number of musical settings and a bibliography of modern editions of 15th-century pieces set to music.

29. Poirion, *Poète*, p. 445.

30. The standard modern work on the history of French pronunciation is Fouché, *Phonétique historique*. A very useful shorter treatise is Bourciez, *Précis*. For a convenient summary of the chief phonetic features of the language from 1100 to 1600, subject to some caution in use, see Alton and Jeffery, *Bele Buche*. See also Poirion, *Poète*, pp. 436–37, discussing certain "alliances de sonorités" in poems of the period.

31. See Bourciez, *Précis*, p. 50; and Alton and Jeffery, *Bele Buche*, p. 16.

32. Christine de Pizan, *Ballades*; Deschaux, *Poète bourguignon*.

33. Marcel Raymond, *De Baudelaire au surréalisme* (1940), 2d ed., rev. (Paris: Corti, 1963).

34. The most recent literary study of Machaut's work is Brownlee, *Poetic Identity*. See also, on the narrative poetry, Calin, *Poet at the Fountain*. Machabey, *Guillaume de Machaut*, vol. 1, gives the most detailed account of Machaut's life. For a convenient study of his music, see Reaney, *Machaut*. Consult the Works Cited (Guillaume de Machaut) for full particulars on the collections of his poetry and for the two complete editions of his musical compositions.

35. Of the ten major manuscript sources for Guillaume de Machaut's lyric poetry, four seem to have been prepared directly under his supervision. In one (BN MS fr. 1584), there is, as we have seen, the important notation, the

first of its kind in French literature: "Vesci l'ordenance que G. de Machaut vuet qu'il ait en son livre."

36. In his edition of *La Louange*, Wilkins includes 282 poems: 206 ballades, 60 rondeaux, 7 virelais, 7 chants royaux, 1 ballade double, and 1 "dit notable," with no underlying musical structure.

37. There are many examples. See, for instance, Deschamps, *Œuvres*, 7: 17–20, 22, 24; Christine de Pizan, *Œuvres*, 1: 59, 93–98, 212, 226; and Charles d'Orléans, *Poésies*, 2: 301, 333, 437, 490, 491.

38. Reproduced in both Guillaume de Machaut, *Poésies lyriques*, 1: 1–13, and Machaut, *Œuvres*, 1: 1–12.

39. Cf. Guillaume de Machaut, *Œuvres*, 2: xxii, where Hoepffner recalls the lyric pieces included in the *De consolatione philosophiae* (see also p. xxxv). Calin, *Poet at the Fountain*, gives a list of medieval authors who, before Machaut, inserted songs into narrative verse.

40. Guillaume de Machaut, *Œuvres*, 1: liv–lv. It is Hoepffner who, following the earlier edition of Tarbé (1849), gave these prefatory pieces the title "Prologue," found only in one late-14th-century manuscript (p. liii). For other recent discussions of the "Prologue," see Brownlee, *Poetic Identity*, pp. 16–18; Calin, *Poet at the Fountain*, pp. 234–37; and Kelly, *Medieval Imagination*, pp. 3–4.

41. Calin, *Poet at the Fountain*, p. 237.

42. Poirion, *Poète*, p. 91.

43. Guillaume de Machaut, *Œuvres*, 2: 12, l. 316.

44. In the late narrative *La Fonteinne amoureuse* (ca. 1360), one finds still that the lover tries to acquire Bon Espoir and Dous Penser, "Car vraiement, qui d'euls deus se derange, / S'il aimme fort, il se gette en la fange" (Machaut, *Œuvres*, 3: 174–75, ll. 887–88).

45. See Camproux, *Joy d'amor*; and Poirion, *Poète*, pp. 90–91.

46. In ballade 1, Nature tells Guillaume "Par Scens aras ton engin enfourmé / De tout ce que tu vorras conformer" (By Sense your mind will be furnished with everything you'll want to fashion; ll. 10–11); in ballade 2, Machaut writes of making "dis amoureus ordenez" (fit amorous poems; l. 6); in the third ballade, Love gives him the possibility of writing many beautiful poems, "et par mainte ordenance" (by many a precept; l. 19); in the last, the poet thanks Love for bringing him his children "pour moy donner avis / Et matere dont c'ordener porray / Dont Nature de vous m'a fait devis" (to give me counsel and argument with which I can put in order what Nature has told me about you; ll. 6–8). This "ordering" of poems,

putting verses together in the right way, seems to be the task of Scens. In *La Fonteinne amoureuse*, it is clear that Scens is wisdom and intelligence, for it is equated with the goddess Pallas (Guillaume de Machaut, *Œuvres*, ll. 1743–44).

47. See the very useful chronology of manuscript sources in *Louange*, pp. 10–11; cf. the table in Avril, "Manuscrits enluminés," p. 133, which includes MS 396, in the Pierpont Morgan Library, New York, not consulted by Wilkins.

48. *Louange*, pp. 18–23.

49. Ibid., p. 19.

50. See Wilkins, "Structure," p. 340. As Wilkins notes, although there is the mathematical possibility of a 19-line rondeau, no example of this is known. Many more apparent types of rondeau structure are found, created, as we have seen, by the suppression of part of the refrain at the repetition points.

51. Delbouille, "En relisant Rutebeuf." Cf. Guiette, "D'une poésie formelle au Moyen-Age" (1949), in Guiette, *Forme et senefiance*, pp. 1–24.

52. Regalado, *Poetic Patterns*, p. 192.

53. See Dragonetti, *Technique*, p. 178, on the variation of traditional topoi by the *trouvères*.

54. This kind of anthology exists, with an excellent selection of texts and very helpful notes: Wilkins, *One Hundred Ballades, Rondeaux and Virelais from the Late Middle Ages*. The evolution of this poetry has been charted for the first time, in great detail and with extraordinary sensitivity, by Poirion in *Le Poète et le Prince*; this work is now one of the cornerstones of any analysis of the courtly lyric in the 14th and 15th centuries, and I have used it abundantly. But Poirion's subject allows him only to consider poetry written in the *formes fixes*.

55. See Simone, *French Renaissance*, especially chap. 5; and Nicholas Mann, "Petrarch's Role as Moralist in Fifteenth-Century France," in Levi, *Humanism*, pp. 6–28.

56. See, for example, Utley, "Must We Abandon the Concept of Courtly Love?"; and Frappier, "Sur un procès."

57. Reaney, "Guillaume de Machaut," pp. 40–42.

58. Dragonetti, *Technique*, pp. 137, 541–42. Cf. Regalado, *Poetic Patterns*, p. 193: "because of . . . changes in our way of thinking about poetry, we can scarcely now conceive of poetry written within a tradition and not against it."

59. Dragonetti, *Technique*, p. 556.

60. See Courcelle, *Consolation*; Lowinsky, "Mathaeus Greiter's *Fortuna*"; and Patch, *Goddess Fortuna*.

61. See also, for the theme of Fortune, *Le Confort d'ami*, another consolation poem, ll. 1854ff (Machaut, *Œuvres*, 3: 1ff); and *Le Voir-Dit*, ll. 8239ff. See also Schilperoot, *Guillaume de Machaut*, pp. 42–45.

62. See Wilkins's remarks on the chronology of the various major manuscripts in *Louange*, pp. 12–13; and Guillaume de Machaut, *Œuvres*, 1: xliv ff. An excellent summary of the problem of the chronology of the poems set to music may be found in Reaney, "Towards a Chronology."

63. See, among others, *Louange*, nos. 9–12, 20, 26, 110, 180, 190, 196.

64. A number of scholars have contested the veracity of *Le Voir-Dit* and its autobiographical nature; the most recent, Calin, sees in it another example of play, of Machaut's creation of a particular persona. See the very interesting chapter he devotes to it in *Poet at the Fountain*, pp. 167–202. We shall return to this point in Chap. 2.

65. In *Louange*, a first-person subject is found in all but two of the 282 poems (nos. 94, 254).

66. Of the 206 ballades in ibid., only five others present the two-rhyme peculiarity, and only seven ballades have real two-line refrains.

67. For the music, see Guillaume de Machaut, *Works*, 3: 118–19. The ballade has been recorded: *The Art of Courtly Love*, Early Music Consort of London, cond. David Munrow, Seraphim Records, sic 6092, 1973; *Chansons*, Studio der Fruhen Musik, cond. Thomas Binkley, Reflexe, c 063-30106, 1972; *Motets, Ballades, Virelais and Rondeaux*, Collegium Musicum of the University of Illinois, cond. George Hunter, Westminster, xwn 181166, 1956. There is a commentary on this poem in Kuhn, *Poétique*, pp. 469–73, in which the author claims (p. 485 n. 2) that stanzas ii and iii are inverted in Chichmaref. He follows the order given in B. Woledge, ed., *The Penguin Book of French Verse* (Penguin Books: Baltimore, 1961), 1: 220–21, i.e., with stanza ii as I have printed the poem becoming stanza iii. Chichmaref is a very careful editor, whose edition follows mainly ms Vg (now in the Wildenstein Gallery in New York). Another careful editor, Schrade, prints the stanzas as I have done, and none of the manuscripts I have checked—bn mss Fr. 853, 1584, 1585 (a copy of Vg), 1587, 9221, 22.545—follow the order Kuhn adopts.

68. Zumthor, *Langue et techniques*, pp. 143–44: "Structure expressive et mentale complexe, le registre procède en quelque manière, quant à sa cohérence, de l'imagination matérielle (au sens où l'entend Bachelard),

tandis que les enchaînements et le dessein général des oeuvres tiennent à l'imagination formelle." See also his *Essai de poétique médiévale*, pp. 231–32.

69. Text of 1587, in Isidore Silver, ed., *Les Œuvres de Pierre de Ronsard* (Paris: Didier, 1966), 2: 179.

70. Translation from Geoffrey Brereton, ed., *The Penguin Book of French Verse* (Harmondsworth, Eng.: Penguin Books, 1958), 2: 56–57. Translation copyright © Geoffrey Brereton, 1958, 1974. Reproduced by permission of Penguin Books, Ltd.

71. Frappier, "*Sur un procès*," p. 192.

72. Calin, *Poet at the Fountain*. See especially, in Poirion, *Poète*, pp. 192–205, 318–33.

73. Reaney, "Poetic Form," p. 29: "The triviality of the Rondeau was the cause of its ultimate abandonment, though in the Middle Ages delicate trifles were greatly admired, and besides Rondeaux were excellent for setting to music." It would be difficult to prove that "triviality" caused the abandonment of the rondeau, considering that other lyric forms—the ballade, the lai, hardly "trivial"—were also given up.

74. Deschamps, *Œuvres*, 7: 269–71. Cf. Reaney, "Guillaume de Machaut," p. 50, who claims that this "natural music" "is clearly exemplified in the poetry of Machaut." I agree—but suggest a larger consequence. Poirion, on the other hand, in *Poète*, p. 438, finds that "Chez Machaut, la musique est ailleurs [que dans les vers], le vers se contente d'alliances de mots."

75. Dragonetti, "Poésie."

CHAPTER 2

1. Deschamps, *Œuvres*, 1: 243–46. The musical setting is by F. Andrieu; see Guillaume de Machaut, *Musikalische Werke*, 1: 49–51.

2. For a convenient brief account of these writer-musicians, see Wilkins, "Post-Machaut Generation." Wilkins gives a selection of their poetry in *One Hundred Ballades*, pp. 39–56.

3. Deschamps, *Œuvres*, 6: 251–52.

4. The fullest bibliographical account of Christine's considerable oeuvre is Solente, "Christine de Pisan," pp. 348–414. See also Pinet, *Christine de Pisan*, pp. xi–xx, and, for an extended literary commentary, pp. 203–456. See also McLeod, *Order of the Rose*. An excellent recent study is Willard, *Christine de Pizan*.

5. See Rigaud, *Idées féministes*; and, for a recent interesting reassessment of Christine's "feminism," Willard, "Fifteenth-Century View."

6. For an attractive evocation of Christine's youth, written with the author's usual verve just before his death as the first chapter of a projected work, see Schmidt, "Christine de Pizan."

7. Indeed, Paulin Paris, in his description of the *Cent Ballades*, takes them all as the direct expression of the author's feeling (*Manuscrits françois*, pp. 149–56).

8. BN MS fr. 1584, fol. 2^r. See the very interesting discussion of this manuscript and its relation to Machaut's poetic practice in Huot, *From Song to Book*, pp. 274–301, especially p. 300: "The *Louange des dames*, the ballades and the lays each open with the image of a man beseeching or embracing a woman. For each of the texts we are given the visual representation of the pure lyric voice of the lover; there is no attempt . . . to identify this figure with the figure of the poet." On the dating of the manuscript, see Avril, "Manuscrits enluminés."

9. The other tradition to which I refer is that of the poet who writes not about love but about what he proposes as his own "life": his misery in marriage, his debts, his sickness, his love of wine, and so forth. One finds it in the Goliardic poets and later, of course, most notably in Villon. As Regalado has shown for Rutebeuf (*Poetic Patterns*), this "mode" is as conventional as the courtly mode.

10. Calin, *Poet at the Fountain*, p. 246. See also pp. 186–89.

11. See especially Roy, *Œuvres*, 1: xxxvii, 271–79.

12. For a list of nearly 30 manuscripts of the *Cité des dames*, see Solente, "Christine de Pisan," pp. 382–84. Eighteen manuscripts of the *Fais d'armes* are listed, pp. 400–402. This work was printed by Antoine Vérard in France in 1488; it was translated and printed by Caxton the following year.

13. See the interesting chapter in Willard, *Christine de Pizan*, "The Search for a Patron," pp. 155–71.

14. Christine de Pizan, *Lavision*, pp. 164–65.

15. Ibid., p. 164. My punctuation. "Adonc me pris a forgier choses iolies, a mon commencement plus legieres; et tout ainsi comme l'ouvrier qui de plus en plus en son oeuvre s'asoubtille comme plus il la frequente, ainsi tousiours estudiant diverses matieres, mon sens de plus en plus s'imbuoit de choses estranges, amendant mon stile en plus grant soubtilleté et plus haulte matiere, depuis l'an 1399 que je commençay jusques à cestui 1405, ouquel encore ie ne cesse. Compilés en ce tandis .xv. volumes principaulx, sanz les autres particuliers petiz dittiez, lesquelx tous ensemble contienent environ .lxx. quayers de grant volume."

16. Willard puts the beginning of her writing career around 1394, about four years after her husband's death (*Christine de Pizan*, p. 43).

17. See the interesting essays in Bornstein, *Ideals for Women*.

18. Christine de Pizan, *Livre de mutacion*, 1: ll. 1319, 1329–97.

19. Willard, *Christine de Pizan*, p. 108. See also p. 48.

20. See "A Feminine Utopia," in ibid., pp. 135–53; and Willard, "Christine de Pizan's *Livre des trois vertus*: Feminine Ideal or Practical Advice?," in Bornstein, *Ideals for Women*, pp. 91–116. See also Richards's Introduction to Christine de Pizan, *Book of the City of Ladies*. For a clear account of the complicated literary quarrel over *Le Roman de la rose*, see Willard, *Christine de Pizan*, pp. 73–89; and for the documents in the case, see Hicks, *Débat*.

21. Hicks, *Débat*, p. 168. See as well Christine's statement in *Lavision*, p. 181. Philosophy is speaking to Christine: "fust meismes converty ton corps foible et femenin en homme" (your weak and feminine body was even changed into that of a man).

22. Poirion, *Poète*, pp. 237–54. See also Poirion, *Moyen Age*, pp. 203–10. Poirion provides the most thorough study of Christine's use of the lyric form; his pages have been invaluable for my own reading of her poetry.

23. Poirion, *Moyen Age*, pp. 207–8. Cf. his *Poète*, p. 250.

24. For one example among many commonplaces, see three ballades on absence and the springtime: Roy, 1: 35 (*Cent Balades*, no. 34); 1: 244 (*Autres Balades*, no. 32); 3: 287 (*Cent Balades d'amant et de dame*, no. 79).

25. Text from Christine de Pizan, *Ballades*, p. 75.

26. Cf. Poirion, *Poète*, pp. 336–42, 357.

27. I amend the punctuation of l. 2, which in Roy is printed "Quant le mary, ma dame, est revenu." The poem does not appear to be addressed to the woman, and the genitive juxtaposition makes more sense. Another slight emendation is the use of dashes instead of commas in l. 7.

28. Zumthor, *Langue, Texte, Enigme*, pp. 68–88.

29. *Louange*, no. 254; Chichmaref, 1: 211.

30. See Roy, *Œuvres*, 3: iv–ix.

31. See Du Bellay, *Œuvres*, p. 35.

32. Ibid., no. 1.

33. Sponde, *Poésies*, p. 244.

34. Translation from Geoffrey Brereton, ed., *The Penguin Book of French Verse* (Harmondsworth, Eng.: Penguin Books, 1958), p. 162. Translation copyright © Geoffrey Brereton, 1958, 1974. Reproduced by permission of Penguin Books, Ltd.

35. Similar poetic *jeux de société* are to be found in the question-and-

answer poems popular at the same time; see Guillaume de Machaut, *Œuvres*, 1: iii, lxi.

36. There are 19 quatrains, 44 sizains, 6 huitains, and 1 dizain in the collection.

37. There is one possible exception: it is not clear in no. 51 (Roy, 1: 200) whether or not the person who answers is a woman or simply a neutral moral voice; the "biens" mentioned could, of course, be those of love.

38. Poirion, *Poète*, p. 82.

39. Huizinga, *Homo Ludens*, p. 122.

40. Such anagram signatures are frequent in late medieval poetry. They are to be found, for example, in Machaut, Villon, and Molinet.

41. "Lay mortel" is what it is called in the manuscript (Roy, 3: 317). See Jacqueline Cerquiglini's very stimulating Introduction to this text (Christine de Pizan, *Cent Ballades*).

42. Zumthor, *Masque*, pp. 244–66. See also Zumthor's examples in *Anthologie*.

43. The dating of Meschinot's religious poetry is Martineau-Génieys's (Meschinot, *Lunettes des Princes*, pp. xxxiii–xxxvii). The poem is printed on p. xxxv, n. 24. It also appears in Zumthor, *Anthologie*, p. 42, in a modernized text that I follow.

44. See Zumthor, *Masque*, p. 259.

45. Zumthor, ibid., claims 1,088 possible combinations. His calculation is perhaps not entirely exact, since he speaks of the line as octosyllabic.

46. Molinet, *Faictz*, 2: 455–56.

47. Ibid., p. 531.

48. Ibid., p. 532.

49. The same historical circumstances provide, in a different way, the impetus for another Marian poem by Molinet, an "Oroison à Nostre Dame" (ibid., 2: 468–75), in which each of the 18 strophes begins and ends with the *incipit* of a secular love song.

CHAPTER 3

1. For a detailed description of the 17th-century edition, see Laidlaw, "André du Chesne's Edition." For other editions, see Walravens, *Alain Chartier*.

2. Chartier, *Quadrilogue*, p. 1. For proof of his reputation for eloquent oratory, see Hoffman, *Alain Chartier*. On the revival of rhetoric in the late Middle Ages and early Renaissance, see "Textes de transition: la poétique comme marge de la rhétorique," in François Rigolot, *Le Texte de la*

Renaissance: des Rhétoriqueurs à Montaigne (Geneva: Droz, 1982), pp. 25–40.

3. For the fullest account of Chartier's life, see Walravens, *Alain Chartier*; for his ambassadorial travels specifically, see pp. 27–34.

4. Poirion, *Poète*, p. 262.

5. For the chronology of the poems, which is far from certain, see Chartier, *Poetical Works*, pp. 28–42; and Walravens, *Alain Chartier*, pp. 92–93.

6. See Chartier, *Poetical Works*, pp. 360–61, for this letter. I shall use the following short titles for Chartier's works in the text and the notes: *Le Lay de plaisance* = *Plaisance*; *Le Lay de paix* = *Paix*; *Le Breviaire des nobles* = *Breviaire*; *La Complainte* = *Complainte*; *Le Debat des deux fortunés d'amours* = *Deux Fortunés*; *Le Livre des quatre dames* = *Quatre Dames*; *Le Debat de reveille matin* = *Reveille Matin*; *La Belle Dame sans mercy* = *Belle Dame*; *Le Debat du herault, du vassault et du villain* = *Herault*; *L'Excusacion aux dames* = *Excusacion*.

7. The definition of what constitutes a *dit* has always been a loose one, and scholars differ on what exactly is meant by the term. After reviewing various definitions, in a recent article that seeks to come to grips with the problem in a new way, Jacqueline Cerquiglini posits the following as constants for the genre: "le dit . . . travaille sur le discontinu"; "le dit est un discours qui met en scène un 'je,' le dit est un discours ou le 'je' est toujours représenté" ("Le Clerc et l'écriture," pp. 158, 160). She goes on to suggest (p. 165) that the "je" represented is that of *le clerc*. All of these criteria fit the poems of Chartier under discussion, with the exception of *Plaisance*.

8. Nesson wrote his *Lay de Guerre* a few years after Chartier's *Paix* (Droz and Piaget, *Pierre de Nesson*, pp. 12–19).

9. Quoted in Poirion, "Lectures," p. 702.

10. Curtius, *European Literature*, p. 158.

11. Machaut in the role of a more or less passive witness is found, however, in *Le Jugement de Behaigne* and in *La Fonteinne amoureuse*; he may well be the model for Chartier here.

12. For summaries of 15th-century and modern views, see Poirion, "Lectures"; and Kibler, "Narrator as Key."

13. I am far from claiming that these courts ever existed as anything more than a literary fiction or, at most, a social divertissement. Machaut varies the tradition by submitting—or pretending to submit—the question to kings: *Le Jugement dou roy de Behaingne*; *Le Jugement dou roy de Navarre*.

14. For the manuscripts, see Chartier, *Poetical Works*, pp. 328–29.

15. Chartier, *La Belle Dame sans mercy et les poésies lyriques*, ed. Arthur Piaget (originally published in 1945). For other editions, see Walravens, *Alain Chartier*, pp. 249–53.

16. For the 15th-century reactions to the work, see Piaget's six-part article, "La Belle Dame sans merci et ses imitations."

17. Chartier, *Belle Dame*, p. viii; Hoffman, *Alain Chartier*, p. 64.

18. Garapon, "Introduction," pp. 97–98.

19. Shapley, *Studies in French Poetry*, p. 116. See especially his conclusion, pp. 114–20.

20. Poirion, "Lectures," pp. 703–5.

21. Kibler, "Narrator as Key," p. 723.

22. This claim of abandoning poetry by a saddened poet is a convention found also in Machaut and Christine de Pizan; obviously it is not put into practice by the authors with those names, although it may be by their poetic personae. It serves here to emphasize the highly literary nature of the personage.

23. Chartier, *Belle Dame*, p. x.

24. See the table in Poirion, *Poète*, pp. 385–86.

25. Shapley, *Studies in French Poetry*, p. 52.

26. Laidlaw thinks that *Reveille Matin* "almost certainly" antedates *Belle Dame*, which was written in 1424 (Chartier, *Poetical Works*, p. 39). But Droz dates it to 1425 (Chartier, *Quadrilogue invectif*, p. viii); Walravens finds it impossible to date (*Alain Chartier*, p. 93). Certainly nothing in the text or in the manuscripts permits dating the poem with any certainty.

27. White, "Conflict of Generations," pp. 232–33.

28. See the table in Poirion, *Poète*, p. 385. Chartier uses the same rhyme scheme in one of his five ballades (see his *Poetical Works*, p. 391). Machaut also uses it, but only once, in the 206 ballades of *La Louange des Dames* (Wilkins ed., no. 112, p. 78).

29. White, "Conflict of Generations," p. 233.

30. The Fat Knight's defense, after a seven-line introductory remark, takes 429 lines, compared with the Thin Knight's 424. The former's reply or rebuttal is stated in 30 lines, the latter's in 4 (ll. 1117–46, 1152–55).

31. We learn in the final part of the poem that the company decided to send it for judgment to Jean de Grailli, Count of Foix. This has been the basis for the attempts to date the poem (see Chartier, *Poetical Works*, pp. 30–31).

32. Ballade no. 27, ll. 1–2.

33. *Belle Dame* dates from 1424; Walravens (*Alain Chartier*, p. 92) and Laidlaw (Chartier, *Poetical Works*, pp. 32–34) agree on 1416 as the year of composition for *Quatre Dames*. See also Hoffman, *Alain Chartier*, pp. 102–3; and Champion, *Histoire poétique*, 1: 11–17. Despite these accounts, I find an absolute dating of the poem impossible, since the references within it are vague and conventional; although the battle referred to is almost certainly Agincourt, there is nothing in the poem itself to indicate that Chartier composed it immediately following that French defeat.

34. The alliteration in ll. 2063–65 combines with the double use of "fortune," first as a substantive and then as a verb, with two meanings of "deserte" (l. 2064: "forsaken"; l. 2065: "ravaged"), and with the unusual rhymes in *creüe* to emphasize strongly the pathetic effect of this passage, with its insistence on the unmerited nature of the second lady's predicament, which is increased by her passionate desire for her lover. Cf. ll. 2098–2113, where the third lady insists on the poignant struggle between hope and desire.

35. The scheme of sixteen lines is clearly an augmentation of the twelve-line strophe: a a b a a b b b c b b c; a a a b a a a b b b b c b b b c. Though they resemble ballade stanzas, these exact schemes are rarely if ever found in the ballades of the 14th and 15th centuries; see the table in Poirion, *Poète*, pp. 386–87.

36. This is not everyone's opinion of the work; see Hoffman, *Alain Chartier*, pp. 96–97, 100, for unfavorable views, based chiefly on the poem's "artificiality" and the belief that it does not reflect as it should the catastrophic public events of the time.

37. See Chartier, *Poetical Works*, p. 328.

38. On the "Querelle du Roman de la rose," see Hicks, *Débat*, Introduction; and on the "Querelle des Amies," M. A. Screech's Introduction to the facsimile edition of *Opuscules d'Amour, par Heroet, La Borderie, et autres divins poëtes* (New York: Johnson Reprint Corp., 1970). Although in my view the Querelle du Roman de la rose was a largely literary affair, the important role played in it by Christine de Pizan certainly represented, for her, a serious manifestation of her authority as a writer and particularly as a woman writer whose opinions—both on women and on Jean de Meung and his influence—were not to be taken lightly.

39. See Walravens, *Alain Chartier*, p. 92, who dates the poem from 1414 (also Champion, *Histoire poétique*, 1: 2); and Chartier, *Poetical Works*, p. 28, where Laidlaw dates it from 1411.

40. Cf. Machaut, *Le Lai de confort, Le Lai de plour,* and *Le Lai de bon espoir.* See Poirion, *Poète,* pp. 400–414, for an interesting analysis of the lai and its affective use by poets.

41. Chartier was particularly celebrated in the 15th and 16th centuries as a writer of lais; see Hoffman, *Alain Chartier,* p. 34 n. 3.

42. *La Complainte* is dated by most scholars to ca. 1424, that is, composed in the same period as *Belle Dame,* in which the poet refers to his lady as being dead. Nothing, of course, proves that this was true—or that the dead lady referred to in both poems is the same one. See Champion, *Histoire poétique,* 1: 62–63; Hoffman, *Alain Chartier,* p. 52; and Walravens, *Alain Chartier,* p. 93 (which gives the date 1424 as uncertain). For the various titles, see Chartier, *Poetical Works,* p. 321; and Hoffman, *Alain Chartier,* p. 48 n. 1.

43. Hoffman, *Alain Chartier,* pp. 48–51, merely summarizes the poem and speculates on its influence on Charles d'Orléans and Villon. Shapley, *Studies,* pp. 47–49, gives a very brief analysis, with no assessment of the poem's literary quality. In the Introduction to Chartier, *Poetical Works,* pp. 40–41, Laidlaw treats it very briefly; he does see it, however, as a "moving poem, in which Chartier's rhetorical and poetic skills are combined most effectively." Even Poirion, in his sensitive analysis of the genre of the complainte (*Poète,* pp. 406–9, 415–22) and his general account of Chartier's work (ibid., pp. 255–70), hardly mentions it.

44. Champion, *Histoire poétique,* 1: 62.

45. Chartier, *Poetical Works,* p. 320; Walravens, *Alain Chartier,* p. 248.

46. Poirion, *Poète,* pp. 406–8.

47. Chartier, *Poetical Works,* pp. 320–21.

48. Zumthor, *Essai,* p. 73.

49. The instability of strophes (and, to some extent, of lines; see Chartier, *Poetical Works,* pp. 320–21) found in *Complainte* is a common feature of medieval texts. It is discussed most pertinently by Pickens in *Songs of Jaufré Rudel,* pp. 19–42. His conclusion concerning the 12th-century troubadour's lyric poems appears to me to be valid for Chartier's complaint: "it is impossible to rediscover Jaufré's intentions (i.e., the extent of his personal involvement in the creation and regeneration of his works)" (p. 39). Cf. Laidlaw: "Although the texts of the *Complainte* differ widely, it is impossible in most cases to find any objective reason for preferring one of the versions available to the others" (Chartier, *Poetical Works,* p. 321). These considerations, of course, go beyond the existence of mere scribal errors, inevitable in any text transmitted in a manuscript tradition.

50. It is interesting to note in this connection that such medieval *artes poeticae* as those of Matthew of Vendôme and Geoffrey of Vinsauf treat literary style, in the words of A. C. Spearing, as "purely . . . a matter of local verbal arrangement. . . . Their remarks about structure . . . consist merely of directions for beginning a work . . . and for attaching the middle to the beginning and the end" (*Criticism*, p. 55). See also Murphy, *Rhetoric*, pp. 168–73.

51. *Ad. C. Herennium, Libri IV*, tr. Harry Caplan (Cambridge, Mass.: Harvard University Press, 1954), pp. 283–85. On the popularity of the *Ad Herennium* in the Middle Ages, see Caplan's Introduction, pp. xxxv–xxxvii, and Murphy, *Rhetoric*, pp. 109ff. and passim. See also Jenkins, *Artful Eloquence*, pp. 41–42.

52. Isidore Silver, ed., *Les Œuvres de Pierre de Ronsard* (Paris: Didier, 1966), 2: 179. My italics.

53. Cf. Christine de Pizan, "De triste cuer chanter joyeusement" (rondeau 11, Roy, 1: 153) and "Je chante par couverture, / Mais mieulx plourassent mi oeil" (virelai 1, Roy, 1: 101–2). For Chartier, see *Quatre Dames*, ll. 352–68.

54. See, for other examples, rondeau 5 (Chartier, *Poetical Works*, p. 376): "Triste plaisir et doloreuse joye, / Aspre doulceur, resconfort ennuyeux, / Ris en plourant, souvenir oblieux, / M'accompaignent combien que seule soye."

55. "Se part y" = "se part-il" (see Chartier, *Poetical Works*, p. 462).

56. See the description of "France" as envisioned in a dream of the Acteur's, in Chartier, *Le Quadrilogue invectif*, pp. 5–10. In the following paragraphs, France laments her situation and harangues the Three Estates, represented by the Peuple, the Chevalier, and the Clergé (pp. 10–19).

CHAPTER 4

1. La Borderie, *Jean Meschinot*, p. 46; Guy, *Ecole*, pp. 140–41.

2. Saint-Gelais, *Séjour*, p. 25. Although James calls the lines from Saint-Gelais a ballade, they are not: they are simply three successive strophes of the poem (ll. 5253–76). The use of his edition of *Le Séjour* is subject to considerable caution; see the severe strictures of Jacques Lemaire, *Bibliothèque d'Humanisme et Renaissance*, 41 (1979): 666–69; and Giuseppe di Stefano, *Le Moyen Français*, 3 (1979): 168–70.

3. Regalado, *Poetic Patterns*, p. 264. Cf. p. 263: "I believe the choice of poetic personality, in the broadest sense, is determined by the poetic genre and themes."

4. Christine Martineau-Génieys, in Meschinot, *Les Lunettes des Princes*, p. xcii. Further references will be to *Lunettes*. *Opus magnum* is the term used by Guy, *Ecole*, p. 102; Zumthor uses the term "prosimètre" (*Masque*, pp. 241–43).

5. For one type of allegorical journey, see Wenzel, "Pilgrimage of Life."

6. It is interesting to note that the lists become longer in the 1542 edition—as if such titles were by then even more amusing.

7. See Fletcher's well-known study *Allegory: The Theory of a Symbolic Mode*; and Sutch, "Allegory and Praise."

8. Guy, *Ecole*, p. 102.

9. Frye, *Anatomy*, pp. 308–14. My argument in the next few pages is heavily indebted to Frye's remarks.

10. Ibid., p. 310.

11. Ibid., p. 312.

12. Ibid., p. 313.

13. For Martineau-Génieys's persuasive argument for the date of composition, see *Lunettes*, pp. cv–cvi.

14. For the early editions, see ibid., pp. lxxix–lxxxiv.

15. The prose passages of Lefranc's *Champion des dames*, for example, are uncharacteristically brief for an *opus magnum*, although the work is clearly an anatomy; moreover, there is only a partial modern edition, published in 1968.

16. For details of Meschinot's life, see *Lunettes*, pp. x–xxviii.

17. This exchange—and whether or not the "prince" of the poems refers to Louis xi—has engendered some controversy among scholars; see Delclos, "*Le Prince* ou *Les Princes*." Since neither poem mentions the king by name, and since castigating bad rulers is a commonplace in literature throughout the Middle Ages, the exchange appears to me not to be political poetry in any narrow sense but rather, like Alain Chartier's *Complainte*, poetic texts that their authors allow to function transhistorically, exactly by avoiding historical particularities. As a result, the picture of the bad ruler is as valid in the 20th century as it was in the 15th.

18. *Lunettes*, pp. xxix–lxx. See also Champion, *Histoire poétique*, 2: 193–238. It is clear from the account books of the dukes of Brittany that Meschinot was known and appreciated as an occasional poet.

19. Frye, *Anatomy*, p. 312.

20. La Borderie, *Meschinot*, pp. 46, 47.

21. *Lunettes*, p. ciii.

22. Ibid.

23. In this respect, it is interesting to note that less time separates *La Nausée* (1939) from *Les Lunettes* (ca. 1464) than separates *Les Lunettes* from the *Consolation* (ca. 524). On the relationship between *Les Lunettes* and the *Consolation*, see Zumthor, *Masque*, p. 242.

24. Frye, *Anatomy*, pp. 307–8.

25. Zumthor, *Masque*, p. 86.

26. Frye, *Anatomy*, p. 308.

27. Ibid.

28. See Jean Dufournet's illuminating studies of Commynes, *Destruction des mythes*, and *Etudes sur Philippe de Commynes*. See also his Introduction to Commynes, *Mémoires sur Louis XI*.

29. In her discussion of the title and its meaning, Martineau-Génieys gives a list of other works of the time whose titles similarly combine an object and a class or abstraction (*Lunettes*, p. xc). We have already seen what use Rabelais makes of this vogue. Since reading glasses were probably used in Europe as early as the 13th century, Meschinot clearly did not count on technological novelty for the effect of his title.

30. Dated 1482, the picture is in the Church of the Ognissanti in Florence.

31. That the "Princes" of the title refers to all men is a point that many scholars have missed and on which Martineau-Génieys rightfully insists (*Lunettes*, pp. xc–xci).

32. Zumthor, *Masque*, p. 155; Zumthor's discussion of the use of proverbs by the Rhétoriqueurs is found on pp. 152–60. See also Meschinot, *Les Lunettes* (ed. Toscani), p. x.

33. See also *-able* (LXVII) and *-table* (xxv); *-esse* (LXXXII, LXXXIV) and *-gesse* (xIV), *-ire* (xI) and *-dire* (xXII), etc.

34. Grammont, in his well-known *Petit Traité de versification française*, first published in 1908, is particularly hard on what he considers excess in rhyme: "La rime trop riche a l'air d'un jeu de mots et doit toujours être évitée dans les genres sérieux" (p. 38).

35. See Langlois, *Recueil d'arts*. Consider, for example, the beginning of the anonymous *Règles de la seconde rhétorique* (p. 11): "Cy commencent les regles de la Seconde Rettorique, c'est assavoir des choses rimées" (Here begin the rules of the Second Rhetoric, that is, of rhymed things).

36. *Lunettes*, p. 96 n. 35. See also p. cxxvi.

37. This designation does not appear, so far as I know, in the manuscripts of *Les Lunettes*.

38. That the persona presented as the author is approaching middle age seems to be indicated in LXXXV, ll. 1–3: "Cecy m'avint entre esté et antonne, / Ung peu avant que les vins on antonne, / Lors que tout fruit maturation prent" (This happened to me between summer and autumn, just before wine is put in the barrel, when all fruits come to ripeness).

39. See Lubienski-Bodenham, "Origins of the Fifteenth-Century View of Poetry."

40. *Lunettes*, p. xcvi.

41. Cf., for example, in *Le Séjour d'honneur*, the first two sentences of Octovien de Saint-Gelais's Prologue, addressed to Charles VIII (James ed., p. 35):

> A la trèshaulte, treschretienne et tresredoubtée imperiale puissance et souveraine majesté de vous, Charles, par la grace de Dieu vivant, roy victorieux et monarque de toute France, huytiesme de ce nom, soit louange perpetuelle, honneur sans fin toujours durant, vie prospere et bien heurée. Et à vous, sire, plaise sçavoir que je, de tout mon cueur et dès le mien primerain aage, dès aussitost que la lumiere de vostre si treshault et grant renom et de vostre incomparable preeminence fut à mes yeulx notifié, et par le vent de fameuse renommée jusques à mes oreilles cheue, ne feiz que penser, et à par moy estriver comment je, de voz treshumbles subgiectz, pourtant le moindre de qui le nom taire de [= je] doiz pour ma trop grande petitesse, pourroye parvenir à si grant heur d'ymaginer ou de comprendre à sçavoir chose ediffier ou mettre en fait par laquelle je sceusse au moins ung coup avoir de vous la veue, et qui vous peust aucunement plaire ou donner ung moment d'aise.

> To the most high, most Christian, and most redoubted imperial power and sovereign majesty of Charles, by the grace of the living God victorious king and monarch of all France, eighth of the name, be perpetual praise, unending eternal honor, prosperous and fortunate life. And may it be known to you, Sire, that, as soon as the light of your eminent and great reputation and of your incomparable preeminence appeared to my eyes and, wafted by famous renown, fell upon my ears, I could only think and contend with myself how I, though the least of your humble servants, whose name I should hide be-

cause of my exceeding lowliness, could reach such good fortune as to imagine or to understand how to erect or set up something by which I could, at least once, gain sight of you, and which could please you a little or give you a moment's delight.

42. Cf. the first sentence of this narration: "En celluy mesme endroit, mon oraison finee, sans aulcune dissimulation ou aultre occupation prendre, moy estant en ma povre et chetive habitation pour satisfaire a mon naturel appetit oppressé et indigent de repos, pour les ennuyeuses peines et dolentes pensees en quoy tout celuy jour avoye esté, me mis sur mon lict, las et traveillé, penssant tous mes affaires regetter pour a reposer entendre" (In this same place, when my prayer was over, with no dissimulation or any other occupation, being in my poor and wretched habitation in order to satisfy my appetite heavy with sleep and needful of it, because of the grievous sorrows and painful thought in which I had spent that whole day, I went to bed, weary and troubled, thinking that I would put aside all my cares; *Lunettes*, p. 33, ll. 53–59).

43. See *Lunettes*, p. 99 n. 71, for references to contemporary texts in which the same *état second* appears. See also the apparition of Sensualité to the Acteur near the beginning of Saint-Gelais's *Séjour* (pp. 45–46): "Et pour ce que bien m'estoye rembarré en ma chambrette, et l'huys fermé pour me celer si n'es ung [= nesung] vint en ce droit lieu, gettay ma veue, lors apperceu dame ou deesse qui ja s'estoit sans porte ouvrir au dedans mise ainsy qu'esperit ou bien fantasme, dont me trouvay assés surprins, ja n'est merveille" (And since I had carefully closed myself in my little room and had locked the door in order to hide myself were anyone to come into that very place, I looked up and saw a lady or goddess who, without opening the door, had already come in, like a spirit or phantom; that surprised me considerably, and it's no wonder).

44. Zumthor makes a useful distinction between allegory as a way of reading and allegorizing ("l'allégorèse") as a way of writing, and he reminds us that in allegorizing the important aspect is showing, not explaining (*Masque*, pp. 79–80).

45. See the very pertinent remarks on Rabelais as "The Olympian Author," in Coleman, *Rabelais*, pp. 45–77.

46. Guy, *Ecole*, p. 21.

47. Champion, *Histoire poétique*, 2: 213, 216, 217. The quote is at p. 211.

48. Ibid., pp. 211, 217.

49. Zumthor, *Masque*, p. 157. In Martineau-Génieys's analysis of the third part, for example, we find such expressions as "les conseils de Prudence," "Justice, comme sa soeur Prudence, commence, elle aussi, par rappeler," and "ainsi commencent les reproches que fait dame Tempérance au poète" (*Lunettes*, pp. xcvii, xcviii, c).

50. Montaigne, *Essais*, 3: 6.

51. Marot, *Œuvres poétiques*, p. 334. The third stanza contains another sort of wordplay, exemplified by the first four lines: "Dieu des amans, de mort me garde, / Me gardant donne moy bonheur, / En le me donnant prens ta darde, / En la prenant navre son coeur" (O god of lovers, save me from death; saving me, give me happiness; giving it to me, take up your arrow; taking it up, wound her heart). See also Marot's early "Petite Epître au Roy," written entirely in *rimes équivoquées* (ibid., p. 45): "En m'esbatant je faiz rondeaulx en rime, / Et en rimant bien souvent je m'enrime; / Brief, c'est pitié d'entre nous rimailleurs, / Car vous trouvez assez de rime ailleurs" (For sport I write rondeaux in rhyme, and while rhyming I often catch cold; in short, it's pitiful amongst us rhymsters, for you find plenty of rhyme elsewhere). And so on for 26 amusing verses. See, too, the chanson in *rimes enchaînées*, "Plaisir n'ay plus, mais vy en desconfort" (Pleasure have I no longer; instead, I live in heaviness of heart; p. 333). A particularly striking example of vertical rhyme-play is the ballade "Du jour de Noël," rhymed in *-ac, -ec, -ic, -oc*, and *-uc* (p. 297).

52. Crétin, *Œuvres poétiques*, p. 276.

53. It is not true that all the rhymes are *équivoquées*, as Martineau-Génieys claims (*Lunettes*, p. cxxv).

54. Martineau-Génieys is slightly in error here, for in her analysis of the structure of the third part of *Les Lunettes*, she lists lying as one of the sins; in fact, it precedes them all (ll. 149–70). As a result, she omits from her list the sin of gluttony (ll. 451–80).

55. See Chatelain, *Recherches*, pp. 144–45.

56. Quoted in *Lunettes*, p. xcviii; cf. Chatelain, *Recherches*, p. 144: "Du quatorzième à la fin du quinzième siècle, le septain terminé par un proverbe a été fort cultivée."

57. See the articles on proverbs in medieval literature in *Revue des Sciences Humaines* 163 (1976): 311–418 and the bibliography of studies on proverbs (pp. 431–36).

58. I have repunctuated line 1136, which in my source reads: "La paour, faveur."

59. Meschinot uses -age as the b rhyme in the second strophe of the section and as the a rhyme in the fourteenth. In the eleventh, one finds -tient in b position, following -ient (preceded by both [t] and [v]) in the a rhyme of 11.

60. Chatelain cites only two other uses of it in the 15th century (*Recherches*, p. 132).

61. Brownlee, *Poetic Identity*. See especially the Introduction, "Machaut and the Concept of *Poète*," p. 16 and passim.

62. Ibid., p. 212.

63. Badel, *Introduction*, p. 149.

64. Ibid., p. 7.

65. I do not mean here to claim for Villon any "modernity"; rather the opposite: I emphasize Baudelaire's association, partly unconscious, perhaps, but also partly conscious (and ironic), with the Christian tradition. His aesthetic difference from a Meschinot or a Villon is, of course, very great.

66. The format and illustrations of many of the printed editions of *Les Lunettes* resemble those of Books of Hours.

67. Meschinot, *Les Lunettes des princes, avec aucunes balades et addicions* . . . (Paris: Philippe Pigouchet, 1495), fol. n2ʳ.

CHAPTER 5

1. Chartier, *Poetical Works*, pp. 391–92. See Hassell, *Middle French Proverbs*. In addition to the references listed in Chap. 4, see also on proverbs in 15th-century French literature, Muhlethaler, *Poétiques*, pp. 65ff.

2. See Villon, *Œuvres*, ed. L. Foulet. 4th ed. (Paris: Champion, 1958), pp. 81–82.

3. Although Hassell lists the expression "de cul et de pointe," he does not refer to this poem (*Middle French Proverbs*, p. 88).

4. See also Droz and Piaget, *Introduction*.

5. See Nykrog, *Les Fabliaux*, p. 18. For an excellent recent account of the fabliau as a genre and its place in medieval French culture, see Muscatine, *The Old French Fabliaux*. In another interesting recent study, *The Scandal of the Fabliaux*, R. Howard Bloch looks at the fabliau in the light of contemporary critical theory and finds, among other things, that its texts can be seen most usefully as referring to themselves and their making rather than to any contingent external reality, either historical or sociological.

6. The poems published by Schwob come from the following manuscripts: BN, fr. 1717, 1719 (the bulk of the collection), 1721, 2264, 2375,

19.165, 24.442, 25.527, fr. n.a. 4237; and Bibliothèque de l'Arsenal, 3521.

7. The major study is still Dupire, *Jean Molinet*. Zumthor, *Anthologie*, pp. 75–108, prints a number of Molinet's poems. Zumthor also refers to Molinet frequently in his study of the Rhétoriqueurs, *Masque*; see especially pp. 135–43.

8. See Zumthor's remarks on this poem in *Masque*, p. 136.

9. Despite Dupire's claim, in *Faictz*, 3: 1169, that green is the color of fools, it is clear here, as elsewhere, that it means new love (whereas blue symbolized true love). Cf. Guillaume de Machaut, *Louange*, ballades 176, 193.

10. For other examples of the "sermon joyeux," see "Sermon nouveau et fort joyeulx, auquel est contenu tous les maulx que l'homme a en mariage," in Montaiglon, *Recueil de poésies*, 2: 5–17, and "Sermon de l'Andouille," ibid., 4: 87–93.

11. Bonnelle is mentioned in Molinet's *Chroniques* as having diverted by his antics the crowd of notables present in 1492 when peace was arranged between Maximilian of Austria and Philip of Cleves (see *Faictz*, 3: 1040–41).

12. For the *Breviaire* and the *Psaultier*, see W. H. Rice, "Deux poèmes sur la chevalerie," *Romania* 75 (1954): 54–65, 82–97. And for other parodies of religious texts in Molinet, see Dupire, *Jean Molinet*, pp. 116–22. For *L'Amant rendu cordelier*, see the edition of A. de Montaiglon (Paris: Société des Anciens Textes Français, 1881).

13. Ed. J. Rychner (Geneva: Droz, 1967). See the interesting comment on this text in the "Sermon nouveau et fort joyeulx" referred to in note 10: "*Matrimonie matrimonia / Mala producunt omnia. /* Le thesme qu'ay ci recité, / Extraict d'ung livre bien dicté, / Nommé les *Joyes de mariage*, / Vault autant en commun languaige / Que qui diroit par mocquerie: / L'homme est bien fol qui se marie" (*Matrimonie matrimonia mala producunt omnia*. The theme I've here repeated, taken from a well-written book called *The Joys of Marriage*, amounts in the common tongue to saying scoffingly, "The man who marries is a fool indeed").

14. Zumthor, *Masque*, p. 136.

15. The metaphor is clear when one looks at Cotgrave's definition of "merrien": "Timber for building, or boords; . . . also, the beame of a Bucke; the branch of a Stag."

16. "Je n'y fays tousjours que penser / A ces ors viés puans cabas" (ll. 141–42).

17. "Marque" = "femme," in jargon, according to Schwob. "Lof-

fue" may mean "folle." "Clappier": "In old time Baudie houses were also tearmed, *Clapiers*" (Cotgrave).

18. Cotgrave defines "broudier" (under *brodier*) as a Norman expression: "The arse, bum, taile."

19. *Louange*, nos. 50, 58, 66.

20. Chartier, *Poetical Works*, p. 336, ll. 147–51.

21. For another example of this kind of language used in poetry, see *Rohan*, p. 347, an injurious rondeau that begins, "Etront de chien en son visage" (Dog shit in his face).

22. Also Schwob, p. 208. Cf. Villon, *Le Testament*, ll. 1122–23: "Mais pour conjoindre culz et coetes, / Et couldre jambons et andoulles" (But to join together asses and tails and sew together hams and sausages). "Coetes" is a diminutive of *queue*.

23. All these terms—and others—are found in *Le Debat du viel gendarme et du viel amoureux*.

24. See, for example, *Œuvres*, 4: 116 (on his fiftieth birthday: "Tout mon bon temps est alé," he claims), 5: 43, 196, 6: 30, 7: 3, and 8: 134–35.

25. This can be compared to a ballade in manuscript 53 in the Stockholm Library, quoted in Schwob, p. 288; the last two lines of the first stanza are very similar to Deschamps's refrain: "Mais quant à moy je souhaitte sans plus / Vit d'Orleans et tousjours dix escus." Schwob, p. 150, prints a comparable ballade (from BN MS fr. 2375), whose envoy expresses the same wish: "Prince, je suis plain de merancolie, / Veu que j'ay ma brocquette amolie / Et qu'argent fault: c'est pour estre mys jus. / Mais je desire, soit ou sens ou folie, / Vit de vint ans et tousjours vint escus" (Prince, I'm full of melancholy, since my prick is soft and I've no money: that's a real put-down. But—be it reason or madness—I want the cock of a 20-year-old and 20 crowns forever).

26. Champion, *Poésies*, 2: 397. The following lines are from p. 536.

27. Ibid., p. 544.

28. Ibid., 1: 136. See also the ballade that begins "Mon cueur est devenu hermite / En l'ermitage de Pensee" (ibid., p. 64).

29. Huizinga, *Waning*, chap. 11. See also Gilson, *Idées*, pp. 9–33.

30. Ibid., p. 139.

31. Except for removing the brackets around the final repetition of the refrain, I print the poem as it is found in Schwob. One must remember, however, that just how much of the refrain of a rondeau should be repeated is not always easy to determine. In this case, it is, of course, conceivable that the entire first line served as the refrain.

32. "Behourt" means "joust" or "tourney"; it is often found in an obscene sense.

33. The version I use is Schwob 194. Cf. a poem printed in Montaiglon, *Recueil de poésies*, 2: 245ff, which begins as a satire of the manner of Charles d'Orléans: "Seulle, esgarée de tout joyeux plaisir, / Dire me puis en amours maleureuse; / Au lit d'ennuy il me convient gesir / Sur l'oreiller de vie langoureuse" (Alone, estranged from every joyous pleasure, I can say I'm unlucky in love; it befits me to lie in the bed of weariness, on the pillow of listless life). But it soon becomes very clear what the source of the lady's "ennuy" really is: "J'ay du *jeu d'amer* grant soufreté" (I greatly lack the game of love).

34. The poem is reprinted in a slightly different version in *Le Jardin de plaisance*, fol. 121ʳ.

35. For an excellent succinct account of the cultural relativism of the idea of obscenity, see La Barre, "Obscenity: An Anthropological Appraisal."

36. See Christine's letter to Jean de Montreuil (Hicks, *Débat*, p. 13): "[Jean de Meung] trop traicte deshonnestement en aucunes pars, et mesmement ou personnage que il claime Raison, laquelle nomme les secrez membres plainement par nom" (Jean de Meung speaks too immodestly in some passages, and even in the character he calls Reason, who calls the private parts openly by name). Cf. *Le Roman de la rose*, ed. Daniel Poirion (Paris: Garnier-Flammarion, 1974), ll. 5537–38, 7108–52. For the punning use of *con* and *vit* in the fabliaux, see Muscatine, *Old French Fabliaux*, pp. 113–15.

37. Kaplan, "Obscenity," p. 554.

38. See another rondeau on the same page of the manuscript: "Quant de foutre me souvyent" (Schwob, p. 131). See also the rondeau beginning "Cons barbus rebondis et noirs" (ibid., p. 164).

39. Also printed in ibid., pp. 232–33.

40. See a text like Molinet's "Chanson sur l'orde de belistrie" (*Faictz*, 2: 725–28), a poem describing the corps of beggars; the language is often indecent (see especially ll. 61ff), but the subject is not.

41. There appears to be an earlier literary tradition of the "catalogue de cons": it is found, for example, in two fabliaux: *Les Quatre Souhaits St. Martin* (Montaiglon and Raynaud, *Recueil général*, p. 206) and *Le Fabliau du moine* (ed. A. Långfors), *Romania* 44 (1915–17): 560–63.

42. For an interesting perspective on sexual punning in the fabliaux, see "The Fabliaux, Fetishism, and the Joke," in Bloch, *Scandal*, pp. 101–28.

43. Reprinted in Zumthor, *Anthologie*, p. 103.

44. Dupire, *Jean Molinet*, p. 140.

45. Zumthor, *Masque*, p. 140.

46. A somewhat different version of the poem is found in Schwob, p. 165.

47. See Zumthor's interesting remarks on this poem in *Masque*, p. 139. And compare another poem by Molinet on "la maladie de Naples," in *Faictz*, 2: 852–53. Another poem on the same subject is found in Montaiglon, *Recueil de poesies*, 2: 99ff.

48. Minta, *Love Poetry*, p. 22.

49. Guiette, *Forme*, p. 65.

50. Ibid., p. 50.

51. See the succinct account of the meaning of the term *courtoisie* in Zumthor, *Essai*, pp. 466–75, to which my discussion is in debt.

52. See Guiette, *Forme*, p. 62: "Ce monde courtois était-ce une classe vivant courtoisement ou tendant seulement vers un idéal courtois? Le rapport entre l'esprit courtois et la réalité pouvait se limiter à un snobisme appelé courtois parce qu'il existerait dans le monde des cours? ou seulement de l'état imaginaire de la société tel que le présentait la littérature, c'est-à-dire une fiction?"

53. See Zumthor, *Essai*, p. 470.

54. Cf. Donoghue, *Courtly Love Tradition*, p. 14: "If the term were abolished, a large body of European literature from different countries and in different languages but with striking common features would be without a name." For a useful summary of the concept and its controversial history, see Boase, *Origin and Meaning of Courtly Love*. See also Newman, *Meaning of Courtly Love*. Frappier, in "Sur un procès," insists rightly, it seems to me, on the distinction between "courtoisie," meaning a set of social virtues, and "amour courtois," which designates an essentially antisocial attitude, in conflict with feudal and Christian morality.

55. Campion, *Poésies*, 2: 358; Chartier, *Poetical Works*, p. 376.

56. Minta, *Love Poetry*, p. 22.

57. Poirion, *Poète*, p. 21.

58. Ibid., p. 20 n. 4, citing Siciliano, *Villon*, p. 421.

59. This was Catherine de l'Isle-Bouchard, whose surprising amourous career is sketched by Poirion, *Poète*, p. 47. On the royal debauchery after the death of Agnès, see also pp. 34 (reference to a ballade of Deschamps concerning a drunken orgy in which Louis d'Orléans participated), and 54–55, 129–30 ("il est vrai que les passions amoureuses se traduisent souvent, dans les milieux aristocratiques, par toutes sortes de violences").

332 Notes to Pages 283–92

60. See Vaughan, *Philip the Good*, pp. 132–33.
61. Poirion, *Poète*, p. 57.
62. Camproux, *Joy d'amor*, p. 156.
63. See Pernoud, *Pour en finir avec le Moyen Age*, p. 73. See also her *Histoire*, vol. 1.
64. Camproux's point of view becomes clear when, after showing how certain troubadours like Aimeric de Peguillan and Folquet de Marseille were bourgeois who became knights, he writes (*Joy d'amor*, p. 34): "On peut estimer que ces gens-là vivaient en une heureuse époque où il était possible d'être, ou de devenir, troubadour et chevalier, quoique né bourgeois, fils de bourgeois!" And he goes on to assert (p. 35) that, "En réalité il n'y avait point de rupture entre les châteaux et les cités en pays d'Oc; point de hiatus entre le bourgeois et le chevalier."
65. The most influential literary critic professing this view has been M. Bakhtin, in his study on the popular elements in Rabelais, published in Russia in 1965, in English in 1968 (Cambridge, Mass.: M.I.T. Press; tr. Hélène Iswolsky), and in French in 1970 (Paris: Gallimard; tr. Andrée Robel).
66. For a summary of his conclusions, see Zumthor, *Masque*, pp. 267ff, and especially pp. 278ff.
67. See Poirion, *Poète*, p. 36, where the author speaks of "la redoutable complexité de l'homme de cette époque: piété, savoir, courtoisie, débauches, comment tout faire tenir dans la même définition?"
68. Baltruşaitis, *Réveils*, pp. 197, 336.
69. In *Literature as Recreation*, Olson demonstrates persuasively that the salutary benefits of laughter (and of the literary production of it) were well known in the late Middle Ages.

EPILOGUE

1. Schmidt, *XIVe et XVe Siècles*, p. 5.
2. Du Bellay, *Deffence*, p. 108.
3. Hommel, *Chastellain*, p. 38.
4. Griffin, *Clément Marot*, p. 26.
5. Minta, *Love Poetry*, p. 12.
6. One of the earliest references to the divine influence received by poets from Apollo is found in the *Instructif de la seconde rhetorique* of Regnaud le Queux, which dates from ca. 1480 and is printed in *Le Jardin de plaisance*, fols. bv^v–ciii^r.

7. Britnell, *Jean Bouchet*, p. ix. Bouchet died in 1557.

8. See Patterson, *Three Centuries*, pp. 227–29, and in general, pp. 216–307.

9. McFarlane, *Renaissance France*, p. 38. The entire section on the Rhétoriqueurs is an excellent summary of their place in literary history.

10. Patterson, *Three Centuries*, p. 227. See Britnell, *Jean Bouchet*, pp. 26–34, on Bouchet's role in establishing some of these rules.

11. I give the *Jardin* poem as it appears on fol. clxiiᵛ, adding only punctuation. The Du Bellay sonnet appears in his *Œuvres poétiques*, 1: 84–85.

12. See Britnell, "Clore et rentrer." The term "ouvert" is Pierre Fabri's; the usual technical terms referring to the rondeau with and without repetition of the refrain are those Britnell uses, "clore" and "rentrer." For Fabri's rule, see his *Grand et Vrai Art*, 1: 63–67.

13. Chartier, *Poetical Works*, pp. 383–84.

14. That the rondeau disappeared for only a brief time is attested by the title of an anthology published in Paris as late as 1552: *Recueil de tout soulas et plaisir pour resjouir et passer temps. Aux amoureux comme Espistres, Rondeaux, Ballades, Epigrames, Dixains, Huistains . . .* (Lachèvre, *Bibliographie des recueils*, pp. 36–37). This collection, reprinted in 1562 or 1563, includes poems by G. Crétin, Charles d'Orléans, André de la Vigne, Jean Molinet, Octovien de Saint-Gelais, and Villon, as well as works by such 16th-century poets as Claude Chappuys, Antoine Du Saix, Clément Marot, and Mellin de Saint-Gelais.

15. See Caldarini in his edition of *L'Olive*, p. 15: "Du Bellay déclare dès le début que son recueil veut être une poésie *bene litterata*. Il écarte par là la nécessité d'une relation entre sa poésie et une vérité biographique qui peut paraître en dernière analyse douteuse et qui est à ses yeux certainement insignifiante pour la création littéraire."

16. *Le Rime*, no. 153, cited in ibid., pp. 121–22.

17. Minta, *Love Poetry*, p. 2. Minta is here contesting—correctly, in my view—the opinion of C. A. Mayer, who finds in Marot's love poetry early and indubitable signs of Petrarchan influence in France. See for example Marot, *Œuvres diverses*, p. 26.

18. Morse, "Medieval Biography," p. 268.

Works Cited

Works Cited

This list omits all anthologies and manuals used mainly for illustration in the text, and a few works cited only once. Full bibliographical references to these sources are given in the Notes.

Alton, Jeannine, and Brian Jeffery. *Bele Buche e Bele Parleure: A Guide to the Pronunciation of Medieval and Renaissance French for Singers and Others*. London: Tecla Editions, 1976.

Avril, François. "Les Manuscrits enluminés de Guillaume de Machaut," in *Guillaume de Machaut*. Colloque-Table ronde organisé par l'Université de Reims, April 19–22, 1978. Paris: Klincksieck, 1982.

Badel, Pierre-Yves. *Introduction à la vie littéraire du Moyen Age*. Paris: Bordas, 1969.

Baltruṣaitis, Jurgis. *Réveils et prodiges: le gothique fantastique*. Paris: Armand Colin, 1960.

Bloch, R. Howard. *The Scandal of the Fabliaux*. Chicago: University of Chicago Press, 1986.

Boase, Roger. *The Origin and Meaning of Courtly Love*. Manchester, Eng.: Manchester University Press, 1977.

Bornstein, Diane, ed. *Ideals for Women in the Works of Christine de Pizan*. Medieval and Renaissance Monograph Series 1. N.p.: Michigan Consortium for Medieval and Early Modern Studies, 1981.

Bourciez, Edouard. *Précis de phonétique française*. 9th ed. Paris: Klincksieck, 1958.

Britnell, Jennifer. "'Clore et rentrer': The Decline of the *Rondeau*," *French Studies* 37 (1983): 285–95.

————. *Jean Bouchet (1476–1557)*. Edinburgh: Edinburgh University Press, 1986.

Brownlee, Kevin. *Poetic Identity in Guillaume de Machaut*. Madison: University of Wisconsin Press, 1984.

Calin, William. *In Defense of French Poetry: An Essay in Revaluation*. University Park: Pennsylvania State University Press, 1987.

————. *A Poet at the Fountain: Essays on the Narrative Verse of Guillaume de Machaut*. Lexington: Kentucky University Press, 1974.

Camproux, Charles. *Joy d'amor (jeu et joie d'amour)*. Montpellier: Causse et Castelnau, 1965.

Cassirer, Ernst. "Some Remarks on the Question of the Originality of the Renaissance," *Journal of the History of Ideas* 4 (1943): 49–56.

Cerquiglini, Jacqueline. "Le Clerc et l'écriture: le *Voir Dit* de Guillaume de Machaut et la définition du *dit*," pp. 151–68 in H. U. Gumbrecht, ed., *Literatur in der Gesellschaft des Spätmittelalters*. Heidelberg: Carl Winter, 1980.

————. "Tension social et tension d'écriture au 14e siècle: les dits de Guillaume de Machaut," pp. 111–29 in Danielle Buschinger, ed., *Littérature et société au Moyen Age*. N.p.: Université de Picardie, Centre d'Etudes Médiévales, 1978.

Champion, Pierre. *Histoire poétique du quinzième siècle*. 2 vols. Paris: H. Champion, 1923.

————. *Le Manuscrit autographe des poésies de Charles d'Orléans*. Paris: H. Champion, 1907.

Charles d'Orléans. *Poésies* (1923–27). 2 vols. Paris: H. Champion, 1971.

Chartier, Alain. *La Belle Dame sans mercy et les poésies lyriques*. Ed. Arthur Piaget. 2d ed. Geneva: Droz, 1949.

————. *Les Œuvres de Maistre Alain Chartier*. Ed. André Du Chesne. Paris: le-Mur or Thiboust, 1617.

————. *The Poetical Works of Alain Chartier*. Ed. J. C. Laidlaw. Cambridge, Eng.: Cambridge University Press, 1974.

————. *Le Quadrilogue invectif*. Ed. E. Droz. 2d ed. rev. Paris: H. Champion, 1950.

Chatelain, Henri. *Recherches sur le vers français au XVe siècle: rimes, mètres et strophes*. Paris: H. Champion, 1908.

Chaytor, Henry J. *From Script to Print*. Cambridge, Eng.: W. Heffer, 1945.

Chichmaref, *see* Guillaume de Machaut, *Poésies lyriques*.

Christine de Pizan. *Ballades, Rondeaux, and Virelais*. Ed. Kenneth Varty. Leicester, Eng.: Leicester University Press, 1965.

————. *The Book of the City of Ladies*. Tr. Earl Jeffery Richards. New York: Persea Books, 1982.

————. *Cent Ballades d'amant et de dame*. Ed. Jacqueline Cerquiglini. Paris: Union Générale d'Editions, 1982.

————. *La Lamentacion sur les maux de la France*. Ed. A. J. Kennedy. Pp. 177–85 in *Mélanges de langue et littérature françaises du Moyen Age et de la Renaissance offerts à Monsieur Charles Foulon . . .* , vol. 1. Rennes: Université de Haute-Bretagne, Institut Français, 1980.

————. *Lavision-Christine*. Ed. M.-L. Towner. Washington, D.C.: Catholic University of America, 1932.

————. *Le Livre de la Mutacion de Fortune*. Ed. Suzanne Solente. 4 vols. Paris: Picard, 1959–66.

————. *Le Livre des fais et bonnes meurs du sage roy Charles V*. Ed. Suzanne Solente. 2 vols. Paris: H. Champion, 1939.

————. *Le Livre du chemin de long estude*. Ed. Robert Püschel. Berlin: Damkoher-Le Soudier, [1881].

————. *Œuvres poétiques*. Ed. Maurice Roy. 3 vols. Paris: Firmin-Didot, 1886–96.

Coleman, Dorothy Gabe. *Rabelais: A Critical Study in Prose Fiction*. Cambridge, Eng.: Cambridge University Press, 1971.

Combes, André. *Jean de Montreuil et le Chancelier Gerson: contribution à l'histoire des rapports de l'humanisme et de la théologie en France au début du XVe siècle*. Paris: Vrin, 1942.

Commynes, Philippe de. *Mémoires sur Louis XI*. Ed. Jean Dufournet. Folio 1078. Paris: Gallimard, 1979.

Courcelle, Pierre. *La Consolation de Philosophie dans la tradition littéraire*. Paris: Etudes Augustiniennes, 1967.

Coville, Alfred. *Gontier et Pierre Col et l'humanisme en France au temps de Charles VI*. Paris: Droz, 1934.

Crétin, Guillaume. *Œuvres poétiques*. Ed. Kathleen Chesney. Paris: Firmin-Didot, 1932.

Curtius, Ernst Robert. *European Literature and the Latin Middle Ages*. Tr. Willard Trask. New York: Pantheon Books, 1953.

Defaux, Gérard. "Charles d'Orléans ou la poétique du secret: à propos du rondeau XXXIII de l'édition Champion," *Romania* 93 (1972): 194–243.

Delbouille, Maurice. "En relisant Rutebeuf," *Marche Romane* 10 (1960): 147–58.

Delclos, Jean-Claude. "*Le Prince* ou *Les Princes* de Georges Chastellain: un poème dirigé contre Louis XI," *Romania* 102 (1981): 46–74.

Deschamps, Eustache. *Œuvres complètes* (1878–1904). Ed. A. de Queux de St. Hilaire and Gaston Raynaud. 11 vols. New York: Johnson Reprint Corp., 1966.

Deschaux, Robert. *Un Poète bourguignon du XVe siècle: Michault Taillevent (édition et étude)*. Geneva: Droz, 1975.

Dragonetti, Roger. "La Poésie . . . ceste musique naturele," pp. 49–64 in *Fin du Moyen Age et Renaissance: mélanges de philologie française offerts à Robert Guiette*. Anvers: Nederlandsche Boekhandel, 1981.

———. *La Technique poétique des trouvères dans la chanson courtoise*. Bruges: De Tempel, 1960.

Droz, Eugénie, and Arthur Piaget. *Le Jardin de plaisance et fleur de rhétorique: introduction et notes*. Paris: E. Champion, 1925.

———. *Pierre de Nesson et ses œuvres*. Paris: Jeanbien, 1925.

Du Bellay, Joachim. *Deffence et illustration de la langue françoyse*. Ed. Henri Chamard. Paris: Didier, 1948.

———. *Œuvres poétiques*, vol. 1 (1908). Ed. Henri Chamard. 2d ed. rev. Paris: Nizet, 1982.

———. *L'Olive*. Ed. E. Caldarini. Geneva: Droz, 1974.

Dufournet, Jean. *La Destruction des mythes dans les Mémoires de Philippe de Commynes*. Geneva: Droz, 1966.

———. *Etudes sur Philippe de Commynes*. Paris: H. Champion, 1975.

Dupire, Noël. *Jean Molinet: la vie, les œuvres*. Paris: Droz, 1932.

Dwyer, Richard A. *Boethian Fictions: Narratives in the Medieval French Versions of the Consolatio Philosophiae*. Cambridge, Mass.: The Medieval Academy of America, 1976.

Fabri, Pierre. *Le Grand et Vrai Art de pleine rhétorique* (1889). Ed. A. Hamon. 3 vols. Geneva: Slatkine, 1969.

Faictz, see Molinet, *Les Faictz et dictz*

Fletcher, Angus. *Allegory: The Theory of a Symbolic Mode*. Ithaca, N.Y.: Cornell University Press, 1964.

Fouché, Pierre. *Phonétique historique du français*. 3 vols. 2d ed. Paris: Klincksieck, 1966.

Frappier, Jean. "Sur un procès fait à l'amour courtois," *Romania* 93 (1972): 145–93.

Frye, Northrop. *Anatomy of Criticism*. New York: Atheneum, 1970.

Garapon, Robert. "Introduction à la lecture d'Alain Chartier," *Annales de Normandie* 9 (1951): 91–108.

Gilson, Etienne. *Les Idées et les lettres*. Paris: J. Vrin, 1955.

Grammont, Maurice. *Petit Traité de versification française*. Paris: A. Colin, 1959.

Griffin, Robert. *Clément Marot and the Inflections of Poetic Voice*. Berkeley: University of California Press, 1974.

Guiette, Robert. *Forme et senefiance*. Geneva: Droz, 1978.

Guillaume de Degulleville. *Le Pèlerinage de vie humaine*. Ed. J. J. Sturzinger. London: Nichols and Sons, 1893.

Guillaume de Lorris and Jean de Meung. *Le Roman de la rose*. Ed. Daniel Poirion. Paris: Garnier-Flammarion, 1974.

Guillaume de Machaut. *Le Livre du Voir-Dit*. Ed. Paulin Paris. Paris: Société des Bibliophiles François, 1875.

———. *La Louange des Dames*. Ed. Nigel Wilkins. Edinburgh: Scottish Academic Press, 1972.

———. *Musikalische Werke*. Ed. Friedrich Ludwig. 4 vols. Leipzig: Breitkopf und Hartel, 1926–54.

———. *Œuvres*. Ed. Ernest Hoepffner. 3 vols. Paris: Firmin-Didot, 1908–21.

———. *Poésies lyriques*. Ed. V. Chichmaref. 2 vols. Paris: H. Champion, 1909.

———. *The Works of Guillaume de Machaut*. Ed. Leo Schrade. Vols. 2 and 3 of *Polyphonic Music of the Fourteenth Century*. Monaco: L'Oiseau-Lyre, 1956.

Guy, Henry. *Histoire de la poésie française*, vol. 1: *L'Ecole des Rhétoriqueurs* (1910). Paris: H. Champion, 1968.

Hassell, James Woodrow. *Middle French Proverbs, Sentences, and Proverbial Phrases*. Toronto: Pontifical Institute of Medieval Studies, 1982.

Hicks, Eric, ed. *Le Débat sur le Roman de la rose*. Bibliothèque du XVe Siècle 43. Paris: H. Champion, 1977.

Hindman, Sandra, and James Douglas Farquhar. *Pen to Press: Illustrated Manuscripts and Printed Books in the First Century of Printing*. College Park: Art Department, University of Maryland, 1977.

Hoffman, Edward J. *Alain Chartier: His Work and Reputation*. New York: Wittes Press, 1942.

Hommel, Luc. *Chastellain, 1415–1474*. Brussels: La Renaissance du Livre, 1945.

Huizinga, Johan. *Homo Ludens: A Study of the Play Element in Culture*. Tr. R. F. C. Hull. London: Routledge, Kegan Paul, 1949.

————. *The Waning of the Middle Ages.* Tr. F. Hopman. New York: Doubleday, 1954.

Huot, Sylvia. *From Song to Book: The Poetics of Writing in Old French Lyric and Lyrical Narrative Poetry.* Ithaca, N.Y.: Cornell University Press, 1987.

Le Jardin de plaisance et fleur de rethorique (ca. 1501). Paris: Firmin-Didot, 1910.

Jenkins, Michael F. O. *Artful Eloquence: Jean Lemaire de Belges and the Rhetorical Tradition.* North Carolina Studies in the Romance Languages and Literatures 217. Chapel Hill: University of North Carolina Press, 1980.

Johnson, Jerah, and William A. Percy. *The Age of Recovery: The Fifteenth Century.* Ithaca, N.Y.: Cornell University Press, 1970.

Kaplan, Abraham. "Obscenity as an Esthetic Category," *Law and Contemporary Problems* 20 (1955): 544–59.

Kelly, Douglas. *Medieval Imagination: Rhetoric and the Poetry of Courtly Love.* Madison: University of Wisconsin Press, 1978.

Kibler, William W. "The Narrator as Key to Alain Chartier's *La Belle Dame sans mercy*," *French Review* 52 (1979): 714–23.

Knapp, Stephen, and Walter Ben Michaels. "Against Theory," *Critical Inquiry* 8 (1982): 732–42.

————. "Against Theory: A Reply to our Critics," *Critical Inquiry* 9 (1983): 790–800.

Kuhn, David. *La Poétique de François Villon.* Paris: A. Colin, 1967.

La Barre, Weston: "Obscenity: An Anthropological Appraisal," *Law and Contemporary Problems* 20 (1955): 533–43.

La Borderie, Arthur de. *Jean Meschinot, sa vie et ses œuvres.* Paris: H. Champion, 1896.

Lachèvre, Frédéric. *Bibliographie des recueils collectifs de poésies du XVIe siècle.* Paris: H. Champion, 1922.

Laidlaw, J. C. "André du Chesne's Edition of Alain Chartier," *Modern Language Review* 63 (1968): 569–74.

Laigle, Mathilde. *Le Livre des trois vertus de Christine de Pisan et son milieu historique et littéraire.* Paris: H. Champion, 1912.

Langlois, Ernest, ed. *Recueil d'arts de seconde rhétorique.* Paris: Imprimerie Nationale, 1902.

Lefranc, Martin. *Le Champion des dames.* Lyons, 1485.

————. *Le Champion des dames.* Ed. Arthur Piaget. Mémoires et documents publiés par la Société d'Histoire de la Suisse Romande, 3d series, 8. Lausanne: Payot, 1968.

Levi, A. H. T., ed. *Humanism in France at the End of the Middle Ages and in the Early Renaissance*. Manchester, Eng.: Manchester University Press, 1970.

Lewis, P. S., ed. *The Recovery of France in the Fifteenth Century*. New York: Harper & Row, 1972.

Löpelmann, Martin, ed. *Die Liederhandschrift des Cardinals de Rohan*. Göttingen: Gesellschaft für Romanische Literatur, 1923.

Louange, see Guillaume de Machaut, *La Louange des Dames*

Lowinsky, Edward. "Mathaeus Greiter's *Fortuna*: An Experiment in Chromaticism and in Musical Iconography," *The Musical Quarterly* (2 parts) 42 (1956): 500–519; 43 (1957): 68–85.

Lubienski-Bodenham, H. "The Origins of the Fifteenth-Century View of Poetry as 'Seconde Rhétorique.'" *Modern Language Review* 74 (1979): 26–38.

Lunettes, see Meschinot, *Les Lunettes des Princes*, ed. Martineau-Génieys.

Machabey, Armand. *Guillaume de Machaut, 130?–1377: la vie et l'œuvre musicale*. 2 vols. Paris: R. Masse, 1955.

Marot, Clément. *Œuvres diverses*. Ed. C. A. Mayer. London: Athlone Press, 1966.

———. *Œuvres poétiques*. Ed. Yves Giraud. Paris: Garnier-Flammarion, 1973.

Matthews, William. "Inherited Impediments in Medieval Literary History," pp. 1–24 in William Matthews, ed., *Medieval Secular Literature*. Berkeley: University of California Press, 1965.

McFarlane, I. D. *Renaissance France: 1470–1589*. London: Ernest Benn, 1974.

McLeod, Enid. *The Order of the Rose*. Totowa, N.J.: Rowman and Littlefield, 1976.

Meiss, Millard. *The Limbourgs and Their Contemporaries*, vol. 1. New York: George Braziller and the Pierpont Morgan Library, 1974.

Meschinot, Jean. *Les Lunettes des Princes*. Ed. Christine Martineau-Génieys. Geneva: Droz, 1972.

———. *Les Lunettes des Princes*. Ed. Bernard Toscani. Paris: Minard, 1971.

Michault, Pierre. *Le Doctrinal du temps présent*. Ed. Thomas Walton. Paris: Droz, 1931.

Michaut, Gustave. *L'Evolution littéraire du Moyen Age français*. Paris: Croville-Morant, 1931.

Minta, Stephen. *Love Poetry in Sixteenth-Century France*. Manchester, Eng.: Manchester University Press, 1977.

Molinet, Jean. *Les Faictz et dictz*. Ed. Noël Dupire. 3 vols. Paris: Société des Anciens Textes Français, 1935–39.

Montaiglon, Anatole de, ed. *Recueil de poésies françoises des XVe et XVIe siècles, morales, facétieuses, historiques*. 13 vols. Paris: P. Jannet, 1855–78.

Montaiglon, Anatole de, and Gaston Raynaud, eds. *Recueil général et complet des fabliaux*, vol. 5. Paris: Librairie des Bibliophiles, 1883.

Morse, Ruth. "Medieval Biography: History as a Branch of Literature," *Modern Language Review* 80 (1985): 257–68.

Muhlethaler, Jean-Claude. *Poétiques du quinzième siècle: situation de François Villon et Michault Taillevent*. Paris: Nizet, 1983.

Murphy, James J. *Rhetoric in the Middle Ages*. Berkeley: University of California Press, 1974.

Muscatine, Charles. *The Old French Fabliaux*. New Haven, Conn.: Yale University Press, 1986.

Nash, Jerry C., ed. *Pre-Pleiade Poetry*. French Forum Monograph 57. Lexington, Ky.: French Forum Publishers, 1985.

Newman, F. X., ed. *The Meaning of Courtly Love*. Albany: State University of New York Press, 1968.

Nykrog, Per. *Les Fabliaux* (1957). Geneva: Droz, 1973.

O'Donoghue, Bernard. *The Courtly Love Tradition*. Manchester, Eng.: Manchester University Press, 1982.

Œuvres, see Deschamps, *Œuvres complètes*

Olson, Glending. *Literature as Recreation in the Later Middle Ages*. Ithaca, N.Y.: Cornell University Press, 1982.

Paris, Gaston. *Esquisse historique de la littérature française au Moyen Age* (1901). 3d ed. Paris: A. Colin, 1922.

———. *La Poésie du Moyen Age*. 2d ed. Paris: Hachette, 1895.

Paris, Paulin. *Manuscrits françois de la Bibliothèque du Roi*, vol. 5. Paris: Techener, 1842.

Patch, Howard R. *The Goddess Fortuna in Medieval Literature*. Cambridge, Mass.: Harvard University Press, 1927.

Patterson, William F. *Three Centuries of French Poetic Theory* (1935), vol. 1. New York: Russell and Russell, 1966.

Pernoud, Régine. *Histoire de la bourgeoisie en France*, vol. 1: *Des origines aux temps modernes*. Paris: Editions du Seuil, 1960.

———. *Pour en finir avec le Moyen Age*. Paris: Editions du Seuil, 1977.

Piaget, Arthur. "La Belle Dame sans merci et ses imitations," *Romania* (6 parts) 30 (1901): 23–48, 314–51; 31 (1902): 315–49; 33 (1904): 179–208; 34 (1905): 421–560, 575–88.

Pickens, Rupert T., ed. *The Songs of Jaufré Rudel.* Studies and Texts 41. Toronto: Pontifical Institute of Medieval Studies, 1978.

Pinet, Marie-Josèphe. *Christine de Pisan, 1364–1430: étude biographique et littéraire.* Paris: H. Champion, 1927.

Poirion, Daniel. "Lectures de la Belle Dame sans mercy," pp. 691–705 in *Mélanges de langue et de littérature médiévales offerts à Pierre Le Gentil.* Paris: Société des Editions d'Enseignement Supérieur, 1973.

———. *Le Moyen Age, II (1300–1480).* Vol. 2 of *La Littérature française.* Paris: Arthaud, 1971.

———. *Le Poète et le prince: l'évolution du lyrisme courtois de Guillaume de Machaut à Charles d'Orléans.* Paris: Presses Universitaires de France, 1965.

Les Quinzes Joyes de mariage. Ed. Jean Rychner. Geneva: Droz, 1967.

Raynaud, Gaston, ed. *Rondeaux et autres poésies du XVe siècle* (1889). New York: Johnson Reprint Corp., 1968.

Reaney, Gilbert. "Guillaume de Machaut: Lyric Poet," *Music and Letters* 39 (1959): 38–51.

———. *Machaut.* London: Oxford University Press, 1971.

———. "The Poetic Form of Machaut's Musical Works, I: The Ballades, Rondeaux and Virelais," *Musica Disciplina* 13 (1959): 25–41.

———. "Towards a Chronology of Machaut's Musical Works," *Musica Disciplina* 20 (1966): 87–96.

Regalado, Nancy. *Poetic Patterns in Rutebeuf: A Study in Non-Courtly Poetic Modes of the Thirteenth Century.* New Haven, Conn.: Yale University Press, 1970.

Rigaud, Rose. *Les Idées féministes de Christine de Pisan.* Neuchâtel: Attinger, 1911.

Rohan, see Löpelmann, *Die Liederhandschrift des Cardinals de Rohan*

Roy, *see* Christine de Pizan, *Œuvres*

Saint-Gelais, Octovien de. *Le Séjour d'honneur.* Paris: Antoine Vérard, 1519.

———. *Le Séjour d'honneur.* Ed. Joseph Alston James. North Carolina Studies in the Romance Languages 181. Chapel Hill: University of North Carolina Press, 1977.

Schilperoot, Johanna C. *Guillaume de Machaut et Christine de Pisan (étude comparative).* The Hague: Swart and Zoon, 1936.

Schmidt, Albert-Marie. "L'Age des Rhétoriqueurs," pp. 175–91 in *Littéra-*

tures françaises, connexes et marginales, vol. 3 of Raymond Queneau, ed., *Histoire des littératures* (1958). Paris: Gallimard, 1972.

——. "Christine de Pizan," *Revue des Sciences Humaines* n.s. 122–23 (1966): 159–74.

——. *XIVe et XVe Siècles français: les sources de l'humanisme*. Paris: Seghers, 1964.

Schwob, Marcel, ed. *Le Parnasse satyrique du XVe siècle* (1905). Geneva: Slatkine, 1969.

Shapley, C. S. *Studies in French Poetry of the Fifteenth Century*. The Hague: Nijhoff, 1970.

Siciliano, Italo. *Villon et les thèmes poétiques du Moyen Age*. Paris: A. Colin, 1934.

Simone, Franco. *The French Renaissance: Medieval Tradition and Italian Influence in Shaping the Renaissance in France*. Tr. H. Gaston Hall. London: Macmillan, 1969. Originally published in 1961 under the title *Il Rinascimento francese*. Turin: Società Editrice Internazionale, 1965.

——. *Umanesimo, Rinascimento, Barocco in Francia*. Milan: Mursia, 1968.

Solente, Suzanne. "Christine de Pisan," pp. 335–442 in *Histoire littéraire de la France*, vol. 40. Paris: Imprimerie Nationale, 1974.

Spearing, A. C. *Criticism and Medieval Poetry*. London: Edward Arnold, 1972.

Sponde, Jean de. *Poésies*. Ed. Alan Boase. Geneva: Cailler, 1949.

Stone, Donald. *Mellin de Saint-Gelais and Literary History*. French Forum Monograph 47. Lexington, Ky.: French Forum Publishers, 1983.

Sutch, Susie Speakman. "Allegory and Praise in the Works of the Grands Rhétoriqueurs." Ph.D. dissertation, University of California (Berkeley), 1983.

Utley, Francis L. "Must We Abandon the Concept of Courtly Love?," *Medievalia et Humanistica* n.s. 3: 299–324.

Vaughan, Richard. *Philip the Good*. London: Longmans, 1970.

Walravens, C. J. H. *Alain Chartier: études biographiques, suivies de pièces justificatives, d'une description des éditions et d'une édition des ouvrages inédits*. Amsterdam: Meulenhoff-Didier, 1971.

Wenzel, Siegfried. "The Pilgrimage of Life as a Late Medieval Genre," *Medieval Studies* 35 (1973): 370–88.

White, Julian Eugene, Jr. "The Conflict of Generations in the *Débat patriotique*," *French Review* 39 (1965): 230–33.

Wilkins, Nigel. "The Post-Machaut Generation of Poet-Musicians," *Nottingham Medieval Studies* 12 (1968): 40–84.

————. "The Structure of Ballades, Rondeaux and Virelais in Froissart and in Christine de Pisan," *French Studies* 23 (1969): 337–48.

————, ed. *One Hundred Ballades, Rondeaux and Virelais from the late Middle Ages*. Cambridge, Eng.: Cambridge University Press, 1969.

Willard, Charity Cannon. *Christine de Pizan: Her Life and Works*. New York: Persea Books, 1984.

————. "A Fifteenth-Century View of Women's Role in Medieval Society: Christine de Pizan's *Livre des trois vertus*," pp. 90–120 in Rosemarie Thee Morewedge, ed., *The Role of Woman in the Middle Ages*. Albany: State University of New York Press, 1975.

Zumthor, Paul. *Essai de poétique médiévale*. Paris: Editions du Seuil, 1972.

————. *Langue et techniques poétiques à l'époque romane*. Paris: Klincksieck, 1963.

————. *Langue, texte, énigme*. Paris: Editions du Seuil, 1975.

————. *Le Masque et la lumière: la poétique des Grands Rhétoriqueurs*. Paris: Editions du Seuil, 1978.

————, ed. *Anthologie des Grands Rhétoriqueurs*. Paris: Union Générale d'Editions, 1978.

Index

Index

In this index an "f" after a number indicates a separate reference on the next page, and an "ff" indicates separate references on the next two pages. A continuous discussion over two or more pages is indicated by a span of page numbers, e.g., "pp. 57–58." *Passim* is used for a cluster of references in close but not consecutive sequence.

138; in Chartier, 155; in *Lunettes*,
185, 189, 225
François I, duke of Brittany, 196
François II, duke of Brittany, 174
François I, king of France, 289
Frappier, Jean, 55
Froissart, Jean, 14, 26, 60, 68, 115, 170
Frye, Northrup, 172f, 176–79

Garapon, Robert, 122
Geoffrey of Vinsauf, 321
Gower, John, 169
Grammont, Maurice, 323
Griffin, Robert, 290, 292
Guénée, Bertrand, 307
Guiette, Robert, 280
Guillaume d'Aquitaine, 243
Guillaume de Machaut: as exemplary
figure, 3f, 10, 14, 25–26; and order-
ing of poems, 15; Acteur in, 28, 227;
and Petrarch, 38–39; as female
voice, 45–46; death of, 59; influence
of, 60; manuscripts of works of, 66;
persona of, 66–67, 246; and patron-
age, 69; Poirion on, 107, 313
—Works: "Ami, je t'ay tant amé . . ."
(chant royal), 45–46; *Ballades no-
tées*, 42, 51; ballades on Fortune,
41–56, 299; *Confort d'ami*, 38; *Dit
de la fonteinne amoureuse*, 56; *Dit
dou verger*, 34; *Jugement dou roy de
Behaigne*, 317; *Jugement dou roy de
Navarre*, 317; *Louange*, 26–27, 34f,
47, 66, 251, 264; *Prise d'Alexandrie*,
26, 38, 169; "Prologue," 28–35;
Remede de Fortune, 28, 32, 34, 41;
"Sans cuer, dolens . . ." (rondeau),
56–57
Guy, Henri, 11, 168, 171ff, 203, 306

Hassell, James W., 327
History: in relation to this book, 1–2;
and poetic conventions, 75, 162f; as

condition of literary persona, 115–
16; and Chartier's *Complainte*, 160–
61; in Chartier's poetry, 165–66; in
Commynes's *Mémoires*, 180
Hoepffner, Ernest, 310
Hoffman, E. J., 122–23
Hommel, Luc, 290ff, 293
Horace, 215, 301
Hugo, Victor, 2, 115, 300
Huizinga, Johan, 9ff, 92, 259, 285, 305
Huot, Sylvia, 66

James, Joseph A., 168, 321
Jardin de plaisance et fleur de rethorique:
as heterogeneous anthology, 21, 27,
236, 279; bawdy in, 233, 255; Char-
tier rondeau in, 291–96 *passim*
Jean V, duke of Brittany, 196
Jean de Garancières, 39
Jean de Grailli, count of Foix, 318
Jean de Meung, 69, 73, 173
Jean de Montreuil, 330
Jeanroy, Alfred, 306
Joyce, James, 178

Kibler, William, 123
Kuhn, David, 312

Labé, Louise, 67
La Borderie, Arthur de, 168, 177, 194
La Borderie, Bertrand de, 144
La Ceppède, Jean de, 300
La Fontaine, Jean de, 208, 292
Laforgue, Jules, 115
Laidlaw, J. C., 148, 318, 320
Lamartine, Alphonse de, 115f
Lanson, Gustave, 11, 306
"Late medieval," as term, 13
Laumonier, Paul, 293
Le Fèvre de Ressons, Jean, 170
Lefranc, Martin, 26–27, 169, 204
Leonardo da Vinci, 249
Le Queux, Regnaud, 332